D1244585

A Holistic Approach to the Treatment of Learning Disorders

Barbara M. Knickerbocker, OTR, FAOTA

This book is dedicated to the many children and their parents, whose trials and hopes, tireless interest and concern have inspired me to gain a greater understanding of learning disorders.

I am especially indebted to James P., Robert S., Tricia J., Michael P., and Erica C.

Acknowledgment

I am deeply indebted to A. Jean Ayres, Ph.D., for her dedicated work in the field of learning disorders. The research contributions she has made in the diagnosis and treatment of sensory integrative dysfunction has been of great importance to occupational therapists, psychologists, and educators who are concerned with learning problems. The work of Dr. Ayres has been fundamental to the work which I have done. Through my study of her methods, my interest in her contributions to research and professional literature, as well as through most valued personal communications and friendship with her, I have sought to understand and apply much of what she proposes with regard to problems of learning disorders. Without her prior accomplishments, it would not have been possible for me to conduct as effective a treatment program for learning-disordered children, nor to conceptualize these experiences as I have done.

I further wish to acknowledge my appreciation to Joy Huss, M.S., O.T.R., and Helen Dahlstrom, O.T.R., for reviewing portions of the manuscript; to Anne Henderson, Ph.D., O.T.R., for her support; to Eleanor Mathews for her help in editing; to Linda Abromovici, O.T.R., for helping compile numerical data; and to Rona Fernandez, M.S., O.T.R., for her long-standing encouragement and helpful discussions. I wish to thank my staff assistant Beth Slotnik, O.T.R., for her review of the manuscript and Beth Seybold, M.H.S., O.T.R., who shared important professional discussions.

My thanks goes to Howard Farmer, M.D., Otolaryngologist, for his time and interest in this work and Julio de Quiros, M.D., whose enthusiastic encouragement was most helpful.

To Glen Doyle, photographer, and to the children who willingly served as models to demonstrate treatment techniques, I give my appreciation. To Joan Bailey and Florence Faith my thanks for typing the manuscript.

To my husband, Harry Beskind, M.D., I wish to express my deepest gratitude for his sustained and devoted support and encouragement, and to my step-sons, Mark and Daniel, for their patience with me while completing this incredibly long task.

Preface

My primary concerns are to meet the need for practical evaluation and treatment procedures for children with learning disorders and, hopefully, to encourage clinical observation and research in the occupational therapy field. By observing and studying spontaneous responses of children with learning disorders in a therapeutic setting over the past decade, a general sequence in which they began to overcome their developmental obstacles became apparent. From this, a hypothesis was evolved.

On the basis of these observations and my hypothesis, I brought together a comprehensive, cohesive, holistic approach to treatment.* A practical, ongoing, dynamic, diagnostic evaluation was developed which coincides step by step with the sequential program plans which are used to correct the problem. Through this cohesive program I have established means to aid in the unfolding and the developing of the normal psychoneurological autonomous functions of the ego. Children with learning disorders have, through specified techniques and approaches, been helped to overcome those developmental obstacles or arrests and to accelerate their rate of change in the direction of normal maturation.

*The term holistic as I have used it is in no way related to the recently emerging holistic approach to health care, advocating a naturalistic, anti-medical point of view. The use of the term holistic was first introduced by me in relation to the treatment of learning disorders at the conference held March 23-24, 1973, in Detroit, Michigan, and sponsored by the Michigan Occupational Therapy Association.

Foreword

Some years ago an American university invited me to lecture in its Department of Pediatric Neurology. I was pleased to have such an invitation. When I arrived, I was surprised to find a very small audience, so I soon refocused my lecture material into more of a round table discussion about the topic of learning disabilities. I was grateful to discover many friendly participants who willingly shared their own views and interests in this topic. Barbara M. Knickerbocker was one of those outstanding professional people who made a lasting impression on me.

A Holistic Approach to Treatment of Learning Disorders is an excellent and practical book for use by a wide range of readers who are concerned with preschool and school-aged, learning-disordered children. The author presents a "holistic" approach through which to facilitate change along the hierarchy of growth and development, which she has recognized from her clinical observations in occupational therapy.

In my opinion, Knickerbocker's approach is a major contribution for therapy in learning disabilities. She accepts the principal avenues of thinking in this regard but applying her own various and sometimes unique methods, she is able to draw new conclusions. In her approach, she develops a suitable therapeutic program while balancing the focus on various factors to include professional role function, clinical evaluation, social aspects, sensory integration, and psychophysiology. Some portions of this book will surely attract the attention of many professional people concerned with treatment of learning disabilities, as for instance, "Reduction of Avoidance Behavior in the Visuo-Vestibular Dyad" (Program Plan 2).

The holistic approach has moved away from the earlier tenets which were concerned essentially with postures and movements through which to elicit better learning abilities. It is understood, of course, that postures and movements are still important because they tend to reduce the extent to which motor responses are restricted by abnormal reflexes. The Bobaths, Rood, Ayres, and others have written excellent books and papers on this subject. Undoubtedly Knickerbocker's comments are based on an understanding and application of much of what these researchers and clinicians have presented, but her approach goes beyond this. In a practical, original kind of programming, she enables the child to make the step-by-step transition between the early movement patterns and academic adjustment.

This is a most useful book which, in my opinion, is a milestone in the difficult path of helping children to establish solid foundations for academic performance. It will, without doubt, be consulted widely by professional people in relation to learning disabilities and motor skills.

Julio B. de Quiros, MD, PhD
Dean, School of Science of Human Rehabilitation
Buenos Aires, Argentina

Table of Contents

Legend of Illustrations*

*Out of respect for the rights of privacy, none of the children seen in these photographs have ever been in therapy here. The primary intent of these pictures is to depict the type of equipment and the techniques used in this program rather than to demonstrate clinical pathology.

Introduction

My original interest in learning disorders came about in 1962 when I was stationed at Walson Army Hospital, Fort Dix, New Jersey as an occupational therapist in the United States Army. I was asked to institute a treatment program for young dependents of military personnel who were designated as mental retardates. In addition to those children who conformed to the usual range of behavior of retardates, there were others whose characteristic behavior clearly mystified their parents, the teachers, and me. These children often scored below the normal level of intellect, but the range between their high and low subscores, reported by the psychologist on the Weschler Intelligence Scale for Children* and the Vineland Social Maturity Scale† and other measurements, were clearly inconsistent with mental retardation. I became aware of the work of A. Jean Ayres, Ph.D., and my interest was quickly aroused in perceptual-motor dysfunction and its effect on children's learning capabilities.

I have since used the work of Dr. Ayres as my background when I watch children's behavior as they play with toys and equipment normal to childhood and as they perform certain academic tasks. Throughout my observations, the kinds of aberrant behavior described by Ayers is always uppermost in my mind. By observing the spontaneous responses of these children to specific tasks, I am able to formulate a functional theoretical base to mitigate the problems. In other words, I utilize functional criteria for the most practical application to these clinical and educational needs.

Definition of Terms

The term *learning disorder* is inclusive of the more widespread and traditional terms *perceptual-motor handicaps* and *perceptual-motor dysfunction* used in the 1960s. In recent years, primarily in relation to the work of Dr. Ayres,[1] the term *sensory-integrative dysfunction* has been used in the literature in the fields of occupational therapy and psychology. The term *sensorimotor* is used here to mean roughly the equivalent of sensory integration, referring to early organization and integration of the sensory systems and the developmental

*Weschler D: The Weschler Intelligence Scale for Children. The Psychological Corporation, 1949.

†Doll EA: Vineland Maturity Scale. Circle Pines, Mn. American Guidance Service Inc, 1965.

motor patterns from which perceptions about our environment arise. The term learning disorders as used here is meant to encompass the early sensorimotor, sensory integrative, perceptual-motor, precognitive, and early cognitive functions upon which learning can take place. The term learning disorder is equivalent to the term learning disability currently used by educators. For clearer understanding, however, the term learning disorder is definitely advantageous. Inherent within this term is the concept of the disorganization, the failure, or an arrest in the ability to bring about an orderly sequence of movements and to assemble order in objects, in events, and in ideas.

Purpose

For Occupational Therapists

The holistic approach — holistic used in this text as meaning cohesive, composite, and comprehensive — is compatible with the activity orientation of occupational therapists. The foremost purpose of this book is to provide the clinical therapist and occupational therapy student with a tangible means of focusing on the problems of learning disorders. Heretofore, a comprehensive behavioral treatment program based on functional criteria has not been available.

I have arrived at a holistic viewpoint through my own strong identity as a clinical therapist. Occupational therapists work with behavioral responses and focus primarily on the way in which the modalities of treatment they use can foster changes in a patient's behavior. This book is similarly designed to provide a behavioral, ie, holistic, model of learning and a detailed presentation of its therapeutic application. The application of this holistic model of learning through behavior techniques modifies the child's disorder through a corrective behavioral experience. This application meets the needs of occupational therapists to conceptualize clinical information and provides them with a point of departure for their own research.

The holistic approach offers many practical aspects to therapeutic programming. All methods of therapy, with certain few exceptions, can be suitably accommodated within a limited physical facility. Much of the equipment is practical for use in the child's home. The holistic approach can be used not only as a primary treatment program, but also can be used supplementarily with other programs, eg, in a cerebral palsy clinic. Occupational therapists who are consultants to school systems will find a suitable use of this material to communicate with teachers, so as to utilize a team approach, or to personally conduct a systematic daily treatment program of occupational therapy within an educational facility.

For Educators

The material of this book will be of obvious importance to the special educator who works with the learning-disordered child or the retardate. The material can serve as a "bridge of communication" between the educator and the therapist who looks at functional responses in terms of delayed neurodevelopmental maturation. In a clear manner, means are outlined by which the talents and skills in areas such as physical therapy, speech therapy, optometry, and to some extent recreational therapy and physical education may be closely interwoven. Through a dynamic interdisciplinary approach to learning, greater coordination can be achieved between the foundations of preacademic sensorimotor function and cognitive learning.

A unique reference is provided for pediatricians who are confronted by the subtleties of the problems parents describe. The significance of delayed sensorimotor function is clarified in relation to its effect on a child's social and academic adjustments. Physicians, psychologists, social workers, and occupational therapists who counsel parents of learning-disordered children will find parts of this book suitable reading for the more sophisticated parent as well as a helpful reference for themselves.

To meet a more widespread need this text will also be helpful throughout curricula for primary education and for teachers in the field. Valuable clues taken from this study can make the learning process easier and more effective for the normal child, as well as prevent early casualties for the child who has only marginal learning problems.

Prevention

Another purpose of this book is to indicate means of prevention. We can prevent the potentially vulnerable child from developing symptoms of a learning disorder if early learning material is presented on a time schedule and in a sequential order which is compatible with the neurodevelopmental maturation needed for the task.

Within the large group of learning-disordered children is a functional subgroup which is largely the product of educational, communicative, and cultural aspects of our society. I refer to them as *pseudo learning-disordered children;* they differ not only in suspected causality, but often are less severely involved and make a more rapid and complete resolution of their problems. These problems are best resolved if they are recognized before the child starts the elementary grades; thereafter there is a more fixed secondary problem which becomes intensified as he begins to miss the cognitive aspects of academic work.

Therefore, portions of this text dealing with early prevention will be of special importance for nursing school curricula. For instance, public health nurses who supervise day care centers or teach child care should be aware of the importance of early prone positioning so that the child will have adequate opportunity for preambulatory neuromuscular development.

One of the most recent developments in education is the federal legislation which stipulates that whenever possible, with the exception of severely disturbed and disabled children, those with special problems should be placed in the "mainstream" of learning in the normal classroom. This means that there will be many teachers whose past experience and formal training has not prepared them to cope with these special problems. Learning-disordered children will need greater understanding by more people than ever before.

Pioneering Professional Endeavors

Throughout the unfolding process of my clinical research, I have directed much of my attention to teaching the methods and the theoretical material on which these are based. I have, over this ten-year period, conducted numerous workshops lasting one to three days which have been sponsored by state and local Occupational Therapy Associations, as well as private schools and public school systems. I have been guest lecturer and consultant in more than ten Occupational Therapy Curricula during this time. My work has been recognized by the American Occupational Therapy Association in several ways, one being that this program was one of three depicting occupational therapy in the film "Making A Difference," released in 1972. In 1973 I was designated as a Charter Fellow of the American Occupational Therapy Association. I have been consultant on problems of learning for numerous school systems throughout New Jersey, New York, and Pennsylvania.

At the 1970 Conference of the World Federation of Occupational Therapists in Zurich, I presented a paper, accompanied by a film, entitled, "A Perceptual-Motor Program in a Private Setting." Prior to that I had organized and privately sponsored a six-day conference in Princeton about perceptual-motor problems of learning, to which 300 therapists and other professionals from the United States and six foreign countries attended; the faculty of 25 was headed by Dr. Ayres.

By 1972 the theoretical basis for my research into learning disorders began to take form. At the Annual Occupational Therapy Conference that year, held in Los Angeles, I presented a paper entitled "Bridging the Gap between Avoidance and Exploration," in which I emphasized the crucial role of the therapist to expedite this aspect of early therapy.

Format

The book is divided into three parts. Part I sets forth the philosophy and the rationale of a holistic approach. It develops the working hypothesis and describes five sequential processes of learning and the therapeutic principles used to promote change.

Part II is comprised of a series of protocols which are the tools of evaluation and programming. The foremost purpose of these is to enable the therapist to make a meaningful and dynamic diagnostic assessment of a child's performance along a graded hierarchy, and at the same time to use these tasks to promote effective therapy. For the therapist, and to some extent the educator, conscientious use of these protocols provides a built-in, self-training method. With a background of understanding of neurodevelopmental maturation and proper use of these protocols, the occupational therapist should be adequately prepared to conduct a holistic program of therapy for the learning-disordered child.

Implementation of the Program, Part III, depicts how to put into action the principles of therapy, emphasizing a nondirective, invitational technique to stimulate the child's spontaneous involvement. Eight program plans are presented. Described in these plans are specific procedures to be followed, the proposed order of programming, and the interrelationship between the various program plans. Parts, or all, of these plans may be required to activate or accelerate the normal cyclic processing identified in the working hypothesis. A summary inventory of foundation skills for academic performance is presented according to subject so that problems in these areas may be traced to their earlier origins by therapists and educators.

Reference

1. Ayres AJ: Sensory Integration and Learning Disorders. Los Angeles, Western Psychological Services, 1972.

Part I: Presenting a Holistic Approach

1

Introduction to a Holistic Approach

Research Setting

Throughout the past decade I have conducted a private practice and research-oriented program for learning-disordered children. To make such a comprehensive study of clinical performance and develop suitable therapeutic procedures would not have been possible in a general clinic where the demands of administration and programming are widely diverse. In a setting where this condition was treated exclusively, it was possible to conduct empirical research which then became the basis on which to establish a viable hypothesis.

I conducted close clinical observations of children on a one-to-one basis at weekly intervals. The case load was restricted to a maximum of five one-hour therapy sessions a day.

At the time when I began my independent endeavors in 1967, private practice for occupational therapists was unknown in my profession. Few occupational therapists currently are engaged in a self-supporting private practice for this or any other treatment specialty. It is, and continues to be, a pioneer endeavor in therapeutic practice, in originating and developing effective, practical therapy techniques, in designing and developing equipment to expedite therapy, and in evolving clinically-oriented research methodology.

Original Intent and Purpose

Without consciously adhering to any specific theory of behavior or learning, I permitted myself to be freely guided by the child's spontaneous responses to selected equipment and toys normal to childhood. From their spontaneous responses, I attempted to understand children's assets and deficits in terms of sensorimotor organization. My recognition of these needs was based on a background of knowledge and experience of sensorimotor dysfunction described by Ayres.

Setting forth on this self-supported clinical program for learning-disordered children ranging from four to ten years of age, I observed a myriad of problems which varied in degree from mild to severe. Originally the purpose of the empirical research from observation was to accomplish three things: 1) systematize clinical observations, 2) arrive at useful insights about the processes of learning, and 3) ascertain treatment methods whereby the development of these processes might be expedited. From this study, five sequential processes have become evident. These are identified in the working hypothesis (see Chapter 4).

Among the useful insights which emerged were data to support two basic premises about a child's exposure to early learning experiences. First, it appeared that learning-disordered children often were exposed prematurely to learning experiences for which they were not developmentally mature. Without the necessary underlying foundations, they could not involve themselves spontaneously to learn from the experience. If they tried and were unsuccessful, their feelings of failure and frustration were increased. In either event, a child would soon recognize the face-saving technique of simply avoiding those physical and academic experiences to which he was exposed, but with which he would anticipate or actually experience failure.

The second premise suggests that because of his need* to avoid involvement with these potentially frustrating experiences, the child would be less likely to develop the broad-based foundation for learning which comes from a smooth progression in neurodevelopmental maturation. If early learning skills are insufficient, new learning, which depends on these, is acquired in an inconsistent, intermittent pattern. Kephart[1] refers to learning acquired as a separate entity as a "splinter skill." By this he means that the child cannot generalize from, nor apply, these isolated kinds of learning experience to other situations. Learning patterns such as these are often found among retardates as well as among learning-disordered children of normal intellect.

Outcome of the Empirical Form of Clinical Research

From the clinical observations of children's abilities to use one toy or activity successfully before another, a hierarchy of steps along the learning continuum became evident. To enable myself to recognize what this hierarchy would finally be, I drew heavily on the two basic premises of why children fail to learn, cited earlier. It then became obvious that there would be a dynamic diagnostic value from the child's performance on certain selected activities which had been graded along the natural hierarchy of development. At the same time, successful completion of each step would imply readiness for exposure to each successive one. A dynamic, diagnostic evaluation tool was born, and with it, a concurrent projected therapy plan. Together, they offered implicit practical value for both therapy and education.

References

1. Kephart NC: The Slow Learner in the Classroom. Columbus, Ohio, Merrill, 1960.

*For ease and clarity in reading I have, throughout this book, used the male pronoun to designate the child in treatment and the female pronoun to identify the therapist.

2

The Philosophy

Three unique and interrelated features characterize the philosophy of this therapeutic program: the first feature emphasizes parent orientation through which to extend the maximum benefits of therapy; the second stresses the use of toys and activities normal to childhood as the principal treatment modalities; the third recommends a holistic approach to facilitate change along the hierarchy of growth and development.

Parent-Oriented Programming

The first step in fostering a parent-oriented participatory program is the creation of a climate for communication. The therapist who feels secure and comfortable in what she is doing can be relaxed and open in her responsiveness, thus more sensitive about her interaction with the parents of the child with whom she works.

In this setting the parent attends each treatment hour, observing the therapist's work with the child. The parent can see an *action model* through which the child's response may be improved and his counterproductive behavior may be modified. For instance, parents of a slow-moving, reluctant young child will recognize methods the therapist utilizes which enable the child to become more actively involved with a heretofore unexplored piece of equipment. Parents of a hyperactive, hyperverbal, anxious child will be relieved to see the positive effects of certain specific techniques which enable him to exercise some self-restraint. With an action model as a guide and armed with a better understanding of the problems, the mother and father may then begin to employ some of these same methods at home.

In addition to recognizing new means of coping with aberrant behavior, the parent also observes the way certain pieces of equipment are used in therapy; the parent learns how to continue the same kind of activity on equipment used at home between therapy sessions. I often stress to the parents that extended practice at home will have a greater impact on the rate of the child's progress — with the early motor activities especially — than his brief weekly exposure to them during therapy. Often the therapist need only check progress on those gross motor activities he has at home so that valuable time during therapy can then be directed to other important parts of the program. Beneficial aspects of this are obvious to the parents in terms of economy. Of far greater importance is the accelerated rate of progress which will hasten the child's academic adjustment.

It is the purpose of this parent-oriented program to provide a practical understanding of the way in which sensory systems function both independently and in relation to each other and how they influence not only the child's movement patterns but also his social responses and academic skills. As parents come to recognize — and to anticipate in advance — those experiences which may cause their child to react negatively or unproductively, they are better equipped to reduce the frequency of such occurrences.

Sound parent orientation and understanding depends to a significant degree upon the availability of related written material. This book contains material which will be helpful to some parents as background reading. Many parents who have a therapist to guide their child's overall program can follow the specific procedures at home which are outlined in the program plans. As the parents develop a better awareness of what it is they are observing and the meaning of such observations through discussion with the therapist and their own reading, they can develop greater objectivity about the problem and understand changes as they take place.

In a parent-oriented program such as this, the parents are encouraged to record for themselves and for the therapist positive and negative changes in the child's behavior which occur outside of therapy. Such observations relate to a wide range of contacts with peers, siblings, parents, and teachers, and furnish the therapist with a more complete picture of the child's progress and changing needs.

As parents become personally involved in recognizing and reporting the changes they notice, they sense not only the importance of conducting a meaningful home program, but also they realize that they have an important part in promoting such changes. Among the principal values of a parent-oriented program is the fact that it helps to reduce their feelings of guilt by involving themselves and being directly responsible for promoting change in their child's condition. This helps to relieve the narcissistic blow to the parents which they may incur through their child's problems. Direct, tangible involvement in programming serves to elevate their self-esteem and restore confidence in their own child-rearing capabilities. A home program tends to draw upon and maximize the effect of the supportive functions throughout the family. The joy and excitement of the child's progress may then be shared by the child, his parents, and the therapist. With notably rare exceptions, the parents in this program have demonstrated that they are appropriately concerned and highly motivated to help their child.

It is also important for those with whom the child has contact in a social setting, such as the Scoutmaster, Sunday School teacher, and camp or sports leader, to understand the nature of those aberrant responses which children who have a learning disorder may exhibit. For instance, in social settings where there is less structure than in school, the hyperactive child may easily become overstimulated. Some children overreact to and are highly stimulated by certain kinds of sound; others are distracted by and made restless by close physical contact and unpredictable movements of children around them. Their unruly behavior can be extremely taxing to even the most patient leader. By understanding the nature of the problem he may be able to take steps to mitigate it so as to maintain a positive relationship with the child. Then those social experiences in the community which are so important in fostering a child's maturation and ego development will be more apt to be successful.

Parents, leaders in extracurricular activities, and teachers who realize that certain experiences are potentially disorganizing for the child can limit or temporarily help him to avoid unnecessary exposure to such experiences. For instance, parents of a child who is auditorily defensive would try to keep to a minimum his exposure to sounds which are especially distracting, irritating, or overstimulating. Parents of a child who is tactually defensive would stop their playful tickling of him. Concurrently during therapeutic sessions, positive therapeutic action is being taken to reduce the effect of these irritating and disorganizing experiences on the child. Obviously, change can be hastened if the problem is attacked from several sides at once. In later chapters more will be said about identifying those experiences which are disorganizing to a learning-disordered child.

Toys as Tools of Therapy

The second feature which characterizes the philosophy of this program is the unique use of toys and activities which are normally enjoyed in childhood as the primary tools of therapy. The modalities of therapy must "speak to the child." When they do, there is greater likelihood that the child will, without persuasion, spontaneously involve himself and be self-motivated to explore its possibilities for enjoyment.

If we use toys and certain motor activities common to childhood, why are the children with whom we are concerned not attracted to them? Why don't learning-disordered children learn by themselves to organize their motor behavior and go through the normal heirarchy or progression without the assistance of the therapist?

Toys or childhood activities require various sets of underlying sensorimotor skills. Toys will appeal to a child and sustain his interest and involvement only if he has the necessary matching skills to be successful in his play. For instance, it is not uncommon to find that the learning-disordered child had no interest in nesting toys or manipulative tasks such as puzzles or climbing experiences when they were appropriate for his age. Not only will such a child terminate his involvement with those toys or playground equipment which yield no satisfaction at the time, but subsequently he will be apt to avoid those academic tasks which clearly depend on the same early foundations.

Through documented accounts of therapy hours it became apparent that certain toys and desk activities could be analyzed according to various skills required in their use. This clinical use of toys and equipment normal to childhood heightened my awareness of the degree of fixation, or arrest, in learning-disordered children at earlier levels of development. I became aware that the primary equipment, especially, for early therapy need not be other than the normal toys of childhood. With some exceptions to be discussed later, the toys of childhood have proven to be the best diagnostic and therapeutic tools available.

7

The thrust of the holistic approach is to elicit spontaneous responses to selected activities. The activities are graded so as to then assess where the child's ability ranks among three levels of proficiency. It is the successful performance with tasks graded over these three levels of proficiency which gives assurance that (1) the underlying skills for each successive task have been mastered previously, and (2) that the proposed underlying skills on which academic performance depends have now been attained. It is the successful progression along the graded heirarchy, and *not* a predetermined age level of expected performance, which is the foremost concern and of primary relevance in the holistic approach to therapy.

Toys and activities normal to childhood — the primary modalities of therapy — are grouped into Phase I and Phase II tasks. Activities from these two phases are used concomitantly, although within a therapy hour either phase may be initiated first; the emphasis allocated to one may be greater one time than the other, varying throughout the program.

Phase I utilizes five basic pieces of gross motor equipment. A nondirective, invitational approach is used to inspire the child to become involved, but at his own speed, wherein he feels less threatened because he is in control. Through this technique, the therapist enables the child to "bridge the gap" between the inactive, avoidance response and the active, exploratory response.

In contrast to the gross motor activities of Phase I, Phase II is comprised primarily of desk tasks through which the child learns to organize and to apply early sensorimotor foundation skills. Once these organizing processes are set in motion to reduce the disorganized quality of behavior, the child tends to progress along the developmental hierarchy of preacademic and academic skills.

The key to successful therapeutic use of these toys is to select those which require a low enough level of motor or organizational response so that the child can spontaneously involve himself in play. As long as the child can find joy and satisfaction from playing with those toys which are within his capability, he will, through play, continue to improve those skills which the toys require. At the same time, he is laying down some of the sensorimotor foundations which he will need to acquire subsequent academic skills.

From among hundreds of toys and childhood activities which are commercially available, each of those recommended has been screened and carefully selected for its potential in promoting early sensorimotor development. In some instances the needs for specific therapy through gross motor equipment and desk activities or toys could not be met by items already on the market. This necessitated devising equipment specifically designed to meet such needs.

A Holistic Approach

The rationale for a holistic approach embraces the fact that there is a close inter-relationship between primary sensory system dysfunction and the secondary symptoms which affect the child adversely in adapting to everyday life. A composite approach which would alter behavior in a more positive direction in the primary problem would therefore mediate the secondary symptomatology as well.

The neurophysiological model has been developed by others and has furnished a very valuable foundation for "conceptualizing" evaluation results. The holistic approach attempts to integrate evaluation and therapy as an ongoing dynamic process which is conceptualized primarily around behavioral rather than neurophysiological information. While continuing to draw heavily upon the latter source for a background of knowledge and understanding of neural integration and sensorimotor performance, the holistic approach to the treatment of learning disorders goes beyond this to integrate with it a behavioral, pragmatic approach. In the holistic approach it would seem more relevant to the treatment to be concerned with how well the individual functions with respect to his own needs, and not how well he functions in comparison with the performance of others, established by normative data.

Bibliography

Knickerbocker B: Gaining a perspective about perceptual-motor dysfunction. Proceedings of the HEW Seminar on Perceptual-Motor Dysfunction. University of Wisconsin, Madison, Wisconsin, 1966.

Knickerbocker B: A parent-oriented program for the multiply handicapped child. Proceedings of the Occupational Therapy Conference for the Multiply Handicapped Child. University of Illinois, Chicago, Illinois, 1965.

3

Rationale of a Holistic Approach

The holistic approach takes into account the specific findings of the medical model but approaches their resolution from a broader, more generalized viewpoint to build on the positive, healthy aspects.

In the occupational therapy profession, a remarkable amount of energy and effort has been invested in documenting a formal evaluation and interpreting the findings as a prerequisite to instituting therapy. Therapists whose interests are strongly identified with formal evaluations often let this overshadow, or even replace, a commitment to remedial programming. This can be at the expense of the child's needs and best interests. It can also be at the expense of losing sight of our professional identity as therapists, unless we also establish a sufficiently broad and suitably integrated professional body of knowledge with regard to therapeutic effectiveness.

Inherent in the holistic approach is the opportunity for therapists to add to the professional body of knowledge information about the effectiveness of therapeutic techniques. Through "process analysis" clinicians are able to recognize which, among the five processes of the clinical hypothesis I have proposed, is represented by the child's behavior as he responds to therapeutic tasks.

If as occupational therapists we are to also maintain our identity with the role of clinical therapists, and if we are to expedite therapy more effectively, it will be essential that both the basis on which to grade our modalities of therapy and the principles of conducting therapy be thoroughly investigated. This book does not pretend to do such an investigation; it does structure the gradation and identify effective principles so that qualitative and quantitative evaluation of these methods can be carried out through further clinical research.

Research into clinical methods of treating learning-disordered children has never reached the level of concern and interest in our profession as has formal research in evaluation. Application of the scientific methods to these broader clinical areas is perhaps more difficult; conditions in formal research are much more readily controlled than in the clinical setting. But there may be other, more personal, reasons for the lack of clinical research.

Personal Attributes and Role Function

In the conventional approach based on the medical model, there is a close interrelationship of evaluation and therapy and a logical conclusion that the therapy is directly dependent upon evaluation. Implied in this statement is the general assumption that, if a therapist is well trained in evaluation, it will automatically prepare her to conduct therapy effectively. Before proceeding on any such assumption, it would be wise to look at the personal demands as well as professional requirements of these separate skills. These relative qualities are cited here only as a point of reference and are by no means thought of as absolute. However, it is important to recognize that since the personal qualifications do differ considerably, therapists may find themselves in conflict when they are expected to become equally proficient in each.

Proficiency in conducting evaluations is aided by these personal traits:

1. An ability to adhere to the scientific method requiring accuracy, attention to detail, and little deviation from prescribed procedures;
2. An analytical mind, interested in arriving at new conclusions and concepts by means which are measurable and precise;
3. A feeling of gratification derived through these endeavors.

Proficiency in conducting clinical therapy is aided by these personal traits:

1. An analytical point of view sufficient to understand and utilize the procedures of formal evaluation and to interpret adequately the significance of those findings;
2. An ability to understand the underlying theoretical premises upon which the therapy modalities are used to reduce sensorimotor dysfunction;
3. An ability to recognize evidence of change in sensorimotor dysfunction during therapy and from reports of the child's behavior outside the treatment setting;
4. An ability to analyze the sensory and motor attributes of a given treatment modality and grade its use so as to assure a successful progression of achievement;
5. An ability to be innovative in adjusting available modalities of therapy upward or downward in relation to the child's age, function, and other factors;
6. An ability to enjoy the variables and to cope spontaneously, intuitively, and creatively to meet the immediate needs revealed through the child's actions and behavior;
7. An ability to organize observations and draw conclusions from them;
8. A personality which will reflect warm, positive feelings toward the child so that his own ego development is nourished.

It would appear, therefore, that whereas there are a number of personal attributes which therapists may share in common, there are certain definite qualities which would make one therapist more compatible with the role of an evaluator and another with the role of clinical therapist. It is suggested that the contrast of these personal qualifications may offer some insights as to why therapists tend to perform in one area better than, or more exclusively than, the other.

Aside from the actual training needed to perform valid evaluations, it also requires quite a different emotional "set" for the individual to administer evaluations from that which is best suited to conduct clinical therapy. Patience for the sake of exactitude is required for the former since boundaries are set both in time and procedure. In clinical therapy extreme patience, emotional aplomb, and prolonged physical stamina are necessary to cope with the complexities of a wide range of changing behaviors and boundless energies of young, often hyperactive children. It is advisable for a therapist to be well aware of both the physical and emotional demands of these two roles.

Role Function in Evaluation and Therapy

To expect therapists to shift from one emotional and professional "set" to the other with equal skill and investment is unrealistic. To perform dual roles within a daily clinic routine can create in one a feeling of conflict. To divert one's energies so is distracting, and it prevents a therapist from fully developing her professional expertise in either. From the point of view of clinical management, such fragmentation of the therapist's responsibilities could feasibly reduce the program's efficiency as well.

Speaking from personal experience, at the time when I was performing both roles I suddenly recognized the adverse effect on one child in particular; I was then re-evaluating him after the first six months of therapy. Instead of finding the warm, accepting, freely communicative and approbative response to which he had become accustomed throughout therapy, the child felt suddenly thrust into an unresponsive, formal evaluation milieu because of my own eagerness to obtain objective data. This was both confusing and anxiety-producing for him. The reversal of roles from therapist back to evaluator had an adverse effect on the results of the evaluation. Scores on some tests were lower than the initial evaluation had shown, yet observations of this child throughout therapy and reports from home and school seemed to verify progress in the areas which were most closely related to these same tests. Young children would especially often perceive my reserved attitude as punishment for being "bad," despite my attempts to allay their anxieties over the change in my role during their re-evaluation. The testing procedures did not involve the customary pleasurable activities with which they associated their therapy. The initial role change, however, from evaluation to therapy had presented no such problems. Therefore, it would seem appropriate to have a person other than the one conducting the child's therapy program to follow through with the formal re-evaluation when it is required. In this way, test-retest reliability is more apt to be assured.

Following an adequate exposure to formal evaluation procedures for the purpose of either specializing along that vein or to use this as valuable background experience for clinical observations, a therapist would want to consider how his or her own personal traits aligned with those best suited to one role or the other. In so doing, a therapist can then function most effectively in the emotional "set" most compatible to role function. In a singular role, the individual will then be able to direct full attention toward mastering the most pertinent skills.

Formal Evaluation —
A Prerequisite to Therapy or Clinical Training?

The purpose, and the foremost value, of a formal evaluation using standardized tests is to diagnose specific areas of sensory intergrative dysfunction. On the basis of test findings and relevant observations, a therapist would verify the need for treatment and determine suitable therapy techniques. One of the most important values of administering a formal evaluation using standardized data is that re-evaluation on the same battery will yield a statistical index of change. It is the general consensus of therapists who subscribe to the medical model that evaluation by means of a formal battery is a necessary diagnostic prerequisitie to instituting therapy.

While the holistic approach subscribes to a somewhat different point of view as regards the need for a formal evaluation as a prerequisite to therapy, it considers that the background of experience which a therapist acquires by evaluating learning-disordered children by means of standardized tests is invaluable. The discipline and the method of making critical observations is unobtainable by any other means. It is therefore recommended that any occupational therapist who follows a holistic approach do so only after having attained an adequate background of training and experience in administering the formal battery of tests by Ayres,[1] and other related tests of visual-motor integration.

Factors which determine administrative decisions as to whether or not a formal test battery will be a prerequisite to instituting therapy will be governed by the goals and the philosophy of the particular setting in which the program is conducted. If the emphasis is directed toward research, then the need to substantiate changes statistically would be obvious. If the clinic is charged with a training mission for occupational therapy students, the same could be true. More commonly, however, the realistic demand in many school and clinic facilities would be to yield results for the greatest number of children with a limited professional staff.

The numbers of learning-disordered children far exceed the supply of trained professionals in this specialty of treatment. Practical, economical, and efficient means whereby more therapists can help a large number of children are urgently needed. Otherwise, a small number of therapists qualified in specifics will be invested in the care of a privileged few.

A More Generalized Approach

For many years, I, like my colleagues, administered an extensive formal evaluation on every child before starting treatment. I subscribed at that time to the medical model and planned each child's program on the basis of the various syndromes defined by Ayres and suggested by the standardized data. This experience over many years provided me a valuable background for observing the child in therapy.

Eventually I reassessed my position and challenged my procedure. It became necessary for me to determine whether the form of therapy I provided one child differed significantly from another in relation to his formal evaluation. It was clear that in clinical practice the modalities of treatment used for one child in many ways paralleled those used for others: the scooter board, the inflatables, or the barrel. For instance, I used the barrel in many different ways to treat various needs for symptoms revealed by a wide range of children.

It was in 1968 at a training program conducted by Ayres that I was first introduced to the therapeutic merits of the carpeted barrel. I have continued using it as one of the five basic pieces of early motor equipment because of the range of therapeutic benefits which can be derived therefrom, including:

1. improved vestibular bilateral integration* by rolling inside, (Part III, Program Plan 2);
2. same, by straddling the outside of the barrel as it is laid on its side;
3. concomitantly stimulate awareness and focus of extraoccular musculature;
4. reduce tactile defensiveness through skin sufaces contacting the carpet lining the inside and outside, (Part III, Program Plan 1);
5. stimulate the co-contraction of the muscles and the joint compression by pushing the barrel;
6. improve sensory system organization and integration among the tactile, vestibular, and visual systems with resulting improvement in motor development and skill.

Protective arm extension is also activated as the child lies prone over the midpoint of the barrel with the therapist holding him by the feet and rolling him forward. In yet another special way, I could foster better awareness of spatial relations in the world around him in conjunction with auditory localization by asking the child to roll in the direction of the sound he heard but did not see (Part III, Program Plan 2.2).

Gradually I realized that I was depending more and more on the observations I made from the child's performance as my criteria to guide his course of therapy. I then began to observe the child's spontaneous responses to a given piece of equipment more closely, comparing it with that of other children in the program. Often a child would be overjoyed to find some pieces of equipment in which he could perform well. Before, I had felt that time spent on areas of better function were unworthy of valuable therapy time when there were other, more urgent, areas of deficit which merited a directed effort.

Out of these systematic clinical observations, a more generalized approach

*The syndrome defined by Ayres originally as postural and bilateral motor integration has now been redesignated by her as vestibular bilateral integration.[2] When I refer to this syndrome by name, I generally include in my thinking the various neurophysiological pathways and mechanisms specified by Ayres. However, within this text, I also use the terms bilateral, bimanual, and two-sided integration to refer to those aspects of this syndrome which are clinically observable. Changes in the child's voluntary, spontaneous integrated actions can be recognized by clinicians and laymen and documented accordingly. In the holistic approach I have identified the functional linkage between the visual and vestibular systems which clinically parallels the syndrome of vestibular bilateral integration, and have termed it the Visuo-Vestibular Dyad (See Chapter 7).

15

evolved which encompasses a wide spectrum of problems of learning-disordered children. Hence it has been named a "holistic approach."

The holistic approach proposes that the need for therapy may be effectively identified through empirical judgment of the child's ability to perform on certain selected pieces of gross motor equipment and to function with key desk tasks. The principal difference in assessment through the holistic approach is that the same kinds of activities are utilized for treatment as for evaluation. Thus evaluation is not separate from the program, but continues as a dynamic and integral part of it throughout therapy.

Parent-Oriented Program

One of the strongest influences in shifting to a more generalized approach was my strong feeling that the parents should be able to participate in an increasingly active role. I clearly had to adopt methods of assessing the problem and defining solutions in a way which was readily apparent to the layman. For certain important reasons, the methods I used to communicate with the parents would often be nonverbal, and thus depend greatly upon my actions. My appraisal of the child's function would be derived more from his spontaneous response to a task than through verbal communications. Reasons for using these techniques are as follows:

1. Despite the fact that a child seems to verbalize adequately, one must not depend on his comprehension of spoken language to assess his performance of a task.

2. Some children prefer to talk about, rather than perform simple motor tasks because they find them difficult to do.

3. Many learning-disordered children are distracted by conversation; verbal communication with the parents during therapy must be kept to a minimum.

4. The hyperverbal child may be using this as a means to avoid a task, or more subtly, to adroitly distract the adult's attention from it.

5. In the presence of the child direct discussion in terms of dysfunction is avoided. However, the criteria for performance cited in "The Ongoing Evaluation and Performance Scale" (See Part II) is a helpful vehicle of communication. The parent can follow the steps depicting performance on a given piece of equipment and can easily see how far along the hierarchy their child is functioning initially in relation to it; they can begin to recognize changes as they occur in therapy.

Constant Factors in Holistic Programming

The rationale of the holistic approach is predicated on the idea that regardless of the etiology of the child's learning disorder, be it organic, systemic, genetic, or environmental, the therapeutic procedures vary insignificantly.

The causes of learning disorders are often unidentifiable in relation to the individual child. Known causes of some of these problems would include nutritional deficits, incidence of rubella during the mother's pregnancy, trauma or oxygen deficiency at birth, genetic factors, a high febrile condition in infancy,

16

and any inflammatory process of the brain such as measles encephalitis. The effects of smoking and drinking during pregnancy have come under attack more recently. A clear clinical history will often yield no specific cause; soft neurological signs may be the strongest available evidence. In the case of organic lesions which are irreversible, the end result will be determined by their severity but the basic treatment procedures and the sequential order of their use would remain constant; one would proceed as far as possible until an insurmountable plateau had been reached. In general, the format and the therapeutic procedures remain constant because they concern function and performance.

Contributory Social Factors

After working with learning-disordered children for a number of years, I began to wonder if there were certain ways in which our society now functions which may have created a different impact on childhood development. It is my own hypothesis that in recent decades there have been important changes which may contribute a dilatory effect on normal learning processes. These factors are 1) a mobile society, 2) the age of plastics, 3) acceleration of education, and 4) television. Of these, the first two and the last two factors seem to have a paired relationship. Since these factors operate independently of any socioeconomic stratification, there would be greater likelihood of, and more credibility for, environmental or societal influence on the incidence of learning disorders. If this hypothesis is found to be valid, it would figure significantly in terms of early prevention.

A Mobile Society

The trend towards a mobile society which was heightened during World War II has continued. The corporate community, like the military, makes demands upon families to move on a national and international scale. In recent decades young families subject to military and industrial mobility have been less apt to raise their children within close proximity to relatives, where members of the extended family are available to help in caring for the infant. The current, universal trend, in this country especially, has been for mothers to bring infants along shopping, to restaurants, and to most outings. The amount of time in an infant's first six months of life which he may spend outside the home environment seems to have greatly increased by comparison with the prewar society.

The Age of Plastics

Concomitant with our becoming a mobile society was the development of consumer products molded from chemical compounds. It would seem quite unnatural today to take an infant across town or across the country without using a plastic infant carrier or car seat. Indeed, it is indispensable to a busy mother for it insures the baby's safety from falling or sustaining other self-

17

incurred mishaps. The child appears comfortable and content as he is propped up to view his surroundings. It would seem obvious that there would be greater opportunity for a child to be visually stimulated and be more responsive to the people and events going on around him. Thus the plastic infant carrier might seem to be an ideal adjunct to good infant care and development. A word of caution would be "moderation in all things."

During the first six months of life, the rate of change in neurological development proceeds at a faster pace than at any other similar span of time throughout life. Therefore, it is urgent that the infant be unrestricted in this course so he can fulfill the predesigned pattern and timetable of normal neurological development. Interference in this process should not be imposed by factors of the environment. If the early antigravity motor exploration is restricted and the preambulatory patterns of motion are interrupted, the child may be robbed of important opportunities for normal sensorimotor development.

When the infant is transported in the plastic infant carrier, the head is passively supported in a semireclined position. This reduces the opportunity to facilitate the neck-righting reflexes. When these righting reflexes are less active, the visual system functions in a more isolated manner. Shifts of motion in the vertical position requires muscular responses to stabilize the head, which aid in the proprioceptive stimulation of the extraocular muscles. Dr. Ayres states that "It is believed that strong contraction of the neck muscles results in better neural integration in the brain stem oculomotor mechanisms."[2]

In contrast to the restricted static positioning of the infant in the carrier or car seat, when the infant is lying on a flat surface in the crib, playpen, or floor he is free to move. He should be able to raise his head, roll over, pivot on his abdomen, and freely respond to the natural urge to move and to explore his environment. There are specific reasons why prone positioning of the infant is so important; he can push himself up on his arms to gradually overcome the effect of the early tonic neck reflexes (TNR) and tonic labyrinthine reflexes (TVR). These reflexes are normal in infancy; they must be gradually overcome and be integrated in the nervous system so that equilibrium responses may develop. This prone positioning stimulates the neck extensor muscles to contract against the pull of gravity; the proprioceptive stimulation from this action is important in integrating the visual response. Dr. Ayres states that:

> Activities which simultaneously involve assuming the quadruped position and evincing equilibrium responses provide a large quantity of the proprioceptive stimuli, which basic research has indicated are critical to the visual space perception process.[1]

In addition to the value of proprioceptive stimulation through movement of the neck and head, being held by the adult also yields touch-pressure information which activates the tactile-kinesthetic receptors in the infant. This contact both nurtures good body image and the natural feelings of warmth and affection so important to a child's early development. Before the age of plastics, when a baby was fed he was frequently in direct physical contact with the adult. When one relies on the use of the plastic infant carrier for prolonged periods of time there will be a substantially smaller portion of time when the infant is being touched and handled. As compared to the natural shifts in touch and pressure on the body when being held and frequently repositioned by an adult, the static quality of touch-pressure of the infant carrier on the child's body greatly reduces the impact of essential sensory stimulation.

It would seem that the interrelationship and the timing between the trend toward a more mobile society and the widespread use of plastic infant carriers in child care would be a relevant consideration when investigating causes and prevention of the high incidence of learning disorders.

Acceleration of Early Education

There are three developments in our society since World War II which have had a dramatic influence on the acceleration of early education. The first is the almost universal accessibility of children to prolonged television viewing; second is the heightened stress and tempo to compete educationally, following "Spuntnik";[3] and third is the fact that kindergarten education became publicly funded. There are both positive and negative effects of each of these influences; the last feature will be my principal focus of the acceleration of education.

Kindergarten

On the positive side, it is incontestable that public funding of kindergarten offers more equal opportunity for all children; at the same time, there is reason to suggest that this change may indirectly, and inadvertently, also contribute to the incidence of symptoms of learning disorders in today's schools. The reason cited here is the change to a curriculum-oriented kindergarten. Heretofore, when kindergartens were not publicly supported, formal introduction of reading and writing skills were introduced in the first grade curriculum. When this training was first instituted at the age of six, the child was much more apt to have acquired the normal neurological development these skills required. These children had had more time in the years prior to entering first grade to develop the gross motor skills through their own outdoor play and exploration of their environment, or on supervised playgrounds, or in some cases under the jurisdiction of private kindergartens where there was no prescribed academic curriculum. This is not to say that some children, girls especially, will not be sufficiently adept and mature to master these academic skills early. The problem arises when such training is curriculum-directed, creating an expectation and requirement for all children to master tasks for which many are not developmentally mature. Such an expectation causes a high risk that a sense of failure will be imposed on children at this early age. When a greater emphasis is placed on gross motor experiences and constructive kindergarten play, the children will then be neurologically more mature and, in a great percentage of cases, able to successfully undertake and master the early academic skills in writing and reading as they are introduced in the first grade. By this time, they presumably would have established the preacademic foundations for determining hand dominance before being required to also maintain control of the direction and the sequence of fine movement patterns. The chance of developing hand dominance as a poorly founded splinter skill would be dramatically reduced; the child would experience little, if any, confusion over left and right, especially as it is applied to forming letters, words, and for reading.

With kindergartens becoming incorporated into the public school system, the tendency to train academic skills earlier has intensified over the years. It is not this factor alone, but also because of the social pressures of the adult world, which after "Sputnik" focused on the educational system both as the cause of our national problems and the hope of their solutions. As this pressure quickly filtered down to the kindergarten level, these teachers felt pressured to produce, ie, the child must be "prepared for first grade." Nursery schools, in turn, felt the pressure to prepare the child for kindergarten. The teachers themselves feel that their success as a teacher is at stake and unwittingly pass this on to the child. The child finds himself at the mercy of pressures from the educational system, from the parents, and from his own strivings to "please." The feeling of urgency "to prepare," and as a child, "to be prepared," now even pervades some nursery schools which start handwriting skills at age four.

It would seem then that when the orientation of the kindergarten school shifted dramatically away from its former emphasis on nurturing good child development, certain early foundations of learning through play were somehow sacrificed. When playing with three-dimensional toys and objects, which kindergartens can provide in rich measure, the child usually learns to use manipulative hand skills, to sense the organization and structure of the physical world, and the natural cause-and-effect relationship of his actions within it. When these early experiences are bypassed, the child at a later time may still be unable to fill in these underlying experiences on his own so as to subsequently organize himself adequately in an academic atmosphere.

Television

The influence, both good and bad, of the content of television entertainment on young children is not the subject of discussion here. Rather, it is the passive, almost addictive quality of involvement of children which can have a deleterious effect on learning when it saps the child's available time and motivation to investigate more active participatory learning experiences.

The advent of educationally-oriented commercial television programs for preschoolers provides both benefits and liabilities. The greatest advantage is in offering additional exposure to young underprivileged children who have access to these programs. If these were the only programs a child watched, the extent of time spent passively would be less significant. But there are other more specific reasons why, in my opinion, these television programs can present problems. Much of the learning is a passive, as opposed to a more dynamic, personally involved visual and auditory experience. By watching television, children may attempt to form their letters, but this is often in the absence of adult supervision, and the skill may be acquired on a random, haphazard basis. It would be more beneficial if, after building the proper foundations motorically in order to develop hand dominance, the child learned under supervision and in a consistent manner the directional orientation of top-bottom and left-right on which to orient the numbers and printed letters. Another adverse effect teachers may find is that by the time the child is ready for formal instruction in these pencil skills, he is apt to be resistive, ie, bored, with further attempts to teach these skills. The child may then persist in making the forms incorrectly, eg, numbers 3,5, 7, 9 from bottom to top or backwards.

Premature training to form numbers and letters in either nursery school, kindergarten, or through exposure to television programs can cause the child to develop splinter skills. These splinter skills are acquired at an early age by children who are alert and bright; however, the undesirable results may be seen in the residual learning problems when reversals in reading and printing persist far longer than would be normal, eg, into second grade. In my opinion, this is one of the primary reasons behind the paradoxical situation in which learning disorders often appear among highly intelligent children.

Pseudo Learning Disorders

In the schools of this country an estimated 12% to 20% of children in the normal classrooms suffer from symptoms of learning disorders.[4] This statistic does not include those in special programs. From my experience, in only a small percentage of these can genetic, organic, or systemic etiology be clearly documented as the cause of the problems. Among those whose etiology is not discernible, there is a sizable percentage of children whose problems must have stemmed from certain detrimental influences of our environment. It would seem reasonable that the earlier an environmental influence (eg, the protracted use of the plastic infant carrier) makes an impact on the human organism, the more pronounced the resulting learning disorder will be. The impact of this could be so significant in arresting normal sequential development that the children thus affected would be considered to have a "classical learning disorder."

There is also a group of children whom I have labeled *pseudo learning-disordered* whose learning problems I feel stem directly from the adverse effects of the accelerated rate of learning promoted in this country. These effects, together with the attendant anxieties of all concerned, eg, the parents, the teachers, and the child, can so aggravate the child's learning milieu that problems arise which truly resemble those of classical learning disorders. The impact resulting from the deterrent effect of accelerated education falls on the child after the most critical early stages of infant growth and development have taken place. Thus the problems are more superficial and more apt to be successfully mediated with proper and prompt intervention. The problems these children exhibit are usually more mild in degree, and they often relate to confused dominance and its secondary effect on directionality and spatial relations; problems are also seen in the inability to direct movement and to master organization tasks. These children tend to be less affected by sensory defensiveness and the distraction and disorganization which often accompany the defensive condition.

Children who demonstrate psuedo learning disorders usually have a normal or higher intellectual level, are quite conscious of the uniqueness of their problems in relation to their peers, are highly motivated, and respond well to therapy. Although these may often be relatively mild cases, they have nevertheless suffered emotionally and academically from their learning disorder. Without intervention, the effect in most cases would be further compounded as time passed; the child would be able to master many of these problems from an intellectual, cognitive approach but not always without some residual emotional scarring.

There is a definite relevance in distinguishing pseudo learning disorders from the classical form. The importance of the term pseudo learning disorder lies in the presumption that measures can be taken by way of prevention. Also, this term identifies a subgroup for whom the holistic approach can have a profound beneficial effect. Much of the holistic programming can be conducted by educators in the preschool and elementary grades to prevent further development of and bring early mediation to a pseudo learning disorder in a child.

References

1. Ayres AJ: Southern California Sensory Integration Tests. Los Angeles, Western Psychological Services, 1972.
2. Ayres AJ: Sensory Integration and Learning Disorders. Los Angeles, Western Psychological Services, 1972, pp 134-145, 202-203.
3. Ley W: Events in Space. New York, David McKay Co Inc, 1969, p 165.
4. John, ER et al: Neurometrics. Science Magazine 196:1393, June 24, 1977.

4

Development of a
Working Hypothesis

Observation of the spontaneous behavior of learning-disordered children to toys and equipment which normally would attract a child's interest gave rise to the impression that there are two clearly antithetical responses: *avoidance* and *exploration.* In Chapter 1 I stated two basic premises as to why a child fails to respond to and explore the objects of his environment: 1) learning-disordered children were often exposed prematurely to learning experiences and 2) the child would be less likely to develop a foundation for learning because of his need to avoid frustration and failure.

Under these conditions, the balance between success and failure soon tilts overwhelmingly on the side of failure rather than increasing on the side of successful learning. The only response then open to the child is to avoid engaging in tasks which portend failure; he may even withdraw from experiences with which he had previously coped successfully if his anxiety becomes too intense. Corrective measures, therefore, would focus on these two points: (1) revert to an earlier level of physical and/or academic skills to expose the child to the tasks with which he can involve himself voluntarily and begin again to perform with success, and (2) adhere to applicable principles of grading to assure continued success as the child is brought up to his potential.

Finding a substitute level of difficulty to assure the child success helps him to mitigate the insults to his fragile ego; it can spark his incentive to more age-appropriate tasks in due time so as to eventually compete on a more equitable basis. Without therapeutic intervention the child may overcome much of the symptomatology of the problem as he matures. However, by then he will have passed the optimal point of sensorimotor integration on which to build cognitive learning. A broad-based foundation for learning can be instituted by task achievement which follows the expected neurodevelopmental progression and which helps the child to approximate more closely the maturational schedule.

Goal Definition in a Holistic Approach

The goal for the learning-disordered child from a holistic point of view is *to enable him to bring organization out of disorganization in sensory input, motor output, social responses, and academic performance so that, insofar as possible, he can function as an equal among his peers.*

The Hypothesis

Gradually a series of processes became apparent through the observations of many children as they performed with the same equipment under similar conditions. A predictably sequential pattern emerged; a hypothesis was formulated. This hypothesis has provided a suitable structure from which to further organize my observations, to plan better means of intervention, and to conceptualize these ideas. The hypothesis has proven to be a practical vehicle of communication through which to convey information to parents, teachers and other therapists. In some respects it can be applied to our society as well.

Careful documentation of my observations throughout this therapy program supports the theory of a natural sequence of processing of information. Early learning processes must be activated in sequence if the child is to eventually assimilate cognitive information. This sequence is evident in the hypothesis to follow:

Once the avoidance response in a learning task is overcome, learning takes place through those processes which evolve in an orderly sequence and continue thereafter in a cyclic pattern, initially providing the foundation skills for learning continuity. The processes in this sequence are presented in order: avoid, explore, organize, integrate, and conceptualize.[1]

Defining the Processes

The five processes of the working hypothesis will be presented in detail in the chapters to follow. It is expedient, however, to define the meaning of these processes as they are used here.

*Avoid** — protect or defend oneself from sensory input which is perceived as being threatening, offensive, noxious; prevent direct contact with offensive sensory input; defend oneself by consciously closing off or shutting out contact with sensory stimuli which are disturbing, distracting, ie, disorganizing; withdraw from those experiences involving sensory input which is perceived as potentially harmful, irritating, or disorganizing; be insensitive to, or unaware of, sensory input.

Explore — become more aware of sensations or conscious of experiences which were previously inactive or dormant; tolerate increased contact with stimuli or experiences previously interpreted from sensory input which were perceived by the individual as being threatening, irritating, noxious, and potentially harmful; initiate action, involve oneself voluntarily and spontaneously; seek those experiences which were previously shunned.

Organize† — recognize elementary likenesses and differences of stimuli within a sensory system, eg, manual form perception, visual form perception, auditory discrimination; match, sort, classify, and group kinds of sensory stimuli, objects, symbols, or ideas by "like" attributes; establish a constancy in the meaning represented by different symbolic form; arrange objects, ideas in a sequential order, ie, by size, shape, in time, numerically or alphabetically, or by other classification.

*Integrate*** — unify present impressions among various sensory systems; unify past experiences with present impressions within one sensory system and together with other sensory systems; perceive, as a result, a more complete "whole" of one's "sensory picture" of the environment and one's emotional "set" in relation to it; establish a sensory foundation for recollection and recall as a prerequisite to associative memory of cognitive information.

Conceptualize — recognize the abstract words and ideas which convey concepts about early concrete, tangible sensory and motor experiences;

---

*The term avoidance, *meaning to stay clear of, was selected in preference to* aversive behavior *which implies dislike, repugnance, or antipathy. The negative attitude suggested by such a term fails to take into account the lack of sensory awareness, or dormancy as the term is applied here, as an underlying reason for the lack of a child's involvement with a task or experience.*

†*Whereas it is often highly desirable to have multisensory stimulation, eg, visual with the vestibular systems on an early sensory integrative level, when it comes to organizing more discriminative qualities of information, ie, tactile, auditory, visual, olfactory, the organization of individual sensory systems without added confusion and distraction is advocated. The use of the terms here, to organize and integrate, are defined with this in mind.*

**The word* integrate *is used by Ayres in neurophysiological terms; it is used here in a behavioral context, to include the 1) early sensory integration, 2) its influence on sensory system organization and integration applied to task performance, and 3) the effect on social and academic adjustment.*

develop a capacity for cognition as an outgrowth of sensory and motor organization and integration; assess likenesses and differences of ideas or abstract information; establish critical common denominators between abstract elements drawing from this process new analogies, developing working hypotheses to arrive at new conclusions and concepts.

Patterns, Processes, and Modes

The term *pattern* is used here to refer to a child's response to a specific task. As an example, a young child may be unable to direct his attention to anything but the simplest piece of equipment, such as an infant hourglass. The pattern of behavior in response to other tasks is identified as avoidance, whereas his emerging pattern of attention and interest in turning this toy upside down would be a part of the exploratory process.

Here is a further example of observing patterns of response: the therapist will recognize that when a task is analyzed and broken down into its component skills, the child's response may be quite adequately organized in some respects — for instance, by using a good tripod grip on the pencil in writing his numbers. On the other hand, he would show a very poor directional pattern if at the same time he were to draw the number "one" from bottom to top.

The term *process* implies the activation of behavioral responses, recognizing both the ones which are negative, such as an avoidance response and those which facilitate learning, as designated in the hypothesis.

As soon as there is no longer any need for a child to respond to a given task by an avoidance pattern, each of the other four processes can be activated. By observing the varied patterns of response a child gives to a task, the therapist can identify which process is being activated. Also, the child may respond with avoidance to one task while at the same time demonstrating that in other tasks he is able to explore, organize, integrate, and conceptualize.

The child's condition is never static; neither is it representative of only one process. However, when the child's condition at the beginning of a therapy program is generally more characteristic of avoidance than any of the other processes, his behavior is referred to in a collective term as the avoidance mode.

Early avoidance patterns which involve motor skills are quite distinct and easy to recognize; at an older age, a child may incorporate his need to avoid in rather elaborate, subtly evasive techniques which are more difficult to identify but can, nevertheless, be traced back to the common roots of early sensorimotor disorganization. Without a doubt, the most difficult step for the child in this sequential learning pattern is "bridging the gap" between the avoidance mode of behavior and an exploratory mode; enabling him to do so is the single most critical step in the therapy program. Gradually, as a child acquires impressions from his exploratory experience he can organize these by discerning their general similarities and differences. In time he learns to integrate the simultaneous input of one sensory system with the information received from another. As these kinds of information from the sensory systems become integrated, the significance of the ongoing experience may be compared with that of the past. In this way the child can begin to develop broad, general concepts from his impressions.

Cyclic Continuity

Subsequently, the child cycles back again and again to proceed through the same sequential pattern, each time at a slightly higher level. At each successive cycle he explores further to organize new information with more accurate discrimination and refinement of differences and to integrate it with current and past sensorimotor and/or cognitive information so as to draw further conclusions and arrive at new concepts. It would appear that once the child has overcome the original need to avoid exposure to or involvement with a given sensory, motor, or cognitive task, learning can continue in this sequential pattern. Through cyclic progression to gradually higher levels of skill, the child is able to establish a foundation for a smoothly integrated learning experience. This continuity allows him to become better organized so that he can develop his ideas and also establish a basis for deductive reasoning and creative expression. This hypothesis seems equally applicable to the pursuit of advanced education and research as it does to the early learning patterns of children. In fact, the dynamics of this hypothesis have been confirmed to me repeatedly as the material presented here has evolved to its present form.

Activating the Process

The terms avoid, explore, organize, integrate, and conceptualize describe processes which may be observed sequentially in sensorimotor development. My greatest concern here is to precipitate change rather than focus on the causality of the problems and the arrest of the child's development in static terms. It is the redundancy of function and the adaptive quality of the central nervous system that makes it possible for these last four processes to be activated. Once these processes are activated they will be able to provide to a greater extent the foundation skills out of which a relatively normal progression will follow along the learning continuum. It is not unusual that the developmental gaps can be closed. Following proper procedures, this can be done with regard to a given skill or skills, in many cases at a rate which may well exceed the normal pace of development.

Illustration of the Sequential Learning Pattern

So that the reader may have some grasp of the practicality of this hypothesis, the following brief illustrations of responses within the tactile system will typify how easily one can recognize characteristic responses within each of these five processes. One can then appreciate how the tactile system undergoes change and what these changes represent throughout the sequential learning pattern. This illustration will indicate also how these progressively changing responses ultimately prepare the foundation skills for academic performance.

Avoid

An avoidance response is exhibited in the infant who is hypersensitive to tactile stimulation or who, to use Ayres' term, is *tactually defensive*.[2] He will often reject cuddling and normal fondling; tickling the infant may create profound excitation or even send him into a sudden rage, which may puzzle the family. The infant may withdraw by moving his head and extremities away from the stimulus while registering an expression of anxiety and discomfort. An adverse response to being held or touched is normal for healthy, happy toddlers when they are temporarily expressing irritability from fatigue. The tactile defensive child will respond to touch in this manner more consistently and profoundly.

Even adults who have an overly sensitive avoidance response in the tactile system will often reject being touched and find it emotionally distasteful and disorganizing to be in close human contact. Light touch especially causes them to be excessively ticklish. Clothing may be irritating, especially that which clings or feels stiff and new. Children who persist in removing their clothes may be expressing such discomfort. Others will feel exposed and more vulnerable to touch unless they are wearing tops with long sleeves. With maturity the tendency to overt discomfort is greatly reduced; with or without therapy, there may be certain hypersensitive responses which may carry over into adulthood.

Explore

An indication that the child has bridged the gap from avoidance to exploration may be seen in a child who, having shown earlier signs of oversensitivity to touch, will begin to tolerate being hugged or touched as his nervous system matures. He first accepts closer contact from close family members, whose movement and contact with him are predictable and evoke his trust. He will then begin to explore his environment by reaching out to touch it. He gradually accepts contact with people and pets as long as he can maintain control, ie, be free either to continue or to withdraw from this contact. A strong tendency in him to touch everyone and everything is the next step along the learning continuum. It suggests that touching is now beginning to yield for the child useful information and newly pleasurable experiences; when this response is reached, often after prolonged delay, it too may reach excessive proportions for a temporary period. In some cases, the natural sequence in the learning pattern portrayed here may have begun to resolve itself by the time therapy is initiated. This finding, which is easily derived from a sensorimotor history, can be hailed as an important and spontaneous indication of progress along the learning continuum, which can then be further accelerated by suitable therapy procedures.

Organize

Through the purposeful, exploratory touching and feeling cited above, the child begins to organize gross impressions of likenesses and differences of his tactile experience. He then learns to correlate what he feels with what he sees by discriminating gross differences in texture and form. During subsequent cyclic progression to higher levels, this ability to discriminate differences in form through touch alone, while vision is occluded, is gradually refined. The child learns to identify increasingly obscure and subtle differences in manual form discrimination, as depicted in the Program Plans of Part III.

Integrate

Out of the process of early sensory organization develops the process of integration. This term is used in its broad application within the behavioral context. In addition to the concurrent validation, ie, integration of one sensory system with another, the child also develops an experience factor in therapy through which to integrate present with past sensory experience. By establishing greater sensory validation and matching current and past sensory impressions, the child experiences a more integrated "whole" with which he can cope with his environment.

At a very early and primitive level a child normally begins to store sensory impressions regarding emotional tone which imbues his experience. Retrieval of sensory information helps the child build the optimal foundation for recollection and recall of information in the academic setting.

Conceptualize

The child who has been tactually defensive will now be able to make continuous and immediate deductions about what is transpiring about him with regard to his tactile system. He will recognize whether the quality of touch he is experiencing is harmful or innocuous, irritating or pleasant, without necessarily giving any cognitive attention to it. He can assimilate this into the total environmental Gestalt of the moment. Since the tactile stimulus no longer requires his undue attention, he can concentrate more fully on the task at hand and become better organized in his academic performance.

Relevance

The five processes contained in the hypothesis are of value not only to the therapist and educator, but also to parents and to laymen concerned with the fringes of this problem in society. For example, the terms which depict these processes are intended to convey to the scoutmaster or to the juvenile authorities some understanding of the nature and the meaning of certain kinds of impulsive behavior among learning-disordered children.

In therapy, these five processes have further relevance; they help to unify in our thinking those characteristic responses which sensory systems share in common. In this way, we can more easily envision methods by which change can be implemented along the broadest base. The extended effects resulting from therapeutic measures to organize the tactile system is one illustration. Because the tactile system is easily accessible to constructive, external stimulation and because the quality of its responses can be readily understood by a knowledge-able observer, this system is often a primary focus of therapy. Efforts to establish better organization within this system can effect a change within the organization of the central nervous system; the effects of this are demonstrated through more predictable responses in other sensory systems and in motor behavior. This exemplifies the goal definition of the holistic point of view which is to bring organization out of disorganization in sensory, motor, social, and academic areas.

References

1. Knickerbocker BM: Reduction of disorganized behavior in children with learning disabilities. Proceedings of the Workshop on Perceptual-Motor Dysfunction. Detroit, Michigan, March 23-24, 1973.
2. Ayres AJ: Tactile functions: their relation to hyperactive and perceptual motor behavior. Am J Occup Ther 18:6-11, 1964.

5

Clustered Clinical Patterns Among Sensory Systems

The holistic approach to mediating learning disorders is directed first toward recognizing the clinical manifestations symptomatic of the problem and then recognizing those clinical features which share common characteristics between and among the sensory systems, as well as to propose primary and secondary linkage between the various symptoms. The term *clustered clinical patterns* is preferred over the term *syndrome* for a number of reasons. The clinical symptoms range over a wide spectrum of symptomatology (see Chapters 6 and 7) rather than being limited to a precise parameter. The holistic assessment of these symptoms is focused on a dynamic, clinically-oriented point of view rather than the more classical use of the term in diagnosing syndromes. Recognition of symptoms by their clustered clinical pattern is of direct value to the clinician; with these clusters she can begin to construct an overall conceptual framework for observation and programming of the learning-disordered child.

During the years in which I have observed these children I have noticed that there are clearly clustered clinical patterns between and among sensory systems which combine in a triadic and a dyadic relationship. Three sensory systems which have the clearest pattern of clustered clinical symptoms are the olfactory, tactile, and auditory sensory systems. I refer to this constellation as *The Olfactory-Tactile-Auditory Sensory Triad,* or, for convenience, *The OTA Triad.* Two other systems form a dyadic clinical picture; *The Visuo-Vestibular Dyad* is so named for the close clinical relationship these sensory systems share.

There is a wide parameter of responses which span these sensory systems — hypersensitivity on the one hand to hyposensitivity on the other. The similarity of behavioral responses to the sensory input within a given sensory system and its likeness to or its contrast to responses of other systems helps us to envision what may be the child's Gestalt about his environs and thus guide us toward the most effective treatment of him as a learning-disordered child.

Sensory Defensiveness

I have continued to be impressed by the clinical significance of the condition Ayres describes so well as tactile defensiveness. In my experience, a more generalized term, *sensory defensiveness,* is likewise applicable to denote heightened sensitivity which can be applied to clinical behavior of other systems as well. Use of the term sensory defensiveness helps to bring into a clearer focus the similarities of clinical behavior between and among sensory systems.

The reason for a disorganized clinical response to sensory information is that there is an imbalance between the inhibitory and the excitatory forces within the nervous system. There is too little inhibition, which is the same as too much excitation, when the sensory message is transmitted too easily, and an excess of sensory information floods the higher centers of the central nervous system. In other words, since this information is not properly monitored along the way nor suitably integrated with other incoming sensory data, it is undifferentiated and overwhelming to the human organism. Disorganization created by the inaccurate quality of sensory data causes the individual to respond excessively; the clinical picture is characterized by the disorganized, immature quality of sensorimotor responses.

Sensory Dormancy

On the other side of the coin, sensory and motor responses may also be disorganized and immature because there is too much monitoring, ie, inhibition of incoming sensory stimuli. I have applied the term *dormant* to this clinical manifestation, signifying a relative, rather than an absolute, condition; that is, the senses are less alert than one would normally expect and are not easily aroused. The individual is less sensitive to or sometimes virtually unaware of sensory information which arises from normal contact with his environment. In the extreme, a sensory system may fail to be aroused despite efforts to directly impose sensory stimuli. This is seen, for example, with the vestibular system when a child is twirled in a suspended chair and demonstrates no lateral nystagmus upon being stopped.

The OTA Triad

The Olfactory-Tactile-Auditory Sensory Triad was so named after I noticed that the children's responses to olfactory stimuli were often disruptive to them and, in quality, not unlike their heightened response to being touched. They would demonstrate a hypersensitivity, an aversion, or avoidance; this often interfered with their being able to direct their attention to other sensory information at that time. In a similar manner, with the auditory system a child may show overconcern, some form of disorganization, or an overt avoidance of this stimuli. In some children the defensive response of either the olfactory or the auditory systems may be more overt than that expressed in the tactile system. Clinically, however, whenever there is a hypersensitive quality in either the olfactory or the auditory systems, one should also suspect there may be a subtle, less pervasive tactile defensiveness as well. In an older child, this tendency might have been outgrown and may currently be revealed only through specific questions on the sensorimotor history; it may also indicate the degree of control the child exerts so that the symptom may become apparent only after therapy has been in progress long enough for him to "let down his guard."

Similarity in clinical manifestations of the sensory systems throughout the OTA Triad is apparent not only in a defensive mode but may also be revealed in the dormant mode as well. For instance, the child who has a hyposensitive response to tactile stimuli may have a similar dormant, or sluggish, response to olfactory input. He may be unaware of the quality and meaning of sounds, or fail to comprehend clearly what is said to him. The child who has a hyposensitive tactile response, referred to here as *tactile dormancy* is apt to be motorically slow and sluggish.

The greater the number of sensory systems functioning in a hyposensitive manner, the less information the child will receive from his environment to stimulate, or direct, a response. These children are often incorrectly considered to be retarded. Whether or not the child is later proven to have adequate intellect or is, in fact, mentally retarded, the program goals and the therapeutic approach would be the same.

As I intensified a therapeutic emphasis on the tactile system the interdependent integrative relationship among the systems of the OTA Triad became increasingly apparent. I then proceeded to cast the tactile system more definitely in the pivotal role as a means of normalizing either the defensive or the dormant responses of the olfactory and auditory systems. While bringing better organization to these two systems selectively, intervention such as this contributed more far-reaching effects by enabling the child to develop a better degree of organization and overall function throughout his central nervous system.

The clinical picture shifts — sometimes subtly, sometimes dynamically. Indications of preclinical responses of defensiveness or dormancy in various sensory systems can often be ascertained by giving close attention to a detailed sensorimotor history. With growth and maturity some of these aberrant forms of behavior will have decreased or disappeared. The inference then, therapeutically, would be to emulate the kinds of sensory stimulation which can help to hasten the rate of maturation. Responses to sensory stimulation may be considerably different after instituting therapy than at the outset; these changes should be documented throughout so as to guide the therapist as to when and where to heighten or reduce the therapeutic emphasis. Usually those systems which are functioning at the dormant end of the scale at the beginning of therapy will follow an undulating course through a temporary defensive mode before being resolved into a more nearly normal pattern of good sensory integration.

It should also be noted that when the child faces a new and potentially stressful situation, such as therapy, he will often manifest anxiety. Under the influence of this anxiety, the nervous system tends to regress and the earlier sensorimotor defects become more manifest. Put another way, when a child's sensory defensiveness has been largely overcome in the course of maturation, its temporary re-emergence under stress is considered to be a significant remnant of the earlier defensive behavior.

Visuo-Vestibular Dyad

The importance of the righting reflexes and the equilibrium responses, plus the proprioceptive facilitation of the extraoccular muscles, already identifies the close relationship of the visual and vestibular system. This dyadic relationship is readily observed clinically. Parallel to the pivotal role of the tactile system in the OTA Triad, the vestibular system follows a similar function to facilitate better integration with the visual system in the Visuo-Vestibular Dyad.

Avoidance Patterns

It is essential to try to trace as directly as possible the relationship between early, or primary, sensory avoidance patterns of behavior and those forms of adaptive motoric, social, and academic responses which are thus influenced. Based on close clinical observations over the past decade, I am proposing the linkage of various forms of adaptive behavior to the primary sensory deficits within the OTA Triad and the V-V Dyad. Arbitrarily I have designated the levels of intensity of this primary sensory influence by the terms *secondary* and *tertiary* *avoidance patterns*.

The avoidance pattern is precipitated by either the defensive or the dormant sensory mode of behavior. The primary, secondary, and tertiary avoidance patterns for both dormant and defensive modes will be discussed in detail in relation to the OTA Triad in Chapter 6, and the V-V Dyad in Chapter 7.

The terms as defined for use in the holistic approach are as follows:

Primary Avoidance:
Patterns of behavior which are directly related to a hyper- or hyposensitive response which are further identified here as a sensory defensiveness or sensory dormancy.

Secondary Avoidance:
This refers to behavior in motor output, social interaction, or academic performance which is disorganized or interfered with because of the child's sensory defensive or dormant response.

Tertiary Avoidance:
This term implies that more serious emotional disturbances exist; these may be related in part or originate in large measure from the primary sensory defensive and/or sensory dormancy responses.

6

The OTA Triad

Primary Avoidance Due to Sensory Defensiveness

Hypersensitivity, the result of too much stimulation reaching the brain due to poor functioning of the filtering or monitoring process, causes too many stimuli to reach the brain with the same degree of intensity and relevancy. The central nervous system is overwhelmed, and the child overreacts. He responds to incoming stimuli from one or more of the sensory systems cited in the *OTA Defensive Triad* in a primitive, protective manner. If any one system, especially the tactile, is operating in such an exaggerated way, the child often acts as though his very existence or survival is hanging in the balance.

The order in which these three systems will be discussed follows that which is best known and documented — the tactile system — to the next most easily recognized and documented — the auditory system. The last to be discussed is the olfactory system; manifestations of this defensive behavior are often overlooked or not recognized as a part of a pattern in conjunction with the other two.

Primary Avoidance Due to Tactile Defensiveness

Tactile defensiveness causes the child such discomfort and alarm that he wants to "fight" or "take flight." This attitude is often observed in a child's withdrawal from human touch. Teachers will recognize, for example, that their efforts to communicate warmth and understanding by the mere placing a hand on a child's shoulders will cause him to quickly move out of range. A child who is tactually defensive will interpret this gesture as potentially threatening or, at least, irritating and uncomfortable. By understanding the reasons behind this response, the concerned and alert teacher will curb her own instinct to touch the sensitive student. She will recognize, too, why this child tends to be disruptive and pick fights with those behind him when standing in line. The threat of being touched — especially in those areas of the body which he cannot see — requires continued alertness on the part of the tactually defensive child.

As he sits at the desk in class, he is alert to the presence of others who, in passing his desk, may touch him. Even the movement of the air as they pass, or the sound of approaching footsteps, require that his attention focus on the possibility that they "could" touch him overtly or inadvertently. Of course, once the classmates of a tactually defensive child discover how ticklish he is, he becomes fair game; they delight in seeing how wildly he responds to their tantalizing actions.

On the playground the tactually defensive child may overreact physically to the unpredictable movements of his playmates or merely to their proximity to him. He may react with either a fight or flight response; the latter seems to indicate that the chance of contact is so overwhelming that he cannot risk the possibility. He may thus begin to retreat farther and farther into a shell of safety, away from interpersonal contact and communication both physically and emotionally. The stage is set for him to start the life of a loner.

Primary Avoidance Due to Auditory Defensiveness

The child who is tactually defensive is also apt to be overly sensitive in the auditory system, and vice versa. The adult would be well advised to recognize the possible significance of a child's hyperverbal response; this is often a signal that he is auditorily defensive.

In therapy, if a hyperverbal response occurs briefly at the beginning of the first sessions and subsides, it may simply signify the child's insecurity and anxiety over being observed. On the other hand, this response could be a remnant of a hyperverbal symptom which the stress of the occasion reawakens. If, however, the child immediately initiates a continuing, sometimes intense, verbal response or asks the adults not to talk when the therapist and the parents begin to discuss matters about the program, this may be indicative of auditory defensiveness. Such behavior must be weighed carefully by the therapist to determine if the child is only expressing jealousy and his demand for either the parents' or the therapist's undivided attention. If the auditory stimulation of any communication sets off an excessive verbal barrage from the child, and if the quality of his voice reveals irritation or discomfort which subsides when no one is speaking, this may be a positive clue to the presence of auditory defensiveness. If, in addition, his attention to other sounds which are irrelevant is observed in therapy, or documented on the sensorimotor history, then there is strong likelihood that the child does indeed have auditory defensiveness.

It is important to look further into the possible reasons why auditory defensiveness may bring on a stream of verbalization from the child. Such a verbal torrent may consist of an unrelenting sequence of loosely related and often irrelevant questions or statements. From long observation of this behavior, it would appear that such a response is the signal that the child uses this technique as a shield. He uses it virtually to protect himself against auditory input.

This protective shield has two functions for him. First, it is a means of alleviating auditory input over which he has no control. The sensory input in and of itself may be irritating, disorganizing, and distracting. Secondly, the child seems to be clearly aware that, as long as he is talking, no one can talk to him, make demands on him, or require him to listen. This may be his adaptive response to an earlier awareness that he is unable to easily interpret the meaning of words; his misunderstanding of directions or failure to follow a request can, in addition, evoke the anger of others. If, for these reasons or because his motor skills also do not permit him to function well, it would then seem preferable to him, whenever possible, to avoid such demands; thus, his solution to "keep talking" can be seen as a protective or defensive pattern of behavior.

A second and cardinal characteristic of auditorily defensive behavior is overattention to and the distraction of sounds, even those which are faint or distant. Since, for the most of us, these sounds are an irrelevant part of the environmental background, they go unnoticed. For the auditorily distractible child, they become an all-encompassing focus of attention. The sounds of a refrigerator, a heating system, or outdoor sounds of a car, truck, airplane, birds, or dogs, become distracting. In addition, the parents may tell you there are certain sounds which have a pitch which is particularly irritating or alarming to their child, such as the hum of a fluorescent light bulb, the noise as he is being driven through a tunnel, or the sound of the vacuum cleaner or electric mixer.

These extreme sensitivities interfere with the child's ability to disregard their presence and refocus his attention on matters at hand — especially in the classroom. Undue attention to sounds which are irrelevant at the time is characteristic of auditory defensiveness and would confirm any earlier suspicions about the hyperverbal response. Methods of coping with the hyperverbal behavior on an immediate level, and the long-term treatment procedures to reduce auditory defensiveness, will be discussed in Part III, Program Plan 1.

Speech pathologists refer to audition as "distant touch."* It is not surprising that if the tactile system is responding in a defensive manner, the auditory system is affected in a similar way. Disorganized tactile and auditory defensive responses account in large measure for much hyperkinetic and distractible behavior. It is this extreme restlessness, poor concentration, and the inability to carry out instructions and assignments which interfere so drastically with the child's academic adjustment.

Primary Avoidance Due to Olfactory Defensiveness

Along with either tactile or auditory defensiveness, there often occurs an olfactory defensive response. It is not uncommon that young children will react defensively to scents; with normal maturation this reaction to scents changes from a global, negative reaction to a more discriminating one. The child who is olfactorily defensive will continue well past this early childhood period to react with an immature response to olfactory stimuli. He will often respond with a strong verbal comment about everything, saying "It stinks!"

Children who are olfactorily defensive are acutely aware of even the faintest suggestion of an offensive odor and are unlikely to endear themselves to friends or strangers by their vehement pronouncements to this effect. They overreact to bathroom odors, to personal hygiene, and to scents which are not recognized as offensive by most people. The learning-disordered child who has limited understanding of the more subtle aspects of our language and who cannot

*Semel E: Lecture at Perceptual Motor Study Course. Princeton, NJ, June 1969.

discern their use of the word "smell," can unwittingly offend those adults whose perfume or powder may stimulate a remark from him such as, "She smells!" Olfactory defensiveness causes the child's parents greater embarrassment in public than behavior which may emanate from either tactile or auditory defensiveness.

Discussion

Whenever the history of the child's development or current reactions to sensory stimuli give any hint that one of these three systems may be functioning in a defensive mode, it is wise to look closely for signs of defensiveness in the other two. As mentioned earlier, it is possible for one system to be in a defensive mode, while the other two may be dormant. As we will see in Part III, the treatment for sensory defensiveness and sensory dormancy does not differ substantially in method, for basically the same techniques are used — to bring organization out of disorganized expressions of behavior, in either case. However, the timing for using these methods does differ in some instances when treating sensory defensiveness compared to treating sensory dormancy.

The child who is functioning in a generally defensive mode usually gives the impression of being intelligent, and often he is. If two or all three of these sensory systems of the OTA Triad are performing in a defensive mode, the child is apt to be hyperactive, hyperverbal, and readily distracted and disorganized by what is going on about him. Such a child is aptly described as being "like someone who jumps on his horse and rides off in all four directions." Because of having to be on the defensive to protect himself from what he interprets as irritating, potentially harmful stimuli, he cannot give his full attention to tasks or to decisions. His actions are impulsive and often show poor judgment. Such a child is so inconsistent in his behavior, it is hard to understand the rationale of his reasoning. Adults find it hard to keep up with him and are baffled as to how he can get into so much trouble. At times, parents have stated they feel that "he is attracted to trouble like a magnet."

Paradoxically, one may find that a child who is hyperactive and hyperverbal at school can function surprisingly well when he is in a quiet setting which is unthreatened by tactile or auditory stimuli. Such a child can often do his school assignments on a one-to-one basis with tutor or parent, but when in class amid so many distracting and threatening sensory stimuli, he is unable to organize himself to concentrate and function. Such extremes in his ability to apply himself seem so paradoxical to teachers and parents alike that they may misinterpret his disorganized behavior. It is easy to look upon the child's activities as willful misbehavior or a way to seek attention.

"He could do it, if only he would try," is a frequent response when teachers and parents discuss the child's class assignments. Having observed and worked with such children over an extended period of time, it would be safe to say that these children often do try; perhaps they try even more than their peers, but they can function only within the limitations imposed upon them by their learning disorder. They desperately want to be able to perform as well as their classmates without needing special conditions. As soon as they are able to do so, they will normally move in the direction of independence and engage in more and more avenues of interaction and healthy competition with their peers.

Parents are further mystified to see their child, who is wildly distractible in the classroom, sit by himself at home of his own volition and be fully engrossed for long periods of time in an activity of interest to him. The key to this phenomenon is the possibility that the child has found a task for which he does have sufficient underlying foundation skills so that his involvement with the activity can be satisfying. The quiet surroundings of a home setting help him to focus his attention, since he is not threatened by the movements of other children. This permits his tactile system to function in a more normal manner, so that he can master those motor skills required for the task. When information regarding the child's varied behavior in different settings (as revealed on the Sensorimotor History†) is analyzed, the therapist achieves a greater understanding about the child and the way his sensory systems function to aid or deter him in his academic performance.

Where there is a severe degree of sensory defensiveness, therapy can measurably reduce the degree of disorganization, but this may not be to the extent desired in every case. Unresolved portions of sensory defensiveness may further subside after puberty.

The child who has a relatively severe degree of sensory defensiveness occurring in two or more sensory systems will have a greater likelihood of suffering concomitant emotional disturbances; this condition may require additional psychiatric therapy. The child who is less severely involved in sensory defensiveness can be expected to make an adequate social and academic adjustment.

Many learning-disordered children who are distracted by the environment of the normal classroom may be of normal intellectual capability; often they are above average. With prompt and early intervention, most of these children can make a suitable adjustment to a study setting which is more conducive to concentration. Unfortunately, the environment of many classrooms, especially the "open" classroom, is not in my experience conducive to this. Whereas it may deter good performance of students in general, for the learning-disordered child the absence of a clearly structured environment feeds into his disorganization. A stable, quiet setting with a minimum of auditory distraction is strongly recommended. But, if it is necessary to remove the child from the classroom setting in order to provide a quiet place for study, every effort should be made to avoid stigmatizing the child for special treatment.

Primary Avoidance Due to Sensory Dormancy

While less apparent to the untrained observer, the condition of sensory dormancy is equally disabling and disorganizing to the child. The olfactory, tactile, and auditory systems are combined in the dormant mode and collectively referred to as *The OTA Dormancy Triad.*

One or more systems — often all three — may be functioning in a relatively dulled, dormant state. The greater the number of systems which appear to be functioning in the dormant mode, the greater the severity of the overall condition,

†*See Appendix F*

and the more extensive will be the duration of treatment required. There is a stronger likelihood that such a child will appear to be retarded, often quite severely. The child who is less severely involved but functioning in a dormant mode in two or even three of these sensory systems will often come out of a course of therapy well organized and responsive to his surroundings. In school, such a child may always seem to grasp new material and concepts more slowly, but once learned, these can be retained and suitably applied by him.

There are sharp contrasts in the social behavior of the child who is functioning primarily in the defensive mode as opposed to one who operates primarily on the dormant mode. Whereas the former child has a marked affinity for trouble, the latter is quiet, compliant, and rarely gets into trouble at all. To the teacher and parent he is more often the "model child" just because he causes no disturbance. Parents have often described such a child in infancy and early childhood as "being too good," meaning, of course, docile. His needs, which are equally profound, may easily be overlooked in the classroom, while the hyperactive child, like the "squeaky wheel which gets the oil," comes to one's attention quickly. It is clear that professional personnel have a unique obligation to be keenly alert to recognize the special needs of the child who may be hypoactive and functioning in a sensory dormant mode.

Primary Avoidance Due to Tactile Dormancy

As one might expect, the clinical picture of tactile dormancy is in exact contrast to that of tactile defensiveness. Rather than being hypersensitive to touch, the child who has a tactile dormant response seems almost to be wearing a thick casing which interferes with his awareness of touch. Consequently, he has a poor awareness of his body image.

Whenever there is disturbance of the tactile system resulting in a hyposensitive response, there is inadequate sensory information available at the motor center of the brain to provide information about past movements and to further direct movement which is about to take place. When there is diminished feedback to indicate the quality of movement, the child cannot judge the amount of force which may be needed to execute the action, as in early pencil tasks.

In a similar manner, the child may lack sufficient feedback as to the proper sequence of movements in which to perform a task. Necessary to this movement plan is the child's awareness of his position in space and the spatial relationship of his body to his immediate surroundings.

The child who is hyposensitive to incoming tactile information plans his movement so poorly that he gives the distinct clinical impression that his brain never got the message. He reacts in a sluggish, uncertain manner, seeming to be unable to establish the pattern, order or sequence of his movements. In fact, watching him suggests a movie in slow motion — halting, fragmented, and unable to put it all together.

The child whose tactile system is hyperactive and hypersensitive is also apt to have very poor motor planning skill. His movements are fast and erratic; the information yielded by the tactile system is so inaccurate and distorted he is unable to develop a good body image or spatial orientation. He, too, is unable to develop the proper sequencing of his movement patterns.

Even when the tactually dormant child is touched firmly, he is less responsive than the child whose tactile system functions normally. He may be extremely insensitive not only to touch, but also to pain, being oblivious to the bumps, gashes, and bruises he receives while playing. He is often lauded by adults for never whimpering when he has stitches for his cuts or when he has shots. In an extreme case, one child was so unaware of discomfort in the dentist's chair, he was known to have fallen asleep. Another was unaware of any pain in the ear until the ear oozed with infection.

By contrast with the child who is tactually defensive and often wiry or on the move, the tactually dormant child has a diminished awareness of movement, derives little satisfaction through motor skills, and generally shuns those activities he needs most to accelerate his rate of motor development. The tactually dormant child has to exert more effort to move, tires easily from his exertion, and often requires more sleep than others.

The muscles of the hypoactive, tactually dormant child are apt to be hypotonic; they look and even feel flabby. Data obtained from a careful clinical history of these children would suggest that in infancy, they would have been labeled "floppy" babies, slow to reach early milestones from the beginning.

Because the tactually dormant child is less inclined to move around, he can easily become overweight, further compounding the problem. Because the whole range of proprioceptive receptors in the skin, the joints, and muscle bellies is diminished in their responsiveness to normal stimulation, the tactually dormant child's body image, spatial relations, and sequential patterns of movement are deficient.

The tactually dormant, hypoactive child often lacks appropriate affect, and may even be depressed. During early therapy sessions these children are often heard to say "I can't." Significant progress has been made when this expression is replaced increasingly with the phrase, "I'll try." It is important to note that this change comes about without being urged by the therapist. As soon as the child has sufficient underlying skills to perform the task, he will try to do it spontaneously. Nothing is to be gained by telling him "to try" as others may have done in the past. A more appropriate attitude on the part of the therapist is to tell him, "Do what is comfortable, ie, right for you."

Primary Avoidance Due to Auditory Dormancy

The term auditory dormancy refers not to loss of hearing but rather to the inability to adequately receive stimuli at the proper centers for interpretation of the input so that language formation, on which this depends, is not disrupted. Children who seem to have such a problem should be thoroughly checked in an audiological evaluation to rule out a hearing deficit. Speech pathologists are responsible for specific therapy for auditory perception problems. In a holistic approach, however, the auditory system should be integrated into the total program at the same time as one emphasizes the organizing of the other sensory systems and gross motor development. In a therapy setting such as the one depicted here, there are unusually rich opportunities to assess how well the child comprehends such words as *under, over, through, behind,* by the way the child moves in response to these simple words. If there is evidence of confusion and poor auditory language comprehension, then the therapist's appropriate use of these words which depict movement in relation to the child's action would enhance the child's awareness of early communication skills.

Other simple means are used to integrate the child's auditory perception skills with the other sensory systems, in particular the visual and auditory-verbal communication skills. Children whose speech is significantly delayed would be highly suspect of having some problems in auditory perception. When hearing is found to be normal, those children who exhibit no signs of auditory defensiveness but seem not to comprehend verbal communication at the expected age level are, from a holistic point of view, said to be functioning in an auditorily dormant sensory mode.

Primary Avoidance Due to Olfactory Dormancy

Olfactory dormancy is not commonly considered clinically important to occupational therapists. It is important to realize, though, that when this sytem is not operating normally, the child lacks yet another avenue of information about his environment. More importantly, where there is olfactory dormancy, there would most likely be an imbalance of sensory input with concomitant lack of optimal integration throughout the sensory systems. It behooves therapists to observe whether the olfactory system is totally dormant or only partially so, and to watch for changes in the child's ability to take in and interpret olfactory information adequately. Therapy methods to implement this change and record progress are discussed in P.P. 1 (Program Plan 1).

Secondary Avoidance Due to Sensory Defensiveness or Dormancy

Disorganization within the central nervous system due to the imbalance between the excitation and the inhibitory forces is clinically observed by an overly reactive, defensive response to stimuli as contrasted with the unresponsive, dormant reactions. The clinician must be able to recognize the direct relationship between the problems in motor skills, social interaction, and academic adjustment which are called secondary avoidance responses and to link them with the underlying primary sensory dysfunction which would appear to precipitate them.

These secondary avoidance responses may be clearly and overtly demonstrated by a child's reluctance to involve himself in a task. On the other hand, it may not be so clear if he has developed subtle, sometimes elaborate schemes of avoidance which may be quite obscure and difficult for adults to understand until such behavior is considered in light of the primary sensory defensive and dormancy responses.

Secondary avoidance patterns of behavior which develop out of poor underlying sensory organization are manifested in a wide range of problems at home, at school, and at play. In the pages to follow, problems in motor skills, social interaction, and academic adjustment will be discussed in light of the underlying primary sensory dysfunction which is proposed as a direct causal factor.

Secondary Avoidance in Motor Skills

Secondary avoidance of motor skills of the upper extremities is related to the tactile system deficits and the lack of vestibular bilateral integration. Additional details about the function of the vestibular system will be pointed out in the following chapter. However, the tactile and vestibular systems cannot be separated when speaking of avoidance of motor skills. The importance here is to identify kinds of avoidance behavior which occurs in infancy, in early childhood, and at the grade school level.

Starting in infancy and early childhood, the child who has inadequate tactile input through his hands will find little enjoyment and satisfaction in manipulating toys. He may demonstrate no interest in nesting and stacking toys when he is exposed to them. These toys require not only hand manipulation, which is often difficult, but an early spatial relationship of one item with another and, in nested toys for instance, some primitive conceptual awareness of their graded sequential order. If the child has little success or satisfaction, he will not pursue it further. By continuing to avoid involvement with graded nesting toys, the child misses an important early learning opportunity regarding the irreversible constancy of size relationships. When this early organizational opportunity is missed at the normal stage of development, it is essential to go back and again provide this experience.

Indifference to toys in general and to puzzles in particular is common among these children who have poor manual dexterity and inadequate awareness of spatial relations. Avoidance of contact with three-dimensional assembly blocks causes the child to miss another of the important opportunities to develop early gross grasp and finger movements. This in part is attributable to a deficiency in the vestibular bilateral integration together with, or independent from, the tactile system problems. Out of the two-sided integration in gross movement patterns develops the preliminary bimanual skills which form the necessary foundation for subsequent development of hand dominance. Otherwise hand dominance, an important preacademic requirement, will be delayed and much confusion in directionality will ensue.

The secondary avoidance pattern in learning-disordered children with regard to handwriting lies not only in their poor grasp and awareness of the spatial relations, but quite specifically in an awareness of how to properly sequence the fine movement patterns. While it is the sensory dysfunction which prevents them from automatically developing these sequential patterns, it is hypothesized that there is a direct relationship between the unfolding of large sequential movement patterns in the slow motions used on the indoor climber, and the child's subsequent, more natural acquisition of the sequential patterns of fine movement. It is this foundation from which the child will then be able to master script writing. The term *sequential patterns of movement* is used here to convey this viable, practical concept. Sequencing is an element of coordination which has not been given the attention in therapy it deserves.

Another manifestation of secondary avoidance is the lack of normal playful gross motor activity during infancy and childhood. For example, while most toddlers can often be seen standing with their heads hanging down as they look between their legs, or standing on their heads, or doing somersaults, learning-disordered children experience these activities to a very limited extent. Clinically it is felt that this inverted posture is the motor response stimulated by the normal, instinctive developmental need to activate the vestibular system. The learning-disordered child who suffers from poor balance will tend to avoid this posture at the same age as his counterparts because it is too threatening to him. Proprioceptive information about the position and movement of body parts in relation to each other and to one's shifting center of gravity may also be insufficient. Therefore, he will be reluctant to even attempt the inverted posture since he will need to depend on the accuracy of information from the weight-bearing joints to inform him how to maintain his balance or adjust his position to keep from falling.

Arrest in the development of vestibular bilateral integration and motor planning skills in keeping with the normal time schedule is apt to cause the child to subsequently avoid age-appropriate games and other peer competition in childhood activities which depend on good early developmental patterns. At varying ages these activities would include hopping, skipping, playing leap frog, doing somersaults, jumping rope, and riding a two-wheel bicycle. The child's situation is compounded if he prolongs his avoidance of these childhood activities, for the mastery of each of these activities in turn helps to mature his vestibular bilateral integration capability even further.

Secondary Avoidance in Social Interaction

The failure, frustration, and rejection of the child by his playmates results most often in relation to the motor requirements of games and sports. The child is prevented from engaging in the usual activities of his peer group if he lacks the foundation skills of spatial relations, hand-eye coordination, and gross motor skills. This lack of skill immediately sets him apart. The chance of failure and ridicule for his clumsiness prevents him from enjoying the activity and from obtaining the ultra important and coveted rewards of peer approval in competition. The humiliation can be devastating to his ego.

There may be other reasons which also exclude him from friendly neighborhood play, such as auditory perception problems, if these prevent him from easily understanding the rules of a game and its goals. One little girl was excluded from her playmates' games because she could not grasp the concept of "stand beside" and "crawl over," which compounded their anger and her despair. An older boy was rejected from the backyard soccer game because he readily got confused in his spatial orientation and would run toward the wrong goal post.

The child may respond to such experiences by withdrawing from those activities or even retreating altogether from playing with children of his own age. He will sometimes prefer playing with a younger age group since these children will offer him less competition. He may choose to stay close to adults because their expectations are neither as realistic nor competitive as are those of his peers. To seek out adult company instead of his peer group is an unfortunate outcome which reduces the child's opportunity to share experiences, develop good peer relationships, and improve childhood communication skills. In nursery school and kindergarten they often become loners. They tend to avoid those play-yard activities which require more balance and control than they can then command. They recognize they cannot perform adequately or safely. The quick and unpredictable movements of many young children who dash around pose a threat to them if their own balance is poor, and it increases their anxiety if they also are tactually defensive.

As a direct result of tactile defensiveness, or because of his feelings of frustration, or both, he may become overtly aggressive. These aggressive responses may also alternate with periods of social withdrawal. Withdrawal behavior may be further compounded and reinforced by his peers' social rejection because of his motor ineptitude, thus furthering his inclination to become asocial and a loner.

Secondary Avoidance of Academic Performance

Disorganized behavior manifested by the child's short attention span and hyperkinetic behavior makes school adjustment difficult. Because of his own distractibility, as well as his lack of fine motor skills in writing, he is often unable to complete tasks and assignments. He tends to divert and distract adults from making demands on him to complete a task and he often becomes quite masterful in this process. One can observe the way some hyperverbal children skillfully divert the adult's attention from the task at hand by asking a myriad of questions about irrelevant matters. Techniques which help to curtail and reverse this behavior are described in P.P. 1.

In addition, the child often postpones or tries to escape academic demands; perhaps this is to protect himself against further frustration and failure. He may know better than anyone that he clearly does not have the underlying skills for a given academic requirement, so he is really forced into additional secondary avoidance behavior.

Often one of the most basic reasons why the child tries to avoid academic work is because he lacks the foundation skills for handwriting. As part of this problem the child often fails to organize his spatial relationships adequately to space letters and words or to align numbers vertically, as in adding. He may also fail to differentiate clearly the orientation of the plus sign versus the multiplication sign. Poor organization of written content is a carryover which manifests itself increasingly as he must cope more often with abstract information in his studies.

Tertiary Avoidance Due to Sensory Defensiveness or Dormancy

Tertiary avoidance responses, as the term is used here, indicates a more serious accompanying emotional manifestation than that seen in either the primary or secondary avoidance responses. The origins of certain emotional manifestations may be directly traceable to primary sensory defensive or dormant reactions. Secondary complications erupt from the primary reactions if left untreated and can become too difficult for the child to cope with. He is forced toward more and more entrenched, protective responses to avoid the need of involvement or to make an adaptive response in the offending defensive or dormant sensory system(s). The severity of these responses, which often occur in many of the sensory systems concomitantly, is delineated progressively as follows: focal symptoms, phobic responses, and global responses. The children with whom I have worked, who also displayed the severity of symptomatology indicated here, are vastly more limited in numbers than those who demonstrated the less severe primary and secondary avoidance symptoms. Despite this I feel it is the concept of how these features present themselves in graded intensity which can be most useful in conducting treatment for this group.

Tertiary Avoidance Demonstrated Through Focal Symptoms

Focal symptoms may take the form of anxiety, irritability, and depression. Stress from the environment may cause volatile feelings of the child to erupt quickly. Disorganized behavior may range out of control and can be destructive. Such behavior on occasion suggests a postical rage, which can follow a seizure.

The intensity of this negativistic behavior will be more likely to erupt if the child must function within a highly directive, instructional, demanding milieu at home, at school, or in therapy. It is indeed unfortunate if his behavior is looked upon solely in relation to the disciplinary aspects. Parents are thrust in the position of feeling guilt for their own ineffectiveness and can overreact to suggestions from counselors that firmer discipline is the answer.

While it is inadvisable to use firm discipline as the foremost method of handling the child's difficult behavior, this should definitely not be misconstrued, nor confused with the need of the child for a stable, firm, clearcut structure. It is precisely because the child is unable to structure his own environment satisfactorily which causes him through his behavior to require others to do so. By structuring for him in simplistic language, one step at a time, exactly what is to happen and when he should start preparing for this, and what is required of him at each step of the way, he will be able to function in a better organized, more responsible manner. Outbursts of his anger may be a direct reaction to demands put upon him which he cannot meet because his sensory dysfunction makes this impossible. Temperamental outbursts may be cumulative. One young child was under such strain to conform and try to succeed each day at school, that upon reaching home he would burst into angry tears for the next hour.

Extreme negativism, or even volatile outbursts, may be a direct response to irritating tactile or auditory stimuli. Adults must learn to understand and respect children who become tense and who withdraw from their touch. As therapists and teachers, we have many other ways to communicate our warmth and acceptance. The therapist must try to recognize those stimuli which are excitatory and cause the child to become disorganized so as to take whatever measures can be effective to reduce or prevent it.

During therapy the therapist should observe whether a change in the order of presenting therapeutic tasks is helpful in preventing the onset of disorganized behavior. Some children do desk work better prior to the gross motor tasks, which may be too excitatory to be followed by those tasks which require greater concentration. Their disorganized behavior may take the form of hyperactivity and boisterousness. Still other children may respond to gross motor activities with faster, louder, and longer verbal outbursts. It may be impossible for the child to control his responses and difficult for him to quiet down under the most skilled efforts of the therapist. Certain techniques — heavy brushing and slow supine rocking on the inflatables, described in P.P. 1 and 2, respectively — are often useful to quiet the child. Also, the therapist's use of a quiet, almost whispered voice has a tranquilizing effect on the child who is hyperverbal, as described in P.P. 1.

Paradoxically, the movement on the inflatables will arouse an excitable, hyperactive behavior in some children, necessitating that this portion of the therapy, which is still necessary, not precede the desk work. This hypersensitivity to vestibular stimulation will gradually diminish over the weeks to follow; periodically the order of this and the quiet tasks should again be reversed to determine at what point this effect has been overcome.

It is most important that the therapist is aware of what measures may be helpful and also be on the alert to recognize any paradoxical effects. There is no one answer or panacea, but rather it is the therapist's sensitivity to a child's response which will help her to select one or a combination of the suggested methods. As the child's central nervous system becomes better organized through therapy, these specific quieting techniques will become increasingly effective in reducing his erratic behavior in the clinic and at home.

Tertiary Avoidance Demonstrated Through a Phobic Response

A phobic response is truly an extreme example of avoidance behavior. It is the child's way of protecting himself from external demands at school, at home, or at play — demands with which he is almost completely at a loss in being able to cope with. Avoiding the requested performance or preventing contact with the offending source of sensory stimulation is, to the child, necessary for his emotional survival.

Too often a serious problem is created where only a minor, perhaps a primary or secondary avoidance response, had originally existed. In my own experience, it appears that when writing skills are expected too early — before the foundation skills are developed — the seeds are planted for a phobic response to writing, to school, and to other situations with a similar demand. If corrected in time, these phobic reactions may be mitigated and reversed without a lasting effect. If therapists or teachers attempt to remediate the phobic symptoms by direct remediation, in reading or writing, without first addressing the child's need for sound sensorimotor foundation skills, they can intensify the academic and the emotional aspects of his problem.

Tertiary Avoidance Through Global Response

The child finds the sensory stimulation to one or more sensory systems so overwhelming, he is unable to react to it in a purposeful, productive manner; therefore, he feels compelled to withdraw from his contact with the environment in order to protect himself from both the stimulation and the demands upon him which require sensory organization and sensory integration. It is possible that the roots of childhood schizophrenia and autism may, in some cases, stem from this deficit. Cases I have treated which were described by others in many instances as being autistic also had what I would call tertiary avoidance patterns. The severity of symptoms requires that one treat the child with the same methods otherwise used to develop greater sensory organization and integration. However, one would treat the child slowly, with great caution and sensitivity, and "read" the child's response minute by minute in order to respond most appropriately. Since many sensory systems may be affected, even minimal stimulation can be overwhelming for the child, causing him to again withdraw.

7

Avoidance Responses
in the Visuo-Vestibular Dyad

Among the learning-disordered individuals studied, the most frequent and fundamental problems encountered arose from dysfunction within and between the visual and vestibular systems. In the holistic approach this functional relationship is designated as the Visuo-Vestibular Dyad. This dyad represents the single most important focus for remediation and for prevention of learning problems in children.

The concept of avoidance offers the therapist a means of identifying and measuring the child's initial level of function in the Visuo-Vestibular Dyad through clinical observations. Through the child's need to avoid characteristic kinds of involvement, she will be able to recognize critical developmental deficits and subsequent motoric changes throughout therapy which signal the child's progress along the developmental hierarchy. Rather than treat these deficits individually, efforts are directed in the holistic approach to facilitate a more cohesive, comprehensive, and naturally simultaneous inclusion of various sensorimotor needs. It is his exposure to Phase I activities which can provide this opportunity and stimulate the natural unfolding of the neurodevelopmental processes.

In the same way that the tactile system in the OTA Triad is seen in a pivotal role, the vestibular system in the Visuo-Vestibular Dyad is seen as serving in a pivotal function. For instance, if only those two systems were the focus of therapeutic effort, the other systems in their respective triadic and dyadic groups would also undergo some maturational change as the result. Clinically this is important since both the tactile and vestibular systems are readily accessible for direct therapeutic intervention. Each of these two systems can be stimulated from external sources and in a manner so that the input can be cautiously controlled, easily observed, and appropriately graded by the therapist.

The function of the vestibular system, together with the visual system, is important in relation to the problems of the learning-disordered child; whatever clinical understanding may be fostered through the therapist's own knowledge of the neurophysiological aspects of this dyad is highly encouraged. One of the most recent contributions to clinical application is found in deQuiros' work.[1] However, despite the avid attempts of many to comprehend what is presently known about these highly complex functions of the visual and the vestibular system interactions, it must be recognized that all the available information may still be but a fraction of what remains to be understood. In lieu of this and the demonstrated results using the holistic approach, it is advocated that the child's spontaneous responses remain the most reliable indicators for application of therapeutic procedures.

Guidelines for Clinical Observations
of the Visuo-Vestibular Dyad

The characteristics of faulty neurodevelopmental function in the Visuo-Vestibular Dyad are apparent from the child's initial spontaneous responses to Phase I pieces of equipment. These characteristics may be identified in four main areas. It is relevant for the therapist to recognize their manifestations separately, but in the clinical application these features are so intertwined that treatment of each in isolation is not advocated. As mentioned previously, therapeutic effort is directed primarily toward replication of the natural progression along the hierarchy of neurodevelopment.

Delayed Resolution of the Infantile Postural Reflexes

A delay in the maturation of the early postural reflexes will interfere with the child's ability to integrate function and produce purposeful motor acts.

The *tonic labyrinthine reflexes* (TLR) in the first six months of life are stimulated to pull in the direction of gravity; if the child is prone, the neck flexors are activated to pull the head downward into flexion by action of the TLR. Conversely, the TLR acts to pull the head down and back into extension when, during the early stages, the infant is supine. By the age of six months, voluntary control begins to replace the infantile reflex patterns. Now the infant begins to counteract the gravitational pull to maintain his equilibrium and to prepare for locomotion.

To enable the child to supplant the early reflex patterns, he needs ample unrestricted opportunity to move. Rolling over from the supine to the prone position begins the process by which the voluntary muscle control helps to break up and replace the previously gravity-activated tonic labyrinthine reflex patterns with gravity-activated neck extension. For the child to roll from supine to the prone position, there must be partial flexion of the head against gravitational pull, accomplished by pulling the chin forward and toward the chest.

As previously mentioned, there may be deleterious effects of prolonged use and restriction of movement from infant carriers, strollers, and car seats. Other factors may impose restrictions on him at critical points along his timetable of development. These will sometimes have even more far-reaching effects on his expected development. For example, orthopedic devices to correct bone deformities or injuries will restrict the normal trunk movement of a young infant.

Traction and splinting which prevent prone positioning or preambulation crawling patterns may interrupt the natural schedule and sequence of the ambulation patterns.

In addition to the infant's increased control of active head and neck extension in the prone position, the trunk and hips begin to come into action. The term *pivot prone,* as first identified by Rood, depicts this characteristic posture of the preambulating six-month-old infant. As he pivots or rocks on his belly, the antigravity extensor muscles throughout the neck, trunk, and hips are activated; the arms, flexed at the elbows, are raised at the shoulders. It is this pivot-prone posture which the therapist looks for but which the learning-disordered child is often unable to perform initially, eg, when kicking off from the wall, prone, on the scooter board.

The term *tonic neck reflex* must next be explored in order that we might become aware of its influence and understand how curtailment of movement may lead to abnormal or delayed development. The term tonic neck reflex (TNR) refers to the involuntary change in muscle tone of an extremity, which is altered by the relative position of the head and neck with respect to that extremity. The asymmetrical TNR is more commonly recognized than the symmetrical. In the former, as the head is rotated to face one shoulder, the arm and sometimes the leg on that side becomes extended, while the opposite limbs are flexed.

The symmetrical tonic neck reflex occurs normally in early infancy by moving the head down toward the chest; the upper limbs go into flexion and the lower limbs extend. When the head is moved up and back, the opposite is true; the arms go into extension and the legs flex. If this primitive motor pattern has not been resolved by the time the child normally would be crawling, it is obvious that he will be unable to put his arms out to hold his weight because the flexion of the head acts to pull the shoulders and elbows in toward the body.

Also, as long as the asymmetrical tonic neck reflex remains active, creeping and crawling will be curtailed also because support of the trunk weight on the extended arm will be possible only if the head is rotated in that direction. Altering the head position toward the opposite side causes the extended arm to collapse. Obviously, creeping in the homolateral pattern (with arm and leg extended on the same side) will be necessary until these reflexes are replaced by voluntary motor control. Only then can the normal sequential development of a reciprocal crawling pattern, with one arm and the opposite leg, take place. Avoiding or bypassing this important developmental step will interfere with and deter the normal early integration of the two sides of the body which is stimulated by this reciprocal movement pattern. It will also retard the further development of postural mechanisms.

In normal development the upper trunk is first raised on both extended arms. As the infant's attention is drawn from side to side he moves his head, thus breaking up the tonic neck reflex control. In the crawling pattern, head movement away from the flexed arm may occur for a time. As the total weight is maintained by one arm at a time, greater resistance is put on the extended arm and the head begins to move more freely toward a flexed arm; in eating and in play, the child may then bring objects in front of him for close inspection.

A further complication of the unresolved symmetrical tonic neck reflex patterns is that the arms cling to the body and would not be free to reach out protectively against falling. The protective arm extension reflex is then delayed in developing and often is inactive or sluggish in the young learning-disordered child. The result of this can be seen both in injury from falls and in the resulting fear which would deter the child in his early stages of motor exploration.

Poor protective arm extension due to unresolved early reflex patterns will also delay the necessary development of strength and stabilization of the shoulder girdle against the ribcage. This remains clinically evident by the "winged scapula" which occurs when the child leans forward to support the weight of the body on the arms. The more relevant issue for the learning-disordered child is the fact that when there is instability in the proximal muscles, stability to control the distal joints is secondarily affected. The minute finger movements to control a pencil can be executed within the distal joints if the arm is supported on the desk, and thus appear not to depend on scapular stability. However, it is difficult for an individual who has adequate scapular function to envision the extent to which this deficit can influence the eventual development of smooth, efficient distal motor patterns. One cannot maintain the level of endurance needed for prolonged handwriting demands in the educational setting without an early onset of fatigue.

Equilibrium Responses

Equilibrium responses cannot be well developed until infantile postural reflex activity is satisfactorily resolved. Until such time, the child must give his conscious attention to controlling his balance. In school, when so much effort must be expended to maintain good sitting balance, the child's attention is diverted from academics. On a more advanced level the child is unable to associate and integrate current information with past knowledge or experience.

Adequate Vestibular Bilateral Integration (Ayres), of which equilibrium responses are a primary ingredient, is a critical prerequisite to the natural development of cerebral dominance. Delay in its maturation causes a compounding of related problems crucial to the learning processes: confusion and delay in establishing hand dominance, prolonged directional confusion, and reversals in reading and writing.

Therapeutic activities which require use of the equilibrium responses activate the inner ear, the visual system, and the proprioceptors. Balancing experiences will stimulate quantities of sensory information relative to gravitational pull; this information is processed and integrated in the cerebellum so that the motor response can be regulated more and more smoothly. Balancing activity on the inflatables and carpeted barrel help to mature these equilibrium responses. In order to maintain body balance, muscle action from both sides of the body must be brought into action, ie, involvement of both cerebral hemispheres.

Before this can occur, early reflex control of the TLR and TNR must be at least partially resolved or modified sufficiently to permit free bodily movement. Then the head and trunk are able to rotate, and the arms can move freely to counterbalance and shift the weight of the body so that one's balance can be maintained even as the center of gravity shifts. With this, the equilibrium responses become less sluggish and respond appropriately to more minute shifts of balance.

In the sitting position, as the trunk rotates, the arms, as an automatic extension of the trunk rotation pattern, will cross the midline. In the kneeling posture, action of the head and trunk to maintain balance will exert force against the extended arm on first one side and then the other, which will further reduce the effects of any unresolved tonic neck reflex pattern. By this time, the child will begin moving his arms across the midline of his body when using the prone twirling pattern in the suspended tires or scooterboard.

Adaptive Postural Responses

Whenever a child continues to have poor equilibrium responses, together with residual early postural reflex activity, this deters his normal development of good adaptive postural responses. As a part of this picture, the extensor muscles of the spine are slow to gain sufficient strength and muscle endurance to support and stabilize the upper trunk. Characteristic of a poor postural response at the desk is the slouched posture of the trunk and weak neck muscles. This will cause a child to lean on the nondominant hand to relieve his early fatigue; it alone can inhibit good bilateral integration of the two hands. The direct effect of this is to prevent him from automatically stabilizing his paper for writing. Whenever there is an obvious lack of awareness of the needed postural adjustment, such as good positioning on the chair and suitable head posture for reading and writing, this signals that problems in the Visuo-Vestibular Dyad are present.

The child's awareness of his position in space and the position of one body part relative to that of another is what enables him to make an adaptive postural response when engaging in purposeful tasks. These arise from information derived from these sources: the proprioceptors, the inner ear, and other parts of the vestibular system, together with the visual system. Lack of awareness to make a suitable adaptive posture at the desk is often characteristic of learning-disordered children in the classroom.

Therapeutic emphasis is placed on activities which will integrate the two sides of the body more naturally. This is done initially by stimulating the equilibrium responses as the individual becomes free of primitive reflex activity. Additional emphasis is directed to activities which will activate the muscle, joint and tendon proprioceptors. This stimulation is achieved through activities which stretch, compress, and provide deep pressure to these areas. One obvious example of the way in which children stimulate these receptors is their own natural propensity for jumping up and down on bed springs. It is a natural course of development, for little girls especially, to respond to a strong drive for such stimulation by jumping rope. At the point which is appropriate in therapy, this action is provided by use of a jumping board.

To promote better adaptive postural responses at the desk, specific attention is directed to the strengthening of the proprioceptors in the neck by encouraging the quadrupedal position or the protective arm extension posture with weights of up to three pounds applied to the neck. An alternative age-appropriate method of applying weight to the neck is to have the child wear a motorcycle helmet. He is also encouraged to wear it during the Phase II desk tasks and while doing part of his homework. It serves as a reminder for him to keep his head in position for more balanced, lateral movements in the eyes while reading.

Vestibular-Oculomotor Function

In the learning-disordered child the involuntary lateral movement of the eyes, or nystagmus, normally resulting from a twirling motion is often absent. Nystagmus may be absent in either the defensive or the dormant mode, as described in the holistic approach. The powerful drive of children to stimulate the connections between the inner ear and the extraoccular muscles is often characteristic of their spontaneous clinical behavior. For clinicians to better conceptualize what presumably is taking place, they should review the medical literature, particularly with regard to the anatomical structure and the alignment of the vertical and the horizontal relationships of the semicircular canals and the functions of the inner ear. For diagrams of the semicircular canals, two highly recommended sources are listed.[2,3]

It is not the intent of this presentation to try to correlate the planes of movement of the child's action during a therapy procedure with isolated portions of the semicircular canals, even though to try to do so might be ideal. What is intended is to describe the kinds of behavior which the child seeks and repeats when given ample opportunity and to recognize that this drive subsequently seems to wane over the course of therapy as the nystagmus response appears.

Spontaneous Efforts to Stimulate the Vestibular System

Exactly what portions of the vestibular system the child is trying to stimulate by his spontaneous efforts remains uncertain. The therapist is in a better position to document what consistent patterns emerge and then pose the question as to why these movements are so often sought. One might assume that the planes of motion used in therapy could identify those areas of the semicircular canals which are receiving the primary stimulation. However, in therapy procedures and in life situations, actions are usually not repeated within a prescribed arc. Patterns of movement are comprised of many vectors which will approximate the optimal point for stimulation of one set of semicircular canals more than the others, but exactly what takes place at a given time within the vestibular system remains theoretical. There are many alternative mechanisms within the central nervous system which can duplicate primary functions or compensate for deficits.

The natural redundancy of function reinforces the position that it is clinical performance which best reveals the degree to which the principal and the necessary compensatory functions are integrated. Clinically it may never be clear exactly which function the child is using at any given moment. Until the clinician has access to precise methods for assessing central nervous system function in direct relation to therapy techniques, the position of the holistic approach continues to be that procedures for therapy are best determined by behavioral observation of spontaneous responses.

The kinds of stimulation the child needs are revealed clearly and overtly through the specific bodily movements or position which he seeks; the extent of these needs is demonstrated by his repetitions and the duration and intensity of his involvement. As a part of this clinical documentation, three characteristic patterns of movement have been consistently observed.

Spontaneous Stimulation in the Inverted Vertical Posture

Within the first six weeks of therapy and often during the first and second therapy hours, many learning-disordered children will discover some means by which to position themselves upside down. Theoretically the effect of this position is the change in gravitational pull of the fluid of the semicircular canals and a direct source of stimulation of the vestibular system.

Inverted positioning may be observed on the indoor climber as the child leans over one of the long, low crossbars, or at a more advanced level when he spontaneously hangs upside down by the knees from the overhead bars (P.P. 3.1). As there is a more adequate integration of proprioceptive information from the joint receptors so the child can keep his balance free of supporting structure such as the climber, he will turn somersaults and intensify the frequency of such action over a peak period often lasting weeks before it subsides.

In the young child, particularly, the inverted positioning is observed as he lies across the long, low inflated roll, which provides safe positioning for him to put his head down and sometimes do a somersault from it. A similar posture in prone and supine positions will be spontaneously initiated lying over the outside of the carpeted barrel. The therapist must be alert and responsive to those unspoken, implicit requests for further stimulation (P.P. 2.2).

Another instance where these indications are observed is in using the inflated rectangular pillow (36 inches by 48 inches). When the child is asked to sit on the pillow, he will often have an immediate sense of the potential this situation offers for supine and inverted positioning of the head. Taking this clue, the therapist responds by offering further stimulation through rocking (P.P. 2.3).

The most dramatic demonstration of a child's drive to satisfy a need for stimulation in the inverted position may be seen by his response to the double suspended tires. After becoming accustomed to prone twirling, he will turn over to lie supine either of his own volition or in response to a softly worded invitation. When asked if he wants to be twirled, he generally will not only accept the idea but relish the feeling it generates. Soon the child will completely relax, lay his head back, and ask for continued twirling. Many children drop their heads down and back so far that their long hair touches the floor. The children, during subsequent therapy sessions, will be observed to spontaneously assume this position and again indicate that they want to be twirled.

Stimulation in the Upright Vertical Posture

The desire of children for stimulation in the vertical upright posture has already been mentioned. It has been observed as part of normal growth and development which most children seek throughout early childhood and then outgrow. In therapy, opportunity is provided the learning-disordered child whose needs to stimulate the vestibular systems have not yet been satiated. This is a symptom which is characteristically found among hyperactive children. With treatment this symptomatology, which is so disruptive in the classroom, can be somewhat, if not markedly, subdued.

When such a child is provided the limitless opportunity for prone twirling in the double suspended tires or the scooter board, there is often an immediate response to twirl spontaneously at speeds which sometimes reach 60 RPM. These movements would normally stimulate the vestibular system sufficiently. It is this persistence to stimulate the vestibular system which characterizes many learning-disordered children, particularly the hyperactive child. The extent of each child's needs will vary, but the intensity of this drive gradually begins to wane over the course of therapy. Then it may be speculated that the gradual reduction of this need for horizontal rotation, or twirling, together with the subjective sensation of vertigo and emerging nystagmus patterns, would be clinical indication of better vestibular bilateral integration as defined by Ayres and improved function in the Visuo-Vestibular Dyad defined in holistic terms.

Avoidance in the Visuo-Vestibular Dyad

The term *avoidance* is used in a broad sense to mean a dislike of, or distaste for, involvement with tasks, the purposeful performance of which requires adequate and/or automatic function of the body in relation to the force of gravity. Secondarily, the term avoidance indicates a reluctance to attempt or an effort to circumvent those motoric, social, and academic activities which are dependent on a well-integrated, gravity-activated, visuo-vestibular response. The term *defensive* is used to mean hyperactive and hypersensitive; the term *dormant* is used to mean hypoactive and hyposensitive — each in regard to behavior and performance within the visuo-vestibular dyad. The terms are not rigidly applied but are used to convey a conceptual frame of reference which is clinically useful.

Characteristic avoidance behavior is described here both in terms of the defensive and the dormant modes. The common feature often present is the absence of the sluggish response of lateral nystagmus to horizontal rotation.

Clinical observations of hypoactive children suggest that while there is a definite need to activate the vestibular system, the equilibrium responses are often so poor that a child is fearful of moving "off dead center" to do so. Any challenge to his precarious balance is disorganizing and may create fear and injury. He tends to remain in a protected, more immobile state, unable to adequately stimulate the vestibular system within the normal developmental time-table. Concomitant with this, a further detrimental effect on the tactile system is seen since it too responds and matures through movement. In this situation the systems throughout the OTA Triad are frequently seen to be functioning in the dormant mode.

Paradoxically, other children respond hyperactively many times as a means to provide the needed stimulation to the vestibular system; they also may have poor equilibrium responses, but they use movement to avoid having to maintain their equilibrium. If the sensory systems of the OTA Triad are also functioning in a disorganized, defensive mode, the distraction which this can cause will further intensify the extent of the child's hyperactivity.

Clinical Evidence in the Visual System

Poor performance, ie, an avoidance response to visual attention, is shared by children whose visual system is functioning in either the dormant or the defensive mode. The clinical picture of the dormant response to visual stimuli appears to be a lack of conscious awareness to the presence of objects of his environment, whereas in the defensive response the child's attention is drawn in various directions by fleeting awareness to many objects, ie, a visual figure-ground impairment. Either type of response will present serious problems with regard to organizing visuo-motor skills for reading and handwriting.

Visual Attention

Young children who also may be severely disorganized may be so distractible they are unable to focus their visual attention on an object for more than a fleeting moment. To help them do so, the therapist offers them an object which provides an attractive and colorful moving stimulus and which also utilizes a predictably rhythmic, simultaneous auditory feedback, eg, a liquid hourglass or marble railway (P.P. 2.7).

Visual Fixation

After being able to direct the child's visual attention to objects in front of him, one should observe and overcome any tendency to avoidance of visual fixation. For this, an object is held an appropriate distance from the eyes in each of the four quadrants (upper left, etc.) of the visual field. Often the child will be unable to maintain the midline position of the head and move the eyes out to the target; instead, he will just turn his head. An important underlying skill for reading is controlled movement of the eyes independently from head motion.

Visual Pursuits

Children who come to therapy at a point where avoidance of visual fixation has been surmounted will often continue to reveal an avoidance of crossing the midline with the eyes. Their eye movements become easily disorganized as they approach the midpoint, thus averting their gaze elsewhere. Visual pursuits are observed and then trained as needed by asking the child to follow the horizontally moving bead in a transparent plastic tube as it rolls from one side to the other in front of him.

Clinical Evidence of Primary Avoidance in the Vestibular System

Failure to resolve the early infantile reflex patterns and to be able to develop active equilibrium responses also impedes development of the capacity to freely cross the midline of the body with eye movements, hand action, or to rotate the trunk. Failure to cross the midline has been mentioned above as part of the primary avoidance in the visual system.

Influence of a poorly developed vestibular system can be seen clinically by the primary avoidance responses observed in using Phase I equipment. Besides poor balance on the inflatables, the inability to rotate the trunk and cross the midline with the arms to maintain balance astride the carpeted barrel and the need for the hands to avoid the midline of the body during prone twirling on the scooter board and double suspended tires are clear statements of primary avoidance. For instance, on the scooter board and tires a child will often be seen early in his therapy propelling himself in a circular twirling pattern with his arms stretched out from his sides. Over the ensuing weeks he will gradually move the hands closer to the midline of the body and eventually establish a distinct and consistent crossover pattern.

In evaluating the possibility of this avoidance pattern still remaining in the child of ten years old or older, one can observe the performance on a more age-appropriate task. For example, when asked to follow a large figure-eight pattern positioned vertically in front of him, the child who still has remnants of this early avoidance pattern will at least initially use an hourglass pattern rather than the usual crossover pattern to follow the figure "eight." This is an important assessment which points out the need for further work to integrate the two sides of the body.

The primary avoidance responses of both the dormant and defensive modes share commonalities regarding the lack of nystagmus and the inability to cross the midline. The defensive qualities of visual figure-ground are often shared by the defensive quality of the vestibular system and show up together in the hyperactive, distractible child. It is essentially the equilibrium responses which offer a contrast in terms of primary avoidance — the sluggish, unresponsive, dormant quality of one versus a hypersensitive, overactive, defensive quality of the other. What they share in common is poor balance; the secondary and tertiary avoidance effects are not discernibly different academically and socially. What is relevant here is the suggested broad effects which impaired visual and vestibular system function can exert on life situations. The holistic approach focuses on the behavioral changes which can be the result of improvement in this form of sensorimotor integration.

Secondary Avoidance

Poor vestibular bilateral motor integration which interferes with sound development of sound visuo-motor skills is the single most disruptive factor to affect academic performance. Poor visual attention has already been cited; it produces distraction in the classroom and inability to attend to and to complete academic tasks.

The inability of the child to suppress from his conscious attention the irrelevant background stimuli so as to direct himself to the visual object at hand represents a visual figure-ground problem. This problem prevents him from organizing himself to concentrate on a task, and it interferes with task completion. Many teachers realize that such a child has the ability to perform the task if he could only give it his attention.

A subsequent manifestation of the visual figure-ground problem complex is the inability of the older student to identify pertinent issues and cardinal points from reading material in order to write term papers and book reports.

The hyperactive, erratic movements related to poor trunk balance and poor postural adaptation are all deterrents to good learning. The most customary indication of poor postural adjustment, secondary to poor two-sided integration, is failure to automatically secure the paper for writing.

Poor vestibular bilateral integration seems to interfere with the natural development of cerebral dominance and, secondary to this, hand dominance. There is then prolonged ambivalence and confusion over handedness, resulting in directional confusion and the lack of a foundation for good spatial orientation. Directional confusion is often evident in top-bottom and left-right orientation of numbers and letters. From clinical experience it has been observed that many children entering first grade will occasionally make these reversals. By contrast, the hallmark of the learning-disordered child is the frequency and persistence of these reversals throughout first and second grade.

The same types of problems characterize those children who have a "pseudo-learning disorder," because the necessary foundation skills had not been adequately formulated in the child prior to the premature introduction of hand-writing and reading skills in nursery school and kindergarten.

Tertiary Avoidance

Forms of tertiary avoidance are more severe and often more fixed than if the disability had been reversed at the primary or secondary avoidance level. In other words, what may have started out as a minor reading difficulty now becomes a more entrenched form of dyslexia. In addition to this, failure, frustration, and loss of self-confidence set the child on a course which can easily deteriorate and cause a significant emotional overlay to the basic problem.

School phobias may in part result from the escalation of the academic problems, but efforts to train the child solely in the related educational material will not solve the learning problem. The traditional educational approach should be augmented with psychological treatment to reduce the emotional aspect and with suitable therapy to enable the child to handle the academic work which is more difficult because of poor vestibular bilateral integration.

Separate from the emotional aspect of dyslexia and school phobia is the more severe, global condition of the autistic child. This is of concern for its possible relationship to the Visuo-Vestibular Dyad because of the bizarre motor behavior often associated with the autistic child. In addition to trying to twirl objects and stimulate himself visually, the autistic child also tries to stimulate the vestibular system by his characteristic head banging, rocking, and twirling action. Efforts to provide him with more suitable means to provide this kind of stimulation to the point of being satiated would be one method used in the holistic approach.

References

1. de Quiros JB, Schranger OL: Neuropsychological Fundamentals in Learning Disabilities. San Rafael, California, Academic Therapy Publications, 1978.
2. English G (ed): Otolaryngology. Hagerstown, Md, Harper & Row Pub Co, 1977, vol 1, p 3.
3. Maximow, Bloom: Textbook of Histology, ed 6. Philadelphia, WB Saunders Co, 1953, p 577.

8

Bridging the Gap
Between Avoidance and Exploration

The term *explore,* a process cited in the hypothesis of the holistic approach, means:

1) to become more aware of sensations or experiences previously dormant;

2) to tolerate increased contact with stimuli or experiences previously interpreted from sensory input, ie, perceived by the individual as being irritating, noxious, or potentially harmful;

3) to initiate action and involve oneself voluntarily.

Role of the Therapist

The paramount role a therapist can perform for the learning-disordered child is to skillfully enable him to overcome his need to avoid and to develop in him a desire to explore his environment. There are certain specific therapeutic techniques in implementing a program so that a child can bridge the gap between the avoidance mode and the exploratory mode. Until a child is able to bridge this gap and tolerate contact with the stimuli of his environment or become awakened to their presence, he will be unable to advance in his ability to organize, integrate, and conceptualize information derived from his environment.

Applicable Therapeutic Principles

The principles of promoting change in a holistic approach are more completely defined and discussed in Chapter 12 of Part I. The first two principles are particularly pertinent in enabling the child to bridge the gap between the avoidance mode and the exploratory mode. Together these two early therapeutic principles are characterized in the phrase: "More structure, and less instruction."

The first of these principles stipulates that progression along the learning continuum advances from use of maximal to minimal external structure. Equipment has been selected which is so simply structured that its use is self-evident to the child and readily invites his involvement. Five basic kinds of equipment have been selected precisely for the manner in which their use promotes the pivotal role function of the tactile and the vestibular systems in conjunction with movement, as described in the OTA Triad and the V-V Dyad.

The second principle stipulates that bridging the gap between avoidance and exploration is best facilitated by use of a nondirective, invitational approach. The child's voluntary, spontaneous responses are the therapist's best clinical means of assessing sensorimotor function. It is therefore important that one not risk confusing this picture. Such clouding of the picture can be prevented by scrupulously adhering to the principle which suggests that the therapist refrain from telling the child, or teaching him, or in any way showing the child how to do a task through which she is seeking to understand how his sensory systems either inhibit or facilitate his function. (See Chapter 12, Principles 1 and 2)

Unstated Goals

In implementing these two principles, no goal is verbalized to the child. Therefore, no values are set up against which the child might recognize possible failure. The child must be permitted the freedom to explore, to discover for himself what he can do. In this way he can demonstrate to the therapist what is comfortable for him in his current state of organization or disorganization. Given the freedom to do so, a child will automatically function at the highest level of central nervous system organization at the time.

In a minimally directive approach, the crucial benefit to be derived from not stating the goal is the child's emerging perception that he is in control. He feels unthreatened. Finding this to be true he will openly involve himself further. He will make the essential transition from avoidance to exploration quite automatically. He will expand his exploration further and will discover it is fun. Fun and success are self-motivating forces. Success helps the child extend the duration of interest and involvement with the task and facilitates his development of a consistent, dependable, organized pattern of voluntary movement.

Praise

A word of caution is recommended to therapists, teachers, and to parents alike whenever an additional step of progress has been achieved. Positive feelings should be appropriately verbalized to the child at the time of his achievement, but it is important to simply use a single, broad statement, such as "I like what I see." This may be accompanied by a mildly-spoken invitation, such as "Can you show me more?" Such a broad, nonspecific comment tends to convey to the child not only a general feeling tone that he is accepted, but also that his efforts, no matter how small, are approved of and generally successful. When one becomes specific about the child's achieving what was heretofore impossible, it sets goals in retrospect.

Undoubtedly, parents, teachers, and therapists have been puzzled to find that many learning-disordered children cannot tolerate praise for their accomplishments. Aside from the possible insecurity often attributed to such a response, this seemingly paradoxical reaction bears a closer look so that further negative effects on the learning-disordered child can be prevented. (See Chapter 12, p 6 regarding the effect of predetermined goals.)

Upon hearing words of praise from an adult, the child may show signs of withdrawal from the situation or regress to his previous level of performance. In the first place, these children have often endured longstanding and overwhelming experiences of failure; drawing attention to success may be too striking and overwhelming an experience for them to tolerate; they may be embarrassed. It is also possible that the adults, in relief of their own anxiety over the problem, may be too lavish in their acclaim, magnifying the importance. These children are extremely sensitive to the emotions of those about them. They have their antennae out in all directions. They are likely to pick up the anxiety of those about them and can become more disorganized by the surrounding attitudes. By using the suggested low-key approach to positive expression, which can be tolerated by the child, the paradoxical behavior of rejecting praise can in some measure be prevented.

Adults may quite properly question the appropriateness of such broad, nondefinitive positive feedback in which there is virtual absence of negative or corrective responses to the child. Both facets are important for the growth, maturation, and judgment of any child; yet, at this early point in the therapeutic process, wherever there are still gaps to be bridged between the avoidance and exploratory modes, positive, supportive feedback is used almost exclusively. Further comments about the use of positive and negative feedback will be made in conjunction with the discussion of the program plans.

9

Promoting the Learning Processes: Organization

The term *organize,* a process cited in the hypothesis of the holistic approach, means:

1) to recognize elementary likenesses and differences of stimuli within a sensory system;

2) to match, sort, classify, and group sensory input, objects, symbols, or ideas of their "like" attributes;

3) to establish a constancy in the meaning represented by different symbolic forms;

4) to arrange in a sequential order, ie, by size, by shape, in time, numerically, and alphabetically, or by other classification.

Sensory Discrimination of Likenesses and Differences

In helping the child to recognize elementary differences among stimuli within a sensory system, we look first at the OTA Sensory Triad with particular attention to the pivotal role of the tactile system. According to Ayres,[1] the more accurately the tactile discriminative system functions, the less defensively the child responds, and the more organized the central nervous system becomes. Discrimination in the olfactory and the auditory systems can also be better organized by techniques which are designed to enhance their discriminative function. Techniques to help the child to identify likenesses and differences in sensory input and organize these impressions is described in the program plans, Part III. Olfactory discrimination, manual form perception, and auditory discrimination are depicted in P.P. 1, and visual form perception is presented in P.P. 5. These techniques are suitable for sensory system organization whether the system is clinically functioning in the sensory defensive or the sensory dormant mode.

Not only is the tactile system seen in a pivotal role with respect to the OTA Triad, but it is clearly advantageous from the point of view of the therapist to start the process of organizing sensory information in the tactile system first. Activities can be devised which are graded appropriately to assure success at the lower end of the spectrum; tactile discrimination of textures and objects with wide variations alert the child to his initial awareness that these differences, eg, between a pine cone and a wad of cotton, can be perceived through touch alone. In organizing the tactile system through manual form perception, the child is asked to feel its shape under a barrier or table top and match it to one from among a number in view. A procedure such as this requires minimal explanation from the therapist and minimal language comprehension on the part of the child; it allows the child accurate and immediate nonverbal validation of his perception through the touch system. For the therapist this is an important starting point because she can make accurate observations of performance through the child's motor response alone.

The easy accessibility of the tactile system makes it advantageous as a primary avenue of approach with many therapeutic procedures. If the child is minimally clothed, for example, broad areas of the skin may be comfortably exposed to contact and stimulation when rolling the carpeted barrel. Since such tactile contact arises from his own movements, he feels in control and can determine the action or lessen its intensity at will. These same broad areas can be accessible to the therapist for carefully executed therapeutic brushing to further reduce tactile system disorganization.

Sensory organization in the olfactory and auditory systems is pursued at appropriate points in the therapeutic process, starting at the most obvious elementary level. Efforts to activate the child's awareness of differences perceived visually can be initiated with determining color differences and then progressed to matching simple shapes and forms.

The child's ability to organize information from his environment is gradually upgraded by presenting him stimuli with less apparent differences in the olfactory, tactile, auditory, and visual systems. The graded hierarchy suggests matching pairs of like stimuli until increasing numbers of stimuli can be successfully differentiated. Later in this cyclic process along the learning continuum, the child reaches the level of organizing objects, then symbols, and gradually ideas by their similarities and differences. He will gradually recognize that the small *a* differs in form but not in meaning from the capital *A*. Based on this skill, he will then be able to recognize that there is a constancy in the meaning of the same word which may be written in a different way or found in a different location but still conveys the same intent.

The Marianne Frostig Developmental Test of Visual Perception, Subtest III, Form Constancy,[2] tests the ability by which a child can perceive circles and squares under varying positions and interrelationships with another form. The source of such a visual problem is believed to be the lack of prior or supplementary sensory perception of manual form. The awareness of the intersensory confirmation of manual with visual form would establish a sound foundation from which one could easily build the understanding of visual form constancy, a prerequisite for reading skill. The ability to organize one's perceptions adequately to arrive at increasingly accurate perceptual constancy with reference to the environment at large, and learning material in particular, is essential to the building of sound academic skills.

Sequential Organization Through Tactile Sequence and Assembly

As an outgrowth of the increasingly subtle likenesses and differences, the child is prepared to recognize that differences can be arranged so as to represent a sequential order or pattern. The most elementary awareness of such a sequential order of differences can be derived from early nesting tasks. In P.P. 4, it is advocated that the therapist start at this level again, even though on the surface it might appear to be inappropriately childish for the older child to do so.

The most effective way to help the child establish a more accurate awareness of subsequent sequential organization is through a carefully selected series of tactile assembly tasks. These tasks provide immediate and simultaneous physical and visual feedback to signal the child whether his order of placement of each piece on the center post is correct. The child is first made aware of the fact that when it is correctly assembled, the outer contour is smooth, but whenever there is an obvious bump the piece is out of order.

The merits of tactile sequencing and assembly experiences are twofold. Not only does the sequential organization through tactile assembly tasks provide vivid feedback, but it stimulates the tactile discrimination as well. It would seem that tactile sequencing and assembly tasks could be equally significant in mitigating the disorganization expressed through the tactile defensive system, as do those tactile perception and manual form discrimination tasks mentioned earlier.

Sequential Order of Time

Concomitant with the child's increasing ability to organize himself in relation to his environment is the awareness of the sequential order of time, beginning with learning the simple application of the words *before* and *after*. The terms before and after have concrete parallels with regard to spatial orientation, for example, with the child's experience of the words *ahead* and *behind*. The child soon learns that those children standing in line ahead of him get their turn at play or at school before him, and those behind him must wait their turn. The desire to be first in the fun reinforces the earliest awareness of an established order of time through positive emotional effects. Supportive measures that reinforce this concept by visuo-spatial means are included in P.P. 4. Many learning-disordered children are significantly delayed beyond others in their age group in learning to tell time. At a later point in school there are further problems, since they often fail to develop awareness of the ongoing passage of time. As a result, they do not cope well or learn to pace themselves with respect to time limits imposed by examinations.

Alphabetical Sequencing

Although children often learn at a very early age to reel off their numbers and the letters of the alphabet, it may be much, much later that the child becomes factually aware that the letters do exist independently and in a sequence. Only after the child can recognize the existence of each individual letter does a sequential order and relationship have any value for him. Delay, reluctance, and secondary avoidance responses which deter efficient use of the dictionary, phone book, or any alphabetically filed system can be recognized in individuals in high school, college, and throughout the professional lives of some adults.

Structuring the Environment for Learning

The ability of a child to bring organization out of his own disorganization depends largely on how adults can help structure the environment and learning experiences for him. The adult must first furnish enough structure for the child to derive a sense of organization within his external environment so as to increase the degree of organization he can begin to bring to the situation himself. When problems occur, whether at school, in the home, or the therapy milieu, it may be that the adult and the child are out of phase. The adult may be providing more structure than the child needs, thus stifling the creative, self-initiating, well-motivated attitudes. More commonly among learning-disordered children, insufficient structure for early learning is provided. If the child is unable to establish such structure within himself, greater structure than would be ordinarily desired is necessary throughout the subsequent grades, and possibly into adulthood.

To enable the child to sense a better structure of his environment, he should be given simple, carefully graded desk activities, starting with the tactile and visual systems. These activities provide him the opportunity to match, sort, and organize objects of his environment according to their likenesses and differences. In the program plans described in Part III, the methods used in therapy provide this early structure; they help the child to establish a sound organization of his environment. Teachers in nursery, kindergarten, and primary grades should find these methods applicable within their classrooms for any child, but they are especially relevant to the learning-disordered child.

Following the early matching phase just mentioned, the child is helped to analyze simple relationships between objects and to identify their common denominators such as size, color, form, weight, and function. In analyzing contrasting aspects between those objects which are dissimilar, a foundation is being laid for a much later and more abstract level of thinking within this cyclic process along the learning continuum.

In secondary schools and later, the preparation of academic material in essays and book reports depends largely on the ability to organize one's ideas, correlate similarities, and identify contrasting aspects. Under pressure of time during essay exams, this skill is tested more acutely. It would appear from observations among learning-disordered children that this may be made less difficult if the child is helped to establish such an analytical base through these early concrete experiences.

Organizing Motor Patterns Within a Structure

Through a concrete learning experience, such as on the indoor climber, a child is encouraged to explore and to recognize that there might be new variables or movement patterns within the structure of that equipment. The therapist watches and listens for accounts from home and from school for signs of the child's expanding ability to create new organizational relationships. New play experiences will challenge him to develop additional motor skills. When a young child, who has previously not involved himself spontaneously in play, suddenly begins exploring new activities at home and on the playgrounds he is becoming more capable of organizing perceptions about his environment and responding appropriately to them. As he moves along the developmental hierarchy in a more independent fashion he will start the exploratory process at a slightly higher level, gathering new organizational impressions from it, integrating this with prior experience, and beginning to conceptualize new ideas from these actions.

In one respect, the key to unlocking the exploratory urge lies in the structure of each of the five basic pieces of motor equipment selected for use in Phase I of the holistic approach. This equipment is so simple it requires no instruction for the child. The possibilities are unlimited; he can readily explore imaginative new relationships within and beyond the existing structure. This type of structure is of great importance because the learning-disordered child does not make transitions easily. He tends not to extend himself toward the more imaginative outside possibilities because he is so locked into concrete forms of thinking and relating to the objects of his environment.

Organized Versus Compulsive Behavior

At this point one could ask if this method might not overemphasize organization, causing the child to become compulsive in his behavior. In both gross motor and early desk activities, the equipment is usually designed or selected because the structure speaks for itself. This structure permits the therapist to keep verbal instructions to a minimum. Generally, children try to perform; they want to succeed and to win approval. However, if they are in a situation where it is expected of them to function compliantly, in accord with the adult's instructions, the implied goal expectations and value judgment can easily cause the child to become overly anxious and compulsive; such is not the case in the holistic approach.

On his own, the learning-disordered child often does become compulsive. This behavior can be decreased by improving the child's organizational ability. It is because he has such poor organization and erroneous concepts of incoming sensory stimuli that he cannot cope comfortably with his environment; thus, he compulsively tries to control its impact on him. As he gains better internal control through improved sensory organization, he is less apt to need to exercise efforts to control his external world. On the basis of observation, it would seem that proper application of the recommended therapy techniques would be helpful in mitigating a compulsive response.

References

1. Ayres JA: Tactile functions: Their relation to hyperactive and perceptual motor behavior. AJOT 18:6-11, 1964.
2. Frostig M: The Marianne Frostig Test of Visual Perception. Chicago, Follett Pub Co, 1964.

10

Promoting the Learning Processes: Integration

The term *integrate,* a process cited in the hypothesis of the holistic approach, means:

1) to unify present impressions among various sensory systems;

2) to unify past with present impressions within one sensory system and combine these with the impressions arising in other sensory systems;

3) to perceive, as the result of the above, a more complete whole of one's sensory picture of the environment and one's own emotional set in relation to it;

4) to establish a sensory foundation for recollection as a prerequisite to associative memory of cognitive information.

Simultaneous Sensory Impressions

The first step on which to build a foundation for more general recollection and recall of facts and events is to establish a clear recognition of and discrimination of current ongoing sensory impressions within each system. In this program the child's first exposure to such information is in matching the tactile sensation derived from rubbing the variously textured blocks, as described in P.P. 1. Such an experience helps the child to retain the brief, immediate past recollection from those blocks in view to then match it to the one which is visually obscured.

In addition to integration within a sensory system of present with the immediate past, integrated use of the visual with the tactile system is found in manual form perception experiences, especially in the more difficult levels of this skill, depicted in P.P. 1.7. In the motor skills, vigorous use of the jumping board in P.P. 3.4 will be likely to greatly activate and integrate simultaneous sensory input from the vestibular, kinesthetic, tactile, visual, and auditory systems. It would appear that recollection and recall evolve from multiple experiences garnered from each of the sensory systems, individually and in concert with one another.

Present with Past

An example of unifying present with distant-past impressions within one sensory system is demonstrated in the following incident. A child, after passing through the early olfactory dormant mode into the subsequent, but transitory, olfactorily defensive mode, could discriminate food scents, matching them quite adequately. On one occasion during therapy, when presented with cinnamon oil scent, he said that it smelled like the French toast his big brother used to make. This experience had, in fact, transpired several months before, during the brother's college vacation.

It is anticipated that as the natural result of establishing a clear recognition and recall of sensory information, this will provide a sound foundation upon which associative memory and recall of cognitive information may later develop. Hopefully it will reduce the frequency by which the child seems one day to grasp certain academic content, only to have it at a later date appear to be a totally new learning experience for him. When such occurrences arise, review and reinforcement of sensory discrimination of these various sensory systems will provide a better foundation on which the child will be able to establish recent and past recollections.

Ego Building

The more effectively the sensory systems can function to provide the child with accurate, well-balanced, or integrated sensory information, the more the child will sense a feeling of inner security and dependability about the perceptions of his immediate environment. Notable changes have been observed among the numerous learning-disordered children in this program which confirm that well-integrated sensory perceptions yield increased self-confidence and more consistent social responses, especially among their peers. In effect, sensory organization can provide a direct route toward building a stronger ego in the learning-disordered child.

Paradoxically, one of the most frequent manifestations of better ego strength which is reported from home is the seemingly increased conflict between the child in therapy and the older siblings. Heretofore, the learning-disordered child may have been less assertive in articulating his own needs so that others could easily override his wishes. As this balance changes, the older child becomes aware of stress because he is unaccustomed to having to cope with the expressed interests and demands of the one in treatment. It should be pointed out to the parents what may be happening and that, although it may be more difficult in some ways for them to cope with the new aspects of the problem, this is often a very significant indication of the learning-disordered child's progress.

Siblings and peers are often the most accurate bellwethers of change in social interaction with the learning-disordered child. When they discover he no longer must be handled with deference, or coddled because he cannot function, or ignored and prohibited from playing with them, other children will quite accurately perceive that he is becoming a force to be reckoned with. This change and assertiveness bodes more of a competitive threat to them. They then react in a normal manner to protect their own self-interests.

These conflicting forces, set in motion from time to time, are the most natural ways to forge a stronger ego, for the child in therapy can begin to stand his own ground. Wise parents will be cautious not to rescue their child from this battleground prematurely, nor convey through their own anxiety that normal conflicts should be curtailed.

11

Promoting the Learning Process: Conceptualization

The term *conceptualize,* * cited in the holistic approach, means:

1) to become aware of the correlation between symbolic language and the ideas or concepts conveyed about early concrete, tangible sensory and motor experiences of childhood;

2) to develop a capacity for cognition as an outgrowth of the organization and integration of sensory and motor experience;

3) to assess the likenesses and differences of ideas, to establish characteristic abstract common denominators;

4) to draw analogies, develop working hypotheses, and arrive at new conclusions and concepts.

Tangible Concepts from Sensorimotor Experience

Among the most elementary concepts the child is helped to recognize is the meaning of the *same* as opposed to *different*. These early tangible, concrete sensory experiences are derived through the olfactory, tactile, auditory, and visual systems, most notably manual and visual form perception tasks.

Early motor experiences in the exploratory phase promote involvement and action on the part of the child before expecting him to respond to words which define the specific movement or position. As soon as practical, one would ascertain how well a child understands the words which depict movements or positions in relation to the external environment. In a simple, clear request the therapist asks the child to stand, for example, at the end of the climber. (The therapist must be cautious to avoid any gesture demonstrating the action.) When the child moves in accord with the meaning of the request, a simple affirmation such as this is given: "Yes, that is what the words told you." It may be necessary at this point to enable the young child to recognize the relationship between his actions and the idea conveyed by the simple instructions. If these simple words of movement or position are incorrectly interpreted, procedures are instituted to correct any confusion.

*The term is defined here as it applies to children and adults.

After the child comprehends the meaning and executes the action of words which relate to his own position in space, he should be ready to cope next with words which relate to things external to himself, such as the position of one object in relation to another. This often involves application to more distant space, with increasingly abstract terms such as *nearer, farther,* or *beyond.* As an outgrowth of these foundations laid in early sensory and motor experiences, the child is enabled to move from the concrete toward the more abstract forms of thinking, which encourages the development of the capacity for cognition in academic skills.

Organizing Cognitive Information

The ability to select relevant information out of a myriad of details or kinds of information is not unlike the sorting out of the visual or auditory foreground from the background stimuli, the visual figure-ground, or the auditory foreground-background stimuli. In these stimuli, overlapping units, shapes, or themes must be isolated for identification. Developing the ability to organize information in this way is essential so that one is prepared to write critiques, book reports, essays, and examinations proficiently. This is a skill which children and adults frequently labor over far more than might be necessary if they had been better prepared to establish a method of selection based on earlier, more concrete experiences.

Abstract Conceptualization

Establishing critical common denominators between abstract ideas is part of the organizational ability required for academic and intellectual pursuits. At the more advanced level, through independent thinking, one can develop new working hypotheses, which lead to further, more complex conclusions and concepts.

Application to the Holistic Hypothesis

A hypothesis embodying a holistic approach has been stated which suggests that learning takes place in a sequential pattern through cyclic progression to provide the foundation skills needed for learning continuity. The processes through which this hypothesis has evolved has clearly unfolded through the same sequence, namely: explore, organize, integrate, and conceptualize. The material in this book has been developed in a continuous cyclic spiral to come to its final stage of completion.

12

Principles Used to Promote Change

The philosophy of programming in a holistic (cohesive and composite) approach supports a) a parent-oriented method and b) use of toys and play equipment as the primary therapeutic media. Within this philosophy are seven basic principles through which to implement change.

1. Progress from maximal to minimal external structure.
2. Bridge the gap between avoidance and exploration through an early nondirective, invitational approach.

(Together, these two principles may be characterized by the phrase "more structure and less instruction" in the initial stages of therapy.)

3. Select a task which speaks to the process.
4. Feed the need.
5. Let the child be your guide.
6. Reduce symptoms by means of the "4 + 4" Scale.
7. Implement a half-step progression to success.

More Structure and Less Instruction

Principles 1 and 2 are closely interdependent and will therefore be discussed together. In the holistic approach the motto *more structure and less instruction* signifies that the success of the learning-disordered child's ability to organize gross movement patterns in the beginning is primarily dependent upon the structuring of the environment through equipment rather than by the use of verbal instruction. This philosophy contrasts the direct use of instruction (in calisthenics, for instance) to provide structure and direct a motor response.

The extent to which the desired response depends upon the external structure versus the use of instruction proceeds in an inverse proportion as the child advances. Starting with motor performance in Phase I as well as in the desk activities of Phase II, and extending into the academic setting, the external structure should shift from maximal to moderate or minimal extent. At the same time, the success should initially depend to a minimal degree on language comprehension and gradually increase in accord with the child's ability so as to allow for a smoothly orchestrated success pattern along the learning continuum.

Because the learning-disordered child often has such poor language comprehension, he needs the structure and the simple function of the motor activities to speak to him in a natural way which automatically invites his involvement. The Phase I equipment has been carefully selected with this need for involvement in mind. The therapist is then able to assume a nondirective, invitational role to enable the child to bridge the gap between avoidance and exploration.

The invitational approach clearly suggests to the child the open-ended, limitless, unstated goals of the task; it is this unstrained atmosphere which accurately promotes his perception that it is indeed he who is in control of the situation. Since he feels less threatened, he can openly engage in the activity to the extent in which he feels comfortable. Soon he realizes that whenever he reaches a point he cannot tolerate, he is free to retreat, returning when he is ready to make the natural transition to the next step. Being free to expand his range of exploration further and further, he soon discovers that the experience can be fun. Through this enjoyment and success, the child will spontaneously prolong the duration of his involvement with the task.

Phase I — Success Through the Invitational Method

The therapist can communicate this open-ended invitation to the child by introducing him to the indoor climber (P.P. 3.1). Introductory remarks can include: "How can you play on this?" "What can you do with this?" "Show me what you can do." "Show me your tricks." Performance at any level is fully acknowledged by the therapist. She even accepts a complete rejection of the task, for she understands that presently the child cannot comfortably involve himself. The child should receive the message that he is accepted as a person, and not accepted only at the times when he performs a certain task. As the child is involved with any of the five pieces of equipment, positive statements are appropriate, such as: "I like what I see." "I like your tricks." "Can you show me that fine trick again?" "Can you show me more?" These comments do not identify any goals. Spoken objectives make the overly-sensitive child believe that he is under close scrutiny.

The therapist makes an effort to refrain from making customary motivating statements such as "Come on, I know you can do thus." Her restraint also sets the tone for parents who are anxious to see their child progress.

As the child demonstrates that he is becoming more comfortable on the climber, for instance, the extent to which he will further involve himself is largely dependent upon the close therapeutic interaction which is established between the therapist and the child. With experience, the therapist will acquire a whole bag of tricks which arise spontaneously to meet the needs of individual situations. For instance, some young children will respond aptly to "hunting for the elves and brownies," climbing quite unconcerned throughout the structure; others will be able to refocus their attention on climbing if the therapist merely taps her ring on the metal bar when they have become distracted.

The most effective therapy comes from using techniques with which the therapist feels most attuned emotionally. As she spontaneously originates new techniques, she will incorporate these into a repertoire which is most closely integrated with her own personality. Most important, each therapist must be genuinely sincere with herself as to whether her emotional makeup is suited to use of these techniques and to a deep involvement with this particular specialty. Therapists will find that a close therapeutic relationship with the child and his parents can be emotionally taxing.

Although the principle of "more structure and less instruction" during early therapy is important, it is just as important for the therapist to be communicative. The interpersonal interaction between therapist and child is crucial to his involvement with the activity and his emerging self-confidence. The communication from the therapist is not dependent upon verbal comprehension; in fact, she must show purposeful restraint to curtail the extent of verbal exchange when the child is hyperverbal. This restraint is an important key to effective therapy with the highly distractible, disorganized child.

The first way a therapist uses nonverbal communication is in maintaining an appropriately close physical proximity to the equipment throughout the time the child is involved with it. The more distant the therapist is from the child physically, the more her communication with him will depend upon verbal means. Because of the vital importance of a close, supportive, nondirective form of communication, the therapist cannot sit comfortably on the sidelines; rather, she is kneeling or standing beside the climber and on the floor continually as the child works on the carpeted barrel, the inflatables, the suspended equipment, and the scooterboard. The therapist's full attention is always directed toward the child. She often expresses her positive affirmation of the child's progress through facial expressions. Brief comments such as "I see how hard you and Mommy have been working this week," help to maintain communication emotionally with the parent during this phase. The parents realize that the focus of the therapist's attention must be directed toward the child and that there will also be time for a brief discussion with them later in the hour.

Under these circumstances the child has no need to dramatize his needs through overt, attention-seeking behavior. The therapist conveys her complete attention to the child in a positive way and maintains close personal contact with him as he performs. This by no means suggests that it is only because he is getting attention that he performs and behaves better. Few of these children, especially the hyperactive ones, have failed to receive sufficient attention from concerned parents, teachers, and psychologists. The attention directed toward him now will not alter his condition. It is the kind of sensorimotor experiences provided him which, together with a scrupulously governed kind of attention, will support the child's positive involvement instead of fostering overt demands for attention through his negative behavior.

From this experience it is my firm belief that, given the freedom to perform without external direction or interference, a child will quite naturally demonstrate the highest level of function which his sensorimotor integration, or neurological maturation, permits him to perform with ease and confidence; children do not willfully hold back. On the contrary, there is an endless striving of the developing human organism to forge ahead to break new ground in motor skills. The observant therapist will welcome and leave undisturbed this clear view of the learning-disordered child's spontaneous responses; they provide a valuable operational viewpoint of the week-by-week advances in his sensori-motor function.

Phase II — Success Through Gradations of Tasks

In Phase II activities, which are simple in nature and require little instruction at the beginning, the structure is derived through careful analysis of the activities, which are then graded according to their degree of difficulty. Here the burden of responsibility lies with the therapist. Within the sequential order and structure provided by each program plan, the success of therapy for any child will depend upon correctly determining the increment of difficulty — between one task and the next — which he can perform. By determining these graded increments appropriately, the child is enabled in bridging the gap from avoidance of Phase II tasks, to involving himself and exploring an emerging interest in them. As the child demonstrates the ability to organize himself, the organization of the therapeutic environment by structuring of tasks is decreased.

Success in Language Skills

In this program, acquisition of language skills progresses from the concrete to the abstract. The language development program has no specific emphasis on naming of objects but there is a focus on helping the child become acutely aware of the words which symbolize movement and direction. The words are first spoken to the child at the precise moment he is experiencing the action, such as *under, over, through;* thereafter, the therapist observes how consistently the child can respond to these words through his own actions. Eventually he is helped to volunteer these same words in direct conjunction with his movement until he can verbalize his plans with *I'm going to crawl through the ladder.* The therapist may be able to start at the point of asking the child to follow a simply stated request involving movement to determine how well the words are comprehended. Such a request might be stated as follows: *Can you move to the other side of the inflated pillow and sit down on it?* When the therapist is evaluating the way her words are interpreted by the child, she cautiously avoids using any facial expression or gestures to convey the meaning.

The therapist gradually increases the use of simply stated requests which involve action in gross motor skills and desk tasks, giving brief confirmatory feedback such as *Yes, that is what the words (mean) tell you.* Language comprehension skills are upgraded in accord with what the child is experiencing through these tasks so that he can organize and integrate these experiences to formulate and express concepts he is sensing, feeling, and learning about himself and his environment.

The Task Must Speak to the Process

The five basic pieces of equipment in Phase I have been selected because of the action which is derived from their use. For example, unresolved remnants of the tonic neck and tonic labyrinthine reflex control are reduced by prone twirling; vestibular bilateral integration is incurred in balance on the inflatables, rolling in the carpeted barrel, and by the twirling action of the scooter board and double suspended tires (P.P. 2). These tasks speak to the process desired to overcome the need to avoid motor involvement and begin to explore, a phenomenon which is clearly exemplified in day-to-day changes on the indoor climber.

Tasks in Phase II which speak to the process of early organization would include the sequential ordering of size in which there is constant, concrete feedback (P.P. 4.1), tactile sequence and assembly (P.P. 4.2), and problem solving through assembly (P.P. 4.3).

An example of the task speaking to the process to integrate information between tactile and visual sensory systems would be early manual form discrimination in P.P. 1.4. Early concepts of the elementary words *push* and *pull* are emphasized at the time when the young child is physically exerting his entire body weight against the indoor climber to move it forward or backward, as found in P.P. 3.1; here in a few moments a concept may be firmly sensed or the meaning of the words directly confirmed. A single activity such as this, when fully analyzed for its merits, has so many elements that it may work for more than one of the five processes; sometimes several may be occurring simultaneously.

Any activity which fails to speak to the process at the point of need may be considered superficial, ie, a splinter skill. For example, use of the walking beam would be contraindicated and premature if the prone and sitting balance were still poorly organized in the child (P.P. 2). Its premature use would not be speaking to the process needed at that point and could cause the child to develop an undesirable splinter skill. At a later point, however, when the child was fully ready for a more advanced level of vertical balance (P.P. 3.3.), the walking beam would be speaking to the process.

Feed the Need

The therapist must be skillfully attuned to recognize subtleties of behavior which convey the needs of a child. The relatively quiet, nonintrusive atmosphere recommended here permits the child to freely reveal the sensorimotor demands which he feels compelled to satisfy. One such demand which is often obvious is his need to assume the inverted or upside down posture. This the child may do by hanging upside down from the bars of the indoor climber (P.P. 3.1); he may also be seen continuously returning to lie supine with his head lowered on the inflatables (P.P. 2.3) or to dangle his head back from the supine posture in the double suspended tires (P.P. 2.1). The imperative role of the therapist should be to not only guard herself against interrupting this drive, but to nurture and feed the need he is expressing. Whenever any slight suggestion of this need is observed, the therapist watches carefully to see how frequently the child spontaneously resumes this position within the therapy hour. On the basis of his expressed need, she would then incorporate into the treatment program additional purposeful stimulation, such as prolonged supine rocking on the inflatables, through his daily home program.

Furthermore, when the child is observed lying supine across the double tires with his head dropped back, it would be incumbent upon the therapist to ask if he would like to be twirled around. The answer will often be *Yes...Go fast...Faster!* (P.P. 2.1).

The tendency for autistic children to twirl themselves and objects as well as to rock and bang their heads is usually looked upon as being an undesirable characteristic which should be interrupted in the therapeutic milieu. Behavior such as this is considered to be representative of an excessive need for stimulation of the vestibular system and a means of facilitating sensory integration. When this need is satiated, the tendency to twirl himself and objects will then be greatly diminished or may cease altogether. It is then a clear example of what is meant by the therapeutic principle to feed the need.

The holistic approach views the intensity of the child's spontaneous responses and the duration of his period of involvement with these activities as an indication of the depth of the need. Prone twirling, for instance, on the scooter board and the double suspended tires provide a tremendous opportunity to observe the intensity of this drive. Changes in the rate of speed or duration can be an important index. This can shift from an initial disinterest or rejection to a growing involvement over the weeks and an intense driving behavior extending over a prolonged period of 15 to 20 minutes' duration in therapy. One can quite often observe a dramatic crescendo of interest in first one activity and then another, waning as the needs which that particular movement supplied are apparently fulfilled.

The principle of feed the need applies equally well to Phase II activities; what may seem to be an inordinately long period of interest in certain activities may be easily observed. For instance, one child of age seven, with better than average intellect, was fascinated by the numerous size sequencing tasks. A period of three or four weeks of daily work with these at home truly amazed the mother, who as a trained nurse was knowledgeable about the child development from a professional point of view. She was able to recall clearly that when these toys were available to him as a preschooler, the child would exhibit no interest in them whatsoever, and she finally gave them away. This is an example of how his disorganization at the preschool age was too great to enable him to cope with these tasks successfully. When he was able to do so, this involvement seemed to be fulfilling a nearly unquenchable need. When this was finally satisfied, he moved on to a new interest at a higher level along the continuum.

Although many of the early activities of Phase II seem to be juvenile in nature, children who are beyond the age where their interest in these activities are expected will spontaneously engage in the tasks and seem to enjoy their successes. In individual therapy, as contrasted to other therapy or school settings, there are no other children in the immediate vicinity who might ridicule the child about what he is doing. To minimize any feeling the child might have about these tasks being too childish, they are often removed from their boxes in the beginning so that the advertising which suggests the toy is suitable for a much younger child does not upset him. If this point arises, the therapist can say very confidently that this may be true for play purposes, but here the toys are used in a different way. In jest, the therapist may laughingly agree that it does say so on the box, but the manufacturer may not know many children, implying this should not be taken seriously.

The child may feel insulted through the use of these toys unless the situation is skillfully handled and the therapist is fully cognizant of the purpose and in agreement with the treatment philosophy. The use of these juvenile toys with children who are older may arouse in adults considerable anxiety; they may view their child's activity as a form of regressive behavior. The therapist should explain to the parents the need for their child to build a sound underlying foundation through such experiences.

The therapist must also analyze her own attitude about use of toys and activities at a level which is considerably below a child's chronological age; her unconscious feelings may act to deter the desired atmosphere and therapeutic benefit to the child. In working with adolescents, especially, the therapist must be honest with herself and with the student, explaining that obviously the childish nature of the tasks is not appropriate but since others which speak to the process in the same way are not available, these are used as a vehicle for change.

Let the Child Be Your Guide

Lest one immediately conjure up the image of a child walking into the therapy room with free access to the toy cabinet, or freedom to rush hastily from one piece of gross motor equipment to the next in rapid succession, be assured this is not the meaning of the phrase. In fact, before pursuing this very important principle by which to conduct effective therapy, it would be helpful to start at the opposite end of the pole. A therapist must recognize when not to follow the lead of the highly distractible child and how to try to cope constructively with such behavior.

Ideally, there is relatively little in view in the therapy room; the toy cabinets have closed doors and are off limits to children. Some gross motor equipment such as inflatables or climber may be stored elsewhere, being brought out only at the time of use. A single Phase I piece of equipment is centrally placed, and the therapist, in close proximity to it, focuses her attention there. As a natural outcome, the child will usually be drawn to it, especially since there is little else available to him. Within this setting, and with the simplicity of structure of the equipment, he is then free to respond in whatever manner benefits him at that time.

Should he begin to wander, as young, highly distractible, poorly organized children will do, the therapist is best advised to try to simply stay near the piece of equipment, focusing her attention on it rather than on the child; she then waits to see if he focuses his own attention there also and returns to the task.

If the child simply rejects any involvement with the gross motor tasks initially, the most suitable action for the therapist is to just sit on the floor, playing with a colorful, age-appropriate Phase II toy herself. She waits to see if the child will come over to take it and begin to play. If the child strays out of sight of the therapist, a toy with an appealing sound such as a musical telephone or marble railway may bring him back out of curiosity. In circumstances such as those, it is preferable if the therapist does not accede to the child's persistent efforts to distract her or pull her away by chasing him. In the optimal therapeutic setting in which to alter such behavior, the problems of safety should be alleviated as much as possible. This enables the therapist to relax and patiently wait for the child to return. If she remains physically unmoved rather than following in his direction, the highly distractible child will relocate to this stable point. The therapist still has all the toys which can be used as a ploy to get him involved. As mentioned before, a few taps of her ring against metal will help him refocus his attention to that spot; this means will be more effective than urging him to cooperate. It is also more effective if he has otherwise been bombarded by barrages of words from adults who have tried to control his difficult behavior in conventional ways.

In a difficult situation, the therapist may have to temporarily abandon any plans she had for using Phase I activities for that session. She will focus then on those early Phase II tasks which will enable her to establish initial rapport and then determine what simple activities at that point can be effective in helping him focus his attention.

In those introductory methods, the child is quite obviously not the guide of the therapist. But use of the noninstructive technique with each of the Phase I tasks enables the child to be his own guide by following the natural hierarchical sequence in performance from the earliest hesitant contact to the fully developed range of fancy maneuvers. In Phase II the therapist makes an educated guess as to where she senses the child might function successfully within this sequential hierarchy. For example, she selects a certain point in the sequence of visual form recognition tasks and is fully prepared to move to a lower level if the task is not smoothly performed, or she moves the level higher if it is. As the therapist gains experience in these techniques, she will be better able to determine how large an increment the child can span within each series of desk activities, but the pace must always be governed by the child's smooth, successful performance.

Within the treatment hour there will be some days when the child is making an obvious breakthrough on a particular activity. On days when the intensity of action seems to be paramount to the child, as for instance, in twirling or rolling in the barrel, the duration is extended, temporarily omitting some of the Phase II activities. This is what is meant by allowing the child to determine from his innermost urgent needs what tasks are the most appropriate.

On the otherhand, if the therapist knows that the child has always hated to do puzzles, she should put this kind of activity aside for the present. It will often surprise the child and parent alike to discover that, once he has acquired the necessary prerequisite skills in graded visual form, spatial relations, and visual figure-ground through other means, puzzles will be much easier for him; they may also be fun. He may even challenge his skills at home with puzzles which are more complex and time consuming than those used during therapy.

The author envisions the structure of this program as being of foremost value to occupational therapists so that they can make relevant clinical observations in a systematic way. A systematic method such as this is provided in the Ongoing Evaluation and Performance Scale (Appendix A) and the Program Plans in Part III. Through such a structure the therapist can freely permit the child to be her guide, following him along tangents which his behavior and her own informed observations would suggest.

Reduce Symptoms by Means of the "4 + 4 Scale"

The *4 + 4 Scale* is a hypothetical means of illustrating that the disorganization demonstrated in a child can be the result not only of the state of his sensorimotor dysfunction, but also of external factors within the environment. Four points on this hypothetical scale are assigned to the internal factors within the child and four to the influences which are created by the environment or, more specifcally, people within it. Therefore, whenever environmental factors can be mitigated and symptom reduction can result in as many areas as possible, the magnitude of the child's overall problem can be brought within more manageable proportions. However, if the external factors which can be modified are not properly reduced, the entire burden of change rests with the child. Not only will changes take longer, the results will be less profound.

The following example of a tactually defensive child who hypothetically is functioning with a marked level of severity is designated by a three on the scale of four.

> The child is awakened each morning by his father who gives him a "double grinder" or a playful twist of his fist in the child's abdomen. Since the child giggles profusely, the father does not consider his action as upsetting to the child or inappropriate on his part. The child, therefore, is sent to school in a heightened state of disorganization.

If this external influence is hypothetically scored as a three, the two factors added together illustrate that, on a scale of eight, the six represented in this child's situation is significant. By helping the parent to become more aware and understanding of their own actions in light of the child's problems, the extent of his disorganization can be reduced to a marked degree. Thus, the effectiveness of the therapy directed to the tactile system is enhanced.

In a much different way, the degree to which a child who is poorly organized in visual perception and fine motor skills will find his problems prolonged or even made worse when the primitive method of teaching printing by sticks and circles is used in some elementary schools. This problem can be greatly mitigated through efforts of the therapists and teachers to institute a method (P.P. 8.8) which is designed specifically to counteract disorganized performance of this kind. In so doing they are meeting the child halfway rather than expecting him to make all the adjustments.

The 4 + 4 Scale then may be applied to the extent of disorganization evident in behavior generally or in a specific skill such as printing. It is presented as a stark reminder to adults, be they parents, teachers, or therapists, that it is incumbent upon them to examine their own actions in relation to the manifestations of the child's problem and to review methods of school instruction and techniques in therapy to ascertain whether or not these might impede progress. In so doing, they may discover new and more viable means of expediting change. In other words, the 4 + 4 Scale is really a reminder to the adult to challenge his or her own actions.

Half-Step Progression to Success

Tasks which are therapeutic and those which are scholastic in nature should be analyzed for those underlying component skills which the task requires. (See

Part III, Summary Inventory of Foundation Skills for Academic Performance.) The principle of *half-step progression* means simply that if the child finds the task is too difficult when two or more components are encountered simultaneously, then by breaking down the task into separate and distinct parts, the skill level of each can be developed independently at a lower level before combining them in a designated task.

Spatial relations and visual figure-ground skills are the components in the familiar task of assembling picture puzzles. In therapy, each of these two factors are graded separately within a series of puzzles. One factor, as for instance in visual figure-ground, is kept at a low level while the child's skill in the spatial relations factor is upgraded (P.P. 5.3 and 5.9). In addition, other tasks directed solely to spatial relations (P.P. 5.2 and 5.7) and to visual figure-ground skill (P.P. 5.8) are also emphasized.

An example in a scholastic task at a more advanced level would be to help the student to organize concrete and abstract information while taking lecture notes or writing a book report. The proposed method is an example of half-step progression, reverting to textbook material or even storybooks several grade levels below the child's current grade. These are used to enable the child to learn to recognize, select, and organize relevant points from irrelevant materials without having to work at the same time toward reading comprehension at his own level.

Teachers are accustomed to grading the performance of their students along clearly defined lines, comparing the way in which they cope with curriculum content and materials which is expected for students of their age and grade. By contrast, occupational therapists have no prescribed curriculum to follow for skills development. However, their professional training to meet the demands of rehabilitation for physically handicapped and emotionally disturbed individuals enables them to bring a rich background of experience in observation, analysis, and gradation of factors entailed in performing a task. In treating the learning-disordered child, there must be a close interface between the gradation within the task and the developing capabilities the child brings to it. The therapist will find that the program plans to follow offer one such curriculum for graded skills development. The teacher will find in these plans a new dimension in teaching, which will be helpful in understanding and fulfilling those underlying skills which are involved in a particular academic task. Within these program plans, half-step progression is one principle by which both therapist and teacher can foster a child's potential for greater academic success.

Part II: Tools for Evaluating and Programming

Introduction

A series of protocols for evaluation and programming are presented. They serve many purposes. The foremost purpose is to enable the therapist to make a meaningful and dynamic diagnostic assessment of a child's performance along a graded hierarchy of activities, and to provide effective therapy through use of these same tasks. Another purpose, of equal value and importance, is that these tools provide a direct means of training the therapist in how to conduct therapy for the learning-disordered child from a holistic approach.

These protocols are interdependent, but they may be used selectively according to the level of experience of the therapist. The inexperienced therapist will need to formally document her findings on each of these protocols initially to realize their maximum value. Gradually her ability to conduct effective treatment will be based more on her observations and assessment of clinical change, and it will be less necessary to make a formal documentation of this in each child's program. Experienced therapists who are first becoming acquainted with a holistic approach will readily discover which, from among these protocols, they will need to keep formal records. Adequate documentation of the child's performance on the Ongoing Evaluation and Performance Scale, as well as the Program Plans, fosters the smoothest progressions toward each child's therapeutic goals.

The therapeutic program is basically structured into Phases I and II. The following protocols are based on this structure: The Ongoing Evaluation and Performance Scale, The Summary Record Sheets, The Program Plans, and The Integrated Program Matrix. The Sensorimotor History and a key to recognizing the relevance and significance of the data are valuable and adjunctive tools.

Before presenting the details of these protocols, a composite view of the program is provided through the following analyses of the purpose and the goals of Phase I and the three sections of Phase II.

Analysis of the Program

Purpose and Goals of Phase I

The emphasis in Phase I is on the use of the five basic pieces of equipment: the indoor climber, carpeted barrel, scooter board, inflatables, and suspended equipment for twirling. Use of these by the child helps to stimulate the proprioceptive information arising from the tactile, kinesthetic, and vestibular receptors, and to integrate this with information arising simultaneously from the visual system. Exposure to these pieces of equipment promotes the spontaneous exploration on the part of the child and, through it, better organization and integration of movement into smooth, sequentially ordered patterns.

Of particular significance is the use of the indoor climber from which the child can clearly establish an internal awareness and concept of the sequential order of movement in large, slowly executed motor patterns. These slow, sequentially-ordered movements are the basic foundation from which will later emerge the rapidly-executed, sequentially-ordered, fine movements needed to master script writing. In these five basic pieces of equipment the goal is simple, and the structure of the equipment focuses the child's attention toward that goal. In this way the therapist is able to use a minimally-directive, invitational approach toward the child.

The initial purpose in presenting Phase I activities is to provide the observer with an opportunity to gain insight into the manner in which the child appears to receive sensory information and how he then acts upon it. Close observation will enable the therapist to determine the presence or absence of avoidance responses in relation to each of the sensory systems in the Olfactory-Tactile-Auditory Sensory Triad, and the Visual-Vestibular Dyad.

Through a properly graded program of therapy the child can be enabled to reduce his need to avoid and to replace this with the desire to explore. The goal of Phase I is to bring organization out of disorganized responses at the most primitive, elemental level of sensation and movement, so that the need to avoid would not remain the prevailing behavioral "set" for his motor, social, and academic performance which is secondary to it. Early gross motor organization and integration involving two sides of the body helps to lay the foundation for cerebral dominance and those academic activities which depend on the child's having established hand dominance.

Purpose and Goals of Phase II, Section A

(See schematic plan by referring to Appendix G, The Hourly Record Sheet)

Phase II, Section A, is concerned with refining the sensory system organization and the integration of multiple sensory input primarily through their application to desk activities. With the exception of the vestibular system, all those systems cited in the OTA Triad and the V-V Dyad are actively engaged through use of these activities; in many instances, there is an integrated action from three or more sensory systems. In Phase II, the vestibular system is involved in a less dynamic role — to maintain sitting balance; by contrast, a primary emphasis is placed on activating this system in Phase I.

Purpose and Goals of Phase II, Section B

(See Appendix G)

The child is first made aware of a sequential order and organization within the environment through the most primitive, concrete, and direct cause-and-effect experiences, eg, sequencing of toys or containers which are graded in size from large to small. Added to this experience, the child is presented three dimensional toys which yield tactile information about their sequential order and correct assembly; then toys or concrete tasks involving sequential steps to problem-solving are presented as preparation for easier mastery of the steps in abstract problem-solving. The immediate value in this procedure is that the objects themselves yield continual feedback to validate to the child whether or not his response is in error and nurtures his initiative to correct it.

Experiences with sequencing concrete objects may lay the foundation for the conceptualization of the abstract sequential order of temporal events. This section of Phase II also helps set the stage for the child to acquire academic skills by using many activities which involve auditory sequence, visual sequence, and alphabetical sequence.

Purpose and Goals of Phase II, Section C

(See Appendix G)

In normal development, sufficient gross motor organization is achieved by the young child to adequately integrate the two hemispheres of the brain, and thereupon to establish cerebral dominance quite automatically. When it has not taken place in the normal course of events, this arrest can, in large measure, be overcome through the activities of the Phase I portion of the program. Concomitantly, in this section of Phase II ample opportunity is also provided for a child who is still lacking adequate hand dominance; this deficit is corrected through bimanual motor integration — by replicating the early forceful pushing-together and pulling-apart of hand toys, so designed. Free exploration of hand dominance, using either hand, is encouraged at this point through random hammering. Use of large movements on a vertical scribble board is also urged in an attempt to fulfill the early developmental stage of undirected scribbling prior to establishing hand dominance.

In this program it is presumed that a dominant hand has been adequately determined by the child when the performance of one hand definitely contrasts that of the other. This is measured by timed hammering and crayoning samples described in Part III. The balancing skills which can be acquired in Phase I provide the child with a definite internal awareness of one side of the body as opposed to the other, ie, laterality. Only after this point is each side identified to the child by its proper name: *right* and *left*. To reinforce this awareness, special techniques are used which will yield further confirmatory sensory identification to the right and left sides of the child on himself. All these measures help him to get a sense of his body image, but more specific measures are used in conjunction with The Positional Model, described in Part III, to confirm and stabilize it. In The Positional Model the child gains a concrete left-right association of position and direction in front of him, and then the association of left and right with those letters (b-d; p-q) which are readily reversed because of these directional problems. Further application of The Positional Model provides a sound foundation for the child's spatial orientation of his external world, such as top-bottom relationships, as well as right and left, upper and lower, plus lower left-hand corner, for example.

Consistent with this, the geographical orientation, such as "Southwest" is added when this is age appropriate.

Techniques to train the child to print the alphabet are based on a directional orientation consistent with the foregoing methods to build a sound foundation. Script letters are analyzed and grouped according to their similarity of motor patterns for ease in their mastery by the learning-disordered child. Mastery of speed and efficiency in script writing is absolutely necessary if the child is to advance academically.

Ongoing Evaluation and Performance Scale

Origin and Development

As a clinical therapist, I had long been concerned that the emphasis on static diagnoses such as learning disorders, dyslexia, mental retardation, and others are of little clinical or educational value since they do not specify the functional problem. Whereas it may be helpful to know the medical diagnosis which describes a lesion or general dysfunction, this too often becomes an end-point in itself. For instance, a diagnostic label of mental retardation tends to obscure the true nature of the problem and to consider the child's condition to be fixated. It may even put him outside the range of help or deter him from getting into the most effective educational environment. Broad diagnostic categories not only do not address themselves to the specific functional impairments, which are subject to change, but also they imply the concept of defectiveness.

It was clear that there was a need for a dynamic, diagnostic tool which allowed for constant re-evaluation and revision according to the child's performance. Standardized data yields information in relation to the broad population; for a functional assessment of clinical and educational value I felt the urgent need to view the child's performance in relation to himself. The Ongoing Evaluation and Performance Scale* has been designed as such a dynamic, diagnostic instrument. This tool includes the means for constant re-evaluation and revision, the direction to follow therapeutically and a means to chart the flow of progress toward the desired function. In addition, the functional assessment of the Ongoing Evaluation and Performance Scale permits the child to be continuously assessed by himself; throughout the program he is able to recognize his improvements over his previous performance. With proper selection of activities by the therapist, the child is almost always spared any feelings of failure and frustration; instead he experiences growing self-confidence and a stronger ego.

This material has evolved out of the clinical experience of working with an estimated 500 children. The experience began initially with groups of young military dependents, then in private practice for ten years, and also in consultation roles with various school systems which are specifically concerned with the education and care of children having serious learning disorders and language dysfunction. The Ongoing Evaluation and Performance Scale, or Performance Scale as it is often referred to, has been developed over the last seven

*The Ongoing Evaluation and Performance Scale (OEPS) appears in Appendix A. This may be used for record keeping of individual children.

years as a direct result of clinical experience with learning-disordered children being treated in private practice, on a one-to-one relationship.

Application

The content of this instrument for programming and for evaluation relates primarily to children from four to ten years, but its application can easily be extended for use with adolescents. Portions will also apply to adults who present historical data from their childhood and evidence of a difficult academic adjustment which is compatible with that of the learning-disordered child.

Obviously, not all the units of this program would be included in the therapy of any one child. This provides a chance to see his areas of strength as well as his deficits.

Portions of this program may be applied to children who are already engaged in therapy to meet their special requirements due to cerebral palsy, mental retardation, or blindness, for example. Selected portions may also be helpful in treating adult patients following a stroke or other cerebral insult. Some of these methods and principles would have a bearing on prevocational testing and vocational training for the handicapped and also for the adult retardate.

Purpose

The Ongoing Evaluation and Performance Scale is prepared primarily for use by therapists, but also serves as an easily understood guide for teachers and parents. It is designed to:

1) provide a frame of reference to observe, measure, and record behavior for the purpose of making dynamic diagnostic evaluations and conducting therapy and/or clinical research;
2) establish a tangible means of coping with a wide array of interdependent and inter-related material;
3) contribute to program planning within the scope of this sensorimotor program and be dovetailed with other therapeutic and educational programs in the same setting;
4) provide a focal point of reference to facilitate communication when responsibilities for programming are shared by a team, which may include several therapists, the child's teacher, and his parents.

Observing Clinical Performance

The Ongoing Evaluation and Performance Scale is designed to enable professional personnel to record observations about the nature and the quality of a child's performance quickly and accurately. It provides a baseline diagnostic evaluation of the child's early performance and an ongoing measurement of his status at any time.

Three levels of performance have been arbitrarily established. The hierarchy of performance skills upon which these three levels were determined is the result of a decade of close clinical observation of learning-disordered children on a one-to-one basis in private therapy. A consistent pattern has emerged in the hierarchy of Phase I motor performance and in the graded difficulty of the skills required in the Phase II activities along the continuum specified in the OEPS. Through simple descriptive statements of Phase I, the therapist is made aware of what to look for and how to assess what she sees. Among the wide range of possibilities within any one level of performance, only a portion of these may apply to a given child. In private practice, it has often been helpful for the parents to follow these descriptions in the OEPS while also observing their child in therapy. These easily comprehended statements enable them to understand the kinds of performance currently in progress and to see indications of emerging levels of function as they undergo change.

The Ongoing Evaluation and Performance Scale is designed so that it can be used by one therapist or by a multidisciplinary team. When the latter is the case, predetermined areas of their programming responsibilities would be established. Base-line evaluations and the follow-up therapeutic or educational programming would then be conducted by respective members of the team.

Scoring and Recording Clinical Performance

In Phase I a series of simple narrative statements describe the performance which has been arbitrarily designated for Level I, the least difficult, to Level III, the most advanced. In Phase II similar descriptive statements indicate the kind of performance and often the sequence of activities suggested for successful upgrading within that skill. In the left margin is a line, where a dash (-) is placed if the statement applies in part, but the skill is not fully mastered. When it is mastered, the dash is converted to a plus sign (+). Beside the plus sign, the recorder can indicate the therapy hour when this was mastered, eg, H6. Up until then, whenever this performance had been observed to be partially fulfilled, the hour would be recorded in a similar manner alongside the ending of the statement. Some statements are more appropriately answered *Yes* or *No,* especially in Level I, where manifestations of dysfunction are more apparent. In such instances, it is important to record either the avoidance or the lack of performance which should normally be expected.

In the long range picture it is anticipated that by being able to look back over a number of children's programs, the data about the sequence, the continuity, and the duration will provide the therapist with new insights for improving the methods and accelerating the rate at which the learning processes in these children may be activated.

The Summary Record Sheets

The Summary Record Sheets (Appendix B) are designed to present a consolidated picture of the child's level of performance in each of the subdivisions of Phase I and II. In essence the Summary Record Sheets present a visible structure, or foreground pattern, of the relationship of one skill to another. Through this structure one can also comprehend at a glance the graded hierarchy among the subdivisions of the program. Such a visible structure as this continually reinforces the therapist's awareness of the foundations needed for later achievement of academic goals.

Through the Summary Record Sheets the therapist has a continual, composite picture of the summary strengths and deficiencies of each child. Change can be easily observed as these sheets are updated at appropriate monthly or quarterly intervals.

As the therapist becomes totally familiar with the program she will become competent in maintaining the proper gradation of many of the activities from memory. Charting of a child's performance on the sub-steps cited in the OEPS can then be dropped in lieu of charting in a brief fashion on the Summary Record Sheets.

Scoring of the Summary Record Sheets follows the same procedure as that described for the Ongoing Evaluation and Performance Scale, namely, a dash (-) indicates the required performance is partially fulfilled and when converted to a plus (+) the skill has been satisfactorily accomplished.

The Program Plans

There are eight program plans (Appendix C) within the holistic approach to therapy. A dynamic diagnostic evaluation can be made within each program plan to determine how far along the graded hierarchy the child can successfully perform the specified tasks. Such an assessment on each program plan enables the therapist to determine where the therapeutic emphasis should be placed initially and as changes take place throughout the course of therapy. This helps to continually update the child's program and maintain a perspective which is relevant to his changing needs. The close interface between the diagnostic assessment and the treatment procedures, made possible through the eight program plans, assures a smooth progression toward the therapeutic goals. Adherence to this well-integrated progression is essential to sound therapy.

The program plans enable the beginning therapist to conduct a reasonably effective therapy program. It keeps to a minimum the element of disorganization which is bound to occur until considerable experience can be gained. This feature is of great clinical importance; any confusion or disorganization in the immediate environment will cause the adverse condition and disorganization of the learning-disordered child to be intensified.

The program plans are clearly defined in a step-by-step progression of subdivisions, labeled 1.1 through 1.9, for instance, in Program Plan 1. These numerical headings correspond to a detailed description of procedures in Part III of this book.

In the program plans there are three blocks along the right-hand side of the page, corresponding to graded performance levels I, II, and III. The heavy dot in the lower left-hand corner indicates that, for instance, Program Plan 1.4 (tactile discrimination and manual form perception) would require satisfactory performance only at Level I, whereas Program Plan 1.7 would include more difficult activities for mastery at Levels II and III, as indicated by the dots in those blocks.

Scoring procedures within the blocks which correspond to performance levels I, II, and III are consistent with the dash(-) and plus(+) designations described earlier in the OEPS.

The Integrated Program Matrix

The one-page Integrated Program Matrix (Appendix D) establishes at a glance an overview of the eight program plans. The horizontal placement of numbered blocks, #1 through #9 in the top row, for example, corresponds to Program Plan #1 subdivisions 1.1 through 1.9. The placement of the initial block within each program plan indicates, as in Plans #1 through #6, that the first step may be introduced from the outset of the programs. This sequence continues until the child reaches a plateau, returning subsequently to try again to move on.

Program Plans 7 and 8, by contrast, must not be introduced until there has been successful performance on specified prior steps. In Program Plan 7, introduction of the first step is dependent upon successful prior performance of Program Plan 6.5. In Program Plan 8, in addition to the general prerequisites listed at the bottom of the outline page of the plan, there are specific requirements for individual units. Introduction of 8.3 depends on completion of 6.5, and 8.8 depends upon satisfactory understanding and function in 7.3, as shown by the numbers in parentheses in these respective blocks.

Through graphic representation on the Integrated Program Matrix, the horizontal sequence of program steps and the vertical alignment of prerequisite skills together signify the highly integrated quality of the holistic approach to treating learning disorders.

Scoring of this instrument again is consistent with the previously described dash and plus signs; for convenience, the therapist may wish to use a red pencil to indicate the point where the child can function successfully upon entering the program. Steps which are irrelevant to the individual child's program are marked N/A, or not applicable.

A look at the child's record on the Integrated Program Matrix clearly identifies those skills the child has brought to the program, and indicates where continued emphasis is needed. It is always helpful to see the child's areas of strength; to the parent it gives important rays of hope; to the teacher it may suggest alternative avenues of instruction; to the therapist it can indicate areas of strength from which to encourage activities the child can enjoy with his siblings and peers.

As time goes on, plateaus in one or more program plans may appear. At such times, emphasis would be continued on those program plans where he is still advancing. Plateaus on a broad scale may indicate that the child should be scheduled for a temporary hold pattern of six to eight weeks with resumption of weekly therapy as indicated (See Part III, Conclusions). The Integrated Program Matrix allows for obvious assessment of not only the temporary plateaus but also the more fixed points, as in working with the retarded child. Termination of the treatment program, either because of completion of the needed treatment goals or a plateau which is apparently fixed, can be clearly seen by charting the

Integrated Program Matrix. Often the program may be terminated when the child is functioning satisfactorily at grade level, even though not all the points in the latter stages of the program have been completed. Brief resumption of weekly therapy sessions would be reinstituted when a new area of performance, eg, script writing, is introduced in the school curriculum.

Therapists who are experienced in this specialty of treatment can quickly acquaint themselves with the holistic approach. They will soon find that documentation of change on this chart alone will be sufficient for them to maintain a smooth progression toward treatment goals.

The Sensory Avoidance Profile — Index of Change

The Sensory Avoidance Profile (Appendix E) provides a schematic picture of the defensive and/or dormancy affects on the sensory system of the OTA Triad and the V-V Dyad. Chapters 6 and 7, Part I, depicts characteristic patterns of behavior which represent primary, secondary, and tertiary levels of avoidance behavior stemming from a dormant and/or defensive quality of sensory information being supplied to the brain. Clinical information, together with indications of sensory system dormancy or defensiveness cited on the Sensorimotor History, is studied in terms of what level of intensity these forms of behavior prevail at the onset of therapy. They are checked on the Sensory Avoidance Profile with an x and labeled $H1$ for the first therapy hour.

As changes in the level of intensity of these responses become apparent, an x again pinpoints on the same sheet where the child functions and the hour of therapy. Often in the case of the olfactory system, for example, the response moves from the tertiary dormant mode, in which the child is totally unaware of scents at close range, to a temporarily defensive mode before being resolved within the wide range of normalcy.

Information by which to chart the Sensory Avoidance Profile is gathered from clinical observations and from the Sensorimotor History (Appendix F-2). The key to the Sensorimotor History (Appendix F-3) indicates groupings of answers which coincide with known gross and fine motor problems of learning-disordered children, suggested clinical clusters, and patterns of sensory responses, as well as problems in academics and social behavior. The strength of the historical and clinical evidence about sensory system dysfunction can be documented on the Sensory Avoidance Profile at the beginning of the therapy program and revised as clinical behavior changes. When a substantial amount of evidence from the Sensorimotor History and from clinical observation suggests that one or more sensory systems are functioning in a relatively defensive or dormant manner, then this would be marked with an x and Hour 1 (H1) at either the secondary or tertiary level of the respective sensory systems to indicate the intensity of such a response initially. Related academic problems are secondary to a dormant or defensive quality of sensory performance. The primary level of sensory dysfunction is not used on initial evaluation, for if there is any dysfunction, this would be evidenced by its effect on the academic and behavioral adjustment, hence would be secondary. As these symptoms are reduced, then the child may move up to a mild, primary degree of dysfunction, which is then indistinguishable from the wide range of normalcy only by the fact that under stress, the secondary symptoms may reappear.

The value of the Sensory Avoidance Profile is seen primarily as a learning tool for the therapist. The experienced therapist will soon find that his becomes a useful guide for mentally recording the defensive-dormancy picture of the child as she observes his continued clinical performance. Formal recording becomes unnecessary.

The Sensorimotor History

The Sensorimotor History (Appendix F) was compiled over many years to gather a wide background of information which has a bearing on the child's current clinical picture. This history serves as an efficient means of assembling data about clinical clusters and patterns and provides the therapist a working model for close observation during therapy. If this data is available to the therapist before the child's initial visit, the clinical assessment can focus particular attention toward those areas which suggest problem behavior. Background history such as this can help to confirm or enhance the significance of clinical findings. On the other hand, contrasts in findings may suggest that one should take another look or that the behavior which had been reported in the Sensorimotor History may have since become asymptomatic through the normal maturation.

This Sensorimotor History is often forwarded to the parents, together with the introductory cover letter, before the child's first appointment. The parents can answer these questions simply and quickly. In so doing, they can also begin to develop an awareness of the clinical clusters of behavior which are related and get some feeling for sensory system performance which may be at variance with that of the average child.

The questionnaire is designed so that it can be easily scored; data can be readily computerized for formal research. Follow-up data can be collected on the same questionnaire by asking the parents to answer only those questions which are pertinent at that point in time.

The Key to the Sensorimotor History (Appendix F-3) provides a convenient way in which to see relevant groupings, although not every child will show a clearcut set of responses. Not all parents are good observers or historians, especially if it is an older child and some of the aberrant behavior has been forgotten. However, the general trends will be sufficient evidence if there was any marked symptomatology. On a copy of the key, the numbers which are marked in accord with the groupings suggested are simply underlined or circled with a red pencil. If the Sensorimotor History is taken again, but then refers only to current behavior, some index of the reduction of symptoms will be evident if another color is used to underline the results on the same copy of the key. This would suggest the extent of overall reduction of symptomatology quite clearly.

Hourly Record Sheet

The Hourly Record Sheet is designed to help the therapist make efficient use of valuable time and conduct a timely sequence of activities which are identified in the program plans. A separate sheet is prepared for every hour the child is seen in therapy. The therapist quickly checks or writes in, in advance, those specific activities which she plans to use. As the therapy hour is in progress, she crosses through the check when the activity has been used, marks a (P) for pass if indicated, and immediately carries those activities which should be reviewed (R), or upgraded (↑) to the new sheet. There is an intrinsic value in this procedure. During the therapy hour the therapist is in closest touch with the child's performance relative to each step on the sequential continuum charted in the program plans and the Integrated Program Matrix. To foster optimum continuity of programming, the next Hourly Record Sheet is pre-planned during the child's therapy session, or as soon thereafter as possible.

Gradually the experienced therapist will acquire expertise in using the sequential order of steps of the holistic approach so that she can conduct a well-integrated program. She will then depend primarily on the Hourly Record Sheets for continuity, relying on the program plans and the OEPS to use as a reference more than to formally document change in individual children.

On the back of the Hourly Record Sheet the therapist records in brief narrative form observations and changes in the child's program and performance. One technique which has proven suitable as an ongoing method of updating information between the therapist and parent is to have the parent jot down on the back of the current Hourly Record Sheet observations of significant behavior which has taken place since the previous session. The parent should also review the notes the therapist has recorded about the child's previous therapy hour. This continual two-way communication fosters the most active participatory role for the parents — communication which of necessity is limited verbally by the child's presence.

Part III: Implementing the Program

Experience

The therapy program which is presented here by way of these eight program plans had its origins in the experience I gained as an occupational therapist working principally within this treatment specialty at Walson Army Hospital, Fort Dix, New Jersey, between 1964 and 1966. These methods have evolved into their present and more complete form as the result of treating learning-disordered children in a research-oriented private civilian program exclusively.

The program at Fort Dix was the first to be instituted in any of the Armed Services; it became a model on which other programs were later based. In 1966 a training program was developed under my direction to introduce this specialty to occupational therapists throughout other Army hospitals. Following my retirement from the Army, I served for a number of years as consultant and instructor for this annual training course.

The program at Fort Dix served the treatment needs of learning-disordered children who were dependents of service personnel within a wide geographical range. Through the auspices of this treatment program, I served on a consultancy basis to families referred through the Surgeon General's office to advise and prepare them in understanding and conducting some form of home programming for their child during the time they would be stationed in remote overseas posts.

The dual demand of working with children in a group while at the same time attempting to meet their individual needs led to the development of the unique means I have come to use. Many of my methods were simple and practical so that the parents of these young military dependents, whom I asked to accompany their child to therapy each week, could be effective in conducting portions of the program under my supervision. Besides giving me greater personnel resources the participation of parents helped prepare them to meet as many needs of their child as they could through therapy; there was always the possibility that they could be suddenly transferred to a remote part of the world where they would have to continue the program for their child.

Each parent was paired throughout the therapy session with a child other than his or her own (except in the pre-elementary group, where the children worked with their own mothers). This arrangement was designed to curtail the effect of any outside conflict between a child and his own parent which might otherwise interfere with the therapy. This close involvement in the action helped the parents to gain more objectivity about their own child's problems as they observed other children with the needs which were similar; at the same time they were able to see how their own child was functioning with someone else nearby. The experience cited here taught me how well-motivated and effective parents can be in helping to conduct such a program. They also demonstrated on many occasions how they had become better observers of their child's behavior and had applied their new understanding appropriately in helping him to make a better adjustment socially and academically.

Each program had to be structured for the parents. In preparation for each therapy session a card was prepared for every child listing the tasks he needed to do that day and the suggested level for each one. To keep the feeling of disorganization to an absolute minimum, the parents in the elementary and intermediate groups* moved with the child from task to task; in those activities which were done with the whole group and led by the therapist, the parent could supervise the same child on a one-to-one basis.

In the senior group the parents would remain in a fixed location with one kind of activity, eg, manual form perception or a gross motor task, while the children would rotate to those tasks specified for them. In a long-term, ongoing therapy group, many of the parents became skilled observers in their special tasks; they rotated to a new area from time to time to broaden their experience. In order that a program of this kind would run smoothly and could be managed by supplementary assistance of the parents, I began my efforts to establish criteria for judging a child's level of performance in a way in which change could be easily identified and recorded.

In the program at Fort Dix, which I conducted over a two-year period, up to 40 children were treated a week. The pre-elementary group did not exceed five in number; the other groups ranged in size from seven to twelve. All group sessions were conducted for an hour and a half. If the child was too young or too disorganized to meet with a group, or if an adolescent was too self-conscious to benefit from group work, he was seen for individual hourly sessions.

Since my private practice began in 1967 exclusively for the treatment of learning disorders, I have discontinued treatment of children in groups because more specific and rapid means of change can be expedited on an individual, one-to-one basis.

Structure of a Well-Integrated Program

Therapeutic activities used in this program have been selected for their numerous attributes. Through the eight program plans their merits may be easily recognized; the procedures are so structured that the various attributes of a given activity can be drawn upon at different points throughout the course of the therapy program. The greatest significance of these program plans lies in the organizational structure they provide the therapist so that she can conduct a cohesive, comprehensive program. The structure of the program plans makes it possible for the therapist to assimilate and cope with the wide range of essential

---

There were four groups: children in the pre-elementary group were 4 years old, the elementary group ranged in age from 4 to 6 years old, the intermediate group was 6 to 8 years old, and the senior group was 8 to 10 or 12 years old.

details. Within this structure there is sufficient allowance for flexibility so that it also inspires the therapist to become adept in creating a treatment program which will meet the unique needs of the individual learning-disordered child. It is the program structure, together with the use of highly structured equipment, which allows the young disorganized child the freedom to explore his capabilities and at the same time to feel the stability and constancy which permeates his experience.

The Integrated Program Matrix is designed to furnish the therapist with a quick profile to appraise how well the child can perform, what skills the child had prior to entering the program, and how far he has progressed at any subsequent point. It is the Integrated Program Matrix which provides a graphic composite picture of performance in the individual steps and the relationships between the steps of the eight program plans.

The specific functions of the program plans described in the narrative content of Part III are cited here:

1) to provide a concept of continuity throughout the program,

2) to provide a clear understanding of how the use of a single piece of equipment may provide partial fulfullment of the steps of more than one program plan,

3) to establish procedures for carrying out the specifics of the program,

4) to relate the use of activities to the provisions of the hypothesis,

5) to illustrate by examples the constancies and variables one can anticipate in programming.

Initial Communication with the Parents

Parents usually make an initial contact by phone at the recommendation of their pediatrician, neurologist, psychologist, or psychiatrist; in some, a written or verbal account of their findings alone will follow. Many referrals come directly from parents by word-of-mouth recommendation of family friends already in therapy; a medical referral is not a requirement to initiate therapy, but a doctor's signature is required if insurance companies are to pay benefits. In any event, the therapist asks the family's permission to be in touch with the child's physician should the need arise at any time.

When there is sufficient time before the initial appointment, the Sensorimotor History, together with the cover letter (Appendix F), should be forwarded to the parents to complete and return prior to starting therapy.

In the initial conversation with the parents, the therapist helps them orient their child on what he should expect when he comes to therapy. The therapist explains to them that the child will be using toys and childhood activities which he will enjoy, and that they will be observing the procedures throughout the therapy sessions in order that they will be able to continue some of the same activities at home.

Initial Involvement of the Young Child

Following the usual amenities with the parent and the child, the therapist focuses her attention on the child by inviting him into the activity area where an attractive, colorful indoor climber† is in full view. By asking the child to invite his parents to come with them, the therapist has refocused the child's attention and concern away from himself and what he may fear will be expected of him; also it gives him immediate assurance that he will not have to separate from them.

Also as a part of the effort to provide a comfortable milieu and to reduce the anxiety of the child and the parents, the term *activity room* rather than *treatment room* is used. The children who attend this program are referred to not as patients, but as *my young friends.* The use of these terms helps to avoid needless concern and questions from the child to his parents about whether there is something wrong with him.

In the activity room the therapist indicates that the parents may be seated in the same area, but she does not engage them directly in conversation at the time. Rather, she focuses her attention quickly toward the child, casually offering him the opportunity to play on the climber. These actions of the therapist set the tone, ie, the therapeutic climate. The parents take their cues from her, sensing that it is unnecessary for them to prompt their child to perform or to convince him in any way.

If the child makes no attempt to engage himself with the climber and is reluctant to leave the parent's side, the therapist makes no overt attempt to have him do so at that time. Instead, she takes an unassuming position, sitting on the floor to be near eye level with the child. This is less threatening to him, and the therapist can promote better nonverbal communication this way. The initial stage of involvement of the young, fearful, or distractible child is a slow-moving process. Establishing sufficient trust to allow the child to disengage himself from his parent's side may take 20 minutes or more; to his anxious parents, this interval will seem much longer.

This early involvement stage of a difficult child will be very anxiety-producing for the parents. Naturally they are concerned about their child's condition; they want him to cooperate and to derive full benefit from the session in terms of the time, effort, and expense involved. What makes this first stage so difficult for the parents is that they cannot possibly have any perspective about the equally difficult behavior of other children in similar circumstances. Parents also cannot be expected yet to recognize that although the child's behavior may be demanding and may tax the skills and techniques of the therapist, the therapist does not measure the behavior in the same terms as the parents. They will soon understand that the child's performance or his avoidance of involvement is perfectly legitimate in this setting and that the performance demonstrates to the therapist the nature of his needs.

For the therapist this initial stage can also be an anxious time, for she is actually aware of how much she would like to explore and accomplish in the initial session. It can be extremely anxiety-provoking for even the most experienced therapist to be closely observed by the parents during these early and difficult stages, when one's most erstwhile efforts to establish rapport and inspire cooperation may seem to be unproductive. She must at the same time cope with the rising anxiety of the parents who can easily become concerned over what they

†*Sources of equipment listed in Appendix H.*

view as the child's noncooperation. Paradoxically, parents of some children who are disorganized will be surprised to find how much the setting, the approach to the child's behavior, and the structured equipment permit him to give a meaningful response to some activities from the beginning. Even if the therapist may not feel she has achieved much the first hour, the parents may comment that the child has indeed excelled beyond what they see in his usual pattern of behavior.

Experience indicates that a quiet, accepting, minimally verbal nondirective communication with the child will tend to dispel his heightened anxiety. Verbal communication which urges the child to participate can convey an urgency and great desire of the adults for him to comply; this can precipitate greater resistance on the part of the child. The child may feel threatened if he knows he lacks those skills.

It is important for the therapist to create an accepting milieu or environment, unhurried and devoid of stated expectations for the child. This may not be natural or easy for the therapist, but it is essential in conducting effective therapy in the holistic approach. Therapists must first recognize that at times their own need to communicate verbally may also be in part a release for some uneasiness or anxiety in a situation which naturally can be difficult. Learning-disordered children can quickly pick up such feelings and then act out through their own disorganized, inattentive manner. Efforts to converse with the child who has a language communication disorder can further confuse him. In order to create the optimal milieu, the therapist should speak in slow, soft, almost whispered tones. This soft tone literally invites the child to listen in order to pay attention to and grasp the meaning of her words.

Throughout the therapy hour the therapist's undivided attention is directed toward the child. To re-emphasize, this attention immediately relieves him from the need to perform with any acting out or attention-seeking behavior. The better the quality of communication between therapist and child, even nonverbally, the sooner there will be a productive response. As the therapist gains experience in the use of a minimally directive technique and has acquired skills which enable her to help the child involve himself voluntarily, she can then begin to assess to what extent her input is critical to his being able to maintain this involvement with the task.

In an attempt to keep the young child's anxiety level low and to lay the groundwork for bridging the gap between avoidance and exploration, the therapist brings out several appealing but simple toys. Selection of these would be guided by the need for the toy to be easy enough not to frustrate the child and not so enticing that he will be reluctant to give it up for other activities.

The young child, while still sitting on the parent's lap, may reject a proffered hand toy from the therapist or even the parent. A considerable amount of time may ensue before the child will even hold a toy or play with it. Beyond that, the child's delay in initiating any involvement with the activities which will require that he disengage himself from the parent will vary widely according to the child's age, his fears, and his degree of sensorimotor dysfunction. The child's voluntary contact with a toy the therapist presents reveals his beginning acceptance and trusting involvement with her.

The activity of choice to be presented initially is almost always the indoor climber, because it is less threatening to the child than any of the other pieces of Phase I equipment. The climber is stable, and the child may already be familiar with similar ones at home or school. If the child rejects this completely, one technique the therapist would use to engage his interest and involvement would be to start to play with one of the colorful manipulative toys herself. She might also offer another to the child either verbally or nonverbally. Without making further overt attempts to engage the child, she would continue to quietly play with the toy herself; the child may then decide that the toy has appeal and want it. As another technique, the therapist can appear to direct her attention away from the child while briefly and softly engaging the parents in conversation. The child may then feel less self-conscious and become deeply engaged in playing.

On the surface it may appear to the parent that having another child there to play with might be more helpful to motivate the child. This is not advocated in the therapy setting; usually it creates confusion. The degree of his reluctance will yield information which should be important to the therapist in her overall assessment. Given the skillful nondirective efforts of the therapist, the period of this noninvolvement will be only temporary.

When trying to involve the young child, it is a safe policy to offer the child a choice between two toys or two tasks; the therapist will wisely avoid any questions which could obviously invite a direct "no" and further delay positive interaction. Nonverbal choices are warmly accepted by the therapist. In order to stabilize this still-tenuous involvement, the therapist is cautious to not communicate verbally by prematurely asking him to make another decision or choice. However, a direct "no" to any invitation to play with a toy or piece of equipment should not be taken too literally by the therapist. By simply saying, "You don't mind if I play with it, do you?" the child's attention will remain focused on the object at hand, and often he will come around.

An experience such as this can be an important initial step for the young distractible learning-disordered child. To him it can mean that, even if he is distracted to other stimuli around him, the therapist's fixed attention will help him to relocate and refocus his attention again on the object or task. This will, in many cases, be in marked contrast to previous experiences where such a child, through his own distractibility, has also pulled the attention of the adult away from the task. Here in the structured environment of therapy, the therapist is in a position to take an important first step in breaking up this endless nerve-wracking cycle generated by the hyperactivity and distractibility of these children.

One of the small stuffed animals from among the food-scented and unoffensive members of "The Olfactory Zoo" may spark the necessary appeal for the young or the anxious child. As a last resort, a toy which has almost universal appeal for children who are difficult to involve would be the marble track or marble railway. This is generally not used unless all else fails, because it then may be especially difficult to redirect the child's voluntary attention to any other activity. When this toy is used to spark the initial involvement, subsequent problems can be created; during the therapy sessions which follow, the child's subsequent requests for this toy can then distract him and be counterproductive.

Emphasis here has been directed toward the art of involving the most difficult young, highly disorganized child. I have described not only how to effect a child's productive participation, but I have cited the rationale behind those measures which help to create a therapeutic milieu. Other children who may not be as young but who are highly disorganized and distractible will likewise profit from many of the methods described. In contrast to the hyperactive, highly distractible child, there is the timid, almost fawnlike being who withdraws from the threatening outer world. Such a child will also profit from the same low-keyed approach; the structure is constant enough to be reassuring. As he feels comfortable enough in this security, he will begin to break out of his longstanding avoidance mode of behavior to become actively involved.

Initial Involvement of the Child Nine Years and Older

The early stages of contact with an older child are somewhat different. The therapist must be sensitive to the child's feelings that some of the activities may seem too juvenile to him. One activity, however, which seems uniquely appealing and not "age-identified" would be the inflated pillow on which he can sit, lie, or kneel to balance and feel challenged.

Once rapport has been established, most other gross motor activities in Phase I are generally acceptable. Nevertheless, the therapist is casual in her introduction of each, allowing the child to pass them by for the time being and return to them in the ensuing weeks. It is often preferable to start therapy for the highly sophisticated older child with desk activities until he can feel comfortable with appropriate Phase I tasks. In the Phase II desk activities, many of the manual, visual, and auditory perception tasks are not age-identified; despite his possible predisposed aloofness from things too juvenile, these tasks soon capture his interest and challenge his skills enough that the child's resistance is replaced by the delight of his success. On a one-to-one basis in therapy, there is no apprehension of ridicule by the child's siblings or peers, and he can soon let down his defenses to engage unreservedly at the skill level he needs.

Therapeutic Approach to the Teen-Ager

Although this book pertains primarily to the child of four to ten years, many of the procedures can be applied directly or modified for use with the teen-ager and also the adult who has experienced the problems of a learning disorder in childhood. The best procedure is to state frankly that much of the equipment which is used in a therapy program such as this is obviously designed for children. Little is available which is specifically for the older age group. However, the skills which this program would attempt to develop are the same skills employed earlier in childhood by use of certain carefully selected and graded toys and equipment.

A program designed for teen-agers is often conducted on a weekly basis over a period of several months. It concentrates almost exclusively on Phase II activities, with occasional exceptions in the use of the inflatables to stimulate the vestibular system and establish to whatever degree possible better integration of the two sides of the body and improve left-right orientation. The emphasis on Phase II desk tasks would be to organize a better response to manual form, auditory sequence and memory, visual tracking, visual figure-ground, spatial relations, and any fine motor skills or script writing practice which might be indicated.

It is at the discretion of the teen-ager whether or not the parent is present to observe and to participate in the home programming responsibilities. Often therapy works best if the parent is not present; wherever possible, the teen-ager himself should assume responsibility for carrying out the home program. The approach the therapist takes is to provide some intellectual understanding about the nature of the fundamental sensory and motor problems and how this is treated. This understanding emphasizes the relationship of the therapeutic techniques and the pre-academic and academic skills, with particular respect to the residual disorganization which has continued to interfere with his own higher academic performance. As the therapy program proceeds toward the latter weeks, greater attention is then directed to organizing abstract patterns of information so as to strengthen his ability to absorb and remember the content of academic material.

In many cases the anticipated length of his therapy program would not exceed eight to ten weeks; in some, a more intensive program ranging from 10 to 20 weekly sessions at more frequently scheduled intervals will be indicated. The therapist should explain to the individual that she will guide his therapy, but that the extent to which he can gain from the experience through outside application and practice will be largely up to him. Such an approach helps to structure the program in terms of duration so that an end is clearly within grasp; this relative brevity helps the student to maintain his momentum throughout the course of therapy. While not all of the programs may be resolved to one's satisfaction, whatever changes can be brought about through these means at this late stage can generally take place within the recommended time limit. Experience with treating this age group has been quite rewarding. The appropriateness of therapy for learning-disordered problems at this age is confirmed by their seriousness of purpose and the manner in which they respond to the invitation, so to speak, to "become their own co-therapist."

Physical Attributes of the Treatment Area

Serious study has been given in designing and preparing a therapy milieu which will effectively curtail the distractible qualities and meet the special needs of the learning-disordered child. The Phase I gross motor equipment is usually stored in an adjacent store room, brought out only at the time of use. Keeping the treatment area relatively free of objects which will in themselves be distracting is one of the responsibilties of a good therapist. She will be able to direct the child's attention to the desired activity more easily, and will need only minimal verbal communication for the child to initiate and maintain his involvement.

To keep the child's distractibility and hyperactivity to a minimum it is essential that the Phase II toys be stored behind cabinet doors to which the children are not permitted access. If the toys are not stored, the therapist will discover that the effectiveness of the program has been greatly diminished; the child's anger and frustration in not being allowed to play at will can be

108

counterproductive then and in succeeding hours. The effort required by the adults to divert the child's attention away from such a magnetic attraction will subvert and destroy the therapist's nondirective approach in which she wants to encourage exploration with the particular activity she has selected to meet his needs.

An ironing board has proved to be the most practical and suitable place for a child to work with the Phase II desk activities. Its use has merit at home for both study and therapy, since it is adjustable in height and has an ample working surface; ideally this is covered with a solid, light-colored cloth. During therapy it is advantageous to the therapist if she sits opposite the child so that she can maintain good communication. This is an ideal position from which to observe his performance.

During the Phase II activities the child sits in a small captain's chair; the arms of it provide a natural barrier which helps to curtail the restlessness of the young, hyperactive child. Its size also permits the child with poor trunk balance to feel more secure if he can touch the floor firmly with his feet.

The therapist sits so she has free access to the cabinet which holds all the toys and related equipment. The contents however, should not be in the child's view, distracting him. The therapist sits on a low stool which puts her near eye level with the child. Ideally she should not have to move from it during the therapy session, for as soon as her own focus of attention shifts away from the child's work so his attention may shift. The therapist sitting in front of the toy cabinet automatically indicates that the child does not have free access to the toys. Whenever he gets out of the chair to come to the toy cabinet, the therapist simply says, "As soon as you can sit in the chair, I'll have another toy for you." Once the procedure is established, there is relatively little trouble in maintaining the child's attention and interest since this is a relatively fast turnover of toys and activities planned for his therapy session. A low, enclosed cabinet within arm's reach of the therapist is ideal. Short of this, the therapist can arrange the preselected toys on a tray, and cover this with a towel so that the child cannot see the toys and be further distracted. The tray is placed on the floor beside the therapist, out of the child's reach.

Other than the toy cabinets and several chairs for the parents or cushioned stools for the older children, the furnishings are kept to a bare minimum. Aside from tiled flooring for scooter board work, thick pile carpeting and heavy padding cover the entire floor. This gives the whole area a feeling of warmth, tactual appeal, and also some protection against occasional tumbles the child may take from the inflatables or carpeted barrel.

Preparing for the Initial Therapy Hour

In order that the therapist has the materials she will need and to conserve her use of time, a dozen or so manila folders are set up in advance. Those materials needed for a school-age child would include the Beery-Buktanica Test of Visual-Motor Integration,** sets of 8½ inch x 11 inch plain paper with carbon between

**Beery KI, Buktenica NA: Developmental Test of Visual-Motor Integration: Test Manual. *Chicago, Follett Pub C , 1967.*

for dominance evaluation in hammering and crayoning, plus the body image drawings on which to assess right-left identification. A copy of the Hourly Record Sheet is included, ready for the therapist to check in advance those items she would anticipate using for the child. In doing this she takes into consideration his age and the reported problems.

If the parents can complete the Sensorimotor History Questionnaire (Appendix F) and return it to the therapist before the child's initial appointment, those items which should be assessed immediately as a basis for planning subsequent therapy would be pinpointed with more accuracy. Whether or not one had this advanced kind of information, one would plan to use each of the Phase I activities to see the child's baseline performance on each. Phase II, desk activities, would be selected in part by whether the tasks would be representative of the primary areas of assessment, eg, letter reversals. If the child is younger, the principal concern would be to determine to what extent and by what means the child's attention can be involved and maintained.

Planning the Next Therapy Hours

The Hourly Record Sheet (Appendix G) enables the therapist to have a feeling of ease and security when conducting one treatment session after another throughout the day. While the program plans provide an overall guide, it is the checklist of therapeutic activities provided by the Hourly Record Sheet upon which the therapist depends as an immediate reference throughout the therapy hour. This enables her to keep track of the grading which the child should be ready for in each task. Throughout the session, the therapist checks the activities and the level of their grading on a new sheet; thus she prepares the advanced plan for the next hour while this is fresh in her mind.

The experienced therapist will find that it is expedient to use the reverse blank side of these Hourly Record Sheets to record notes about the most relevant aspects of the child's performance during the therapy hour and to note the reported changes at home and at school which the parents furnish. However, this informal notetaking probably will not suffice until the therapist becomes fully familiar with the graded steps of skill cited in the OEPS and the recommended progression within the program plans. By scoring the performance of individual children's responses on the OEPS, this process becomes a training vehicle for the therapist who is becoming acquainted with the holistic approach. With practice, she will be able to conduct an effective program using the OEPS, the Program Plans, and the Integraded Program Matrix for references.

Program Plan 1

Reduction of Avoidance Behavior in the Olfactory — Tactile — Auditory Triad

The holistic approach emphasizes a conceptualization of patterns of clinical behavior which are apparent between and among groups of sensory systems. In so doing, one lays the foundation for a more cohesive, comprehensive approach to therapy. The OTA Triad (Part I, Chapter 6) describes the nature and the quality, ie, defensive or dormant responses of varying degrees which appear clinically and which are shared in common among the OTA systems. Sensory defensiveness within the systems of the OTA Triad may occur singly or in combination; defensive and dormant responses may also co-exist among these three systems. In any event, avoidance responses occur as the result. The program to follow is designed to reduce these avoidance responses throughout the OTA Triad as rapidly and as effectively as possible.

Initial Phase

Early Tactile System Organization — Pivotal Role (1.1)

As the quality or organization in the tactile system improves, the organization of the central nervous system matures. In the holistic approach, the tactile system is then said to be functioning in a pivotal role. This is manifested clinically when changes become evident in the olfactory system performance and when no specific therapy has been directed to improve the function of that system.

If the learning-disordered child is hyperverbal and auditorily defensive, there is a possibility that there is a subclinical tactile defensive mode if it has not yet been manifested clinically. By putting the therapeutic emphasis on the tactile system and assisting it in its pivotal role to help organize the central nervous system, the extent of auditory defensiveness can be reduced.

Tactile System Organization — Defensive Mode

The tactile system organization should be promoted to reduce the defensive mode. First one must be able to identify the nature and intensity of avoidance responses in the tactile system performance so that their decrease can be easily recognized along the continuum. These steps determine where the tactually defensive child may be functioning along this continuum at any point.

From the Sensorimotor History, characteristics of both past and current behavior can be documented to enable the therapist to see how far along the continuum the child has already progressed. These indicators can be particularly helpful in observing changes throughout a course of therapy. It is important for the therapist to enable the parents to become sensitive observers of the signs and changes in this behavior which take place outside therapy. Then they are prepared to recognize that behavior which may be even more "difficult" for them to cope with may also be part of this normal progression. As long as the parents can be reassured that some undesirable behavior, such as excessively touching people and objects, is only a temporary problem and in fact signifies a step toward better sensory integration, then they are less inclined to overreact.

The following points describe the nature and quality of the child's response with regard to a gradual decrease in the tactile defensive response and identify the level of maturation of the tactile system along the developmental continuum.

1) Rejects human contact: in infancy struggles to get off one's lap; shows continued distaste, discomfort, irritation, or even aggressive responses to being touched; responds in exaggerated terms to minor bumps; a tiny cut or "shot" may assume the proportions, in his eyes, of a major assault.

2) Accepts being touched by parents whom he can trust, but avoids physical contact with other adults and children; may act aggressively when he is obliged to be in close proximity with other children, for their movements are unpredictable and out of his own control.

3) Avoids manipulative skills not only because of clumsiness, but also because tactile defensiveness may cause him discomfort in his hands.

4) As the tactile discriminative system becomes more functional, he initiates touching objects everywhere in his environment, as infants do, in order to now learn from these tactile experiences in a way which is new to him.

5) Initiates touching people, sometimes to an excessive degree, even though he still may reject touch which is intiated by others.

6) Visual sensory information can be sufficiently integrated now with the tactile to create a visual-tactile match. The child becomes able to recall the "feeling" of similar past experiences so that he can associate visual and tactile information adequately, no longer having to depend on actively touching objects to sense their physical qualities.

7) May for extended periods of time seek excessive tactile input from others, as in affectionate hugging, cuddling, rubbing, or brushing.

Organization of the tactile system, either to reduce its protective effect or, if clinically dormant, to alert it to function, would thereafter follow along the same developmental continuum — the goal being to increase the quality of the tactile discrimination system. Inhibition of the tactile protective system occurs with increased tactile system organization, later reverting to its survival function only when there is a threat or when the system malfunctions. As the discriminative system develops along the continuum, it permits the child more freedom to explore his environment and to develop a capacity for coping with it, moving easily within it, and manipulating it for productive use.

The following clinical steps are suggested to reduce avoidance behavior resulting from the dominant role of the tactile protective system. The trend along the continuum starts with purely nonhuman contact through the equipment and gradually enables the child to tolerate being touched. These early steps could occur concomitantly with the desk activities to increase the direct awareness and quality of tactile discrimination; together they would accelerate the rate at which the protective system influence was diminished and the tactile discriminative system was enhanced. The measures to reduce avoidance behavior include:

1) Self-initiated, voluntary heavy touch-pressure along the weight-bearing surfaces, usually on those areas of the body which are outside the child's normal range of vision, eg, sitting on the indoor climber.

2) Self-controlled movement with heavy touch-pressure from nonhuman sources, to include nonvisible and sensitive parts of the body, eg, straddling the outside of, or rolling inside, the carpeted barrel; wherever possible, direct skin contact is desired.

3) Heavy touch-pressure to visible areas and later to the nonvisible areas with indirect human touch, eg, pressure of the inflatables rolled over the extremities and body if the child's responses suggest a desire for it.

4) Heavy touch-pressure involving direct human contact of trusted parent or therapist, eg, rubbing with rough towel.

5) Heavy touch-pressure involving human contact of trusted adult over visible, then non-visible, areas of body using a plastic bristle brush.

Indoor Climber

The indoor climber is one of the most effective and appealing means of heavy touch-pressure as a means to reduce tactile defensiveness. There are significant clues the therapist must be alert to which can reveal the presence of this degree of discomfort. For instance, the therapist would observe whether or not the child resists the suggestion to take off his shoes and socks to go on the climber. While perhaps not saying so, children who experience any skin contact as irritating will resist such a suggestion, or if they take off their socks, they often act as if they were standing on hot pavement, first on one foot, then on the other, in obvious discomfort. When climbing the plastic rungs of the climber, the acutely tactually defensive child will often show great sensitivity to the burr or junction where the molds join during casting. These responses all provide initial clues to the alert therapist and a means of recognizing change in the ensuing weeks as these forms of behavior disappear.

Standing, sitting, and leaning over the rungs of the climber provide intense touch-pressure to various parts of the entire body. The joint receptors of the hip and the muscle receptors throughout the back of the thighs and buttocks enhance the tactile-kinesthetic input. Together this helps the child to develop a better concept of his body image, especially as it relates to size, shape, and position of those parts which are least visible to him. (See P.P. 3.1 for discussion of those specific attributes of the indoor climber, recommended for optimal therapeutic use.)

1. Exploration on the indoor climber allows for body image development and an increased awareness of one's position in space.

2. A child demonstrates the upside down or inverted positioning on the indoor climber.

114

Carpeted Barrel

While the carpeted barrel is used for many purposes, one of the most important is its value in reducing tactile sensitivity because the contact arises entirely from the child's own actions; by contrast, touch which arises from the action of others is more alarming because he feels out of control and vulnerable. Friction created by the child's own body weight against the somewhat harsh texture of the rug acts to reduce the abnormal degree of sensitivity in the touch system and establishes for him a more accurate body image. The child is encouraged to maintain contact with the carpeted barrel for five to ten minutes during therapy, with the maximum skin areas exposed. This early gross contact with the richly textured surface of the carpeted barrel helps directly in establishing a concept of the body size, shape, and form. Rolling inside provides the child an awareness of individual arm positioning, arm positioning in relation to each other, and arm positioning in relation to his trunk.

Inflatables

Early in the course of therapy the inflatables are introduced for their particular merit in stimulating the balance system. The therapist must be alert to recognize subtle clues from the child during this time; for instance, when the child pulls the pillow on top of him while lying on the floor, he may be asking for touch-pressure against his body. Upon witnessing such behavior, the therapist may ask, "Is this what you want?" as she starts to rock the pillow slowly back and forth from the child's chin to his toes. With the transparent surface toward the child's body so that his vision is in no way occluded, the pressure is increased gradually to 10 or 15 pounds, at which point it is not uncommon to hear the child ask for even greater pressure. This activity may appropriately continue for four or five minutes while the child lies prone or supine. Periodically the therapist asks if the pressure is right and if he wants it to continue; otherwise this would be a quiet time in which they would not converse. Light touch feels "ticklish" to the child, but heavy touch-pressure tends to dispel any feeling of irritation or tickling; the use of the inflatables for this touch-pressure is appropriate because it is impersonal and nonhuman, and therefore less threatening. It is the consistently firm, controlled contact which is acceptable to the tactually defensive child and which becomes one of the first steps in normalizing his interpretation of touch stimuli.

Towel Rubbing and Brushing

The one technique for improving tactile system organization from either the tactually defensive or dormant mode is rubbing the child's body with a dry towel. This technique can be introduced at the outset of a therapy program. The simple measure can even be safely applied by parents of hyperactive children without the child necessarily being under professional care. The best kind of towel to use is one which is thin enough to be wrung out to dry so that the wrinkles in it create the rough texture ideal for strong tactile input.

Mothers will frown in disbelief, recalling perhaps how the child has never liked to be dried after his bath. Such a description often confirms the impression that the child is truly tactually defensive. Probably the mother reacted to the tendency of the child to pull away when touched by softening the pressure so as to not hurt him. Paradoxically, this only exacerbated the condition, causing the child to feel he was being tickled. He then reacted by even more overt means to avoid his discomfort. If the mother finds some resistance to the methods suggested, she should alter the rubbing techniques so that they are more acceptable to the child. For instance, the child is asked to take the towel to rub his own arms and legs if the mother's efforts are too disquieting. Gradually he will be able to permit his mother to rub his back and those areas which are difficult to reach.

It is not uncommon to find that the sleep pattern of the tactually defensive child is erratic; frequent or early waking present serious problems to the family. What was originally an unexpected benefit, described by parents of one child in the early 1960s, has since been confirmed by many other families for whom the technique has been purposely prescribed. Parents of one severely retarded five-year-old related how difficult it was for the family since this child slept so little and cried so much; medications had been only partially effective. Rubbing her with a rough towel at night was suggested for its soothing effect and the assurance it might give her about her environment. The child was on no therapy program of any kind. A few months later the father came to me and described with great feeling what had occurred. "You can't imagine what you've done for our family. We've been able to sleep every night. Since we started rubbing her before bed and when she occasionally awakens, she sleeps throughout the night. We haven't used any medication for her to sleep since."

Since that time I have advocated use of this means to help counteract sleep problems in many children; there has often been a high degree of success which usually takes place within the brief period of a week or two. Coupled with rubbing with a rough towel or brushing, to be described, supine rocking on the inflated pillow (P.P. 2.3) before bedtime is also used to induce sleep. The guidelines below, used for brushing, would be the same when rubbing the child with a rough towel.

The therapist first lays a fur coat or soft blanket on the floor; she then sits beside the child as he lies supine on the furry surface and cradles his elbow and extended arm comfortably in one hand. If the child is fearful or reluctant, this procedure may be started from the sitting position. If the child needs help to reduce confusion about direction, he may be asked to also put his hand on the brush as he watches and says, with the therapist, "pull up" and "push back." The therapist applies several pounds of pressure. The child is asked if he wants heavier or lighter pressure and where on his body the therapist should brush next. This degree of control lessens his tendency to respond defensively.

When the child is willing to lie prone, with his shirt off, the therapist starts at the tip of the fingers and pulls the round plastic-tipped hairbrush the length of the child's arms, over the shoulder, and down the back, at which point she reverses the direction. This is done four or five times, with pressure as heavy as the child requests, and is then continued on the opposite side of his body. The continuity of movement from the tip of the fingers to the lower trunk gives the child a feeling of unity of those parts of the body which are not visible to the child.

As soon as the child is comfortable, the legs may also be brushed. The child can begin by brushing his own arms and legs. Then the therapist or parent should brush on the front and then the sides where he can easily observe. Finally the

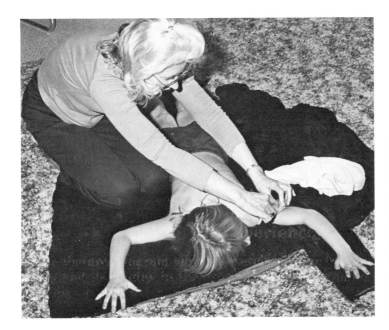

3. Heavy touch pressure with a plastic bristle brush helps to normalize the tactile system. The hypersensitive response of the tactually defensive child is reduced; likewise, the awareness of tactile input is enhanced in the tactually dormant child. The child also senses a striking contrast of tactile input between the firm brush and soft fur.

back is brushed from the foot or ankle region to the hip. The inner borders of the legs and the abdomen are not brushed unless the child wants to do it.

In the young child brushing may not be instituted until long after starting the program. Any child with an intense tactile defensive response may reject attempts to do this for some time; meanwhile rolling in the carpeted barrel would be advocated. Beginning and terminating the brushing routine will depend upon the therapist's judgment, but there are certain guidelines.

During the time brushing is recommended for home use, the brush should be kept in a spot which is obvious to the child so that he may use it to brush himself whenever he feels the need for it. In some children this need will continue for several months and then wane. The child's tactile system may always remain vulnerable to stress. Then there will be periods of greater tension when the tactile defensive symptoms return; a brief resumption of the brushing and manual form discrimination experience would again be advisable. The child who has a history of being "feisty" around other children no longer needs brushing when he stops reacting negatively to touch and when his ability to discriminate the perception of manual form is increased (P.P. 1.7).

Tactile System Organization — Dormant Mode

The following points identify the nature and the quality of the child's response with regard to the tactile system which will help in defining where, along the continuum of developmental change, the tactually dormant child is functioning at a given time. Similarities and contrasts observed in the child with a defensive response and a dormant response should be noted and, in particular, the general parallel in the sequence in which these developmental changes take place.

1) The child lacks awareness of normal touch: often stumbles and falls; suffers numerous bumps and lacerations which he may not notice; reacts stoically to stitches, shots, and other normally painful experiences.

2) Due to the lack of knowing how to move adequately and because these experiences provide little success and satisfaction, he is disinterested in manipulative toys, playing, or crayoning. He is unable to function in games, sports, or motor skills suitable for his age.

3) As discriminative skills are awakened, he begins to touch objects and people. This may temporarily reach excessive proportions and resemble the young child who has a need to touch everything.

4) He begins to recognize that areas of his body have been touched. He may become temporarily defensive and overly sensitive to touch.

5) His demand for hugging and tactile information such as rubbing or brushing may seem insatiable.

6) Visual-tactile match develops. His need to touch things and people to excess lessens.

7) Motor skills gradually improve: diminution of cuts, abrasions, and minor injuries; awareness of pain reaches more normal levels, sometimes preceded by temporary oversensitivity to pain.

Clinically speaking, the procedures already cited to improve tactile organization in the tactile defensive mode also apply. The important difference is that heavy brushing can be initiated at the outset of therapy.

The Olfactory System (1.2)

When the child enters the therapy program, a simple estimate of his baseline olfactory performance is made to determine how well he receives and responds to olfactory stimuli. This is done in two ways: 1) by assessing the data furnished on the Sensorimotor History, and 2) by casually exposing the child to close contact to scents which have been applied to small stuffed animals (P.P. 1.5).

It can be difficult to otherwise assess this olfactory behavior objectively. It is natural for parents to direct a child's attention to "smell the fresh bread" at the bakery. The child may appear to respond as if he did actually smell it, or even make appropriate comments at a later visit. To the surprise of parents, that same child will be totally oblivious to a scent when he is not anticipating any aroma, as when a furry stuffed animal scented with peppermint oil passes near his nose. The seeming contradiction may be the result of initial cognitive association at the bakery instead of sensory awareness and discrimination of scents and odors.

It is normal behavior for children as young as three years who have been presented with a scented animal to comment, "Can I have some gum?" or to respond to a cinnamon scent by asking for a piece of apple pie. Sometimes they take additional sniffs or offer it to the parent to smell too. In contrast to this normal behavior is that of the child who has absolutely no awareness of the pleasurable food aromas or even the more pungent odors which are presented during treatment. Eight-year-old Matthew, who showed a tertiary level of dormancy, was not only unaware of the aromas of "The Olfactory Zoo," a collection of scented animals, but he was even oblivious to powerfully-scented perfume, eucalyptus oil, or shaving lotion applied to a handkerchief. The therapist held the handkerchief in her hand as she rocked the inflated pillow back and forth, as mentioned in P.P. 1.1, coming within several inches of the child's nose, but he discerned no odor.

At the other extreme is a child like Sam who had shown tertiary defensiveness, making frequent comments at inappropriate times to the effect that people or things "stink!" This was a global, nondifferentiated response. It seems that this child interpreted all incoming scents and aromas, even those pleasurable to most others, as offensive, overwhelming, and disorganizing to him. These experiences definitely interfered with his ability to concentrate on other happenings around him. When scents dominated his awareness of the environment, the olfactory system was operating in its primary or survival role and could not forfeit this position. In this same child, the tactile and the auditory systems were also disorganized and functioned in a defensive mode.

The Sensorimotor History of another child, Len, age four, had seemed to be functioning in an olfactorily defensive mode; his parents told how he had frequently commented that they "smell," which was most disconcerting to them. No doubt Len's vocabulary was lacking somewhat in sophistication, but it is clear he was reacting to olfactory stimulation. It may be that he had earlier been defensive, but his words "Mommy smells," may also have been to alert her to a scented object. When presented with the scented animal in therapy he was not defensive. However, he was fascinated with these objects, returning frequently to rub each one against his cheeks. This behavior suggests that there was a trend from defensiveness toward normal organization and maturation of the olfactory system which could be recognized from the clinical behavior. At the same time the parents noted that the frequency of his earlier defensive comments had recently begun to lessen.

The olfactory system has clearly been observed to change spontaneously simply as the result of the efforts to organize the tactile system. This can be recognized 1) by the decreased dormancy, ie, arousal of the olfactory system, or 2) reduction of the olfactory defensiveness to more nearly normal proportions. Until these basic changes take place, the olfactory system is not treated directly; but its change in response resulting from tactile system organization is considered to be a barometer of more widespread, sensory integration. Therefore, the therapist avoids using the word "smell" until it is clear the function is aroused from its dormant state.

If those signs of change in the olfactory system are not forthcoming, after an initial period of several months more direct measures are undertaken to reduce the defensive avoidance response and to activate the discriminative system. Progression along the continuum would follow these steps to:

1) inhibit the protective system by voluntary control of contact with pleasurable sensory stimuli;
2) establish gross discrimination between irritating or noxious stimuli and those which are harmless and pleasurable;
3) discriminate the nature, quality, and identity of aromas and scents (P.P. 1.5).

As the protective function diminishes and the discriminative function increases in the olfactory and tactile systems, more information is available by which the individual may assess his total ongoing environment. With improved function of both the tactile and olfactory systems, the individual has a more complete Gestalt, or picture of the immediate environment. Well-organized sensory system function provides a feeling of greater security in coping with his world. There are other ways in which the tactile and olfactory functions share commonalities.

Ayres points out that the tactile protective system is an old primal system which has served a major survival function to perpetuate the species among the primitive organisms. This protective function, while modified, has not been lost. It conveys information as to the presence of pain and of sexual arousal. It is unfortunate when the primacy of the protective system persists into maturity and causes light touch, especially of the areas of sexual arousal, to be interpreted as threatening and uncomfortable rather than as pleasurable. In the animal kingdom perpetuation of the species is directly dependent on the power of the olfactory system to stimulate sexual arousal. The olfactory and the tactile systems in man function in conjunction to promote sexual pleasure, reproduction, and perpetuation of the species. Thus, in seeking to provide a foundation for behavioral flexibility, adaptability, and pleasure in maturity, it would seem highly relevant to establish a normal balance between inhibition and excitation within the tactile and the olfactory systems with good intersensory integration between them.

The Defensive Response of the Auditory System (1.3)

When the child arrives at the initial therapy session the therapist should immediately begin to collect data about his reponses to auditory stimuli and to determine to what extent, if any, there may be evidence of auditory defensiveness. The therapist must keep in mind that the initial impressions may also be exaggerated because of the child's initial anxiety. If the degree of anxiety, noted through a hyperverbal response for instance, subsides in the next few therapy sessions, then it is possible that anxiety was either the basic underlying factor or that there has been some element of auditory defensiveness which becomes exacerbated with anxiety but otherwise can be held within tolerable limits.

There are certain observations the therapist makes initially from which to identify change:

1) the child's distractibility to sound which is often distant, insignificant, and irrelevant;
2) how well the simple commands of motion are interpreted and acted upon by him;
3) to what extent the child persistently exhibits a hyperverbal response.

In order to do this most effectively the therapist maintains a quiet approach, speaking softly and giving the child her undivided attention.

Beyond this, the therapist actively employs clinical techniques to establish the optimum climate for the child's listening attention and early language comprehension. These measures on the part of the therapist, together with certain specific activities of the child, work in a cohesive, comprehensive manner to reduce the extent of his auditory defensiveness.

The therapist should conscientiously refrain from saying to the child, "pay attention" or "listen" because others have already done this to no avail. In the holistic approach, the therapist who is confronted with a hyperverbal child must recognize how difficult it may be for him to direct his attention, and she tries to acknowledge to him her awareness of this by asking simply, "May I speak with you?" The silence which follows will do more in directing his attention back to the source of the question than any repetition. When she has eye-to-eye contact, she makes a single request or statement in simple, clear tones, again waiting in silence to allow the child ample time to first process the idea and then to act upon it.

Ideally such requests involve movements. Then the child's reaction provides a clear picture of how this information was interpreted, or misinterpreted, by what he does. Upon completion of the task, ample feedback is given to the child to indicate that the movement was in accord with the spoken message. If the movement was in error, then one may simply show the child what the words meant, thus approaching the problem at a simpler level. Even when the proper movement is executed, we can still make no assumptions that he knows the words and movements are truly synonymous. The therapist will provide accurate feedback such as, "Yes, that is what the words told you."

The discriminatory function of the auditory system, like that of the tactile and olfactory systems, again represents a continuum, with the discriminative function evolving as an extension of the protective system. The therapist, having used these subtle clinical techniques to make a general assessment of the way the child functions, then tries to determine from the steps below how far along the continuum the child seems to be functioning. The steps in this progression are as follows:

1) inhibit the protective system;
2) establish gross discrimination between innocuous and irritating kinds of sound;
3) discriminate the spatial quality of sounds to determine direction and distance (P.P. 1.6);
4) discriminate non-verbal sounds (P.P. 1.6);
5) develop recollection and recall of verbal information (P.P. 4.6).

A therapy program of self-controlled sound production, such as hammering and forceful scratching of the textured plastic scribble board with a wooden dowel, provide the kind of sensory experience by which the child's auditory protective function can be mitigated. Such a child, like the young child who pounds the kitchen pots and pans or a toy drum, will show an amazing tolerance to intense sound which he can produce. When the jumping board appropriately meets the child's motoric needs; this also offers the older child, especially, an excellent opportunity to increase his tolerance of self-controlled auditory input.

With these experiences behind him, the child will be observed to become less aware of those sounds, often faint and distant, which previously had seemed important enough to concern and distract him.

Early Sensory Discrimination
Tactile Discrimination and Manual Form Perception (1.4)

Moving along the continuum from the early measures to reduce the effects of the tactile protective system, the therapist would now use those activities which are designed to help the individual recognize and discriminate the qualities of tactile information as follows:

> 1) texture,
> 2) spatial qualities (manual form perception),
> 3) temporal qualities,
> 4) sequential order.

A young child should first be introduced to sources of innocuous, non-threatening, predictable forms of contact such as a cuddly, richly textured, stuffed animal. Subsequently a live kitten, puppy, or rabbit whose movements would be minimally threatening could be suitably introduced. Experiences such as these can be genuinely pleasurable since the young animal will also respond lovingly toward the child and inspire further contact.

The next step would be to help the child actively recognize the widely diverse textures such as a soft fur coat on which to lie for brushing, contrasted with the rough feeling of the brush itself. Increased awareness of these gross differences of tactile input paves the way for the recognition of the spatial qualities of tactile discrimination. A set of 12 kinds of texture, some grossly different, others more subtle, are mounted on thin wooden blocks and placed on the table surface for the child to feel each one in turn. One by one a duplicate is placed in his hands beneath the table for him to rub and then match it with the one it corresponds to on the table. It is important that these blocks be large enough for the whole hand to be rubbed across it, for example 3″ x 6″ for optimal results.

The next step would be to help the young child, or the very disorganized older child, to recognize one of three or four simple three-dimensional objects which differ widely in both texture and form, eg, a pocket comb and a key. (In some children this early awareness of contrasts will have to be introduced prior to their matching even a small number of sharply contrasting texture boards, eg, carpeting and sandpaper.) Manual identification of familiar objects is introduced in the same manner cited above, letting the child feel one beneath the visual barrier, to match it from among the few, until he can gradually become successful using ten to twelve objects.

The spatial quality of touch is developed through manual form perception tasks; the tactile input is validated to the child as he realizes that his manual form perception and visual form perception of the object match.

The tactile discriminative system must also be activated in such a way that both the spatial and temporal qualities of touch are available to the individual. The temporal quality of touch may be less apparent to the therapist; the significance of the temporal aspect of touch is that the sensation alerts the child as to which parts of the body were touched and in what sequential order. From clinical observations, it appears that the tactile discrimination system may provide what is referred to here as a "temporal record" of movement. It indicates to a child which part of the body felt contact first, second, and so on, in a distinct and orderly sequence as he moves, for instance, in rolling over inside the carpeted barrel. It helps to establish an imprint so that this orderly sequence of movement may be reproduced again and again. The temporal-spatial quality of touch is best stimulated by the direct skin contact against the carpeting, as he rolls inside, or straddles its outer surface.

Presumably, this sequential awareness and the orderly acquisition of touch information occurs quite early in the normal infant, at the time of crawling and climbing. In Phase I, the learning-disordered child is exposed to activities which will provide similar experience in serial and repetitious movements which he needs. It is proposed that through these experiences the child will replicate, in part at least, this step in early motor learning.

Undoubtedly, the child's awareness of the temporal aspects of this experience are diffuse, but another type of experience which focuses more clearly on the temporal-spatial quality of tactile discrimination is the graded series of tactile sequence and assembly tasks (P.P. 4.2). In these tasks the child must be able to accurately recognize, for instance, that the pieces of the toy animal are stacked in their proper order when the edges where they meet feel smooth. Active play with the tactile sequential tasks such as these requires a purposeful, cognizant, discriminating decision on the part of the child. Such an experience also serves to integrate the data arising simultaneously in the visual and the tactile systems. Tactile sequence and assembly tasks are considered by this author to be strong contributors in reducing the tactual defensive response; such activites have been successfully used by children as young as four years old. It is suggested also that temporal awareness generated through the tactile sequence and assembly tasks may help significantly in establishing an orderly sequence of steps in cognitive problem solving, logic, and deductive reasoning.

In manual form perception tasks, the procedure at first is for the child to use smaller three-dimensional objects, such as plastic train cars two to three inches in size, again matching the one he feels to one of the set which is in view. Once this expectation is established, the child advances by matching what he feels with the drawings of these same objects. At home a cardboard box can be used to occlude his vision while he is feeling the object. The Manual Form Discrimination Frame is designed for clinic use.

Olfactory Awareness Through "The Olfactory Zoo" (1.5)

"The Olfactory Zoo" consists of approximately six small animals made up of furry or softly textured, appealing material. Most children will find them so inviting that they may rub them on first one cheek and then the other even before the therapist suggests that they do so. When oil of peppermint is applied to the head of the furry animal, for instance, it should dry before it is presented to the child so as to avoid watery and burning eyes. Store the animals in plastic bags.

123

Early Auditory Matching of Nonverbal Sounds (1.6)

The purpose of this level of sound recognition is to enable the severely disorganized child or the young learning-disordered child to first become aware of contrasting sounds and to be able to identify one as opposed to another among obvious contrasts. Use of sound cylinders of bird and animal sounds is described under Auditory Localization, Discrimination and Sequence, Level I, OEPS.

Refining Sensory Discrimination Skills

Manual Form Perception (1.7)

This is the point where the child begins to refine the sensory discrimination skills. Level II and III activities may be pursued as rapidly as successful performance permits. The older child may, following a brief exposure to the textured blocks, begin with small plastic forms, eg, the set of freight cars.

Close observation will reveal that the child who is at first disorganized as to the spatial orientation will move in a haphazard, disorganized manner, being alert to feeling only isolated features while being oblivious to other parts. Gradually he acquires more input through his tactile system, and he begins to organize the parts into a whole. We find that as soon as a child recognizes that most of the pieces have wheels, he will thereafter position them toward the bottom and proceed to search for the other features by which that object may be discriminated from the others. The clear awareness of a top-bottom orientation of these small three-dimensional objects provides a foundation for the child to learn more easily the top-bottom relationship in making his numbers and letters.

After the child has demonstrated successful performance in discriminating three-dimensional forms, the two-dimensional linear forms and designs are introduced, from which the procedure was established in P.P. 1.4. These linear patterns are made by embossing lines and shapes from the back of three-inch squares of heavy aluminum foil. These patterns comprise two complete sets, designed to supplement one another, and are graded in such a way as to provide a broad experience at a highly refined skill level of tactile discrimination. The basic differences in these designs of the two sets is that in set #1 the child must organize the relationship of one line in relation to another within the pattern, whereas in Set #2, while the lines in themselves are simple, correct identification depends also on their position relative to the outer perimeter of the three-inch square. Initially the designs are presented in the same top-bottom spatial arrangement as the child sees pictured in front of him, but as he is more experienced, he is told these may be rotated and that before he brings them out to confirm that his decision is correct, he should turn it to conform with the matching drawing.

Olfactory Discrimination (1.8)

So that color does not suggest the answer to the child, uncolored scented "scratch and sniff" paper is preferred. At Level II, the Olfactory Discrimination Cards, comprised of such a scented paper, is mounted on a card together with pictures of three objects from which to identify the matching one. At Level III, six single cards, each with a different scent, must be matched to a duplicate set. It is also possible for many individuals to identify by name what one scent is, without any pictures from which to select the answer.

Auditory Discrimination (1.9)

Sound cylinders to assess auditory discrimination are easily prepared from plastic medicine bottles which can be acquired from a pharmacy. Half the cylinders are covered with contact paper of one color; the other half which contain matching objects are covered with a contrasting paper. Definite contrasting sounds are arranged in the six cylinders and their matched pairs in Set #1, while sounds which are closer to one another are arranged in Set #2. Among items which can be used in Set #1 are pecan, bell, wooden match stick, pieces of dry macaroni, a cork, teaspoon of dry rice. Set #2 could include a wad of paper, button, paper clip, penny, marble, and a half dozen peppercorns. Therapists must test these to assure that the items in Set #2 are not too close to one another in sound and then change the items accordingly to enhance auditory discrimination but not create needless confusion in the child.

A simple matching procedure is established in which six cylinders of Set #1, for instance, are set on the desk in front of the child and he is asked to shake each one and remember what it sounds like. As the therapist shakes each one of her matching sets, one at a time, he tries to locate the one which matches it in sound, setting them aside in pairs. When all have been matched, the child and the therapist open each pair to visually confirm to him whether the auditory match was in fact correct.

Program Plan 1 spans the spectrum of sensory organization within the OTA Traid. Initially efforts are directed toward tactile system organization and activation of it in a pivotal role. In its pivotal role, its function enhances intersensory integration, with particular reference to the olfactory and auditory systems. Direct means are cited by which to reduce avoidance behavior in the tactile defensive and dormant modes and to enhance the discriminative quality of tactile sensation.

The olfactory system responses are identified as a barometer for identifying better intersensory integration and improved central nervous system function. Methods are documented through which to advance the discriminative quality of sensory organization in the tactile, olfactory, and auditory systems.

Program Plan 2

Reduction of Avoidance Behavior in the Gravity-Activated, Visuo-Vestibular Dyad

This program plan is designed to counteract the residual effects of early postural reflexes which prevent the child from developing smoothly integrated patterns of movement throughout the body. These smooth patterns depend upon good integration between the visual and the vestibular systems. The vestibular system is given a pivotal role in developing this integration; with improved visuo-vestibular integration the incidence of related avoidance responses can be significantly reduced. The broad goals of this program plan are as follows:

1) reduce residual influence of gravity-activated postural reflexes;
2) develop midline stability along the spine and proximal stability at the scapula and shoulder;
3) promote equilibrium responses and motor activity to integrate the two sides of the body;
4) establish smooth motor function across the midline (arm action and oculomotor control).

Through the activities of Phase I, the child is provided opportunity to involve himself in actions which enable him to replicate insofar as possible the early sequence of gravity-related gross motor patterns. The steps which follow give the general pattern of the most important actions the therapist would attempt to stimulate.

1) Expose the young child to activity which stimulates extension of head and neck against gravity, eg, prone rolling over an inflated roll.

2) (In addition to above.) Activate the child's hip and trunk extension as he kicks forward, lying over the inflated roll, together with the protective arm extension pattern as he catches himself and pushes back. He can also be held by the ankles and rolled forward over the carpeted barrel to again push with arms.

3) Activate balance in prone, supine, sitting, and quadrupedal positions on inflatables and carpeted barrel.

4) Expose the child to prone activity such as the double suspended tires which support the body weight and allow an equal gravitational pull on both arms as means of reducing the symmetrical tonic neck influence. (Bilateral voluntary action in the arms and shoulders as the child pushes

himself backwards keeps himself in the midposition and helps to prevent the asymmetrical tonic neck reflexes from being triggered. The child's reversed forceful action of the shoulders and arms to thrust himself forward acts in a similar way to reduce residual reflex influence.)

5) Activate light neck and trunk flexion during supine rocking and by rolling inside the carpeted barrel.

6) As the reflex activity is decreased, further activate neck extensors against gravity by employing the optical righting reflex. When the child is lying prone in the double tires and gently pulled backward, the optical righting reflex will act to tense the neck extensors and elevate the head.

7) Activate anti-gravity extension of the upper trunk and shoulders as the child swings prone in the double suspended tires, producing the desired "pivot-prone posture."

8) Expose the child to early opportunities to use bilateral motor integration and further reduce the asymmetrical tonic neck reflex activity twirling in the double suspended tires. As the arms, being pulled down by gravity, become active and press against the floor to twirl, one arm and then the other gradually comes closer to the vertical midline of the body until the hands overlap.

9) Activate voluntary motor activity in the neck flexors against gravity. Lying supine across the suspended tires, the neck flexors are under tension and active use when holding the head up. The neck muscles are also activated as the head is self-supported when rolling inside the carpeted barrel with only the head out of the barrel.

10) Initiate safe early equilibrium reactions in a kneeling posture, rocking inside the carpeted barrel. The weight-supporting requirement on both arms acts to reduce the asymmetrical tonic neck reflexes; the resulting motor pattern during rolling involves bilateral motor integration.

11) Activate equilibrium reactions by asking the child to balance in a sitting position on a small inflated pillow with feet touching the floor and later with feet off the floor.

12) Reinforce weight-supporting arm extension and reduce asymmetrical tonic neck reflexes by balancing on top of the carpeted barrel or inflatables in the quadrupedal position.

13) Promote prone positioning and activate the total prone extension with kickoffs from the wall on the scooter board, ie, the "pivot-prone position."

14) Activate equilibrium responses in the vertical sitting posture on an unstable base, the scooter board. Pulling himself alone on an overhead rope activates the bilateral motor patterns at the midline.

15) Promote joint compression of weight-bearing joints, the postural and equilibrium responses and bilateral motor integration patterns through use of the jumping board in the kneeling and standing positions.

In keeping with the holistic approach, the Phase I activities are presented to the child through a purposely nondirective, invitational approach; the therapist then discerns to what extent the child demonstrates avoidance responses. Various kinds of childhood performances on these basic pieces of equipment are described in P.P. 2.1-2.7. Therapeutic techniques which have been effective in helping the child to increase his level of performance along the hierarchy are depicted in detail.

In the holistic point of view, emphasis is placed on providing the child opportunity to involve himself spontaneously with those kinds of movement which are directed from within. By observing the quality of his response, the therapist can also see where the child's needs are. Observations can suggest that there is a strong need for stimulation which arises from twirling. Self-imposed movement in the tires, for instance, is the safest; I indicate repeatedly that passively imposed stimulation of this kind must be done only by those who are knowledgeable about this technique and who are also sensitive to the child's responses with regard to changes in heart rate, vasomotor dilation, facial blanching or flushing, and signs of nausea.

It is definitely contraindicated for imposed stimulation such as this to be done when the child with poor trunk balance and equilibrium is poorly supported. For instance, a revolving secretarial chair, whether or not a safety belt is used, is contraindicated for this purpose. It is simply too threatening an experience for any child and can be disturbing to a child who has a poor balance system at the outset. Imposed twirling is not an activity which is carried out by assistants for a set number of revolutions, but is conducted by the most experienced therapists, always with the child knowing he is in control, to indicate the rate of speed and the duration which is within his tolerance. Keeping all these factors in mind, twirling in the suspended tires and the twirling chair has resulted in safe and pleasurable experiences for hundreds of children in my care. An early awareness and sensitivity to any possible discomfort has alleviated experiences by these children which would be undesirable.

Although it would appear that this stimulation is directed to the vestibular apparatus directly, namely the semicircular canals, it is in no way limited to that. While the direct mechanical effect in the semicircular canals is emphasized, the therapy in fact promotes better neural connections between structures at the brain stem level to include the input from the proprioceptors, the kinesthetic input, and the cerebellum where this information is integrated.

Personally, I am quite interested in the drive for vestibular stimulation and the frequency of depressed nystagmus observed among learning-disordered children. Nystagmus frequently arises after a number of weeks of this kind of stimulation. Although the sternocleidomastoid muscles, which stabilize the head and neck, are said to inhibit nystagmus,* nonlearning-disordered children immediately experience subjective feelings of dizziness and demonstrate a clear nystagmus from this kind of twirling.

Using electrodes to the brain, electroneurographic studies permit accurate determination of vestibular responses to scientifically controlled torsion-swing chairs in the laboratory. Since 1954, it was recognized by studies in Belgium that turning movements by hand often were not constant enough to establish levels of vestibular responses which were at scientifically acceptable levels. In laboratory studies, mechanical "torsion-swing chairs" have replaced manually controlled rotation to determine the effects of acceleration and deceleration nystagmus.*

It is unnecessary, however, to be so clinically restricted, since we are not

*Personal communication with Dr. Julio deQuiros

investigating nystagmus from a medical point of view. Therefore, twirling movements from the point of view of stimulating nystagmus is relevant in therapy because we are not studying the effect of twirling on the vestibular apparatus alone. From the holistic point of view, we are responding to an expressed need by the child's spontaneous behavior or his positive receptivity to passive twirling, which may also coincide with the presence of depressed nystagmus. The stimulation the child receives may have a more cumulative effect on the structures of the central nervous system which then creates in the involuntary eye movements the desired response.

Suspended Tires (2.1)

In the beginning the child may only push the tires away with his hands; others may climb up to sit on top of them. If the child is slow to crawl into the tires prone, the therapist, sitting on the floor, looks through the opening to catch his eye. The therapist then holds the tires, saying, "You may climb in if you wish." Double tires rather than a single one are used so that the child can lie in them comfortably. The tires are tied together at the top only, allowing for them to be separated, an important feature for safety in supine twirling.

The therapist observes whether the tonic labyrinthine reflexes are still pulling the head down. The latent reflex activity and/or the poor muscle endurance in the neck extensors may be more apparent when the child lies prone on the suspended tires than on the scooter board, because the head can drop lower here. Conclusions about the head position must not be made too quickly; the child may be looking down at the floor pattern. The therapist tries to determine how well the child lifts the head against gravity voluntarily and to what extent it can be stimulated by the swinging movement in the tires.

If there is no spontaneous activity on the part of the very young or disorganized child, the therapist may ask if he wants her to give him a little ride. With an affirmative answer, she moves the tires back very slowly. The child's head now has been moved by this action to a lower point than before, and the optical righting reflex may then quickly respond to bring the head into a more upright, extended position. The neck extensor pattern can be initially activated by passively swinging the child in this manner.

Action such as this may motivate the child to continue the movement by pushing himself. The action of the shoulder muscles in a downward thrust toward the child's chest, to push himself forward, utilizes the lower trapezius muscles bilaterally. Since the accessory nerve also supplies the upper trapezius and the sternocleidomastoid muscles as well as the lower trapezius, they are inclined to respond simultaneously to stabilize the head in a neutral position against gravity.

The therapist is careful to observe whether the child initiates any twirling and how well organized this pattern may be. Twirling in the suspended tires is totally unresistive and should be made available to the child as early as possible. The duration and the intensity with which the child proceeds gives the therapist some indication of how pressing this need must feel to the child. On occasion, these children have been clocked twirling spontaneously at a speed of 60 RPM for a 20-

second period. A child may spend 20 minutes or more swinging in these tires without interruption.

The therapist would be anxious to observe whether the child who spontaneously twirls himself at intense speeds of 60 RMP demonstrates any nystagmus upon stopping. This can be done by putting a mirror under the child's face. Only the presence, absence, or possibly a gross estimate of the duration or amplitude of the eye movements can be determined in this manner. A more accurate assessment can be made in the twirling chair (P.P. 2.6).

The therapist observes how well developed the twirling pattern is, the characteristic features of the child's prone posture, and the endurance he displays in this position. If the child's most typical posture in the tires is one in which both the arms and legs, as well as the head, are pulled down toward the floor, this signals an immature pattern. It is also undesirable if the legs and lower trunk are actively brought into action to assist in the twirling movement. The child may also use one arm exclusively, or one to propel himself in one direction, one in the other; both should be in use. The hands may at first be outstretched at nearly 180° apart and gradually come closer to the midline of the body until they overlap more and more consistently.

Intermittently, between active twirling motions, the arms and upper trunk will begin to float freely in the "pivot-prone posture." The extension of the upper trunk often precedes the extension of the lower extremities which together should resemble the position of a freefall parachute jump. Until such time the legs will drag, or one at a time will extend, until gradually a more complete and consistent bilateral extension pattern is seen throughout the body.

Many children like to lie supine across the tires, dropping the head far back and down, their hips sunk down in the space between the tires. Their desire is to

4. This position is normal for brief periods when at rest; hips and upper trunk should gradually become extended during twirling. When flexion continues, it suggests residual labyrinthine reflex activity.

5. Hands cross the midline of the body as desired, in prone twirling.

6. The child spontaneously assumes the inverted position for supine twirling in the double suspended tires.

assume the inverted position. This means has proven to be one of the most effective and safe ways of twirling as if one were upside down. (See Part I, Ch. 7.)

Carpeted Barrel (2.2)

Rolling Inside

A 3 foot high fiber drum of approximately 22 inches in diameter is carpeted inside and out by gluing squares or scrap pieces to the surface. Oil drums are too heavy. The inside of the carpeted barrel offers an early, safe means for the child to explore even the most primitive supine rocking patterns. One end is kept closed, motivating the child to use a much higher skill level of postural and bilateral integration than would be used in rolling on the floor or in an open-end tube where the legs are extended while he rolls. It is the wide range of skills possible both in and on this piece of equipment which, from a holistic point of view, makes its use ideal.

Use of a nondirective, invitational technique is most suitable with the carpeted barrel. The learning-disordered child is often confused by instructions. Since this activity needs none, it appeals to children who otherwise feel compelled to reject any attempt of an adult to involve them so as to avoid possible failure and further emotional trauma. By saying, "Show me what you can do," the therapist sets no verbal limits nor goals. So that the therapist can help the hyperactive, distractible child focus his attention, the barrel would ideally be the only activity available to him for that period of time. Within the structure of the equipment and the setting, he is then free to explore his full capabilities. He will demonstrate spontaneously his highest level of function as long as he does not feel threatened by either verbal directives or any unexpected actions of others.

Initially the child may do little more than use his hands to push the barrel, and the therapist should accept this. She does not try to set the pace for the child who is slow to respond, and she is cautious to avoid barraging him verbally with encouragement. Sometimes one can motivate a child to go for a ride in the barrel by offering him a toy animal which is thrown inside. This helps the child become involved, and he may reach in or crawl inside. It may take a number of therapy sessions before some children will even enter the barrel or, if they crawl in, they may simply lie very still without rocking at all. Watching the child's eyes for signs of anxiety, the therapist stabilizes its movement as may be necessary.

From the secure prone or supine positions, the child will begin to move little by little. Then by turning over, he soon finds it is fun to rock a little. Taking cues from the child, the therapist senses when the child is ready for her to release her hold on the barrel as he increases his initiative and range of exploration. Generally the therapist refrains from rocking the barrel to stimulate the child's actions, although it can be done after a while when, for example, a young retarded child's spontaneous efforts are not forthcoming. The barrel should not be used in home programming unless the therapist feels confident that it would be used appropriately. The child should not be rolled or rocked by any other child or adult with sudden, unexpected motion which could cause him to become apprehensive.

Children as old as six or seven years who have poor balance may simply rock the barrel from side to side from the supine position, without rolling it over, for a period of six weeks or longer. Should such a child accidentally lose his balance and fall over, rolling the barrel with him, he could be frightened. More often, although the fall may come as a surprise, he quickly recovers his equilibrium and his emotional aplomb as he and the therapist share a few laughs.

Frequently children from four years or older will crawl into the barrel and, without hesitation, soon roll it over. The therapist, always nearby on the floor, watches quietly and approvingly. Her continued interest and feelings about his accomplishments help him to see himself in a more positive light. A child may at first roll the barrel over in a random, chance experience two or three times; interspersed with this will be a great deal of repositioning of himself without even moving the barrel and climbing out to move the barrel by hand. Quietly the therapist observes this initial exploratory experience from which a more organized, purposeful pattern will emerge.

If the child puts his head in the closed end of the barrel, the therapist watches as he rolls over to see whether he can flex the hips and knees and, if so, how consistently he can maintain this pattern. If he puts his feet in the closed end, the therapist then observes to what extent the head is rested on the floor as he rolls, or whether the neck muscles are able to support the weight of his head. Rolling with the head at each end is encouraged; there may be a noticeable difference in the skill level of one over the other and not infrequently the child will be more skillful in rolling to his right or to his left. This is not interpreted in terms of dominance, however.

In the early rolling pattern the child usually moves in a single, isolated

7. With the child's head in the closed end, he demonstrates the ability to maintain hip and knee flexion as he rolls.

revolution, requiring much readjustment and repositioning of his body before he can roll the barrel over again. Gradually the interval of time needed to readjust his position is reduced, but the movement patterns continue to be awkward and fragmented. In four to six weeks, some children of six to eight years who are exposed to five or ten minutes of this activity once a week can move from a random, fragmented pattern to one in which they can make continuous, smooth revolutions across the room. For others who are younger or who have a slower rate of development, this smooth pattern may take three to six months. For a few, it may never be accomplished well. Children who are large will find the size is too small for easy maneuvering inside. This does not prevent them from gaining the needed benefit from the activity, but the therapist must be cautious in judging the quality of performance.

Other children who are further along the hierarchy will quickly and eagerly start rolling when first introduced to the task. They giggle and seem to thoroughly enjoy themselves. The therapist's task here is to maintain lively communication to reflect this child's pleasure and then to enable him to move as forceably and rapidly as possible to enhance postural and bilateral motor integration to its maximum.

Prone Rocking (Outside)

One of the earliest forms of gravity-related motor patterns which must be developed is the protective arm extension pattern. Children of five, six, and seven years have been observed to lack this spontaneous, automatic arm thrust to protect themselves when falling. Their histories reveal that they are prone to falls and succumb to facial cuts and bruises, broken teeth, and black eyes from their poor balance on the one hand and the inability to protect against it on the other.

The carpeted barrel presents an ideal way of bringing about better use of this pattern, or by eliciting one where it is either sluggish or nonexistent. As the child lies prone over the side of the barrel, the adult eases him forward with caution to determine the point where his hands will comfortably contact the floor and his head will not hit. If the child registers no opposition, this is repeated, gradually adding more force to the forward thrust. If after several weeks the protective arm extension has not been aroused, the therapist may suggest to the child that he push back, together with the therapist's movement. A point of caution would be to always roll the barrel over a nonskid surface, preferably over carpeted flooring.

Ideally the therapist looks into a mirror or a reflective surface to see how close the child's head comes to the floor. Short of that, she must be able to judge the safety range herself. Proper posture of the adult to assure safety for the child would be to hold both ankles and set up a prescribed range forward and back. With a young child who is lightweight, the adult can be comfortable and also see the child's response by placing the right foot at the end of the barrel, shifting the body weight on to it during the forward motion, while rocking back on the left foot which is positioned behind the barrel. Then the forceful thrust may be made through the proper range with skill and safety. With a heavier and older child, the adult would have to stand with both feet behind the barrel to avoid undue back strain to herself.

Because of this swift action, the child can gradually assume arm extension.

8. As the therapist holds the child by the ankles, she rocks him back into the inverted position which learning-disordered children often seek.

Additionally, pressure under the abdomen as the barrel rolls backward stimulates an antigravity reflex action to extend the upper trunk, just the body in space. This pressure presumably also stimulates the neck and upper trunk musculature and, as the result of the movement into this position, also alerts the semicircular canals. This procedure might be lightly referred to as "bouncing him on his head," as he is pulled back slightly and then lowered again. This process will often cause the child to elicit a brief staccato giggle, which I have called the "giggle signal"; it suggests that at that moment something newly integrative is being acutely sensed by the child and implies that similar action should be furthered at that point and in subsequent sessions.

Supine Rocking (Outside)

Supine rocking over the barrel is done in a similar manner. Here it is safest if the child is slowly lowered to within several inches of the floor, and then with a more rapid thrust, pulled up again. This action increases the forceful gravitational pull to stimulate the anterior semicircular canals. The expression on the child's face, as well as his comments, will confirm whether or not he wants this to continue. "Giggle signals" will yeild additional evidence that this is indeed what he wants.

Sitting and Kneeling Balance (Outside)

The learning-disordered child, like most children of five to eight years, like to sit on the barrel and balance. If his legs are long and his feet touch the floor too easily, he is urged to hold them up as if he were riding a horse. As the barrel moves

9. A high level of performance is demonstrated in the kneeling position on the carpeted barrel, illustrating good vestibular bilateral integration.

from left or right, the child's center of gravity shifts. The therapist observes whether the child's response in the head and trunk resembles a stick figure with little flexibility. She watches to see if there is any rotary movement of the head and trunk, and whether the child's arms cross the midline toward the opposite side of the body in a well-integrated, graceful pattern.

While being cautious not to interfere with the exploratory process, the therapist may take certain actions to increase the duration of balancing experience. If the child seems to want to fall off repeatedly, the therapist reduces the amount of time lost in getting the child back on the top of the barrel as follows: sitting or kneeling in front of the open end, she simply holds the barrel with a firm grip but allows a flexible range for the child to rock from side to side. The therapist is cautious to only supplement the amount of control over the rolling action which the child cannot furnish.

Most children between the ages of six and eight who readily take to riding the barrel become "good riders" in a course of two to three months of clinic and daily home use. The steps in the development of skill are fairly consistent among children in this task. The rate may vary considerably and some children may never reach the more advanced and intricate performance described here. It is not considered vital to achieve the highest range, for this activity is used as a means to an end and never an end in itself.

The usual steps are as follows. The child discovers that not only can he balance left and right, but in catching his balance at some point he observes that the barrel can be moved while he stays on top. Sitting upright, he raises himself off the barrel with his hands and soon discovers, as his hands shift to the side, that he can keep his trunk vertical. Sitting again to reposition the hands, he repeats this new-found skill. Quite to his surprise, he finds he can control the speed and the direction in which the barrel moves left or right.

Next he discovers he no longer needs to sit on the barrel and hug the sides with his legs, but that he can move his legs up to the top of the barrel and control its movement from the four point kneeling or quadrupedal posture. Additional voluntary control increases, and he can roll the barrel from one end of the room and back with scarcely any hesitation. Instead of kneeling to roll it side to side, some children kneel across the barrel, so that by controlling the forward movement and momentum of their knees, they can propel the barrel backward over a fair distance. The most elaborate pattern which a number of children have found is to roll the barrel in the kneeling position, and over the course of moving from one end of the room to the other, they will turn a 360° circle in the process without losing their balance. While this is possible, it is not necessary for children in the program to progress beyond the point of controlled movement in either direction in the first kneeling position.

Inflatables (2.3)

The term inflatable refers to a series of transparent and/or opaque vinyl pieces of equipment designed and developed by the author, arising as an outgrowth of therapeutic benefits attributed to the large beachball. Ayres instituted use of the beachball for sensory integrative function for the learning-disordered child subsequent to its extensive and very specific use by the Bobaths in the treatment of cerebral palsied children.

The inflatables which are used in this program are designed to provide the child the opportunity to improve his balance safely and independently, even if his equilibrium responses are still poorly developed. This would yield a feeling of constancy with regard to the force of gravity and the motor response needed to maintain his balance in relation to it. When the adult holds the child on the beachball to stimulate balance, the experience will be variable and the child may even feel a sense of false security.

The earliest kind of action one could expect would be prone rocking across an inflated roll. For toddlers and preschoolers the 18 inch diameter roll which inflates to one foot in height can be used safely; movement of the child is limited to forward-backward so it is stable enough for them when the hands or feet or both touch the floor. For larger children and even adults, the same type of action can be experienced by them across the 36 inch diameter roll which inflates to about two feet in height, called Moby Dick.

This forward-backward rocking action can stimulate the proprioceptors of the neck and upper back as well as a stronger protective arm extension pattern and the extensor thrust throughout the back and lower extremities. The force is intensified on older children and adults by placing sandbags weighing up to four pounds on the back of the neck; some of the boys prefer to wear a heavy motorcycle helmet.

Before the child attempts to balance on the large 48 inch x 48 inch pillow, the forward-backward pattern should be well-established in these long inflated rolls which move in only one plane. This pillow moves in all planes: left-right, back-

10. Repeated activity in the protective arm-extension is encouraged on the inflated roll.

forth, and any combinations between. Here the feet and hands are usually off the floor while balancing. Since the pillow is more mobile, it puts a greater demand on the child's equilibrium responses. The child is encouraged to try his balance in the prone, the supine, and the quadrupedal positions. Occasionally the therapist will need to balance the pillow to prevent the child from becoming frightened or to keep to a minimum any time lost by his falling off when this becomes a part of the child's avoidance response. The therapist watches to see if the child can execute an identifiable pattern of movement back and forth, and left to right; if necessary, some verbal structure such as counting the repeats can be instituted. A smaller, less expensive pillow, 36 inches x 42 inches, is designed for home programming. It is somewhat less stable, however, then the previously mentioned large square.

One inflatable, the Space Ship, is designed and constructed primarily for clinic use to meet the widest range of therapeutic needs with safety for the child with the least strain on the therapist. Each position, prone and supine lying, quadrupedal, and kneeling or sitting, can be used effectively. The Space Ship is basically a large square inflated pillow surrounded on each side by pontoon-like bumpers. By having one set of long and one set of short bumpers, they press upon one another in such a way as to secure the long bumpers down for more longitudinal rocking, less horizontal movement, or up for less stability in the horizontal direction. When, for example, the child lies parallel to the long bumpers and these are put in the down position, they limit the tilt of the Space Ship left and right within a range the less skillful child can control. The child can safely explore his balance at any time because it is virtually impossible for him to fall directly to the floor. Instead, the crevice created between the rounded center pillow and the inflated bumpers breaks the fall.

11. As the child demonstrates balancing ability in the kneeling position, the therapist observes the equilibrium responses and the spontaneous repetition of organized movement forward and backward, left and right.

As with all inflatables, slipping is reduced by not only the indentations which the weight of the child creates, but also the nonskid properties of the vinyl against the skin. These advantages are especially relevant in the treatment of a tactually defensive child who dislikes being touched or held but who, on the other hand, finds the experience of touching this smooth surface to be pleasing.

If the child is too disorganized to initiate any purposeful action on even the small inflated roll, the therapist would then first use the Space Ship to structure this movement for him. The child lies prone with arms outstretched to reach the forward bumper. The therapist activates all the rocking back and forth until such action can be elicited from the child. Thereafter, the child can use the roll or pillow in the manner described earlier and supplement the clinic experience with a valuable home program. The Space Ship can be tilted left and right in the same manner to elicit the child's head and trunk righting responses.

The need for supine positioning and movements to stimulate the semicircular canals has been described in Part I, Chapter 7. The inflatables provide a valuable means of satisfying this need and to quiet the hyperactive child who is seeking this stimulation. The therapist must be alert to observe any spontaneous action of a child which would hint of this need. If no need is initially observed, the therapist should offer the use of the inflatables and watch the child's acceptance and desire for it.

Passive supine rocking can be done on either the large pillow or on the Space Ship (see page 142). On the pillow, for instance, the therapist can test whether this position is appropriate and desired by the child once he has experienced it.

The therapist asks the child to show her how he can sit down on the inflatable and, after he has become comfortable in the sitting balance, she tells the child he

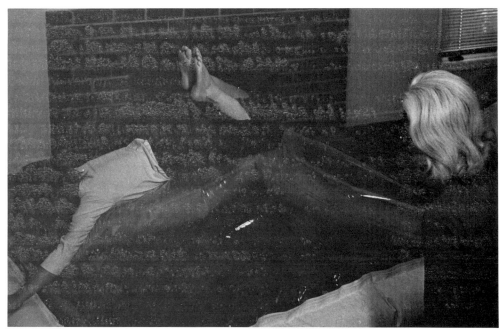

12. In the prone position on the Space Ship, forward-backward movement is organized by a reciprocal pattern of knee flexion and extension, together with properly timed neck and head movements.

may lie down if he wishes. Not only is this invitation often acceptable to him, he may return voluntarily to lie in the supine positions numerous times during that therapy session and in those to follow. As the child lies supine across the full length of the pillow, the therapist kneels on one side grasping the pillow with her left hand, which also rests in the curvature of the child's neck to prevent him from slipping. At the same time, she holds the child's right ankle, together with the edge of the pillow at the end with her right hand. Initially she rocks the pillow in a small arc of movement to avoid surprising or frightening the child. She asks if this is comfortable or "all right" and as soon as the child's eyes and face confirm a lack of anxiety from this position, the arc may be increased until the therapist's hand at either end touches the floor. Again, it is preferable to have direct skin contact with the surface, but even when the child is clothed, the depression from his weight, the nonskid properties, and the proper grip would prevent the child from slipping.

Supine rocking may be a regular part of each weekly therapy session over the first several months with some children; thereafter, it may be used on a symptomatic basis when the child becomes hyperactive and this behavior interferes with performing other activities. For the severely involved child, it is supplemented with frequent or daily home programming; for such a child, who may be as old as eight or ten when entering therapy, continued daily use may be indicated for up to six months. At home this may be recommended for use in the morning before going to school or on returning, especially if significant disorganization in his social and academic behavior is apparent. As long as getting him to sleep remains a problem, supine rocking along with brushing is suggested for use at bedtime. Parents are also encouraged to use this as the most

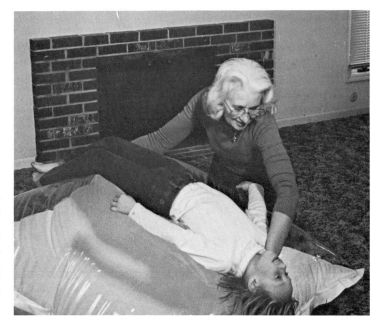

13. After the child spon-
taneously assumes the
supine position, the therapist can provide further
stimulation by rocking the
child in an extended range
on the large pillow; note
the position of her hands
to assure the child's safety.

direct avenue to reduce irritability and to quell temper tantrums. This technique
can be suitable for use by the school nurse under similar circumstances.

Sitting balance, straddling the 18 inch inflated roll, is safely encouraged for
even the young learning-disordered child of three, or an older child who has
poorly developed equilibrium responses. A larger inflated roll such as Moby Dick
gives the same experience for large children. The small pillow (26 inches x 32
inches) is suitable for sitting balance with the child's feet on the floor for stability
while he begins to explore side-to-side movements, even imitating the wings of an
airplane with his arms.

Sitting with the legs folded in Indian fashion on top of the large rectangular
pillow or the Space Ship requires a higher degree of balance since the feet cannot
touch the floor. (The smaller pillow is too unstable for this.) When proficiency
warrants it, the child is then offered a long plastic tube (such as a translucent golf
club cover) closed at both ends containing a wooden bead or marble. Holding it at
eye level with one hand at each end, the child tries to watch the bead roll while at
the same time he must maintain his balance with little conscious thought and
attention to it.

Although balance — prone, supine, and sitting — are all encouraged, it is the
quadrupedal position which seems to be the most enjoyable and controllable to
the children because the greater flexibility of the entire body in this position
enables them to maintain and regain their balance over a wider range. Kneeling
balance is used after his mastery of quadrupedal balance to further challenge the
equilibrium, coupled with use of the bead and tube already mentioned.

Without question, the ultimate challenge to horizontal balance which would
meet the needs of large children and adults would be to lie prone, and later supine,
lengthwise across the large inflated roll called Moby Dick. At least initially, the

therapist or parent will need to stabilize the inflatable at one end until partial or total independent balance can be maintained. Quadrupedal balance is equally difficult but can be mastered.

Another inflatable, called the School of Porpoise, is comprised of a series of inflated rolls which are linked together. When these parallel rolls lie on the floor, the child can crawl, jump, or walk across them. His movement causes a sudden shift of these rolls within a restricted range of several inches. This activates and challenges the child's righting reflexes and equilibrium responses appropriately and safely.

The School of Porpoise also provides a safe opportunity for the more physically impaired cerebral palsied child to experience falling. They usually find the activity nonthreatening and fun. In addition, the School of Porpoise can be lifted at the center and positioned in a circular form. This gives the learning-disordered child a broader range of balancing experience while climbing and jumping on it. He can intentionally roll it to one side through a self-limited range and make the necessary readjustments as his center of gravity shifts. This design provides a self-motivating experience in early climbing experience for children with severe motor impairments.

Among the various inflatables, the most all-round use is derived from the large pillow (36 inches x 42 inches); hence, it is most often recommended for home use. For clinic and home programming the small 18 inch inflated roll is recommended. Moby Dick serves the same purpose for children over 4 feet, 6 inches and for adults. By contrast, the Space Ship and the School of Porpoise are designed for their particular attributes in clinic use to help the more severely involved child activate and develop early equilibrium movements independently and safely.

Scooter Board (2.4)

The scooter board is constructed of a ⅝ inch piece of plywood, 12 inches x 18 inches, curved at one end, padded with a 1 inch layer of sponge rubber, and covered with shag carpeting. Beneath it, at the back corners and at the broad part of the arc, are secured a set of four flat-flange Shephard, Nova castors, 2¼ inches in diameter, with rubber wheels and attached with screws. (See Appendix I).

The therapist observes the child as he lies prone on the scooter board to note evidence of disorganization and the tendency toward avoidance of that position or toward exploration of movement patterns in that posture. For example, the extent of disorganization would be obvious if he is unable to get on independently and needs to have the therapist stabilize the scooter board for him. Also, he may be unable to maintain sufficient trunk balance once he is on it and starts to move, because he exerts so much extraneous trunk motion that he easily rolls off. Early fatigue of the neck extensors, which causes a child to avoid the prone position, suggests that the effects of the tonic labyrinthine reflexes had not been sufficiently overcome to allow these muscles to hold the head up against the pull of gravity.

The therapist approaches the child by saying, "Can you lie down on this and show me what you can do?" Children who have such weak neck muscles will subtly demonstrate an avoidance response within a minute or so by sitting up or

14. As the child forcefully kicks off from the wall, he assumes the desired pivot-prone position.

15. The child demon-strates the desired over-lapping hand pattern while twirling on the scooter board.

leaving this task in favor of another. This is done so quickly and in such a natural way that, unless the adult is trained to recognize it, efforts to counteract this problem in therapy may be overlooked. When the child tries to avoid the prone posture by diverting his attention and attempting to distract the therapist from this activity too, she simply moves toward the scooter board and says, "If you want to get back on, I will hold it for you." The therapist observes whether the child returns of his own volition and whether the periods of endurance continue to be brief. In the weeks which follow, his endurance will increase from a few brief periods, less than a minute each, to periods which extend five minutes or more.

In the initial exposure to the scooter board, the child may twirl inappropriately by using the legs and trunk action, which is unrelated to the movement desired. Often a child will start to twirl spontaneously upon first using the scooter board. If not,he should be asked if he can go around and around, using hand gestures to assure his understanding of the meaning in this particular situation. The therapist observes the position of the arms carefully; in the beginning they may be 180° apart. Over the ensuing weeks the hands come closer to the midline until eventually they overlap consistently when twirling in either direction. Meanwhile, the trunk has become more stable so that the excess activity there and in the legs ceases. At first one will often see the child's hips semiflexed and his knees dragging on the floor. As the motor patterns become better organized, one hip at a time will be extended, then both will assume the desired "pivot-prone" position.

As these children discover how to twirl, one is utterly astonished to see the speed and the duration of their involvement. A speed of 30 to 40 RPM intermittently over a 20-minute duration can represent the peak performance of one child. The tempo and duration gradually reaches a crescendo during home programming and in therapy, lasting three to four weeks, followed by a diminishing interest and involvement with the scooter board. It may take from three months or slightly longer from the time of initial introduction of the scooter board to the point of apparent fulfillment of the child's need to stimulate the semicircular canals for its use to be discontinued.

Sitting balance on the scooter board poses a new set of challenges to the child's equilibrium. Various steps of skill can be observed immediately. The therapist observes whether he can get on independently, whether he sits with his feet crossed in front, and whether he must keep them in touch with the floor for security. If he needs help to get his feet into the Indian-style position, it should be noted if he maintains this posture, keeps his trunk balance while moving, or instead falls over easily.

An important variation in movement on the scooter board is accomplished through an activity which has been named Ferry Boat. The child, sitting on the scooter board, is asked if he can pull himself across the "river" by pulling a rope suspended lengthwise overhead. The therapist watches carefully to see if the child uses only one hand to inch his way along while disregarding the other. If so, nothing is said to the child which would suggest that he should use both hands; this will come about automatically, and when it does, this will be one indication of change in the integrative function between the two hands. Even when the two hands do meet at the rope, the movement may be hesitant and show disorganization by the way in which the forward hand advances several times,

16. The child's trunk balance is stressed, while sitting on the scooter board, to pull himself along the overhead rope.

followed by the second hand moving in the same matter without any evidence of the normal hand-over-hand pattern. Several disorganized children have been seen at times to perform as if they had absolutely no awareness of either the position or the function of their hands. As they "hitch" themselves forward solely by erratic trunk movements, they totally disregard the fact that their hands are left behind them still holding the rope. However, within a few weeks of bringing both hands into action on the rope, this pattern will develop into a smooth, consistent, firm, hand-over-hand pattern, signaling one indication of improved two-sided integration. This is one of the forerunners of holding the paper for writing, which one would see developing along the learning continuum.

At first a child will often use his feet to propel himself along. Then, as the child can sit cross-legged, he will begin to stabilize the trunk to maintain his balance in a still haphazard, random, poorly organized motor response. Gradually he will be able to maintain good balance across a span of more than 15 feet, turn around by means of hand action on the rope, and return without hesitation or accidental movement. As trunk control along with the well-integrated hand-over-hand pattern develop, he will explore further action to swing to and then under the rope to elaborate on this. He will devise a series of "swing throughs" to turn about by one hand and then the other, to swing to and fro in a smooth, rhythmic, skillfully executed sequential pattern of movement.

Jumping Board (2.5)

This jumping board is constructed of a five-eighths inch piece of plywood measuring 16 inches x 96 inches and is attached to end peices 2 feet x 6 inches x 16 inches by means of four ¼-inch bolts and washers; the action of the two surfaces is kept flexible by cutting a slot for each bolt to slide through, 1 inch in length, running parallel to the length of the plywood (see Appendix I). These end pieces are padded underneath with felt or rubber matting to prevent tile floors from being scratched and to reduce the noise. Half-inch felt padding is attached to the under surface of the board also to muffle the sound on impact. Rubber floor matting is attached to the entire top surface of plywood to avoid splinters; a center square of 12 inches is outlined with paint or adhesive tape as an easy reference point.

Rhythm and hand clapping are bimanual integrative functions. The following technique may be used with young retardates or severely involved learning-disordered children to instill their awareness of rhythm through simultaneous impact of several sensory systems. As the child lies supine, the therapist stands with both feet placed on the end of the jumping board and moves herself up and down to activate a rhythmic movement pattern. The child lies with his hips at approximately the center point of the jumping board, facing the therapist. By quietly pressing down and forward with both feet in a slow rhythm, the therapist claps lightly to match the "down-beat." (The therapist must be sensitive to the possibility that from the child's position, the looming figure of an adult may be overwhelming. As long as those precautions are kept in mind, this procedure can be attempted until there is evidence that it is contraindicated.)

The child is encouraged to join in clapping. If this is too difficult, the child can clap each hand against his thigh. Similar hand clapping with this reinforcement technique can be carried out in a sitting position. In this procedure there is simultaneous input of sensory information to the tactile, proprioceptive, and vestibular systems by the firm, sturdy impact throughout the total body as the board contacts the floor. This simultaneous sensory input is further confirmed on the jumping board by the auditory input of this pronounced thud as it hits the floor and by the auditory and visual input from the rhythmic claps and bodily movements of the therapist.

Customarily, use of the jumping board in a vertical standing position is reserved until three or more months of work have been performed on the prone, sitting, and quadrupedal balance on the inflatables, suspended equipment, scooter board, and carpeted barrel. For the child over ten years, movement on the jumping board can be a valuable yardstick. If his motion in jumping soon becomes fluid, rhythmic, and adapts well to meet the balancing requirements of jumping on this unstable base, this activity is used therapeutically for the coming weeks to enhance his rate of development. However, if he tends to stand for the most part in a rigid, fixed, inflexible manner which greatly resembles a stick figure, this would signify that he has not established adequate bilateral integrative function of the two sides of the body and that use of the preceding portions of this program plan are needed before action on the jumping board should be resumed.

Upon introducing the jumping board for its specific therapeutic value for vertical balance skill, the child's jumping pattern may at first be quite fragmented. Assuming that the foundations which the earlier units of this program plan would promote have been adequately developed, the fragmented pattern of jumping which may be observed initially should be only a temporary condition. Instead of jumping once or twice before having to stop and regain his balance, the fragmented pattern will within a few weeks give way to a fairly smooth, rhythmic, prolonged jumping pattern. It is at this point that the child would begin to explore his capabilities on the jumping board which includes jumping in the quadrupedal and kneeling position as well. If the exploratory phase is slow to develop, the therapist may suggest the idea by a question such as, "Would there be any other way you could jump?" Variations might then include "bunny hopping" from one end to the other, on one foot or two, turning 360° while continuing to jump, jumping off and onto the jumping board, or other patterns each child will originate for himself.

Twirling Chair (2.6)

Insofar as possible, voluntary action of the child on Phase I activities such as the scooter board and double suspended tires is advocated over involuntary, passive stimulation to the vestibular system as the means by which to activate the extraocular muscles through the pivotal role of the vestibular system. When there is a voluntary motor component, the process is more integrative than when the stimulus is passively applied, as for instance in the twirling chair. However, it may be that the child does not yet have sufficient motor skills to enable him to twirl on either of these pieces of equipment. It could also be that, while he may have actively established a twirling pattern, the speed of his movement does not provide a sufficiently powerful stimulus to activate the desired nystagmus. The twirling chair has therefore been introduced as the most practical means of providing a more intense stimulation to the semicircular canals so that the lateral nystagmus can be activated.

The twirling chair, made in Hong King of cane and rattan, is available at stores which sell patio furniture. This chair is scoop-shaped and comes in three sizes, of which the middle size has proven most practical for children and adults in therapy. The chair is suspended by its sturdy iron chain into an overhead rope which has been knotted at intervals for quick adjustment in height for this and other suspended equipment. This rope is attached near the ceiling by a swivel hook fastened into an iron eye-hook which has a long bolt extending through the overhead beam and secured by double lock washers. The swivel fastener is of paramount importance in preventing this otherwise strong twisting action on the nut and bolt from accidentally dislodging it from the overhead beam.

The Hong King chair has been selected for use because of its structural advantages. The child can get in unassisted; this is important to the tactually defensive child. In addition, the therapist can push against the sturdy rim of the opening to rotate it with some degree of constancy. As she does so, she counts the number of revolutions within the period of time she measures on a stopwatch. Again, it is the shape of this chair, extending forward from the sides, which provides the child with enough enclosure for security as well as with an open latticelike frame which does not restrict his vision. A webbing seatbelt, threaded through the openings to fasten in the back, prevents small children from trying to get out before the chair is safely stopped. Without needing the seatbelt, the older child is protected by the shape of the chair even if his head or trunk sways and he feels dizzy. The therapist can readily observe these findings and on stopping the twirling movement can measure the presence and duration of any nystagmus. Upon completing the twirling, the child is asked to get out of the chair and walk to his parent. In the beginning therapy sessions, before nystagmus has been aroused, there will be no feeling of dizziness, but the therapist always follows close behind the child to prevent the child from falling in case he becomes unsteady.

Whenever any sensory stimulation is imposed on a child, one proceeds with great caution. This is especially true when twirling a child in a suspended chair. The procedure to be described here in detail should be used only by therapists. In contrast to this, parents may, under the therapist's guidance, provide the child a less regimented format for twirling at home. Therapists who include use of the twirling chair in their programs should be extremely cautious in implementing its use, relying on and being sensitive to the reactions of the child moment by moment.

When the child accepts the idea of the twirling chair by trying to climb in, he is given a cushion on which to sit for greater comfort. To avoid his needless anxiety over being restrained, the therapist might ask if he would like to be a junior astronaut, with a comment about young astronauts who need seatbelts. The child is asked if he would like to swing back and forth or go around. After a brief swing to and fro, a gentle twirl is started while the therapist asks the child if this is what he wants. Usually the answer is, "Go faster." The child is reminded that any time he wishes, the chair can be stopped. The therapist is well advised, at least the first time, not to twirl the child nearly as fast as he may ask for. If the vestibular system is functioning, the stimulation can be cumulative and suddenly make him feel nauseous. More commonly, however, the child whose vestibular function is adequate will not ask to be twirled so fast. The learning-disordered child who has poor vestibular function will rarely feel nauseous despite extensive stimulation in subsequent sessions.

In twirling, the procedure is for the therapist to twirl the suspended chair slowly at first, awaiting some positive indication by the child that not only is this imposed stimulation tolerable, but it is highly desirable. After about 15 seconds of slow twirling, the therapist brings the chair to a stop to reconfirm that this is not overstimulating. If all indications are to proceed, the child is then twirled in the opposite direction for a similar period to further explore the child's potential need and desire for fast twirling.

After the twirling has proceeded satisfactorily in alternate directions at this rate and the child's "command" is strongly in favor of going "faster, faster," the therapist proceeds to twirl him a little longer, possibly 30 seconds at 30 RPM, or 15 revolutions. On stopping the movement, the therapist holds the chair in front of her and, facing the child directly, says to him, "Let me see your pretty eyes." Very often the child will have no trouble focusing directly and immediately.

Within the second or third therapy session when the chair is used, the following procedure is attempted, with intervals of a minute or two spent by the therapist to record the results of the twirling before resuming this action in the opposite direction. The therapist should be ever watchful of any hint that the movement is uncomfortable, stopping the motion or limiting the speed or number of repetitions accordingly. If nystagmus, or the other indicators of being stimulated such as dizziness, have not become evident from the slower twirling, then the therapist could cautiously explore the feasibility of implementing the following procedure:

Clockwise	30 seconds	@	60 RPM
Counterclockwise	30 seconds	@	60 RPM

This procedure may be repeated once or even twice if there is no nystagmus aroused and there are still no contraindications evident. Children will vary in regard to the number of treatment hours which might transpire before any nystagmus can be detected even at the trace level; some will develop a definite but brief period of only a few seconds, others will eventually extend for a period up to 20 seconds.

The duration of input (30 seconds) is then compared to the output, or nystagmus. If there is ten seconds output, then there is said to be a three-to-one ratio. Gradually the goal would be to decrease the duration of input to 20 seconds and strive for a two-to-one ratio, and on until ten seconds of input would produce ten seconds of output.

When a one-to-one ratio of ten seconds duration has been achieved for several sessions, then twirling is discontinued with periodic rechecks at intervals of six to eight weeks to see if the nystagmus could be readily produced. It is not expected to remain at peak performance, for in time the system accommodates to the stimulus so there is a greater tolerance to input.

Visual Attention, Fixation, and Pursuits (2.7)

Whereas efforts have been directed primarily to the vestibular system in the previous units of this program plan, to activate it in a pivotal role in organizing the visual system function it is also indicated to direct specific attention toward the visual system. In no way is this activity program intended to give optometric training. It is intended to provide a smooth transition between the primitive activation of the visual system and the voluntary oculomotor control needed in reading.

Following the repeated oculomotor response during nystagmus, which returns the eyeballs to their neutral position, the extraocular muscles have been activated and strengthened. Thus it would seem feasible that these muscles are better able to act in a more purposeful, concerted manner to direct the child's focus of attention on a visual object. Efforts are directed which will enable the child to reduce the initial and pervasive avoidance response, eg, visual inattention. At first it may be possible for the child to maintain but a momentary, random visual attention to an object, followed by voluntary visual attention to simple moving, colorful objects of interest. Attempts are then made to help the child direct his attention by positioning his eyes briefly on a still object, referred to as visual fixation. Finally attempts are made to help the child advance to a sustained, purposefully directed movement with the eyes on a slowly moving target. This is called visual pursuit. All of this is done as a preparatory foundation to visual tracking and is supportive to academic function, in particular, reading.

The reading process, as viewed in terms of the hierarchy of skills advanced through the holistic approach, is dependent on a series of steps: the ability to make repeated stops, or visual fixation points, in a left-right progression across the page for a long enough period to recognize letter symbols and subsequently clusters of symbols which comprise words or phrases. As the child improves his ability in visual tracking to recognize the letter and word symbols more automatically, his cognitive attention is now freed from the mechanics of reading and can be focused on comprehending the content. Being able to make a smooth transition with the eyes across the midline better prepares him to scan a line or a page with the skill and speed commensurate with his age.

Visual Attention

Early attempts to overcome a visual avoidance response in young children or severely involved older children can be most effectively achieved through the use of an infant's plastic liquid hourglass whenever this is available. This toy is about 6 inches high and filled with colorful tiny plastic chips which float in the viscous liquid as the hourglass is turned from end to end. A soft, bubbling sound attracts the child, which may make him briefly aware of the correlation between this simultaneous visual and auditory input. The child's volitional response may be purposeless and unsustained, such as pounding it on the table in the manner of a young infant. It may, on the other hand, soon invite some manipulation and result by chance at first to inspire his brief visual attention. Gradually the child will begin to realize the cause and effect relationship between his own actions and what happens in the hourglass. A start has been made to bring him toward a more purposeful response to visual fixations.

As another early means of inviting involvement of a timid or reluctant child, or one who is otherwise incapable of focusing any attention, the marble railway is used. This toy, mentioned earlier, comprised of a plastic or wooden downhill, zigzag course, captures the child's attention and yields simultaneous auditory feedback which accentuates and confirms his visual input. The motor performance required to place the marble in the slot at the top is so elementary it can often provide an enjoyable first success experience for poorly organized and also physically handicapped young children. The ultimate goal of P.P. 2.7 is to develop voluntary control of the extraocular muscles, independently of head movement, using a bead and tube a distance of 4 feet from the eyes. Since the marble railway must be within arm's reach for the child, one would not expect independent ocular control.

Visual Fixation

After visual attention has been achieved past the point of a random response, attempts are made to help the child establish voluntary conscious control over the position of his eyes, ie, visual fixation. As much ability as possible is desired so that the child can become more aware of visual images, recognize forms, and identify their likenesses and differences. It is important to realize, however, that some highly disorganized children will be able to perform better at the Phase II desk skills than his ability in a more formal type of visual fixation such as this would suggest. The therapist would proceed to work on both skills; progress in one will further the development of the other.

In visual fixation the procedure would be broken down into three steps. In Step #1, the child lies supine on the floor with the nondistracting ceiling as a background. An object of interest, eg, the infant hourglass, is held 3 to 4 feet above him in an effort to get him to fixate momentarily on it. It is held so that the child looks at an angle of 45° to 60° and not directly overhead at 90°. The therapist counts as the child gazes at it, trying to attain a duration of two to four seconds or longer, moving the object slightly to keep his interest. The therapist watches to see if the child can focus at the midline with both eyes to converge on the target as it is brought slowly to within six or eight inches of his eyes. While holding the object, the therapist remains kneeling or sitting to the side of the child so that she does not appear to him as a large, looming figure overhead.

In Step #2, attempts are made to encourage visual fixation in the upper left and right and the lower left and right visual fields. Keeping the distance between the object and the child's eyes still at 3 to 4 feet, the lateral range should not exceed that which could be normally comfortable without turning the head. As soon as is feasible, the object of interest is replaced with a small penlight, the end of which is covered with colored transparent or translucent vinyl or plexiglass to further dim it. The child is told that as long as he can keep his eyes on the target, the light will stay on, but when his eyes shift away, the light will go off.

This technique provides interest and motivation to yield direct and immediate feedback about the duration of his own visual attention and motivate him to prolong it. As soon as the child can maintain visual fixation in each of these quadrants near his age formula, ie, maintain a response in seconds equal to his age in years, he is ready to advance to the sitting position. Insofar as possible, the child is encouraged to move the eyes without turning the head. The therapist counts silently so as not to distract the child and records her findings in the four quadrants in this simple fashion:

$$
\begin{array}{c|c}
5 & 4 \\
\hline
3 & 4
\end{array}
$$

In Step #3, the procedure used in Step #2 is continued in the sitting position. If necessary, this can be done before a blank wall or relatively nondistracting background at first. In this step greater emphasis is placed on the child's awareness of keeping the head still, moving only his eyes. To do so, the therapist institutes a simple reminder: the word "chins" means for the child to align his chin with the therapist's. Use of this simple term reminds him of this in an instant graphic way and keeps verbal distractions to a minimum. This technique has proven effective in directing the child to isolate eye movement from head movement. If the neck muscles are straining to keep the head in the midline position or if there is tension around the eyes, either it is too early to expect this much control or the target is placed left or right too far from the midpoint at the desired distance of 3 to 4 feet from the child's face.

Visual Pursuits

To train the eyes in visual pursuits, a 3-foot transparent plastic tube one-half inches in diameter is preferred. If this is not available, a translucent polyurethane golf club cover 1 inch in diameter may be substituted. The tube is sealed at each end to contain a marble or wooden bead. It will be easier to attract the visual attention of some children with a moving target such as this, so it can also be tried in the early supine stage just described. However, for smooth pursuits across the midline of the body, as the marble is rolled slowly from one end of the tube to the other, there is much more skill involved than in visual fixation exercises from the supine position.

The steps of difficulty by which one would upgrade visual pursuits would parallel those outlined in visual fixation with respect to posture, the therapist's position to hold the visual object, and the use of the age formula. This time the same number of trips are attempted which would equal his age in years. The therapist records the number of uninterrupted trips the child can make, moving from one end to the other without losing visual contact with the moving target.

In visual pursuits the procedure is broken down into two steps. In Step #1, with the child supine and the therapist kneeling beside him, she holds the tube 3 feet or more above him so that first the bead moves back and forth left to right to observe how well the child can pursue the moving target. When this reaches the age formula, the child is ready to do the same in the sitting position. In the supine position one could also try the movements other than horizontal so that the eye muscles are also exercised in the oblique angles, for example, moving from ten to four on the clock face.

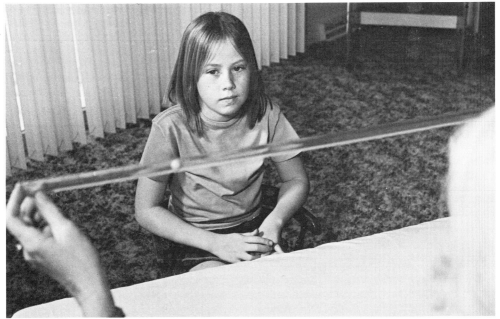

17. With the head maintained in the neutral position, the child is asked to watch the bead as it rolls slowly from one side of the tube to the other.

In Step #2, the therapist sits opposite the child at a distance of four feet and holds the tube at waist level until the skill is fairly well established. At a later point the height can be raised slightly above the child's eyes, coming down little by little with each successive crossing.

The therapist should note if the child can pursue a slow, evenly moving target in a constant manner and continue it up to his age formula. The customary early response in many learning-disordered children is to follow the target at the start, but then dart to the opposite end of the tube. Often a fairly good pattern of control persists up to the midline, at which point a disorganizing form of behavior may be demonstrated in the child's apparent need to avoid the midline. This is characterized by either a sweeping movement toward the end or, in a milder form, a momentary "hump-up" may be seen at midpoint in an otherwise smooth pursuit. As the bead comes in line with the therapist's face, there may be a tendency on the part of the child to look at her. The tube is then held above or below the level of the therapist's face until that tendency is more easily overcome. To be in the optimum position, the therapist sits on a low stool to watch the child's eyes from the same level.

Progress does not always take place in the steady, step-by-step progression one might anticipate. It is crucial to let the child be the guide. The graded steps cited here are to help the therapist establish a framework for analyzing where to begin and how the program can be adjusted upward or downward in a way which will most accurately meet the child's needs at that point in time.

It is also important to point out that a child's visual performance will be no better in this procedure than the control the therapist has in moving the tube. To hold this steadily at a position above the head, for instance, takes practice. Insofar as possible, one should execute an almost imperceptible shift in this position, by which the rolling target proceeds along a slow, uniform, downward zigzag pattern.

Program Plan 3

Bridge the Gap Between Avoidance and Exploration — Organizing Gross Motor Skills

It is consistent with the goals of the holistic approach to bring organization out of a disorganized motor response. The therapist's most important initial function is to enable the child to bridge the gap between an avoidance response and exploration with regard to early motor skills. A highly structured piece of equipment such as the indoor climber provides a safe medium through which the child can do this. On it he can clearly demonstrate the extent to which he must avoid involvement with the task and later, as his tactile and vestibular system function improves, he will then reveal increased ease and motivation to explore and develop gross motor skills into smooth, sequential patterns of movement. (See Part I. Ch 6).

Following this major emphasis on activating the exploratory process through use of the climber, supplementary pieces of equipment are introduced. These pieces are less structured and less stable and thus help the child to organize patterns of movement at a higher level of the learning continuum. It is hoped that this discussion will serve to point out that the walking beam, which is a popular motor task in schools, has the adverse effect of causing the child to develop splinter skills if it is used prematurely or in isolation. This discussion also suggests the appropriate time and purpose for its use.

The Indoor Climber (3.1)

The indoor climber, which in actuality is a small-scale jungle gym, was selected for its therapeutic advantage over equipment of a similar type used on outdoor playgrounds. The indoor climber has proven to be the single most effective activity by which the child can be enabled to bridge the gap between avoidance and exploration in organizing his motor skills. It is recommended for its attractive color, its size, and in particular, one certain feature of its design. The unique aspect of this is the long metal crossbars running parallel to the floor, one on each side at different heights from the floor. This feature greatly expands the possibilities for the child and motivates him to explore a wide range of movement patterns as he climbs. (See page 114.)

The indoor wooden jungle gyms manufactured for schools can be adapted for use by the child who is older or less fearful than many children when they are first seen in therapy. To adapt them suitably, iron pipes can be attached with plumbing hardware; they are placed at points one third and two thirds of the distance from the floor. For a span of 6 feet, 1 inch outside diameter is suitable; larger size is needed for longer spans. In some instances families have constructed a simple indoor climber similar in size and design to the Climber-A-Roo. Working drawings are available.

Because of the successful use of the indoor climber, discussion of these clinical findings refers to it and not to a substitute. The colorful aspects of the climber and the fact that the ladder, the long crossbars, and the overhead bars are easily accessible to the child immediately invite his attention and involvement. Since the equipment speaks for itself and provides sufficient structure to the child's actions, it allows the therapist to maintain a neutral, quiet, and nondirective role. Since there are no goals set for him, the child can feel comfortable to freely explore even his limited range of movement. Even the poorly coordinated, fearful child will feel close enough to the floor to at least begin moving around or sitting on the lower crossbars safely.

These are the critical factors which will enable the learning-disordered child to bridge the gap and to engage in self-directed involvement. Avoidance of such activity may have been a form of survival heretofore. Picture such a child at the top of a playground jungle gym, or even a slide, when other nursery school and kindergarten children would relish the action. Even if he did start to climb up, he might be fearful of going further. As children would come up behind him, any jostling movements of theirs would be threatening to his balance. Furthermore, he may be equally at risk in making his retreat backwards down the ladder if his motor skills, spatial orientation, and balance skills are poor. Thereafter, what can he do but avoid similar experiences whenever he can?

If perchance the learning-disordered child did start to crawl across the overhead bars of a large jungle gym on the playground, he could soon find himself threatened by a swarming, screaming sea of children below. Imagine the tension and fright such an experience could create if, in addition to having poorly developed motor skills, one's orientation in space and a visual figure-ground confusion contributed further problems. From the top of the jungle gym, the most stable point of reference may be the building, which is far removed. If others are also climbing on the equipment at the same time and may even try to "pass" him on the overhead bars, this could be so threatening as to make him freeze in dreaded anticipation of falling off. Surely in the child's eyes these would be experiences to be avoided.

The indoor climbers, by contrast, provide a challenge which is more nearly within his capability, and it is situated within the confines of four walls to offer him a stable, tangible frame of reference. Being able to relate to these spatial surroundings will give him more security with which to explore. In therapy, with no other children around, there are no threats to his safety beyond which he can cope, and there are no auditory distractions to disturb him such as those encountered on the playground.

After observing the performance of hundreds of children on the indoor climber, the steps along a hierarchy which have been generally demonstrated are those which are listed in the OEPS. The progression of an individual child may not coincide exactly with the sequence listed, but the general order will be valid.

Unless there are overriding emotional issues, children are usually eager to push ahead, to function at the peak of their then current motor capabilities. This has been particularly evident among children in their use of the indoor climber.

The procedure for introducing the indoor climber and observing a child's early performance is described here. The equipment is lightweight; a large child could lean far out and tip it, so the therapist keeps her hand on it to prevent this. By her close presence and minimal verbal communication, she readily conveys warmth and approval no matter how meager the child's early efforts may seem. This is not the time for coaxing nor setting of goals, but rather it is the time in which the child must be free to sense that it is he who is in control. Approbating comments may be simply and broadly conveyed to the child in a statement such as this: "I like what I see."

The therapist can further motivate a child by asking him to show her his "tricks." "Can you show me another way?" "How can you play on this?" All of this expresses to the child approval for free exploration without pushing him toward any specific action.

When the exploratory phase is going nicely, the therapist may insert a minimum of instructions to help him correlate the meaning of words which express movement and direction, together with his actions. If there is obvious confusion, she will use these words to first inform him when he is "on top," "under," "between," and so on, prior to asking him if he can move in each of those directions. He may be asked if he can crawl under or over the crossbars, or between the rungs of the ladder, saying, "Can you show me how to___?" "Can you go through the ladder with your feet going first?" Immediately upon fulfilling the specified actions, the therapist says to the child, "Yes, that is what the words tell you." If the action was in error, then the therapist carefully goes back to try to reconstruct for the child 1) what was asked, 2) what he did, and 3) try to help him correlate the words of direction with his body actions.

The therapist carefully observes the child's responses and records what he attempts to do and what he avoids. To instill the feeling of security in therapy, the child works alone. If the climber is considered for home use where there are young siblings in the household, it will be best to wait until the child has reached a high enough level of involvement so that he will not be deterred by seeing that their ability surpasses his, nor again be frightened by actions of others around him. Once he has begun to explore and once he can tolerate a less predictable set of circumstances, he may be suitably motivated and even challenged by playing on it with other children.

Many young children are eager to participate in make-believe games. The green carpet to them quickly becomes an ocean in which they can make believe that every time their foot touches the "water" beneath the climber, a hungry alligator comes up to take a bite. The game is: "Can you get across to the other side without letting the alligator get a bite?"

Some children as old as ten years have demonstrated such poor motor organization that they are unable to climb higher than the second rung of the ladder on the indoor climber. A child such as this who also expresses "fear of heights" reveals how poorly the balance system is serving his needs.

The older child who has poor gross motor skills may be more self-protective and reluctant to explore than the younger child. It is not surprising that he would become fearful of climbing when the tactile and the balance system were inadequate to protect him from previous unfortunate experiences. One ten-year-old girl could do little more than put her feet on the lower crossbar as she sat on the upper one. After a month or two she could be enticed to move from one end to the other along the crossbar without "letting the alligator bite her foot on the floor." However, after six months of therapy it was still impossible for her to climb higher with comfort and ease. By the time she had been referred for therapy, the pattern which had been significantly severe throughout childhood was so rigidly set that she was beyond the point where change in this respect would be possible.

In the process of exploration and organization of gross motor skill, the child gradually develops clear patterns of movement. The crucial point upon which development of smooth patterns of movement seems to hinge lies in the proper sequencing of a series of individual movements. These isolated, distinct, voluntary motions of their limbs, in slow motion, are clearly observable when watching learning-disordered children as they move on the indoor climber. These singular, or compartmented and fragmented, movements with widely spaced intervals of inaction are gradually reduced and a flowing, closely sequenced movement pattern emerges. It is this early slow and obvious sequential pattern of movement which is felt to be the necessary underlying foundation skill upon which the minute, sequential patterns of handwriting are established.

Structured "Near the Floor" Gross Motor Organization (3.2)

If the child is too fearful of climbing up a ladder or the child is very young, a single wooden ladder secured on its side so that he can crawl through the rungs would be suitable. Even more advantageous therapeutically, a simple wooden ladder may be constructed of two-by-fours with 1.5-inch carpeted-covered rungs, spaced at graded intervals from eight to twelve inches. The smaller spaces require that the child turn on his side to get through — action which requires him to organize his gross motor skill; it also enhances his body image, as his bare skin rubs along the rungs.

The same ladder, when attached to the crossbars or the overhead bars on the indoor climber, invites the child to crawl up an incline, which thrusts the head and neck back into extension at the same time that he holds on with his hands, and his shoulders are in forward flexion. This positioning is particularly desirable to reduce the residual tonic neck and tonic labyrinthine reflexes.

Other structured "near the floor" experiences would include the wide open space within a cloth tunnel or the limited openings of the windows in the K-DEE self-assembly wooden playhouse. Even in the simple removal and replacement of the panels on the four sides of this playhouse, there is an unusual set of demands placed on the motor skills of the child. For one thing, these panels measure up to 3 feet in length and weigh 1 to 2 pounds. This weight may extend over a long lever arm as the child lifts or carries it, requiring the child to exert more control over this movement than would normally be required in moving parts of his own body or other objects within close range. A significant new demand for motor organization is presented when the child fits long pieces into the slotted corner posts; one end at least may be at a point quite distant from himself. This activity also puts an increased demand on trunk stability in the kneeling or the upright position and provides a good transition to the activities in P.P. 3.4 and 3.5 to follow.

A number of observations may be made as the child maneuvers in and around and manipulates the pieces of the playhouse. He may have little awareness not only of how much space his own body requires, but the additional space needed to maneuver the long side panels into place, inadvertently hitting them against anything in his path. One's immediate human instinct is to caution him in advance. Within the bounds of human safety, it is preferable for him to discover the limits of space through the direct impact of this sensory experience. As he integrates these sensory experiences and can draw upon them, this will be revealed by his preventing similar collisions from recurring.

While the problem-solving aspects of assembling this playhouse are discussed in P.P. 4.3, the reassembly procedure in and of itself offers important insights as to how well the child has integrated an awareness of the effect of gravity. When this has not developed, the child, upon placing a panel in the slots at the corner posts, will simply let go, being somewhat surprised to see the board go crashing to the bottom. The therapist avoids intervening but watches closely to see how soon

18. This self-assembly play house promotes problem-solving techniques, exploration of various arrangements, opportunity to use it as a large puppet stage, a store, or just to crawl in and around.

the child can alter his response.. This is an opportunity for the child to experience the direct cause-and-effect relationship of his action in relation to gravity without at the same time imperiling persons or objects.

Unstructured "Near the Floor" Gross Motor Organization (3.3)

Self-directed gross motor organization is encouraged by reducing the extent of structure in the activities and to increase the variations which the child himself can implement. For example, obstacle courses can be arranged with chairs, stools, cardboard boxes, and objects in the setting for the child to crawl over, under, or through. Courses can be set up for him to guide himself on the scooter board beneath and between a series of television tables without "hitting" them, thus placing a demand on spatial relations and body image, especially of those body parts which are out of the child's range of vision.

In addition, a set of hula hoops, preferably those made by hand of plumber's polyvinyl drisco pipe, ranging from 12 inches to 20 inches in diameter, can be placed in a row or circle. Here the goal would be for the child to sit on the floor and then, without touching the hoop with any part of his body, move from one to the next. Innovations will be discovered by the child or may be suggested, as for example, "Do this with only one hand on the floor."

Performance depends upon verbal comprehension and auditory memory of the instructions through to goal completion. This is an important step from the holistic point of view, which begins with an early nondirective approach and progresses to those tasks which depend increasingly upon verbal instruction. Children who have poor auditory memory or a poor attention span may be able to execute no more than two repetitions before they lose the established goal and their performance deteriorates to a random type of action. This may be interpreted by some that the child is bored, which may be true, but more often the child who claims boredom really has difficulty or he would do the task quickly and get it done. Most likely, he has problems of motor organization, poor sequential patterning, or the aforementioned problems. The goal would be for him to do only as many repetitions as he can perform successfully so that he can feel positively about having completed the task. Too often adults feel they must challenge the child to do more and more. Although there is a place for this, the primary effect will be defeat and frustration if early goals seem to the child to be continually "out of his reach."

Vertical Balance and Movement from a Stable Base (3.4)

The gross motor organization activities which are listed in Level II of the OEPS have been selected for the purpose of pointing out the proper sequence and gradation of skills. However, many substitutes which have comparable qualities may also be used in therapy, in the classroom, and in a developmental gym program.

As a challenge to his vertical balance and gross motor skill, the child could walk on footprints cut from rubber matting and placed on a course in which the feet may cross over the midline or turn at a 90° angle to one another. The child's balance is further challenged by asking him to walk over an irregular rope pattern or on the colorful plastic stepping stones. If, in any of these activities, the child's balance is so precarious as to evoke erratic arm movements, and he frequently loses his balance, use of these activities would be premature at this time. After they have been mastered, however, the child would then be ready for walking the balance board (or beam), a few inches off the floor, using first the broad side, then the edge.

One-legged standing balance can be suitably challenged by playing Hopscotch and Twister. These activities would usually be socially accepted games and can strengthen peer relationships.

The purpose of each of the remaining activities in P.P. 3.4 is to stimulate the proprioceptors, especially the joint receptors within the weight-bearing joints, and to challenge the body righting and equilibrium responses. Jumping rope is an activity which requires a high degree of postural and bilateral motor integration and can also help in establishing and enhancing body rhythm, which is often difficult for the learning-disordered child. In addition, for little girls jumping rope can provide a means of social interaction within a peer group.

Balance and Movement from an Unstable Base (3.5)

Initial activity on these items may be random and exploratory until motor organization is developed to the point where the child can exert good balance and control. These highly unstable pieces of equipment require greater stabilization throughout the body in order that the child may move his extremities individually and with adequate control. Consider the contrast in motor skill required on unstable, mobile equipment such as the rope ladder, which is constructed of a series of wooden rungs suspended at the sides by rope, compared to the skill required on the indoor climber. The child's movements on such an unstable base as the rope ladder or the single knotted climbing rope would have to be controlled in relation to the mobility which creates unpredictable shifts in his center of gravity.

Program Plan 4

Development of Elementary Concepts Through Sensory Sequence, Order, and Organization

The remaining Program Plans 4 through 8 are comprised exclusively of Phase II activities. The responsibility for grading the levels of difficulty among these tasks falls on the therapist. The critical factor in conducting therapy is to determine the increment of difficulty within which the child will be able to advance. Appropriately graded increments by which the child can organize better foundation skills makes for smooth transition along the steps of the learning continuum so the child can begin to reach his real potential.

There is good reason why the small transition steps within the early learning processes may be easily overlooked by both therapists and educators. The child who has no learning problem will readily organize and assimilate information and do so in such a rapid and automatic fashion that it is difficult for observers to recognize and study the minute gradations in this processing. On the other hand, the learning-disordered child, who lacks the internal organization which stems from good sensory integrative function, will be unable to do this unless the learning experience is structured in a more specific step-by-step process. The units which are presented here are in no way considered a complete coverage of the steps which may be involved. However incomplete these methods may still be, it is a sizable step in the right direction. Changes in clinical performance and in academic adjustment among learning-disordered children in this program indicate that with proper implementation, at least a reasonable degree of change can be expedited. More commonly, a good academic adjustment has been made among children of normal intellect who were able to overcome their specific learning dysfunction sufficiently to advance to grade standards among their peer group.

I wish to re-emphasize the value of these methods for educators. By studying the unique ways in which they have benefited learning-disordered children, the educator will gain new insights for their use as supplemental learning experiences. These would greatly enhance the overall learning process for children generally. These supplemental skills in particular would include developing better awareness of likenesses and differences of the OTA Triad in P.P. 1. Here in P.P. 4, attention is directed toward recognizing within a physically tangible "whole" its parts and the ordered sequence among them. This experience is a suitable forerunner of the visual whole-part relationships stressed in P.P. 5.1 and P.P. 5.6; furthermore, it furnishes the foundation of whole-part relationships of abstract material the child will need in preparing written academic material. Foundation skills in visual figure-ground patterns will also prepare the student to discern in the academic setting the relevant from the extraneous points to study.

It is the purpose of P.P. 4 to help the child make a more viable transition between concrete experiences with a clearly visible, physical sequential organization and those concepts of sequence and order which are intangible and abstract. It is, for example, through the constancy of the physical properties the child experiences with the nested toys that he begins to recognize the irreversibility of this order. Steps 4.1 through 4.4 advance from the physically graded size sequences and tangible feedback of the tactile sequence and assembly tasks — which suggest from an irregularity along its surface that the pieces are not assembled in the correct order — to the more abstract concepts of temporal sequence. This is a basic requirement for establishing a logical progression in problem solving at the concrete level in P.P. 4.3 and subsequently on a more abstract level at school.

While the ultimate goal would be to integrate the sensory systems, one with another at successively higher levels, our attention is directed in P.P. 4 to the need to organize the visual and the auditory systems individually. These are organized first in P.P. 4.5 and 4.6 in the handling of sequential information through each of these systems individually. Then the visual and the auditory symbols of language are correlated in P.P. 4.7 through 4.9, starting with early numerical and alphabetical sequencing in appropriately graded dot-to-dot designs.

Learning the sequential order of numbers is usually not a problem. Learning the sequential order of letters of the alphabet would not be a problem were it not for the frequent need academically to retrieve the isolated, sequential order to two or three letters for filing or use of the dictionary, for example. However inefficient, the age-old tendency is to return to the first letter of the alphabet to get started; this need not be necessary. Helping the child to establish a viable system for storage and easy retrieval of such information is one goal of this program plan; it applies to alphabetical sequencing and to establishing the early skill for the sequential order of letters in spelling, a problem which can greatly handicap the learning-disordered child.

Sequencing by Size (4.1)

The physical constancy of size among the nesting pieces yields to the child a concrete experience about the irreversibility of their order. The child discovers that no matter how hard or how often he tries to force the larger one into the smaller one, it cannot be done. Some children will recognize the sequence visually, others will recognize it only after physically attempting to fit them with much trial and error. Children who are even more disorganized will need prolonged, carefully graded exposure. Long before this action is intentional, the child will, by chance, slip a smaller one inside the larger one. As it does become purposeful, the child often will delight in his ability to exert some control over this portion of his environment, creating in him a curiosity to explore further aspects

19. Nesting open-end hexagonal cups in their proper sequence promotes early sequential organization through consistent, concrete experiences.

of his surroundings as well. Natural curiosity evolves from successful involvement. The learning-disordered child will continue to avoid involvement of his own volition until his efforts meet with some success. Tragically for the learning-disordered child, he will mature in age and be beyond the point where children normally play with these toys long before successful involvement for him is possible. The chance of his being exposed later to these same kinds of activity without help would be unlikely, and so the child still tends not to bridge the gap between the avoidance and the exploratory response.

During the initial therapy hour, the therapist should assess the child's performance in sequential organization through nesting activities. Observations would follow the protocol in the OEPS. The general procedure would follow along these lines or a variation suited to be more age appropriate.

Starting with open-end nesting items and without demonstrating or instructing the child how to proceed, three shallow, round units of the Ring-A-Round toy would be presented to a young child of three or four, or an older child who may still be very disorganized. These three units with the open ends facing up and properly nested would in some cases be alternating in size so as to provide a wider margin of contrast than would be the case with those of each neighboring size. The child's initial response is observed and recorded as it corresponds to the protocol. Some children will show their hesitation or confusion while others will disassemble and reassemble nested pieces in increasing numbers immediately or after a minimal period of trial and error.

The therapist is interested in not only the child's initial response, but also his

20. This set of open-end sequencing or nesting tasks illustrates the graded difficulty within circles, squares, etc.: 1) large buckets, 2) shallow circles, 3) deep circles, 4) baskets, 5) funnels, 6) beakers, 7) nested bowls or drums, 8) infant cubes and squares, or shallow squares, 9) deep squares, 10) indented squares, 11) hexagons.

application of that experience to other similar sets, for instance, the deep round or square units. A wide selection of every available nesting toy is recommended for clinical use to include the skill levels of the older child. If approached with sensitivity, even adolescents will appreciate the fact that the equipment used is simply a means to facilitate the processing of information and that there are no substitutes which are age appropriate.

In addition to offering this breadth of range to include older children's skills, a good therapy program must offer depth. This means that more than one toy must be available at nearly the same level so that the child's response develops not as a splinter skill but so that it is integrated in his experience and can be more broadly applied.

To foster optimum concentration and performance, the child is seated at a low table or adjustable ironing board which is recommended for its ample and stable working surface at a height which easily is adjusted to meet the child's needs. The therapist introduces the low nesting items which are easy for the child to see and later uses the higher stacking toys which may require visual and manual performance above eye level. Here the child must try to stabilize the head and neck, focus the eyes, while also using the shoulder movements and fine motor control in the hands.

When the child's initial performance suggests considerable confusion so that he is unable to grasp the concept of sequential organization, the therapist may, over the weeks which follow, find that a more directed procedure will be necessary to help him achieve the desired result. The child is asked to spread out each piece of the set of nesting or stacking toys on the surface of a cloth-covered, solid-colored cardboard panel measuring 15 inches x 25 inches, referred to as a panelboard. The pieces would all be turned up or turned down. The child is asked to look over the whole group to find the biggest one. Should the child have difficulty in dealing with the concept, then the therapist could liken them to pieces of candy; he would have little trouble searching for the biggest piece. The proper selection having been made, the therapist indicates to him to remove it from the panelboard and place it in front of him on the table. Again, he is asked to look back to see, "Now, which is the largest one left?" As soon as the child shows he has grasped the idea, verbal instructions are automatically curtailed. Occasionally the concept is reinforced by simply saying, "Yes, that is the biggest one left."

The child normally progresses from open-end nesting toys which have the largest increment of difference to those having the smallest, while at the same time increasing the number of units within the toy. When the concept of graded sizes in open-end nesting items is apparent, closed-end nesting is introduced, parallel with either of these stacking tasks which progress in difficulty according to less and less structure and feedback to the child.

Closed-end nesting presents a unique sequencing experience for the child. It puts greater demand on the child's memory to maintain the sequential organization than does open-end nesting. Once the reassembly process is started, the smaller pieces, being visually obscured, cannot provide visual feedback to confirm the continuity of order which the child could see in the open-end nesting items.

In the nesting eggs the child need only push the ends together, as compared to engaging the threads of the barrels, but each egg must be properly oriented from top to bottom for them to fit and may be more difficult for that reason. If, after ample opportunity to explore with trial and error it is obvious that the child cannot recognize that the top and bottom do differ, then simple, crystalline phrases such as "point to point" and "round end to round end" will convey the concept and prevent undue failure and frustration.

Study of this sequential organization yields a range of responses which can be plotted along the hierarchy. For instance, the Handy Boxes, which are like a set of nested plastic jars with matching lids, may be reassembled in two contrasting patterns. The less mature approach would be to carry over the experience from open-end nesting by nesting all the bottoms, capping them one after another later. The more mature approach would be to cap the smaller one each time before inserting it in the next size. Often within a matter of weeks the more mature response will, without any instruction, become evident, and the child will rarely be seen reverting to the more primitive patterns thereafter.

21. This set of closed-end sequencing tasks is graded by difficulty, three and five nested dolls, nested eggs, barrels, seven-unit nested family, sets of five handy boxes and tops, nested bowls, or drums.

22. The surface of the totem pole yields tactile feedback to indicate whether the child's choice of each block is in the correct sequence. This promotes tactile-visual integration and helps to improve tactile system organization.

Likewise, changes in maturation can be observed as the child assembles the inverted bowls. After much trial and error, a child may first nest a series of them open-end up, going back to cap each intervening space with the alternate unit which is turned upside down. The procedure which gradually develops over weeks or months is as follows. Holding the smallest piece in one hand, it is inserted into the next size, progressing up to the largest. However, the most mature pattern, which may be evident in children normally as young as six years, may not be developed in the learning-disordered child until much later and is rarely seen during the initial stages of therapy. This is the alternating pronation-supination movement of the forearms to assemble the units.

Tactile Sequence and Assembly (4.2)

Tactile assembly tasks are comprised of a series of pieces of wood or plastic mounted on a dowel and graded in size and contour to form familiar childhood objects, animals, or personages such as a clown or soldier. The value of tactile assembly tasks would be first to enhance the tactile discriminatory system, thereby diminishing the effects of the tactile survival system, and to establish by tangible means an awareness of a sequential order or arrangement of neighboring units.

Toys which can be suitably used to train tactile sequence and assembly are difficult to find; many on the domestic market are unsuited because the design cannot be assembled from the tactile feedback without also referring to the

168

picture. The objects used as the tactile sequencing tasks must be possible for a child to assemble without reference to the picture. Those toys identified as tactile sequence and assembly tasks in the OEPS have been selected and graded with these features in mind:

1. The activity should be attractive and appeal to the child's curiosity.
2. The activities have been analyzed so that upgrading will yield success.
3. The activity should be simple in design so that the correct sequence is evident and confirmed to him by feeling the contour. Its successful assembly should not depend on a picture.

As soon as it is apparent that the child has become aware of sequential organization in nesting activities, it is appropriate to introduce tactile sequence and assembly tasks. The intact object is placed on the cloth-covered panelboard by the therapist, who cups it in both hands and gently strokes the contour, saying to the child, "Feel it, feel how smooth it is." The child is encouraged to do this with each tactile assembly toy before dissassembling it. The pieces are laid out in full view on the panelboard once the child has demonstrated he has the concept and will not be too frustrated or meet with failure as the pieces are shuffled. In order that the therapist does not convey any feeling of deterring his chance to succeed in their reassembly, she asks if he would like to shuffle them himself. As the child begins to reassemble the toy, he is asked, after adding each new piece, to "feel" it, so as to determine if the juncture is smooth, hence correct, or if there is a "bump" to signal an error.

When toys are selected which yield immediate feedback, the child can, by his own internal sensory information, ascertain whether his performance is correct or incorrect. In this way he is developing the security and self-confidence he needs and is less dependent on the judgment or opinion of others. This is one of the early methods used to nurture and strengthen the ego.

23. This set of tactile sequence and assembly tasks is graded by difficulty: 1) Ring-A-Bell, 2) Pyramid Tree, 3) Cat, 4) Dog, 5) Totem Pole, 6) Giraffe, 7) Duck, 8) Teddy Baby, 9) Parrot, 10) Soldier, 11) Penguin.

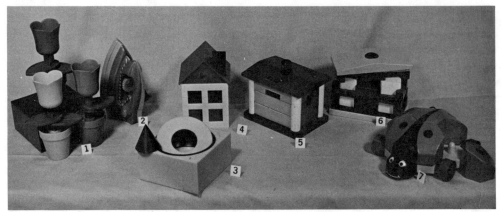

24. This set of problem-solving sequence and assembly tasks is graded by difficulty: 1) Fun Flowers, 2) Iron, 3) Magic Boxes, 4) Ambi House, 5) Build-A-House, 6) Swiss Chalet, 7) Take-Apart Lady Bug.

Problem-Solving Sequence and Assembly (4.3)

As soon as the child has mastered some of the Level I tasks in tactile sequence and assembly, then problem-solving sequence and assembly tasks, which start in Level II, are introduced. Problem-solving tasks are selected from current commercial toys insofar as possible; other foreign toys which have the desired attributes for this aspect of therapy are also used. The following description of the rationale for their selection and the characteristics which are considered in grading difficulty are included so that as new toys come on the market, the therapist will have a better concept of which ones could fulfill these therapeutic requirements.

Foremost would be the need for any toy in this category to be assembled with simple, manipulative efforts; additionally, the parts should be added in a self-indicative sequence. It should be possible in the problem-solving sequence and assembly, as it is with tactile sequence and assembly toys, for the toys to be reassembled by the child without reference to a plan or picture. If this feature is not true, the task will not tap the problem-solving process the child needs.

The early Level II activities are selected because they are elementary enough to facilitate a successful experience; this is possible because there is some latitude for correct responses, as in Fun Flowers. The Activity Engine involves some temporal sequencing on a concrete level; that is, the placement of some pieces must be fitted into place before others. The play iron and the telephone require more exact temporal sequencing, but at the same time, these provide some reinforcement through their tactile sequencing properties as well. In Level II of problem-solving assembly, the Magic Boxes and Ladybug are more difficult. They require some temporal sequencing, but there is little tactile feedback to confirm whether or not his solution is correct.

The House Building Set is a table toy which requires problem-solving through spatial relations skills and some temporal order or sequence in the placement of the corner posts and side pieces. In this 4- by 5-inch toy, the whole-part relationships can be seen within a small unit. The child is then given ample opportunity to apply this experience to the fullscale Self-Assembly Playhouse.

This can take place at various levels, depending on the age of the child. For example, the young child, after crawling into and upon the playhouse as part of his experience in "near the floor" gross motor skills in P.P. 3.2, can explore the possible rearrangement of the end pieces and sides as part of his Level II problem-solving assembly experience. He will discover as part of the problem that the openings of the ends and side pieces are not centered, requiring him to align them properly, or their offset positions will be too small to crawl through.

At Level III the child can be expected to disassemble and reassemble the Self-Assembly Playhouse; to do so draws upon his previous experience in spatial relations, motor planning and organization, temporal sequence, and whole-part relationships. Because of the size, the whole-part relationships are more difficult to perceive as compared with the table task which was similar. To upgrade the task still further in Level III, the Self-Assembly Playhouse may be presented in its completely packaged state at some point after the child has not played with it for several weeks or longer. Here the challenge for problem-solving is greater, and it also draws somewhat upon his memory of prior experience.

To upgrade the task suitably for a teenager, he can be asked to assemble it for use by the younger children, without having ever seen it in its assembled state or

25. This problem-solving sequence and assembly task provides concrete organizational sequencing experience.

at least not having been involved in its use. Its simplistic construction "speaks to the process" so that without drawings or any instructions, he should be able to organize and sequence the steps toward a solution.

Time and Temporal Sequence (4.4)

A child who has a learning disorder often experiences more difficulty than other children in learning the meaning of the abstract concept of before and after, yesterday, today, and tomorrow. Comprehending the sequence and meaning of the relationship of the days of the week, months of the year, or the preceding or succeeding relationship of significant holidays or events may also present subtle problems.

There may be difficulty in learning to grasp the concept of how to tell time. The actual method of helping the child to cope with such a problem rightly follows the introduction of the Positional Model in P.P. 7.2 and is described in P.P. 7.5.

Another indication of problems with time is seen among some children who fail to develop an inner sense of measurable units of time, such as "five minutes," or the ability to estimate the ongoing passage of time, all of which can present problems in excess of those which children normally encounter. The inability of the learning-disordered child to mature in this dimension at the rate of his peers can become a point of friction between parent and child. For instance, he may seem to habitually overextend the time limits since he may sense little difference between five minutes and half an hour.

Poor temporal awareness, sequencing, and organization can create significant problems in academic adjustment. These children often seem to be "out of phase" with what is transpiring from moment to moment; they easily become bewildered and should not have to face the confusion of the "open" classroom. To the older child, poor temporal organization will present problems when taking written examinations, since they tend to spend an inordinate amount of time on the first or second essay questions out of four or five. If the child's class performance far exceeds his examination responses, the question should be raised with regard to his temporal awareness as well as the other component skills which signify learning problems. Also, close attention should be paid to his reading and writing skills and his ability to organize factual and abstract information.

Early Visual Sequence (4.5)

In Level I of this program plan, a very elementary procedure may be introduced quite early as a means of observing the child's performance in following a left-right progression. Without a word of instruction, the therapist arranges in a left-right progression a series of four or five color cubes over a pattern which ideally is placed beneath the plastic grid used principally in P.P. 5.2. Otherwise color cubes are arranged over an open design of colored blocks arranged in a straight line.

The purpose of this is to observe to what extent the child has already developed interhemispheral integration. The child who has integrated the two hemispheres adequately for this prereading skill will imitate the pattern demonstrated or initiate it automatically, having already assimilated this skill. If the child has not arrived at the point where he can imitate the left-right progression, no instruction should be given to correct the problem at this time. Instead, this is used as a yardstick to measure the extent of disorganization which persists. Such periodic observations will signal the time when the pattern is established, so the therapist can continue in Level I of Visual Sequencing. Often this point arises after two or three months of therapy which involve activities of P.P. 2. These early residuals of the directionality problem should be disappearing by the time P.P. 6.5, in which hand dominance is established, and P.P. 7.2 and 7.3, the Positional Model and its application to direction, have been mastered.

If the child is old enough to succeed with horizontal visual sequencing, after the left-right pattern has emerged it is developed through a timed procedure in which the therapist, sitting to the side of the child, arranges a series of four to six 1-inch color blocks in a row. The first few times, the child may observe the therapist as she prepares the blocks in a left-right progression, but subsequently he is to not look at them as long as they are in front of him, a matter of five seconds, at which time the therapist shuffles these together with several more and asks the child to reproduce the pattern. No time limit is set for reassembling the pattern, but for optimum recall, it should be started without interruption or delay. A general left-right orientation is usually evident as the child replaces them. What is stressed here is the ability to retrieve the visual sequence of the pattern. If the child fails, the pattern can be repeated immediately so that he can recognize how to remember it better. By the time the child is ready for this, it is not usually necessary to verbally instruct by identifying the left-right progression. Success is our guide in pacing the child's advancement from four to six blocks in a pattern.

In this same manner a series of three to six pictures are arranged in a left-right progression on a wooden tray such as the one used in a scrabble game, so that the slant can then offer the child better visibility of them. These pictures are obtained from simple single-unit puzzle pieces which illustrate objects familiar to a young child. The therapist draws from lists of objects to avoid any chance of her being confused later about the correct order. Visual memory through visual sequencing is advanced from the recollection and recall of color cube patterns, pictures of objects, and later through the letter order of spelling words in P.P. 4.9.

The academic application of visual sequencing is recognized for its direct benefit to reinforce the left-right progression in early reading and writing patterns, especially for left-handed children who find writing more difficult because it is unnatural for them to write toward the midline. Through a tangible experience such as this, children can more easily establish and retain the proper sequence of the position of letters which are easily transposed, eg, board and broad. It helps the child establish the initial awareness that visual information should be available to him for easy recollection and recall and provides him a means of practicing how to systematically organize such data. Furthermore, it can provide a more tangible structure for the child to depict the sequential order of events or logical progression of an idea, which is helpful in reducing expressive language dysfunction.

Auditory Sequence (4.6)

All of the activities which relate to organizing auditory information, aside from discussion of and defensiveness in the OTA Triad, are grouped under one heading, but each of the three levels, emphasizing a different process, is located in a separate area. Reviewing this for a moment, one recalls that Auditory Localization, representing Level I, is found in P.P. 1.6, and Auditory Discrimination, a Level II skill, is located in P.P. 1.9. It is because of the emphasis on sequential organization throughout P.P. 4 that Auditory Sequencing, at Level III of the overall unit in the OEPS entitled Auditory Localization, Discrimination, and Sequencing, is found here.

It is easier to repeat the sequential order of numbers from memory than to remember the names of objects in a series. Both are used in this program, but only a brief emphasis is placed on sequencing of numbers. For the most effective results in auditory sequencing of words, a method is presented here which first helps the child to correlate the names of familiar objects by auditory stimulus with the visual imagery of them. Once this is firmly established, the child can go on to tap the auditory sequencing at a higher level and to remember words other than nouns, which are more difficult.

During the procedure, the therapist first informs the child that the list of words, numbers, or letters will be said in order slowly and distinctly and will then be repeated the second time; this will no longer be necessary as the child's skill improves. While he is listening, he may close his eyes so as to direct his full attention to the auditory information. The therapist can suggest an alternative method for concentrating by having the child gaze at a blank wall trying to "visually pin" the pictures, for example, in a row, as in the visual sequencing process.

When the child is having trouble with multisyllable words, the therapist helps him become aware of the rhythm and tonal quality of the word on the list he cannot recall. For example, she does this by again reading the list of words with the same intonation she has used for each word, but when she comes to the missing word, the voice intonation of the syllables are made with pursed lips to form the "mm" sound. The child says the words with the therapist, trying to recall the missing one through association with this auditory rhythm and pattern. He is at the same time encouraged to visualize the image he has "pinned" on the blank wall in a further effort to help him reinforce the auditory with the visual input.

The academic application of auditory sequencing is to develop in as tangible a way as possible a foundation for recollection and recall, using visual reinforcement techniques when necessary. As in visual sequencing, this method helps the child to become aware that auditory information can and should be stored for later retrieval and provides him with a means of systematically organizing such information. The awareness of this sequential order should make it easier to recognize the order of facts and events so as to grasp lecture content. By correlating the visual and auditory input through the sequencing experience of P.P. 4.5 and 4.6, this should significantly reinforce the child's comprehension capabilities.

Dot-to-Dot Alphabetical Sequence (4.7)

The cardinal numbers are often learned by the child in an automatic, rote fashion, spieled off with easy abandon by quite young children. This happens long before the child can identify the quantitative concept other than to know they are "this may fingers old." In many commercial toys the child may match cardinal numbers to the equivalent dots or objects which the child can count with a pointed finger. As soon as he can move his fingers in accord with each number one on one, he will be able to recognize that the visual symbols represent the numerical quantity. The ordered sequence of numbers in dot-to-dot drawings should ideally be large, uncluttered, and for this purpose, go no further than 10 in some drawings, 20 in others.

The numerical sequence of ordinal numbers — first, second, and third — comes at a more advanced level of comprehension. The child learns what it means for him "to be first," but beyond that these abstract terms may have little real meaning and in fact may be confusing to him. Their use is not stressed here.

Like the numbers, alphabetical sequencing is often recited in a meaningless, rote fashion long before the child can associate the letters with the visual symbol, aside from early recognition of the first few letters. The unfortunate travesty on the child in perpetuating the nursery school chant is that the letters of the alphabet lose their individual identity and "klmnop" are jammed together as one letter. Unless there is auditory and visual identification of individual letters, their sequence will be hazy at best.

A series of specially designed and suitably graded alphabetical dot-to-dot drawings has been designed for the special purpose of developing in the child a sound awareness of the sequential order of the letters of the alphabet. Circular patterns moving counter-clockwise are designed to be consistent with the direction used to print the *C, G, O, Q, S,* and *U.* This also helps to counteract the more primitive response in which the child starts to make a circle, for example, from the bottom, moving in a clockwise direction. In designing these special dot-to-dot drawings, the need for subjects suitable for older boys in particular has been kept in mind in order to provide them the needed experience also, but with less chance of their being offended by the more customary juvenile drawings. Subjects which are included especially for them include a man's face, a typewriter, a football player, and a lunar module.

During the procedure the therapist, sitting opposite the child at a low table or ironing board, presents an age-appropriate dot-to-dot drawing. These drawings are comprised initially of only the first ten letters, then all of the capitals or all the lower case. Then, at the other end of the spectrum, exercises which include each set within the same drawing, eg, the football player, are included to test the ability of the child to maintain the constancy of each alphabet and not be confused. These exercise pages are covered with a transparent page protector, and a china marking which can be easily rubbed off is used to trace the lines.

In starting the young child, the therapist may hold the pencil and draw the lines so that the child's attention can be directed to the primary aspect of the task, ie, recognition and proper sequencing of letters of the alphabet. The therapist says to the child, "Find the first letter"; then, "After *A* comes____"; "Can you find it?" In the beginning the therapist provides the structure by repeating this last phrase for the child each time. The purpose of doing so is to establish in his mind the correct auditory sequence for automatic auditory recollection and recall, since throughout his schooling he will often have need to use the alphabetical

26. The circular pattern of letters which form the bicycle wheels give subtle suggestions about the sequential order of letters of the alphabet; success and correct auditory feedback should be established prior to a greater challenge where the drawing does not suggest the next letter.

filing system. As the child can assume the additional function of saying the phrase with the therapist and then independently, he derives the auditory-verbal reinforcement of the visual symbol as well as the auditory recall of the letter sequence.

As soon as the child has the concept and is able to control the pencil he connects the dots while the therapist continues to provide some structure by saying, "After_____ comes_____." When the child can assume this function and also maintain the proper sequence, he can be reasonably independent in the task.

In the beginning, however, many children will want to rush from dot-to-dot, in part because they do not yet have the individual identity and the sequential order mastered and are relying on the cadence of the song. In this way they will not have to stop and recall by the individual letter which one follows. At that point the therapist adroitly moves in to prevent the child from proceeding with this haphazard performance. She does this by placing her finger immediately beside the dot which has just been identified and connected by a line from the previous dot. With her finger she prevents the child from moving the pencil ahead until he can try to say, "After_____comes_____."

Visual Tracking of the Alphabet (4.8)

This Level I task touches more closely on academic preparedness than any yet described. It is one of the essential prereading steps which incorporates the child's visual recognition of letter forms, visual tracking along a line, and disregard for distracting stimuli, a figure-ground factor. Prerequisites which

176

27. Early recognition of a single letter throughout the page in Exercises #1 through #7 fosters good visual tracking along a line and is presented as a preliminary step to visual tracking of the complete alphabet in the next illustration.

have helped to prepare the child to do this successfully include:
1) visual fixation and pursuits of P.P. 2.7;
2) early recognition of simple object forms in P.P. 5.1;
3) early single letter identification in the dot-to-dot drawings of P.P. 4.7;
4) the visual figure-ground emphasis on P.P. 5.3 and 5.4.

Over the past decade of observing children with learning disorders, I have found it necessary to analyze the alphabet from a number of viewpoints for the purpose of reading and writing. Here is the analysis of capital letters according to the principal characteristics in form which they share. According to this study, visual form recognition and visual tracking of capitals should be introduced prior to lower case letters because these letters present fewer problems in left-right and top-bottom orientation, the rare exceptions being *J* and *L,* and *M* and *W* respectively. Capital letters are divided into these three groups:

	principal characteristics
C G O Q S U	circular or curved lines
B D E F H I J K L P R T	vertical lines
A K M N V W X Y Z	oblique lines

Using a china marking pencil to mark on the vinyl page protector for the exercise, the child selects a stimulus letter from the group at the top of the page and circles it. He then proceeds in his "letter hunt" to locate as many like this as

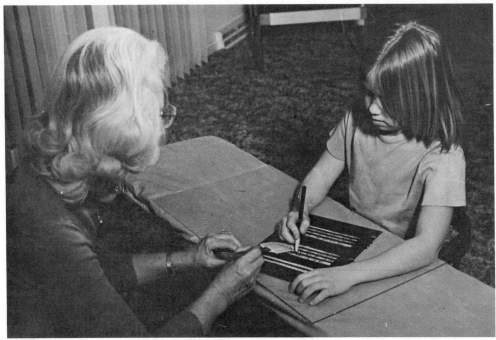

28. The child is assisted during early visual tracking of the alphabet by the therapist holding a spatula until the child says the response correctly for the next letter, ie, "after *f* comes *g*."

he can in the lines below and then marking these with a short downward slash. These lines are comprised entirely of letters from this same group, thus requiring the child to maintain the "form constancy" of the stimulus letter from distracters which differ only slightly. Throughout the Visual Tracking Exercises 1 through 7, space between the letters and between the lines is gradually decreased so that the surrounding letters become increasingly strong competitors for the child's attention; three distinct gradations of difficulty are presented. This provides the young child or the more severely involved child who is older an opportunity to successfully develop this function through the clear and widely spaced letters to build directly on this skill in a consistently graded, appropriate manner. The reading pattern is thus established in a step-by-step progression; the left-right tracking movement can be developed without also requiring the child to attend to the content of reading material.

In the beginning of these exercises, the left-right pattern of progression may not yet be fully established; the child who is disorganized in this way and one who is possibly impulsive and hyperactive can be helped to greatly improve his performance by the following method. The therapist, sitting opposite the child, holds a rubber spatula on which is drawn an arrow to direct the child to focus his visual attention as it is moved slowly along the line ahead of his gaze. This prevents the child from responding with a common form of disorganized response in which his eyes will dart all over the page in a random fashion to find the stimulus letter. The use of the spatula to guide and restrain his actions is discontinued as soon as the child can exercise sufficient internal control and organization to perform the task.

As long as the child fails to establish adequate left-right visual progression along a line of print and continues to be drawn to stimuli throughout the page because of the visual figure-ground distractibility, it can be expected that he will encounter severe reading problems later. How can one then expect the child to concentrate on comprehension of the content of his reading material when he has not yet conquered these and underlying foundation skills for the task? When these residuals are still evident in a child eight years or older, remediation efforts should first be aimed toward correcting the most basic elements of dysfunction, cited here, rather than starting too far along the continuum, to correct the reading problem through material which at the same time requires the child to comprehend the content.

Upon completion of Exercises 1 through 3 using capital letters, Exercises 4 through 7, involving lower case letters, are then introduced for a similar "letter hunt." If problems in reversals appear, this signals that the foundation skills have not been fully mastered. These skills include:

1) P.P. 7.3, Application of the Positional Model to early directionality;
2) P.P. 7.4, Application of the Positional Model to body image;
3) P.P. 8.8, Directional Orientation to number and letter forms to emphasize specifically the frequently reversed letters — *b* and *d* or *p* and *q*.

The lower case letters of the alphabet have been analyzed for similarity of form and grouped by their principal characteristics. These are marked in the same manner described for tracking of the capital letters.

		principal characteristics
Exercise 4	a c e o s	Similarities of form are close and may be initially confused.
Exercise 5	i j l t	Same as above.
Exercise 6	b d f g h k p q y	Similarity of form in letters *g q y* and *f h k;* reversible letters *b-d, p-q.*
Exercise 7	m n r u v w x z	Similarity of form in letters *v x z;* top-bottom directional orientation required for differentiating *m* from *w* and *n* from *u.*

On Levels II and III, visual tracking of the alphabet along a line is used to reinforce the left-right progression, the sequential order of letters and to correlate the visual and the auditory-verbal symbols. These tools are necessary in the development of early reading patterns and subsequently the ability to scan a line or page. If visual tracking is done without the underlying foundations which enable a child to do it with relative ease, the child may develop a splinter skill.

The learning-disordered child needs to master those foundation skills individually which many other children quickly assimilate in the classroom, skills which could be helpful to anyone. To focus on skills individually, the requirements of some elements within the skill are kept to a minimum for the learning-disordered child, or the task is structured in such a way that the child can direct his full attention to whichever performance is paramount at this time. The method by which these individual requirements have been identified and developed one at a time is described here. Performance Levels II and III in visual tracking require a culmination and an integration of those skills which had been stressed and mastered previously.

Having already mastered horizontal visual tracking along a line in which key letters were located, the child is now ready to couple this skill with the alphabetical sequencing established through dot-to-dot drawings. He is ready to identify the sequential order of letters in the alphabet which are embedded among distracters. Initially this is introduced by use of Visual Tracking Exercises 8 and 9. The importance of these exercises is that the stimulus letter comes at a fairly predictable interval, spanning no more than five intervening distracting letters. Soon the child can sense a growing confidence in the rhythmic pattern by which he can identify the mark letters a through z.

Across the top of each page is the complete alphabet in small letters, available for the child to refer to should he need it. A few children may temporarily need the structure of windows cut from a black background page to expose two separate exercises. The spatula may be used at first to guide the child, but this is discontinued as soon as it is evident from the child's performance that he can function adequately without it. In a manner similar to the dot-to-dot drawings, the therapist moves the spatula slowly along the line until the child sees the proper stimulus, marks it with a downward slash, and then says, "After_____ comes_____."

As soon as the child demonstrates he can maintain the sequence adequately in these transition steps in Exercises 8 and 9, he is ready for his skill to be upgraded to *The Ann Arbor Tracking Program.** This workbook is divided into five sections. The first two are used the most; the other three are used for children of 10 years old and into adulthood.

The emphasis now is for the child to maintain stability of alphabetical sequencing amid stronger distractions and the added difficulty of irregular, prolonged spacing between stimuli. As many as 20 to 25 intervening letters may be found. No mention is made to the child about developing speed until he has a consistent, rhythmic response. Then, to keep stress at a minimum, the therapist may "offer an invitation to him" indicating that whenever he feels he is ready, he can be timed. As the child's self-confidence and skill increase, he will frequently ask to be timed. He can now establish a baseline of performance for himself which is meaningful to him, and he can compete with himself to challenge his previous records. Valid feedback such as this reinforces his self-esteem. He is able to

---

Ann Arbor Tracking Program, Letter Tracking. Ann Arbor Pub. Inc, P.O. Box 7249, Naples, Florida 33940.

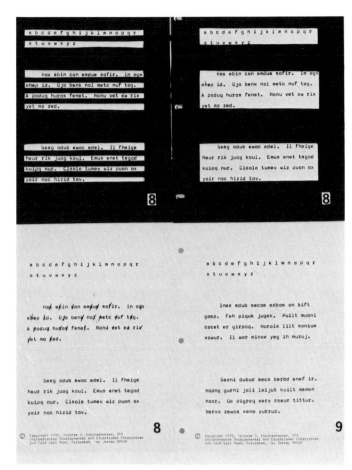

28A. In Exercises #8 and #9, the black sections between each line help the child to stabilize his eye movements along the line while incorporating other foundation skills (or subskills), ie, visual form of letters, alphabetical sequencing and the auditory-verbal component, "after f comes g." As the child can develop his internal organization and master these skills also, the external structure of black framing is reduced, but the intervals between key letters of the alphabetical sequence remains constant. When he can cope with the increasing demands, The Michigan Tracking Book is introduced. This progression illustrates the treatment principle of "half-step progression."

stabilize his function gradually and maintain it under the added stress of being timed.

Over a period of time in which the child upgrades his skill, other fallout benefits from this technique have often been observed. It is felt that there is a significant carryover from this kind of experience which helps to decondition the anxieties produced by other timed and stressful situations. Not only is the speed at which he may read improved, but there is also a substantial reduction in failure experiences which were previously associated with taking examinations. These oft-repeated and timed experiences in visual tracking — over brief periods of one or two minutes — can also serve to develop better temporal awareness and the inner sense of the ongoing passage of time. Unless the child is helped to become cognizant of these factors of timing and their associated problems mentioned under P.P. 4.4, those obscure aspects which tend to exacerbate a difficult situation will only be prolonged.

In Section I of the *Ann Arbor Tracking Program,* timing will range initially for more than two minutes per paragraph. After a period of four to six weeks' practice, the child's timing will often average below one minute. In Section II, timing for most paragraphs will first range between one and one-half and two minutes since the letters are smaller and more difficult to locate amid stronger distracters.

Children 8 years of age and younger who have significant learning disorders would usually not proceed further than Section I and/or the beginning pages of Section II within a therapy program, but at a later time they could proceed further, as would any other child.

In Performance Level III, stress is placed on both accuracy and speed. Children of 10 years of age can feasibly proceed into Section III in a therapy setting or even complete it, but beyond that the skill level required would be more appropriate as a challenge to the adolescent or adult. Individuals at the high school level or above can challenge their scores in Sections IV and V, sometimes as a part of therapy, but usually that level of expertise would follow their course of therapy.

Visual Sequence (4.9)

Following the development of early visual sequencing by color block patterns in Level I (P.P. 4.4), the child will be ready to undertake this unit at Level II. Visual sequence of the letter order in words is an important foundation skill in both spelling and reading. Its relevance in developing more automatic spelling patterns will be discussed first.

Whereas reading depends on the rapid processing of the whole visual image, spelling is more dependent on reaching the more automatic level of function for sequencing the letter order within words. Those who have a better avenue of learning through the auditory system can memorize the sound of the letter order, while others must depend to a larger extent on developing visual skill. Ideally the visual and auditory symbols can be used to reinforce one with another. First it is suggested that the child's attention be focused directly on the visual sequence of the letter form of the word to be spelled. Letters are arranged in front of the child in a tray as in P.P. 4.5. Their sequence spells a short word familiar to the child. After a few seconds of exposure, the letters are first scrambled without any additional distractions, and the child tries to reassemble them in the same sequence to spell the word. When the child's full attention can be focused on the visual and the supplementary auditory feedback by sounding out the letters, the process can become more and more automatic for the child. Then, when he writes the word, he can devote his attention to the motor sequencing of movements to make each letter without losing the correct order of the letters. When a child is having problems in spelling, it is strongly suspected that he may be struggling with mastery of the two or more skills at the same time. It will, therefore, be helpful to break down the task into the component parts identified here for mastery of one at a time.

In his reading, the speed and accuracy with which the child has mastered his recognition of the visual image of individual letters in the visual tracking can now be applied to the rapid processing of the total word image. Before he learns to recognize the word by its whole image or configuration, he recognizes it by the sequence of the individual letters which comprise the word. To do this at a pace which would be required, one must quickly recognize the likenesses and differences which may be subtle and confusing initially. This is especially true when more than one word can be composed of the same letters. The word must be quickly identified by the sequential arrangement of the letters, eg, *sign* for *sing*.

Common reversal problems of one-syllable words, such as *no* and *on* or *was* for *saw* are in actuality a matter of left-right sequencing which normally develops out of bilateral integration of the two hemispheres. Failure to develop adequate left-right sequencing, and the presence of some visual figure-ground distractibility, will cause a variety of problems such as these. Transposition of letters which appear at the beginning or end of the word often occurs because their position makes them more obvious and they attract the child's attention first. A letter which is more prominent because it protrudes above or below the line will pre-empt others for attention, moving it to a forward position, ie, *could* becomes *cloud*. Letters having similar shapes within a word can be visualized out of sequence. By reversing the medial letters, *carve* may easily become *crave*. Words composed of nearly the same letter forms, such as *these* and *those* can be missed when one letter form is replaced by another which is similar.

It is of little wonder that reading comprehension suffers if transpositions or replacement of similar letters either alter the meaning dramatically or simply cause it to "make no sense at all." Reading under these conditions will spark little interest or pleasure and may cause the child to avoid it because it generates in him added confusion and disorganization.

The tendency to read words incorrectly can be greatly reduced when skill is developed in horizontal sequencing of letter forms at Level II. The child develops the ability to recognize visual form in a rapid left-right progression and can process this kind of singular visual image with increasing ability. To strengthen the child's ability to recognize the minute differences within a whole image, Same or Different Design Cards, P-212, DLM are used in Level II, followed by Same or Different Word Cards, P-211, DLM at Level III. The worksheets of Seeing Likenesses and Differences, Level 3, Continental Press are used for the more advanced level of skill of older children and adults; they require the individual to match a stimulus word amid three or more distractions. These worksheets are used in this program also as a means of enabling adolescents and adults to learn to analyze the way in which the words actually differ and to formulate this into a meaningful statement which has application to more than one set of words. In particular, this method has been helpful to adults who have residuals of an expressive language disorder. Examples, drawn from word pairs on pages 20 to 23 of Seeing Likenesses and Differences, Level 3, demonstrate below how statements have been formulated to depict the difference between the first and second words.

night — might:	The first letter is replaced.
spent — spend:	The last letter is replaced.
defend — depend:	The third letter is replaced.
thorough — through:	The third letter is omitted.
other — another:	Two letters are added at the beginning.
cold — clod:	The letters in the second and third positions are reversed.
slave — salve:	The letters in the second and third positions are reversed.

bowls — blows:	The letter in the fourth position is moved to the second position.
except — expect:	The third and fifth letters are reversed.
wired — weird:	A letter is added in the second position.
bread — beard:	The second letter is moved to the fourth position.
haste — hates:	The letter in the third position is moved to the end.

Throughout this program plan, efforts have been made to instill an awareness and a functional application of early concepts such as ordered sequence and orderly arrangement of objects, of steps in early problem-solving, and the awareness of a sequential order of events. The early concept of the sequential ordering of numbers is included primarily to identify its position in the hierarchial scheme. Greater emphasis is placed on the sequential relationship of individual letters within the alphabet and to create a more stable concept of the constancy with which the left-right progression and letter order must be maintained so that reversals in reading, writing, and spelling do not occur.

Program Plan 5

Visual Form, Spatial Relations, and Visual Figure-Ground

As the Integrated Program Matrix indicates, P.P. 5 may be initiated at the outset of therapy, moving along the continuum in accord with the child's successful performance. In this program plan the child is helped to sense a structure about the experiences to which he is exposed as a means of identifying color and simple forms, so that he is helped along the learning continuum from an avoidance response to involve himself, ie, explore these aspects of his environment. Through the methods advocated here and the gradations which allow him to find success, he can begin to organize and integrate these experiences. Gradually he will start to build simple concepts, ie, realizing that the circle, square, and other basic forms which he recognizes can also be found among objects around him, such as the round clock face and square window.

The therapist should note in the OEPS under Visual Form Perception suggested toys and games for proper grading; sources of their manufacturers are listed in Appendix H. These are cited as examples of the level of difficulty which is being tapped so that the therapist can apply this grading to new products as they come on the market.

Color Recognition, Matching, and Sorting (5.1)

One of the earliest means of helping a child to become aware of how he can organize his environment through a purposeful visual-motor response would be in recognizing the differences in color, matching them in pairs, and then sorting them into groups. In therapy, early visual recognition of color and form should parallel the child's other experiences with gross texture contrasts and the likenesses and differences in manual form of common objects such as pine cone, fur, or sandpaper. This initial level of awareness and organization of sensory information must not be overlooked, especially in the young retardate. The child of two or three or the severe retardate who may be considerably older can soon grasp the concept of sorting and matching two or three colors of vivid contrast; for this use, poker chips have proven very appropriate.

To convey to the child a concept of likenesses and differences clearly and effectively, a box 5 inches x9 inches $x2\frac{1}{2}$ inches of $\frac{1}{4}$ inch transparent plastic is used. This box has three compartments and a removable transparent lid with a narrow slot over each compartment so that the child can sort objects by color, eg, poker chips; therefore, the likelihood of becoming confused over taking them out and mixing them is eliminated. This structure provides a learning experience in which the goal is not only simple, but more importantly, it cannot be reversed by the child or confused before the concept is established.

Once the child can maintain goal direction in this way, the lid is removed and the color chips are sorted into the three open compartments. Cupcake tins provide suitable sorting compartments for small objects.

Visual Form (5.2)

Throughout years of observing children under clinical conditions, I have made a concerted effort to analyze how childhood games and toys utilize various components of visual form perception, components which children normally assimilate through play. Since the learning-disordered child often does not engage in these play activities, he would be apt to have poorer foundations of this kind on which to build the early academic requirements. The components which have become evident to me and are included in Level I of Visual Form Perception are as follows:

a) Early pegboard placement,
b) Inserting whole form into a space,
c) Visual matching of simple whole object or form,
d) Matching and sorting form from bold to subtle likenesses and differences,
e) Whole-part relationships,
f) Matching forms by associations or to convey a concept.

Early Pegboard Placement

Young, hyperactive, distractible children may be so grossly disorganized in their behavior and their performance with early visuo-motor tasks and lacking in early language comprehension to such an extent that they tend to respond to even the simplest task in a random, haphazard, disorganized fashion. To convey to them the simple concept of "putting an object into a space," the Hide-A-Peg Set has been designed for this purpose. As the child masters this elementary concept, he can link the meaning of the words with his movement. (If this very early level of activity is necessary, then it would precede even P.P. 5.1).

The Hide-A-Peg Set is designed so that the therapist can follow one of the early treatment principles, "more structure and less instruction." Sixteen round pegs, 1 inch in diameter, 1½ inch high, sink halfway below the surface of the Hide-A-Peg Set. When all the pegs have been removed, the moveable hinged wooden platform of this pegboard is repositioned by the adult so that as the child now replaces each peg, it sinks below the platform. Since the child is unable to grasp them when the platform is in this raised position, he cannot reverse the process part way through, but must continue. The young learning-disordered child tends to have a very short attention span. Later in school the same child will have prolonged problems in task completion. The Hide-A-Peg Set is offered as the initial

186

step to prolong the child's attention span and see a purposeful task through to completion.

It is natural for even infants to grasp and remove objects; it requires visual attention, as well as intent and purpose, however, to place them. In this early task, the object is to focus the child's attention toward the terminal point of action. This identifies for him a recognizable goal, so he can begin to direct his actions toward that goal in a more purposeful manner. As a means of directing the child's limited attention, he is asked to drop the pegs into a container which is designed with several attributes in mind.

This container is a 6 inch transparent plastic cube which has an opening 3 inches in diameter at the top. This is large enough for one hand to reach in. The size of the opening is somewhat of a deterrent to his inadvertently trying to switch goals, and retrieving some of them from this cube-like box before all the pegs had been removed. When they are dropped into an open pan, however, this reversal of goals does occur. Early hand preference can also be observed since only one hand at a time can be used to remove the pegs from this container.

As the child drops the pegs into the opening, the therapist uses the word "in" or "put it in" to coincide with the child's action and the sound as each peg hits the bottom. This is done to develop in the young child an early awareness of the meaning of words, as long as this level of language is needed. To keep confusion of language comprehension to a minimum, the words "take out" are avoided. The child is simply asked to "put the pegs back," using the word "in" as seems appropriate.

As the last peg is replaced, the therapist moves the platform down into its original position; the sudden "return" of these pegs seems to the young child like "magic." Such a surprise rewards him for his sustained effort, a first step toward development of concentration and attention span.

This procedure is described in detail so that one does not overlook the fact that, even in the simplest tasks, there must be no chance of adding confusion, as could be the case if "take out" and "put in" were both used within this very brief span of time and space. One cannot assume that a child will make the transition between steps. For instance, in the therapy situation, if the simple form boards to follow were presented to a child and there was clear evidence of goal reversal, ie, replacing some before all had been removed, then correction of the problem should not rest on verbal instruction. Preferably the task would be put aside until at some future therapy session the prerequisite skills of maintaining the goal without reversing the pattern had been established with the Hide-A-Peg Set while the platform was left down and he could have free access to the pegs.

Inserting Whole Form into a Space

Inserting a form into its matching space is still a highly structured task. It provides the essential starting point in the development of visual form and secondary to that, the application of spatial orientation. Form insertion tasks provide immediate, nonverbal feedback from the visual and tactile systems to inform the child whether or not his performance is correct. The child must first recognize the relationship between the positive, solid form and the matching negative outline of single, isolated units. In fitting an isolated form, the child must align the spatial orientation of this contour, which involves the rotational factor; that is, the child must turn it around a central axis until the positive and negative contours fit together. For some children who are severely involved, this can be quite a difficult task. For this reason, toys have been selected and graded to enable the child to bridge this gap to involve himself at the level where success with single unit forms in Level I is probable.

Visual Matching of Simple Whole Object or Form

Following successful completion of single unit form boards, a less structured task can be undertaken. Visual matching of simple whole objects or form on single cards matched to master cards of six or more pictures from a lotto game would be introduced. This can be upgraded by presenting more than one master card, possibly three or four on the desk before the child. The task is graded so as to require the child to depend increasingly on his own visual validation.

Matching and Sorting Form from Bold to Subtle Likenesses and Differences

Advancing slightly, the tasks here involve matching and sorting of visual form by likenesses and differences which are graded from the more easily recognizable pictures and bold silhouetted form initially to those with more subtle elements of difference. The gradations at the far end of this component require a more advanced skill than do the early tasks of the following components which involve initial whole-part relationships of visual form.

29. This is the third of six sets of cards graded for visual discrimination of likeness and differences. They subtly tap the child's awareness of top-bottom and left-right orientation. (Note the girl with the umbrella.) Errors are not pointed out, but left for the child to recognize at the time or correct spontaneously the next therapy hour. This method promotes a left-right placement pattern.

Whole-Part Relationships

The first element of whole-part relationships to be mastered would be to match halves, first top-bottom, then left-right halves. Combining three or four sections of a whole animal, person, or object would be stressed next.

Matching Forms by Association or to Convey a Concept

Studying missing parts of, for example, a face, which would be recognizable by its association with the surrounding features, is an illustration of this component of visual form perception. Classification of the Animal, Bird, Fish Game helps the child begin to understand the broad concepts by which they are discriminated; other games deal with the concept of opposites, as it relates to the elementary physical properties of familiar objects or situations.

Elementary Spatial Relations (5.3)

Out of the child's body image he develops an awareness of his own position in space with regard to objects of his environment; gradually he begins to determine the relative positions of one object in relation to another or "spatial relations." In Phase I the gross motor activities are used with words of direction and movement to introduce a very elemental awareness of spatial relations. In Phase II the Grid and Peg Set is the most elementary application of spatial relations at the desk, requiring the child to place blocks one in relation to another within a structured grid.[1]

The structure of this task provides the external organization which is necessary to assure early success. This structure provides enough security to enable even the poorly coordinated child to be independent; the task is designed to permit a child to focus his attention on the spatial requirements. Even the very disorganized child with short attention span can feel a sense of successful achievement and task completion when adequate organization or structure of the task makes this possible. In short, the Grid and Peg Set "speak to the child's need" at the level where he can succeed.

The Grid and Peg Set is comprised of a 6 inch x 7½ inch transparent plastic grid, ½ inch and 1 inch pegs to insert into this so as to reproduce the colored block pattern beneath. Pegs are matched by color and by shape, starting with squares, adding round pegs and then triangles within the patterns. The "overlay" method is used throughout this program plan to enable the child to reproduce the patterns of familiar objects in a child's environment.

Here the child is required to integrate several previously acquired skills at a most elementary level: 1) color and 2) form recognition, and 3) spatial relations. If any difficulty is found in any of these areas, then more work on it in an isolated manner should be emphasized.

The color and appealing patterns "speak to the child" to invite his involvement; the goal of the task is so apparent that the child's performance is not dependent upon instruction from the adult. In a task such as this, the results are self-validating to the child. With only a brief exposure, he can begin to recognize whether his response is correct, and if not, how to correct it. If the task

30. The child is copying a grid and peg pattern in the transitional method, which is more advanced than the early overlay method, but not as demanding as the subsequent transfer method using half-size patterns which are placed for more distant visual focus. A well-integrated pattern is seen in her natural use of the two hands.

requires verbal support to maintain the child's interest, or instruction to insure desired performance, the therapist would realize that he is not yet ready to be involved in the task.

Eight simple patterns in this series are comprised initially of squares oriented in a stable, compact arrangement, side by side, above or below one another. In these patterns, triangles are added a few at a time. To start with, the triangles are oriented against the stable edge of squares; subsequent patterns place them more and more tangentially, to require greater visual organization from the child.

When each of the eight colorful patterns can be reproduced by the "overlay" method without problems, then following the same progression, a new and more difficult method is introduced; it is called the "transitional" method. This requires that the child look at the design, which is positioned forward of the plastic grid, and copy it. Explanation and demonstration by the therapist may enable the child to count down and across to find the proper starting place. Often it is appropriate for her to simply place an initial block in place without explanation until the child is ready to also master that.

The purpose of this method, in addition to its spatial relations aspects, is to develop early stages of visual retention and recall — a much-needed skill in copying from the chalkboard. Many learning-disordered children fail in this task at school because they cannot retain the visual image sufficiently to write it on paper. Failure to copy the material before it is erased, or copying it in error, only compounds an already difficult learning situation.

190

Graded Integration of Spatial Relations
and Elementary Visual Figure-Ground (Puzzles) (5.4)

Teachers and therapists already appreciate the use of puzzles as a child's means of developing spatial relations and manipulative hand skills. However, exposure to puzzles on a random basis will guarantee little benefit to a child who has a problem in this area; he will simply avoid engaging in the activity. To be of benefit, the use of puzzles must be properly timed in relation to the rest of the program so that the child has already acquired the necessary sensorimotor organization to enable him to experience success. If he is enabled to bridge the gap from the avoidance mode to involve himself, or explore and begin to organize his response, he is already moving along the continuum to develop subsequent skills which depend upon spatial relations and figure-ground factors.

The foundations for assembling puzzle pieces were laid in P.P. 5.2, Component B, wherein single unit form boards provided early isolated experience with the rotary factor together with confirming feedback from the plastic or wood perimeter; in addition to this, the Grid and Peg Set provided the necessary elementary spatial orientation. Single unit cardboard puzzles make a suitable starting point. When the subject of each piece is the same throughout, eg, forms of transportation such as cars, trucks, tractors, and the contours are quite similar, this can be more difficult for the young child.

Using the cardboard frame-tray puzzles almost exclusively for therapy, upgrading is done through multi-piece puzzles in which there is minimal tactile feedback, and the visual feedback is also less obvious and many pieces within a multi-piece puzzle may be similar in shape. The child's attention may be directed

31. Pieces of a frametray puzzle are first arranged on the panelboard and then assembled in the frame according to the specific method, "green-to-green," described in the text, to reduce visual figure-ground confusion at this level for later application to organization of abstract academic material.

more to the picture for his cues than to the contour of the piece; there is no objection to this, as long as the level of figure-ground difficulty is not beyond his capability. If this happens, he will be easily confused and withdraw from the task as he may often have done before.

When puzzles are properly used, they can provide a most effective means of developing good spatial relations skill, while simultaneously incorporating the visual figure-ground factor; puzzles can be easily graded by suitably small increments of difficulty to assure success. The grading system which has been evolved here is applicable throughout this unit at Level I and P.P. 5.9 at Levels II and III; the system upgrades the spatial relations factor according to the number of pieces, not to exceed 50. This has been found to be a suitable upward limit even for the preadolescent child, because 1) the desired performance can be derived, 2) task completion through short-term goals is an important goal, and 3) the time required for such a task is not out of proportion to the total treatment hour, during which many other kinds of activity must also be accomplished.

Visual figure-ground is graded according to the extent which the active background pattern distracts one's visual attention from the principal subject or content. This may occur because of a busy, bold, active background, or it may be the extent to which the subtlety of color of the subject fades into the background, again making it more difficult to perceive the relevant foreground subject matter from irrelevant background details. For the learning-disordered child, this inability to "see the forest for the trees" is only greater in degree and more specific than that which most people experience. The visual figure-ground factor for some individuals, like the auditory foreground-background confusion for others, appears as a symptom of more generalized disorganization.

It is the experience with the visual figure-ground factor which draws a close parallel to organizing abstract information when ferreting out and focusing one's attention on the principal or dominant features of a situation, a book report, or a problem, and not be confused or distracted by an array of irrelevant details. This kind of organization is a normal part of maturation which is honed to the point of need according to academic or vocational demands. If symptoms of disorganization in the visual and the auditory systems can be recognized and ameliorated in childhood, one might then expect that the normal maturation and ability to organize one's abstract thinking would be less apt to be deterred. Evidence of improvement in organizing abstract thoughts in the academic realm has been observed among high school students in a relatively short period of therapy (less than three months). It was felt that some of this change was related to the use of puzzles in the specific methods to be described, together with the use of other sensorimotor techniques.

Over the years it has seemed that those puzzles which are most suitable for use in this manner are the cardboard frame-tray puzzles by contrast to use of children's large, multi-piece wooden framed puzzles. Reasons for this are cited here:

1) cost of cardboard frame-try puzzles is a fraction of those which are wooden,
2) easy availability in most shopping centers,
3) large numbers of these puzzles may be compactly stacked or

192

conveniently stored in wire racks,

4) ease and low cost of replacement if a piece is lost (use of incomplete puzzles should be avoided since it can create needless confusion for the learning-disordered child),

5) subject content ranges from early childhood interests to those acceptable to the older child,

6) graphic reproduction on paper is preferable to painted design on wood, for it allows a wide range of difficulty in the figure-ground factor.

The spatial relations factor and the visual figure-ground factor are graded independently, permitting the therapist to upgrade in "half-step progression" to stabilize the skill level in one of these at a time. For example, puzzles of elementary and intermediate levels of difficulty in spatial relations may carry either an elementary or an intermediate level of figure-ground difficulty. The therapist can help the child develop his spatial relations skill up to the intermediate level, while the figure-ground factor is kept at the elementary level, going back to the elementary level of spatial relations while the level of figure-ground is being raised. In time, the child will be able to master puzzles which are at the intermediate and the senior levels in both factors.

Graded Progression of Spatial Relations and Visual Figure-Ground

	SPATIAL RELATIONS (No pieces)	VISUAL FIGURE-GROUND
Pre-elementary	9-18 single unit pieces 5-6 multi-piece puzzles	None
Elementary	7-13 pieces	clearly evident subject, with some connective lines, but minimally distracting
Intermediate	13-35 pieces	more active, bold background, competing for attention
Senior	36-50 pieces	wildly active, competing for attention from color contrasts, intersecting lines, and multiple subjects
Advanced	(more than 50 pieces, not indicated within therapy time; may be used at home)	muted, subtle color tones which blend subject into background

Color Coding of Puzzles for
Spatial Relations and Visual Figure-Ground

SPATIAL RELATIONS

Elementary	Intermediate	Senior
Yellow	Orange	Red

VISUAL FIGURE-GROUND

Elementary	Intermediate	Senior	Advanced
Green	Blue	Purple	Black

Along the right edge of each frame tray puzzle, lines are drawn down the entire stack of puzzles at 1½ inch intervals to make three sections at the left and four sections at the right, for color coding. The proper coding for spatial relations is determined by counting the pieces. To determine the figure-ground factor is more difficult and at best can be only relative. One would first assemble the puzzles and arrange them sequentially in their relative degree of difficulty, using the features described for each category in the previous table, insofar as possible. Using the color code above, the color green would represent an elementary level of visual figure-ground confusion. More minute grading may be signified by only the left half of the space colored green, to represent the lower end of the range, while the right half would represent the higher levels of elementary difficulty. Fine grading such as this is often essential to the successful performance of the child who has severe problems.

Generally preschool children are started at the pre-elementary level. For others, the therapist can estimate by the child's age and general performance whether he would be ready to begin at the elementary or intermediate level. Some children of age eight and ten can be appropriately started at the elementary level, moving quickly to higher levels once their performance portrays an organized approach. To determine where his probable level of success would be, one could offer a choice of three or four puzzles with contrasting levels of the two factors to ascertain whether the problem seems more evident in spatial relations or visual figure-ground. The reason for the choice is twofold. Having some choice involves the child in the task and can help him feel more comfortable. There are occasions when the child's choice between puzzles is based principally on appeal of the subject matter. However, children can be fairly good judges of how successfully they can cope with a difficult figure-ground pattern. In fact, their opinion in establishing levels of difficulty of the figure-ground factor can be quite reliable and helpful in confirming or refuting the grading established by the adult.

The puzzle pieces of the elementary level of spatial relations among these cardboard puzzles are large enough for the young child to manipulate easily.

After the child has had opportunity to look at the puzzle in its complete form, he is asked to remove the pieces and place them face up on the panel board so that each piece is clearly visible. Children often tend to stack the pieces; this can cause the learning-disordered child to become confused and frustrated when a piece eludes him. To keep his attention focused on the task, the therapist, sitting opposite the child, can hold the panelboard within reach in front of him. For the child who has not yet established dominance, this permits free exposure for either hand until he has confirmed his dominance.

The large cardboard frame-tray puzzles by Western and others have the outline of each piece imprinted on the bottom of the frame. Preferably this is not used as a principal aid; sometimes the bottom is covered with contact paper to reduce this effect. Any technique is advocated which encourages the child to proceed from information which is "known" to that which is "unknown." To help the child evolve a more organized approach to tasks, he is asked to look at the top of the frame to see what clues he can find about the subject, the color, the linear progression within the pattern or design, and the contour of the piece he needs to search for. The technique of moving "from the known to the unknown" is depicted in more simplified language as well. Abbreviated reminders such as "green to green" or "line to line" are made as needed to reduce the disorganized means to which learning-disordered children may quickly regress. Without this structure they readily lose their goal direction, get confused in the random, trial-and-error process, become frustrated, and again fail in task completion. Here is an example in which the program language comprehension skills are utilized as a means of structuring the experience.

Puzzles, when used with this "known to unknown" technique to maintain goal direction, then become a vehicle for focusing a child's attention on a limited number of factors at a time, amid distracters which are strong competitors. It is certainly not the intent here to develop compulsive, neurotic forms of behavior; rather, the purpose is to provide sufficient external organization and structure to the task until the child can develop adequate internal organization to maintain goal direction independently. The early awareness of the whole-part relationships which was first introduced in P.P. 5.2, Component E, in matching halves or matching parts of the whole, has been extended through this experience, with puzzles, to convey the concept of a larger, more encompassing "whole" with its many parts.

Visual Figure-Ground (5.5)

The singular emphasis here is on the visual figure-ground skill which may require greater skill in directing the eye focus and movement than that which was necessary in the previous program plan. Hand-eye coordination would also be required for pencil control on exercises designed for this, namely, The Visual Figure-Ground Exercise Sheets #1 - 119 from *The Frostig Program for the Development of Visual Perception* by Marianne Frostig and David Horne.[2]

After checking to assure that there is no color blind tendency, on the *Dvorine Psuedo-Isochromatic Plates,* the eight alternate testing plates in the back may be used as a means of enhancing the child's experience, having him trace the course of the submerged trail with a blunt object.

In addition to these two-dimensional tasks, visual figure-ground skill may also be challenged in three dimension by use of a set of large four-strand white beads, the center bead of each strand having been marked with a different color. These strands, when lumped together in a heap, challenge the child to visually trace the course of each strand as they wind over and under.

Some or all of the means mentioned here and in Levels II and III can be utilized to develop and strengthen the child's organization of his visual input. In this holistic approach, a broad range of experience is encouraged; it is felt that this promotes a means of greater flexibility and adaptability to enable the child to organize himself in his daily life.

Visual Form (5.6)

Level II visual form tasks are gradually upgraded to include 1) selection of a single form from a visual figure-ground configuration, 2) more complex whole-part relationships of obvious whole objects or geometric patterns, and 3) matching by more subtle association and abstract concepts.

Assuming that left-right directional orientation has been well established in P.P. 7.1 and 7.4, the child would be ready to engage in Level III tasks which have been upgraded to stress 1) increased complexity of design, 2) subtle differences of position, form, and color, and 3) a left-right component.

Throughout Levels II and III there is an increasing demand placed on the child's ability to sort objects by recognizing and remembering the multiple, subtle, minute visual form differences. It is important to point out that while some of these tools of therapy are obviously designed as toys for young children, eg, the Simplex Inset Boards, the technique used here requires visual form discrimination which is much more difficult. For instance, the five inset pieces, having subtle differences of form and often a left-right component, are removed from the board and, without benefit of confirmatory feedback by inserting each piece, the older child must indicate by visual selection alone where each piece would fit. As a means of further upgrading, the pieces, rather than being oriented along a horizontal baseline, are placed in a random position, not to be moved, while the adolescent or adult copes with the visual rotation factor as well.

To complete Level III, The Continental Press Series, Level II[3] is used to apply the visual form recognition skill to differentiating letters and short words. This skill is refined separately before the child must recognize the word and its meaning in the context of which it is written. In the latter instance, not one skill, but four or five skills must be integrated. (See Part III, Summary Inventory of Foundation Skills for Academic Performance).

Spatial Relations (5.7)

For specific development of spatial relations, continued use of the Grid and Peg Set is recommended. By virtue of its structure and close-step grading, minute intermediate difficulties the child may encounter can be easily recognized so that direct, appropriate adjustments in the program can be provided. The number and the variety of designs offers the child an in-depth experience in which to strengthen his spatial relations skills. The Grid and Peg Set is an excellent example of the way in which one basic piece of equipment can be used for many purposes over the entire age range, from the ages of three to adolescence and adulthood, as techniques described in Level III will indicate.

In P.P. 5.1 the "overlay" method was introduced, followed by the "transitional" method with full scale color designs. Level II begins with full scale black and white designs, again using the transitional method; some children find the shift from color, which is determined for them, to the use of black and white, in which they must determine the choice of colors, too great a step and must revert to the overlay method. Some learning-disordered children find they are unable to make an adaptation to this new factor and that shifting from full scale color designs to the use of black and white is too disorganizing. Then the overlay method with the full scale black and white designs is used until they are ready to move to the less structured, transitional technique.

In Level II the principal shift in grading is the introduction of black and white designs in half-scale. Reproducing the grid and peg design is referred to as the "transfer" method. It requires increased adaptability and skill in spatial relations as well as much greater mental concentration; in short, the task requires a higher level organization. Throughout this series of designs the trend moves from those which are relatively symmetrical and stable to those which are predominantly linear, asymmetrical, and unstable due to the tangential relationship of an increased number of triangles.

In Level III, designs are presented in full scale, but this time by a "coded" method. First the key to the coded symbols is in full view throughout the task; later the key must be recalled after a brief visual exposure prior to attempting the task, or with an increased time lapse from the early part of the therapy hour, or from one week to the next. This method provides the preadolescent and older individual with an opportunity to develop memory retention and recall by means which are brief enough to be practical for use in a limited period of therapy, yet be challenging and colorful enough to be acceptable.

In addition to the Grid and Peg Set, a number of supplementary two- and three-dimensional spatial relations activities are listed in the OEPS. Some of these are suitable for use in a group during therapy, ie, Linjo and Hex. Not only can such experiences enhance the child's spatial relations skills, but when games such as these can be used for recreational purposes with his family or peers, they can provide a suitable transition by helping the child develop better self-confidence and pleasure from participating in a group.

Visual Figure-Ground (5.8)

A series of Visual Figure-Ground Exercises (1-6) have been designed for use in Level II; colored pencil lines which vary in intensity from one end to the other intertwine over a 6 inch x 6 inch square of translucent white paper mounted between two polyvinyl sheets. A circle is placed at either end of each line so that with a china marking pencil the child can place a number in one circle and, by maintaining sufficient visual organization and control to follow the line without being diverted to another line, place the same number at the opposite end. The design, traceable on each side of the paper and square, can be changed each time it is turned, totalling eight variations of each exercise.

At Level III, Dvorine plates are used to identify subtly colored trails embedded in a similar background.

Graded Integration of Spatial Relations and Visual Figure-Ground — Continued (Puzzles) (5.9)

It is anticipated that there will be a smooth, automatic progression between levels of difficulty accorded P.P. 5.4 and this, at 5.9, as defined in the former of these two units. This point may be a logical starting place for some children of age six and older. However, when a task which involves an integration of skills is started at Level II, special attention must be paid to the component skills to assure that an adequate underlying skill level has been attained in spatial relations and visual figure-ground skills indepedently.

Special Note to Educators

In the preceding program plans, appropriate use of the activities may be made by way of prevention in the preschool and elementary school classes to generally enhance the learning skills of children. In particular, I refer to the gross motor activities. The sensory discrimination skills, the sequencing experiences, and the graded use of toys and puzzles to promote early visual perception are also encouraged. The program plans to follow — 6, 7, and 8 — will be of even greater specific value in the classroom. These techniques will be most useful on an individual basis for children who are experiencing particular difficulty with handwriting because of dominance confusion, poor directionality, and inadequate fine motor skills for manuscript print and/or script writing.

References

1. Knickerbocker B: A Central Approach to the Development of Spatial and Temporal Concepts. Seattle, Special Child Pubs, 1968.
2. Frosbig M, Horne D: The Frostig Program for the Development of Visual Perception. Palo Alto, CA, Consulting Psychologist Press Inc, 1963.
3. Continental Press Series, 1966. Elizabethtown, PA, 17023.

Program Plan 6

Dominance Exploration, Selection, and Confirmation

Throughout nursery school and kindergarten it is not abnormal for the young child to be ambivalent over which hand will become dominant. Evidence of this ambivalence is seen in his alternate choice of hands used for unilateral hand activities. A child may write with one hand and eat with the other. Learning-disordered children who have problems crossing the midline of the body will also be seen from time to time writing with one hand up to the midline, and then switching to the other to continue. This is a more significant degree of dominance confusion than that which is only temporary in the normal evolution of dominance selection among preschoolers, who also go through a period of number and letter reversals.

To review briefly, laterality, or the child's awareness of one side of the body as opposed to the other, develops prior to or concomitantly with the gradual development of hand dominance. It is only after this internal awareness has developed in the child that the words *left* and *right* will be meaningful. Directionality, or the awareness of left and right externally, will continue to confuse the child until laterality and hand dominance are firmly established. As long as confusion persists, it will delay the child in his academic adjustment by continued reversals in reading and writing. Even into adulthood remnants of this confusion will persist, preventing the individual from developing an automatic, spontaneous orientation to the left and right.

Ideally, activities recommended in P.P. 2 could be used in the kindergarten as a preventive measure so that better postural and bilateral motor integration could take place among children generally and to offset the depth of problems encountered by children who will suffer the academic effects of a learning disorder. When there is an untimely delay in developing hand dominance which causes the child to reach first grade unprepared to hold and to direct a pencil, then certain carefully designed intervention procedures should be instituted in school or in therapy. These procedures are designed to accelerate the rate of development of hand dominance. The measures to follow would enable the child to explore hand dominance essentially without external influence, and subsequently to identify when he has established a more dominant pattern. Specifically designed follow-up measures can help to confirm this pattern to the child. Of course, the ultimate intent of this is to reduce the left-right confusion of the child's conception of his external world.

Early Bimanual Motor Integration (6.1)

Along the sequential hierarchy of development a young child normally learns to master the combined function of the two sides of the body on a very primitive level such as creeping or crawling. A sound foundation should be developed first in the use of the two sides of the body in reciprocal patterns of the extremities such as crawling, or in therapy, bilateral balance on the inflatables. Likewise, bimanual combined action is encouraged through toys which require both hands to push parts together or pull them apart. These activities which utilize two-sided motor activity help to develop both sides of the brain by sending sensory and motor impulses across the midline to the opposite hemisphere. When sufficient capability has been reached in bilateral integration between the two sides, and especially between the two hands, then one side is ready to assume a more specialized role which is properly referred to as hand dominance.

In the OEPS a series of activities are listed which involve simultaneous pushing together or pulling apart. Most of these would naturally be appropriate only for young children and are introduced simply as a part of providing those foundational skills which are felt to be important prerequisites to dominance selection. The first five items in Level I are particularly suitable as a means of involving young children during initial hours of therapy because the action of "pulling apart" is so simple and natural to them.

Older children who are felt to need this kind of activity but who might be offended by the juvenile character of the first five activities can be started on any of the others which are more age-appropriate. If necessary, the fine skills needed to link the jewelry snap beads may even be used to challenge teenagers if presented in a way by which they can try to better their score of the number assembled in a two-minute period, for example. Boys up to ten or older have shown interest in Build-O-Fun because the construction of some items such as the airplane, dump truck, and camera can be age-appropriate and suitably complex. Build-O-Fun requires force to engage or disengage the pieces, as does the Skaneateles train track. It is because the assembly of the erector set pieces are less stable and usually require less resistance that these are not recommended for the purpose of forceful bimanual integration.

Nondominant "Finger Drawing" and Scribbling (6.2)

Throughout nursery school and kindergarten, children need to be exposed to opportunities which encourage wide, random arm movements both bilaterally and unilaterally. Free, nondirected exposure such as this helps the child make a satisfactory transition between forceful bilateral motor integration patterns of the upper extremity and the initial purposeful direction of gross arm movement. Activities such as finger painting invite free, sweeping movements over a broad surface. Other simple tasks which could offer similar benefit, be more practical at home and school, and which also might have greater appeal to children who dislike contact with finger paints would be as follows:

> Glide the hands over a smooth table top which has been either powdered or sprayed with furniture polish. The child can draw roads in a sand-covered

surface with his fingers. Without needing to concentrate yet on the direction of his movements or on the control of a writing tool, these early exploratory hand movements provide the child nevertheless with important sensory feedback as to how the movement was performed, and through this feedback, the way in which these movements correspond to his simultaneous visual input.

Early nondominant scribbling should be done at eye level so that here also arm movements can be correlated with the visual system. A long piece of brown wrapping paper may be mounted against the wall. The best arrangement, however, for clinic use has been to cover the surface of a hollow door, available at lumber yards, with heavy transparent vinyl; a grease pencil is used to provide the smoothest, most tactually satisfying sensation of movement. A large scribble board such as this can be rested horizontally on two open drawers of proper height. To stimulate the child's interest, age-appropriate subject material such as pictures of animals can be mounted under the vinyl so that the child can hide it by his scribbles.

Observe Presence or Absence of Established Hand Dominance (6.3)

One scale of measurement is presented here as a means of observing whether the child functions equally well with each hand, signifying a lack of hand dominance, or whether there is sufficient contrast in the skill of one over the other to suggest that dominance is either beginning to emerge or has been firmly established. A timed sample within a circular space helps to shed light on this point. While these tests are timed, the supplemental findings are subjective. Therefore, these are considered samples of behavior and should not be considered as absolute.

Timed Hammering Sample

Materials: A piece of carbon paper is turned upside down and sandwiched between two plain sheets of paper, stapled at one edge and secured lengthwise with masking tape to a smooth table surface in front of the child. Using a round template 4″ in diameter, cut from heavy cardboard or 1/8″ Plexiglas, the therapist draws a line around its perimeter; the template is then removed. A child's wooden hammer is placed at the midline, in front of the child, with the handle facing him.

The child is asked first to put both hands under the table. The therapist, sitting opposite him, tells him to wait until she says "go" before picking up the hammer, adjusting it to be comfortable, and then hit the inside of the circle as hard and as fast as he can until told to stop.

With the first blow the therapist starts the stopwatch and counts the number of strikes. The strikes often come in such rapid succession that they are difficult to count; while effort is made to keep the record accurate, it is actually the contrast in the production of the two hands which is more relevant. The duration will be

32. The timed hammering test helps evaluate whether hand dominance has been established; if it is not, subsequent test results often reveal shifts toward one hand or the other.

varied from one child to another; if the child has a short attention span, ten seconds of continuous pounding would be adequate. A longer duration of 15 to 20 or occasionally up to 30 seconds is preferred.

Without stopping to remove the masking tape which secures the papers at the edge nearest the child, the therapist lifts the free edge of the top sheet and carbon to record immediately all the pertinent data while it is fresh in her mind. She does this without revealing to the child the effects of his hammer blows against the carbon, as this will become a needless distraction, possibly invalidating further testing. The kinds of information she gathers during the timed procedure which she would then record would include the following: which hand was used first, the number of strikes, the number of seconds, the amount of control in gripping the handle, the shoulder action, positioning of the forearm, skidding action resulting from gross incoordination and control, the visual attention, facial stress, tongue activity, overflow to the opposite hand, attempts to transfer to the opposite hand, and any verbalized response about which hand he prefers. If desired, a format on the idea of the one below can be mimeographed on the page as a reminder of what to observe and to organize the collection of comparable data. However, with practice it is often easier to simply record pertinent observations at the time. The data and name of the child must be recorded on each sheet at the time of testing, to prevent any future uncertainties.

    Observation format for hammering: Left____Right____
    Initial Set of Hammer Samples/First Repeat/Second Repeat
    Number of strikes____in____seconds
    Attempted to transfer L to R (____x) or R to L (____x)
    Hand grip weak____; handle flipped around____

Hand and arm function:

____wild, uncontrolled; poor visual attention
____barely adequate; evidence of skidding; off target occasionally
____well-directed response in arm and hand

The procedure is repeated for the other hand; the child is again asked to put both hands under the table before starting the second timed sample. The child's response to this request gives one indication about the child's comprehension of early language, and it also helps to provide more objective findings. That is, the selection of the hammer on the initial trail is more apt to be made by the dominant hand if both hands are under the table. Unless this is done, if one hand is at the moment already moving or is closer to the hammer than the other, it might be selected when otherwise the other would be chosen if there were more equal opportunity.

A new set of papers is now secured in front of the child, the circle drawn inside the template, and the stopwatch in hand. This time the handle is directed toward the opposite side and the child is told "now it is this one's turn." If indicated, one can acknowledge that it is often easier for one hand than the other to function, but "let's try this one now." The child is reminded to hammer inside the circle and to keep going until stopped. The duration will be equal to that of the first hammer sample. On retesting in subsequent sessions, the duration of those tests need not remain constant with the first set of samples but would again be dictated by the circumstances and duration of the initial sample of that session.

In clearcut cases where there is a distinct contrast in the frequency, density, and degree of motor control, interpretation of the findings is not difficult. Rarely is it so evident. The hand which is chosen first suggests the idea that this is the dominant hand, and it often is. This single finding is less significant than other observations. Indications of the hand which is nondominant are often more apparent. For example, the child will often fatigue early, stop prematurely, and seem either disinterested or try to transfer to the other hand. Attempts to transfer are noted, but the child is encouraged to continue with the hand which is being timed until told to stop. Having started with both hands under the table, when attempts are made to transfer it is then a more significant finding.

Comparison of the frequency, ie, the total number of strikes, is easy. As the child is hammering with the first hand, the therapist determines whether it will be feasible to strive for more than ten to fifteen seconds' duration. If the child shows minimal attention with the hand chosen first, his attention is likely to be even less on the second hand. Despite the fact that the child may have stopped prematurely, it is the total number of strikes in periods of time as nearly equal as possible which is considered to be a more meaningful indicator.

The density and clarity of the carbon paper impressions created by the impact of the hammer head is one of the most significant findings. Comparison between the two samples may show a clear contrast or even an equal lack of skill. The clarity and crispness of the impressions suggest motor control. Lack of such clarity occurs in "skidding" movements when the hammer head hits the paper with an angular, glancing blow and then slides. This can happen when the child has poor visual attention, being unaware of aligning it properly, or it may be that the hand grasp is too weak to prevent the handle from flipping around uncontrollably. The handle on a toy wooden hammer is approximately ½ inch in diameter. Despite the fact that it may slip around in a weak or poorly functioning hand, it should not be padded, since one is attempting to observe and document function and do so with consistency.

Probably one of the most, if not the most, important single indicators of hand dominance is the contrast in density and motor control which is evidenced by the pattern of clustering versus the dispersal of the strikes. Clustering of marks roughly within a 2 inch space inside the circle indicates a well-controlled arm and hand grasp. By contrast, there may be a distinct lack of clustering in either hand initially and wide, randomly dispersed strikes extending far beyond the target.

If dominance selection has already taken place in a child, this will be evidenced by a relatively consistent contrast between the two sides with respect to frequency, density, and control. For example, if the number of strikes counted on one hand is nearly equal or the lesser number is at least three quarters that of the larger, then there is felt to be a definite lack of hand dominance. However, when the smaller number approximates half that of the larger and there are obvious contrasts in density, and greater clustering and control appear on the same side, then dominance would seem definite. By this time, the dominant hand is usually the one to be selected first. If it is not, and all other signs point consistently to the one hand, the therapist may consider this to be a chance finding, or else due to the possibility that the child's attention is drawn to the problem and he is playing games. This would be the indicator he could alter at his own whim, whereas on the others, he does not know how the findings are assessed.

Any time there is any question about dominance confusion, it is helpful to expose the child to several weeks of daily dominance exploration activities described in P.P. 6.4. At the end of that time the hammering and crayoning samples would be repeated. If there is a more consistent pattern at that time, the desired results would have been attained and the child would be ready to begin P.P. 6.6 with subsequent follow-up of P.P. 7 and 8.

When a definitely inconsistent, disorganized pattern or a nearly equal performance in the frequency, density, and control exists between the samples of each hand in hammering and crayoning, then a minimum of four to six weeks of daily activities to explore the dominance trend, in P.P. 6.4, would naturally follow.

Time Crayoning Sample

Immediately following the timed hammering, the top sheet of these sets of paper may, unless damaged, be used next for the crayoning sample. It is secured in the same manner as described before, and a china marking pencil or heavy crayon is centered on the sheet of paper. To motivate the interest of young children, a red pencil is used to make a "sunset" within a 4 inch round template; preferably this template is cut from 1/8 inch Plexiglas because of its durability.

With both hands again placed under the table, the child is told that when he hears the word "go," he is to reach for the china marking pencil or crayon and crayon as hard and as fast as he can, trying to cover the entire space. He is requested not to stop until told to do so. A sample of 30 seconds is ideal; sometimes a minimum of 15 seconds may have to be accepted from young children.

After recording the appropriate observations on the first sample, it is removed

33. The timed crayoning test also helps to confirm or refute the impression of which hand is dominant and whether there is a shift toward one hand, which is apparent.

and the procedure is repeated. After placing both hands beneath the table once more, to keep to a minimum any chance of the child's transferring the pencil back to the first hand, the therapist points the pencil toward the other hand for "its turn."

Before starting, the child is asked not to change hands; young children may not remember, and others who transfer to the hand chosen initially because of the already emerging patterns of dominance reveal important data. However, for the purpose of comparing the timed samples, after such an interruption the crayon is again positioned in the hand which started the sample with a minimum loss of time. The stopwatch should be stopped during this period and restarted to finish out the remaining time which would total that of the other crayoning sample. The object is to maintain maximum consistency in techniques between samples to be compared.

Observations of performance during the crayoning sample include the hand chosen first, type of grip, control of pencil, and movements of the arm. These may be noted informally at the side of the sample or, if more convenient as reminders to the therapist, a format such as the following may be helpful. Such data provide a basis then for comparison of the performance between the two sides, which is documented in the OEPS in accord with Level I, II, or III in hammering and in crayoning.

     Observation format for crayoning: Left____Right____

    Initial Set of Crayon Samples/First Repeat/Second Repeat
    Was this hand selected first? Yes No
    Attempted to transfer L to R (____x) R to L (____x)
    Duration of crayoning sample____seconds
    Held pencil in clenched fist? Yes No
    Awkward finger position?   Yes No
    Tripod finger position?   Yes No
    Crayon jumped edge   Yes No

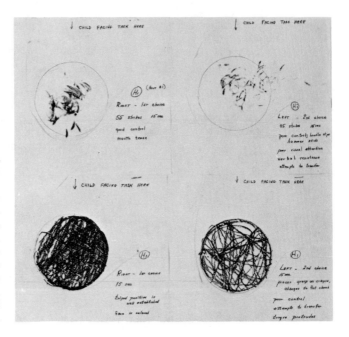

34. The results of the timed hammering and crayoning tests in Hour 1 clearly reveals right hand dominance in this six-year-old boy. During his left handed performance, there was less production and it was of poorer quality; there were attempts to transfer to the other hand, and his tongue protruded during the crayoning test.

Interpretations of the crayoning sample would be made principally by observing density and control. Comparison of the intensity with which the strokes of the crayon are made indicate the strength and thrust of the shoulder and arm as well as the grasp of the china marking pencil. If more lines are parallel than are in opposition to each other in a random, haphazard pattern, or seem to have bounced off at a different angle after hitting the edge too force-fully, then the degree of control is fairly poor. Again, whether the control is poor or even fairly adequate, the more nearly equal the results of the two hands, the more it would suggest that dominance has not been established and further exploration by means of P.P. 6.4 would be in order.

Nondirected Dominance Exploration (6.4)

The purpose of the activities in this unit would be to provide the child the opportunity to use either hand, switching back and forth at will. Activities mentioned below were used in therapy weekly and frequently, if not daily, on the home program. The changes which took place over the four to six weeks of dominance exploration were largely the result of this concerted effort. The child begins to find that one arm is more comfortable and can yield a more sustained effort before fatiguing. Over these weeks the balance would begin to shift from a nearly equal, random choice to a more frequent use of one hand.

The following activities are suitable for home and school use as well as the clinical setting. The method used would be to present the child with a 3 foot long piece of balsa wood, ½ inch thick and 3 inches wide, on which he is encouraged to

206

35. The child crosses the midline to hammer the forms to her far left on the balsa wood board; hammering helps her to establish hand dominance.

hammer as long and as hard as he can but without being timed. The child may freely switch hands as often as he wishes. He is further encouraged to continue and to give his strongest effort by the therapist, who speaks admiringly of how big the dents in the wood are or how hard he can pound. To keep the child's interest and involvement, various common geometric forms 2 inches in size are drawn along the length of the board with colorful marking pens. These act as focal points; the therapist asks him to pound first one, then another.

As a variation, cardboard egg cartons have made excellent "targets"; it seems to be satisfying to the child when he has pounded one to bits. A lump of clay can be pounded with hammer or fist. A punching bag which is suspended or standing on the floor could serve as an alternate, but the most effective method has been hammering balsa. It is at this point of dominance, contraindicated to use hammering of pegs which must be held in place with the other hand, until P.P. 6.6 is put into effect — the time when the dominant and the subdominant roles are purposely combined.

During this period of dominance exploration it is suggested that if at all possible, in kindergarten at least, all handwriting, crayoning, and use of scissors be avoided. In school, instead of cutting when others in class are doing so, this child would benefit more by tearing the contour, thus using his two hands in an integrated manner. Instead of crayoning, he can draw on a powder board, sand tray, or with finger paints. When the importance of curtailing these activities temporarily has been explained to the teachers, they have been most cooperative and helpful in adjusting the child's program so as to augment what was being done in therapy and at home. Children in first grade will often be able to resolve this problem in four to six weeks and quickly catch up with their classwork; children in kindergarten will require longer.

Document Dominance Shift or Selection (6.5)

After the appropriate interval of dominance exploration is felt to have transpired, retesting of the hammering and crayoning is done to determine the child's "writing readiness." As indicated earlier, this may be a problem which a child of eight or nine years can overcome in several weeks of work, or it might require three months of intermittent exposure to these activities for a child of five. During this time it is also helpful if eating utensils are placed at the midline. As parents begin to notice shifts toward one hand, as compared with a previously vacillating pattern, this serves as a clue of emerging dominance and would suggest that retesting of hammering and crayoning might now document this change.

Confirm the Roles of the Dominant and the Subdominant Hand (6.6)

The emphasis now is to introduce an activity which confirms the dominant role for one hand by also furnishing a subdominant role for the other. This particular emphasis is promoted by a certain method in which the child is asked to use the Grid and Peg Set. The therapist picks up a few blocks and offers them to the child to hold in his subdominant hand. This can be done subtly at first to see how automatically this pattern is continued. If necessary, the child is then told that the one hand should hold the pegs which the other hand is to place. This not only fosters a suitably integrated pattern, but also reduces the incidence of placing the pegs actively with the subdominant hand, thus prolonging the status of ambivalence or confusion over hand dominance.

Program Plan 7

Directional Orientation

When two-sided integration is so well developed that the child overlaps his hands when twirling on the double suspended tires or the scooter board, and when hand dominance has been documented in P.P. 6.5, then adequate foundation skills have been laid for the development of directionality. Having established an internal awareness that there are two separate and opposite sides of the body by balancing on the inflatables and kneeling on top of the carpeted barrel, the child has an internal reference point which will enable him to recognize the meaning of the descriptive terms *left* and *right*. Now for the first time they are emphasized verbally in therapy.

Establish a Sensory Identification of Left and Right (7.1)

The terms left and right are introduced by means of distinctly different, easily remembered sensory input. To confirm to the child through strong sensory stimulation what may be a more subtle, nebulous feeling of one side of the body as opposed to the other, the right side of the body is identified for him first through proprioceptive information, ie, by the use of a weight. This weight, a five- or six-ounce fisherman's sinker, covered with blue contact paper, is used to provide additional visual association and to instill a pronounced sensory input by strongly activating the joint and muscle receptors of the right arm.

The fire-engine red by contrast is associated solely with the left side as the most vivid visual stimulation. If only the colors red and blue were to be used, a child could still be confused. It is imperative that the child have a strong proprioceptive stimulus to be distinctly associated with one of the colors, and this stimulus should be introduced and firmly established in association with that color before the other color is mentioned. Then in the child's mind the color blue becomes synonymous with the "heavy blue weight" with which to identify the right hand. To alleviate any possible confusion, the same means of identifying right and left are kept constant whether the child is right-or left-handed, but greater emphasis and time are directed to the red, with which to remember his left and dominant side.

The procedure typical for sensory identification of the left and right would be for the child to stand and face the therapist who kneels so as to be at his eye level. Holding the fisherman's sinker in both hands, the therapist says, in a slow and distinct voice, "I have a weight for you. It is for your right hand. Can you reach for it with your right hand?"

36A. The therapist first holds the weight at the midline in both hands and says, "I have a blue weight; it is for your right hand; can you reach for it with your right hand?"

If the child seems at all confused and alternates between his choice of hands, the therapist curtails this response by simply putting her own hands behind her back and pausing briefly before repeating the procedure. This time, if need be, she reaches forward, placing the weight in the child's right hand, while reinforcing the action verbally with the comment, "This is your right hand. This is the one with the weight. This weight is only for your right hand. Hold it firmly. Do not let it drop."

Then the therapist says, "Watch my hands and do with yours what I do with mine. As I count one-two, raise both hands over your head and hold them there straight while we count together." A slow count of ten is suitable for the 5 or 6-year-old in the beginning; this may be increased to 20 as the child's interest and endurance permit.

At the words "...and down again," both the adult and child drop their hands. "Which one is tired?" Often the answer will be "neither one," which then suggests the further question, "Which hand held the weight?"

Repeat the procedure, this time holding the arms forward at shoulder level. Urge the child to keep his arms steady. At times a third repetition is needed; the arms may then be extended to shoulder level at the sides of the body, each time reviewing the question, "Which arm is tired?" "Which hand held the weight?" One can gather additional information about the child's level of performance in other areas simultaneously and provide variation by asking the child to say the alphabet, repeat the days of the week, months of the year, whichever is appropriate.

After each series, when the child answers that the right hand held the weight, confirm this to him immediately with the phrase, "You are correct." Insofar as possible, the word correct is used rather than "right" to avoid needless confusion.

36B. Both arms are raised while the child holds the "heavy blue weight" in the right hand to establish a proprioceptive sensory identification for this side, whether or not the child is right handed.

This step and the next are briefly reviewed each session prior to any application of the Positional Model.

Whereas the right side is identified primarily through proprioceptive stimulation, in particular the kinesthetic input, the vivid visual impact of bright red has been used to help the child clearly remember the left. Many children will be able to proceed directly to the introduction of the left hand in the same therapy session that the right hand is introduced. Facing the child as before, the therapist now holds a red china marking pencil in both hands at the midline so as not to suggest an answer from her hand. She says, "I have a red pencil for you. It is for your left hand. Can you reach for it with your left hand?"

Whenever there is any confusion, the therapist places the pencil behind her back before trying again. Whether to confirm his selection as being correct or as a means to counteract his confusion, the therapist says, "This is your left hand. The red pencil is for your left hand."

These two steps are conducted as the child stands facing the Positional Model so that the blue and red color coding can be further associated in a clearly visible way. Often these steps should be reviewed over several sessions before moving on. Other children will need this procedure only as a brief introduction to help them establish the proper point of departure for the techniques which follow.

Introduction of the Positional Model[1] (7.2)

Panel 1 of the Positional Model, shown on page 213, is enlarged to 30 x 40 inches for clinical use and mounted on ½ inch thick panelboard obtainable through many art stores. This is placed in front of the child so that the horizontal lines are at

37. The therapist, holding the red grease pencil midline, says, "I have a red pencil; it is for your left hand; can you reach for it with your left hand?"

shoulder height, allowing the child to reach near the top and the bottom. The panel board is braced at a slightly oblique angle and supported at various heights by an open drawer or suitable wall fixture.

The procedure for introducing the Position Model is for the child, as he faces Panel 1, to hold the red and blue china marking pencils in the hands so designated. The therapist then asks the child in slow and very distinct terms to place both hands with the marking pencils at the bottom of Panel 1 and wait for further verbal instructions. If the child is unable to understand, the instructions may be repeated and then, if necessary, the child is helped to place his hands properly.

Whenever the child has moved correctly, this is immediately reaffirmed by saying, "Yes, that is what the words told you" or "Yes, that is what those words mean." A child may respond to a request without being certain that the words he heard and the action he took really mean the same. Make no assumptions! Whenever a young child responds to a new experience which entails early language comprehension, his action is immediately reaffirmed in this way. Every opportunity is used to verify for him that which the child may be unable to confirm for himself. Until he is able to rely on his own internal data, he will need external confirmation to help him correlate action with words.

Getting back to the Positional Model once more, the therapist says to the child, "Listen very carefully to the words and then show me what the words tell you to do." Watching to see how the movement is carried out, the therapist explains that he is to hold the pencils against the panelboard, and in a slow, distinctly rhythmic manner, she says, "ONE, TWO go *up* to the *top*...THREE, FOUR, come *down* to the *bottom*."

212

38. In Panel 1, the Positional Model is introduced to establish the movement pattern which matches the words top, bottom, (hands) apart, and together.

The initial response of a disorganized child is to make a hurried dash or purposeless, random response irrespective of the words or timing. It may be necessary to ask the child to wait at each end, holding the position until he hears the words and gives himself enough time to think through how to act upon them. The task is so structured that the child, who is otherwise unable to establish his own control or direct his attention to the task, gradually is able to do so.

This slow, rhythmic cadence provides enough structure for some children to perform the task at once. This rhythm is coupled simultaneously with the child's own visuo-motor response to promote in him better sensory integration. Another method which has worked well is for the therapist to move her own forearm up and down rhythmically, while lightly snapping her fingers each time at the bottom of the arc of motion. The child can depend on this accentuated visual-auditory input to make him more aware of controlling the speed of his movement.

Some children who are in fact ready for this may in some respects still be severely disorganized when they begin. When the therapist's imposes the following structure, such a child can be helped to develop a more controlled motor response. The therapist begins, for example, by standing behind the child to grasp his hands and guide the color pencils in the manner designated while tapping out a rhythm with her fingers on his hands. As the therapist feels the child is able to control his own responses more and more, she removes her hands. A less pronounced "tactile beat" may then be maintained by tapping the child on each shoulder until words alone are enough for him to control the motor response.

While this "tactile beat" may be helpful in conveying the concept of rhythm to some children, the therapist must always keep alert for the tactually defensive

39. In Panel 2, the Positional Model becomes the base for identification of the left and right relationships of the letters *b* and *d*, *p* and *q*, so that letter and word reversals can be reduced.

child who would find that being touched where he cannot see it would be uncomfortable and disorganizing. Other children may respond negatively to the auditory input of clapping or snapping the fingers. Thus, in using any of these techniques, the therapist must be constantly aware of the individual child's responses, avoiding those which he indicates are inappropriate for him.

After several repeats of the above procedure he is asked to put both hands at the center of the panelboard or where the lines cross. Some children will need assistance here. With both hands at the midpoint of the horizontal line, the therapist says, "ONE TWO (move your) *hands apart*...THREE FOUR (move your) *hands together*." Once the child has established well controlled rhythm, he may begin to speed; this may simply mean he is becoming bored with the task. Such responses are accepted, for the purpose for which the method was developed is no longer needed, and it is important not to let a potentially negative reaction develop.

Early Application of the Positional Model to Directionality (7.3)

The child is asked to touch the top of the panelboard, then the bottom, the left, and the right sides to reaffirm to the child the meaning of these directions. This having been correctly accomplished, Panel 2 is enlarged to 30″ by 40″ size in accord with the color diagram.

The Positional Model is applied first as a means of clearly establishing the

214

40. In Panel 4, body image, back view is superimposed on this stable frame of reference which the **Positional** Model provides for left and right.

directionality of reversible letters. Following a brief review of the sensory identification of left and right and the basic Positional Model, the therapist and child face Panel 2 as she says, "Here is a black circle on top of the dotted line. Along the left side of the circle there is a red line making it the letter *b*."

Speaking slowly and kneeling to be near the child's eye level, she marks the red line up and down to give the child ample time to formulate his answer. Continuing in the same manner and using the appropriate color for each of the letters *d*, *p*, and *q*, she points out that in the latter two the lines extend below the dotted line. In the early stage of this letter identification, confusion can be avoided if the therapist and not the child marks these red and blue lines. In Panel 3, this can be done by the child.

As a variation with Panel 2, the child is asked to point to the letter named. This works well with two children or in two teams. The person at the front of the line on one team names a letter for the one at the front of the line on the other side to point out. The team making the request must confirm whether the answer was right or wrong; children then move to the back of the line.

In application of the Positional Model in Panel 3, there are blank spaces for the child to attach words which apply. He is helped to first recognize how to apply the words — center, upper and lower halves, left and right halves, upper left-hand corner, etc — to those parts of the panelboard. Successful performance here is followed by the introduction of the directions north, south, east, and west on this large panelboard in conjunction with the small grid, Appendix J-7 and J-8 used in P.P. 7.6.

Panels 1, 2, and 3 are shown separately here for the purpose of clarity in conducting these therapy procedures. In practice these three may be combined into one.

Application of the Positional Model to Body Image[1,2] (7.4)

In young children, identification of body parts and the most common joints is encouraged during home programming to help also develop verbal language. In therapy, a quick check is made in Level I to determine if there are any residual problems of this kind. Again it is stressed that while adults in his midst will use the terms left and right themselves, and in a natural manner, their application should not be stressed at home, or in school, or in therapy until hand dominance has been suitably established.

The Left-Right Identification Index has been developed as a means of assessing the baseline of function in a manner which is consistent with the ongoing therapy program. Stylized line drawings of the back view (Panel 4) and front view (Panel 5) of a young boy, emphasizing joints and facial features, are enlarged 8 inches x 10 inches for mimeographing. Using the Left-Right Identification Index together with these drawings, children may be screened individually or in a class or therapy group simply and quickly. This instrument provides an important baseline assessment against which to measure change.

The Left-Right Identification Index: Starting with the back view, the body image drawing is placed on the desk in front of the child; he is asked to place the number in the space designated on the list below. If there appears to be no persistent left-right confusion on the back view, proceed to test with the front view in the same manner.

Back view	*Front view*
1. Right ear	11. Left ear
2. Left elbow	12. Left hip
3. Left knee	13. Right knee
4. Right hip	14. Right elbow
5. Left ankle	15. Left ankle
6. Right wrist	16. Right hip
7. Right shoulder	17. Left shoulder
8. Left wrist	18. Right eye
9. Right elbow	19. Left elbow
10. Left shoulder	20. Right wrist

Scoring: This is scored simply with one point for every correct answer.

Assessment on the back view alone is suitable at first grade level; the front view would normally be presented at the second or third grade level. The Left-Right

Identification Index can be particularly useful as a screening device for those who enter therapy after the age of eight. Results of the procedure are not revealed to the child; in some cases, after the deficiencies have been satisfactorily overcome, these changes may be shared with the individual to help him recognize the extent of his own progress.

Left-right confusion is normal among many children at kindergarten level and early first grade, but it soon subsides. In therapy when there is a stable point of reference such as that provided through early sensory identification and color coding in the Positional Model, this confusion disappears very quickly. Competence equal to that of their peer group may not be achieved by children receiving therapy until they have had extensive experience in the foundation steps which were previously mentioned and in other therapy to follow. It is suggested that all these techniques and, specifically, the next one, could feasibly be adopted for routine classwork in first grade so as to provide the average child a similar point of reference on which to establish good directionality.

The procedure is conducted with an enlarged version of Panel 4, the back view of the body image drawing which is secured at an appropriate height in a near-vertical position. Having briefly reviewed the sensory identity of the "heavy blue weight (or china marking pencil) for the right," and "red for left," the therapist says, "Here is a drawing of a little boy. He is facing in the same direction you are, looking straight ahead. Touch the back of the boy's head in the drawing. Now touch the back of your own head. You and the boy in the drawing are looking in the same direction."

The purpose in asking for the ear first would be to prevent early confusion of having to cross the midline to touch a joint on the opposite arm; this will disorganize some children. Continuing throughout the drawing, the child is asked to identify the joints one by one, beginning with those which are familiar and easily visible, eg, the knees and elbows. The more obscure joints which may also be less familiar to the child follow, eg, the hip, ankle, and wrist. The therapist reminds him to take his time if he tends to rush and get disorganized. The therapist says to him, "Touch your left elbow. Take your time. Yes, that is your left elbow. Squeeze it so you know what your left elbow feels like." Having progressed satisfactorily to this point, the therapist now says to the child, "Find this boy's left elbow in the drawing." As the child points to the circle surrounding the joint of this stick-figure, the therapist colors in the area. There is less chance of disrupting the continuity of the child's thoughts and associations if at first the therapist does this. As the age of the child and his proficiency permit, this function can be readily assumed by him, at least to color in the side which for him is dominant. For children of ten and over they will usually be able to color both without becoming confused.

Body image work with the large drawing can be fun and motivating in a group. A child should, however, not be included in a group until he is functioning with better than a 50% chance of responding with the correct answer. When he can, a group experience such as this can provide positive feedback which these children often need so desperately.

Assessment of the Left-Right Identification Index may be conducted during the initial evaluation for children who are 8 years old and older. When there is obvious confusion on the back view there is no need to check his response on the front view at that time. When training begins in cross over identification, it is not necessary to make an assessment either, for one would expect to include the procedure as a part of therapy anyway.

Recognition of left and right on a person facing the opposite direction is considerably more difficult than when two persons face the same way. Residual confusion occurs into adulthood. The method I have devised is simple and tangible; it has been helpful in clarifying the problem by providing a stable point of reference.

The therapist offers the child a blue weight in the method previously described for his right hand. She turns, with her back to the child, and as she picks up another blue weight in her own right hand, she points out to the child that they each have a weight in the right hand. He is reminded to keep his eyes on the blue weight she holds up in full view for him to watch as she turns around to face him. They then touch their blue weights together with their right hands. Subsequently they shake hands and use that as a supplementary aide to confirm quickly that the right and left sides of the other person are always diagonally opposite. The adult may continue at an appropriate pace thereafter to have the child identify right and left joints on himself first and then on the person or the front view drawing. The enlarged front view drawing is mounted on the reverse side of the first one and both are covered with transparent vinyl for easy marking with the china marker.

Application of the Positional Model to Telling Time (7.5)

Learning to tell time often presents difficulty for the learning-disordered child because it is based on directionality. Children have little difficulty in understanding the hour hand once the numbers 1-12 have been learned. It is the abstract application of directionality to identify the position of the minute hand "before" and "after" the hour which leaves them confused. Again, the early sensory identification of left and right and their color coding on the Positional Model provide a stable, constant frame of reference so that the child can comprehend the meaning of "how long" before or after the hour with less confusion.

Panel 6 is color coded and is enlarged for school or clinic use. It is designed for early use to convey the basic concepts of before and after to help the child understand that there are many words used to express the same idea, and to show that the line segments of the dial represent five-minute intervals. These concepts need to be established before the child is confronted with the potentially confusing numerical arrangement of the dial.

Facing the nearly vertical panelboard, the child's attention is directed to the parallel vertical red and blue lines similar to those of the Positional Model. After being instructed that when the short hand is on a number, eg, the three, and the long hand is at the top, it means "on the hour of three" or "three o'clock," and when the long hand points to the bottom, it is half past the hour. These relatively concrete concepts can be mastered with little difficulty by comparison with coping with the minutes in between.

Beyond this, the more severely disordered child or the retardate will sometimes need a definitive means of mastering the additional aspects of telling time, such as telling the quarter hour. Directing the child's attention to the horizontal red line, he is asked to lift his arm from his side to shoulder heights to the position equivalent to the nine on the clockface. He is helped to recognize that the position of the long hand anywhere along the left, or red side, from the bottom to the top would signify minutes before the hour. At this point, the word "quarter" is used only because it is the accepted way of expressing time, and no attempt is made with the child who is just learning to tell time that the hour is divided into four quarters. However, he is helped to understand that the numbers nine and three correspond to the horizontal position of his extended arms; this will enable him in due time to recognize the quarter before and after the hour by associating it with the earlier sensory identification and the Positional Model.

Starting on the hour, it is next pointed out that each minute is marked by a tiny line, there being five between each big number or larger line. To make it easy, one learns that when the long hand is on the number one, this means "five minutes *after* the hour," and so on. The words "past the hour" are also used to mean "after"; simple as this seems, one cannot assume that these transition steps will be made automatically by the learning-disordered child. The line to the upper right in Panel 4 is put there so that the words after and past can be written as temporary reminders if the child can benefit from reading them at this point.

Application of the Positional Model to Geographic Orientation[1] (7.6)

The older child will be ready to apply the geographical positions to the Positional Model, Panel 3 following 7.3. While the words north and south are easy enough, east and west may cause him confusion since this is the usual order in which they are stated, and it is just the reverse of the left-right horizontal progression which has been stressed. The child must become clearly aware of the fact that west and east are the directions which match the left-right orientations. One association which can help the child remember is that the sun sets in the west; in this procedure both left and west are represented by red. To become fully accomplished in recognizing geographical orientation, the following exercise is recommended.

Using a black and white graphic representation (Appendix J-9) of the plastic grid of the Grid and Peg Set from P.P. 5.2, the structure of the Positional Model is superimposed with dotted lines to designate the North-South and West-East axes. On this grid, drawn in ½″ squares, 10 blocks by 13 blocks in size, a series of exercises is introduced on Panel 7 which carries the labels of the directions and the axes. Using a china marking pencil, the child is required to follow a designated route on this panel, which has been slipped into a vinyl page protector. Many children would be able to start this exercise on Panel 8 in which there are no labels, expecting the child to have already integrated this information adequately.

These patterns are graded in difficulty starting with the most stable ones, moving North, South, West, East, to patterns which include occasional diagonal directions such as Northeast, and eventually to those which include a predominance of oblique lines to make a less and less stable pattern. The directions are stated in a clear voice, instructing the child to move, for example, "North three blocks...Southwest four blocks." The task requires integration of numerous skills, to include recognition of geographical orientation, while at the same time keeping control of the pencil while listening for the auditory information which includes two steps, the direction, and the number of blocks. This is upgraded for the adolescent and adult by giving several instructions in sequence to further develop skill in auditory recollection and recall in order to prepare the individual for increased demands in retaining the content of lecture material and to assist him in note taking.

It should be noted that throughout the latter portions of the program, there has been a gradual increase in verbal instruction. The child is able to demonstrate by his actions what the words mean, allowing the therapist to continually monitor his responses for any confusion in the ideas or concepts being conveyed.

Through these geographical orientation exercises, the ability to formulate and express the direction is also emphasized. Upon completion of the task, according to the verbal instructions, the individual is then asked to reverse the route and say them back at each change of direction. This requires yet another process to be integrated.

The essential point throughout the holistic approach to therapeutic programming is to break down the task into distinct, closely interlocked steps which will enable the child to make the transitions necessary. In this case it is to learn directionality; after a sound internal sensory base was established and the structure of the Positional Model was provided as a stable frame of reference, the child can easily acquire directionality in his body image, reversible letters, telling time, and now geographical locations.

Problems in reading, writing, and other hurdles throughout a broad range of academic application arise when there has been an incomplete analysis and breakdown of steps according to the essential sensorimotor elements within the total learning process. Whenever a child needs repeated instruction to learn, chances are that the concept the instructor is trying to convey is too far above the child's foundation skills, eg, when "saw" and "was" were thought to be mastered one day but were lost the next. Experience suggests that children who heretofore have been unable to grasp this early academic material through traditional instruction will be enabled to do so through the early sensory integrative means described here.

References

1. Knickerbocker B: A Central Approach to the Development of Spatial and Temporal Concepts. Seattle, Special Child Pubs, 1968.
2. Knickerbocker B: "The significance of body schema and body image in perceptual-motor dysfunction." Proceedings of the Conference on Body Image. Cleveland, Cleveland District, Ohio Occupational Therapy Association, Box 7173, Cleveland, Ohio, 1966.

Program Plan 8

Scribbles to Script

Many of the previously stressed underlying foundation skills culminate in this last program plan. A brief review is in order to demonstrate how the various prerequisite skills have been carefully integrated. P.P. 1.4 and 1.7 help the child to organize better tactile system function within himself, for the development of prehension, to grasp and control the direction of a pencil in order to produce number and letter forms. P.P. 2 stresses the all-important bilateral and postural motor integration. P.P. 6 helps the child to develop hand dominance. In P.P. 7, through the use of the Positional Model, the child develops sound directional orientation for numbers and letters on which the specifics of this program plan will be based.

Before turning our attention to training the child in specific directional orientation of number and letter forms in P.P. 8.8, much emphasis must be placed on the gradual progression from gross motor control of body movements all the way up to fine movements of the dominant hand which must be properly sequenced for manuscript print and script writing. Problems of motor function which have been observed in learning-disordered children have been analyzed from a holistic, composite point of view. To review momentarily, it is proposed in the hypothesis that learning takes place through cyclic processing and learning continuity. It further proposes that five processes are identifiable in this sequential learning pattern, the first being the process of overcoming an avoidance response, and then going on to explore, organize, integrate, and conceptualize.

The concept of cyclic processing and learning continuity becomes apparent in tracing the development of motor skills from those early patterns which were originally under residual reflex control progressing all the way to the sequencing of fine motor patterns in script writing. The program plans presented here have been designed so that this processing and continuity can take place in the most natural and self-motivating way for children. Through the implementation of these methods, those aspects of motor behavior which are deficient or slow to develop can be accelerated and enhanced. Thus, one aspect of the overall goal of therapy has been met, namely, to enable the learning-disordered child to bring organization out of disorganization so that he can function as an equal among his peers as much as possible. Reduction of disorganized motor responses and academic adjustment are two of the four specific areas of performance included in the goal definition for this therapy.

The hypothesis (Part I, Chapter 4) proposes that learning takes place through cyclic processing and learning continuity. The route by which the learning-disordered child has been enabled to organize motor behavior illustrates this point. Following the activation of the sensory systems in P.P. 1 and 2, which emphasize in particular the tactile and vestibular systems, P.P. 3 proposes means to enable the child to bridge the gap between avoidance and exploration to organize the gross motor skills into large, sequential movement patterns. Initial experiences in P.P. 3 were first structured by the equipment, ie, the indoor climber, followed by a decrease of structure to unstructured "near the floor" activities. The demands on balance increased as the structure decreased in order to involve standing balance and movement in the vertical position, ie, use of the balance beam and the highly unstable suspended equipment such as the rope ladder.

Postural and bilateral integration involving use of both sides of the body through gross motor skills was emphasized in activities of P.P. 2 to include the double suspended tires, the carpeted barrel, scooter board, and inflatables. Prior to dominance exploration in P.P. 6, early bimanual motor integration was stressed using such toys as the plastic interlocking Fun-EE Men.

In P.P. 7, emphasis is placed on gross motor organization of the upper extremities to develop awareness of position and direction. This is carried out by means of the Positional Model and the application of this as a stable frame of reference. As a follow-up of the early bimanual motor integration in P.P. 1, bimanual motor integration is introduced in P.P. 8.2 at a higher level using the bimanual circles. Thereafter, gross motor organization of the dominant hand is introduced in P.P. 8.3 with template training, in P.P. 8.4 with kinesthetic "tag" and "baseball," and in P.P. 8.5 with the large figure-eight patterns. Each of these aforementioned tasks involves a gradual increase in control of movement throughout the shoulder and arm; the normal developmental progression advances from stabilization and control of proximal, gross movements to the distal, fine patterns of finger movement such as those which follow.

In P.P. 8.6, fine motor integration between the two hands is stressed. Young children can suitably use the small interlocking pieces such as found in Lego or Tinkertoy Sets of wood or metal, while a very high level of the skills would be required for older children and adults in the bimanual control of the familiar recreational games of Labyrinth or Roll-A-Score.

Following some development of fine motor integration between the two hands, specific training of the dominant hand begins. To help a child print his letters with a minimum of directional confusion, one would first establish an awareness of a simple ordered sequence and direction of movements. This would be found in Practice Sheet 1 for P.P. 8.7. It emphasizes the simple verbal and motor sequential patterns "top-to-bottom" and "left-to-right" in preparation for training directional orientation to numbers and printed letter forms in P.P. 8.8. The ordered sequence of minute finger movements for script follow in P.P. 8.9. A semiautomatic level of function must be mastered in forming the sequential pattern of individual letters and letter combinations if the child is to develop writing speed commensurate with increasing academic demands.

The child who normally experiences no learning problems with regard to directionality, motor function, or the sequence of movement patterns will presumably have followed much the same progression in learning to write. Since he is able to assimilate and integrate new information and experiences so rapidly, these distinct intermediate steps are relatively obscure to observers. Close observation of the learning-disordered child makes these steps more apparent; the interdependent factors can be isolated and analyzed. If the learning-disordered child is to succeed in acquiring adequate writing function, then the experience must be structured for him in such a way that there are no significant gaps in these critical transitional steps.

The therapist and the educator must be able to identify which of these steps is deficient in the individual child. She must evaluate his performance in early writing skills through a procedure which makes his needs readily apparent and which is sufficiently constant to document change. Such a method is described in P.P. 8.1

Scribble Boards

P.P. 8 spans the development of pencil skills from the early scribbling stage and beginning finger prehension of preschoolers to the refinements of script writing. The latter stage can be of value even to the high school student who is still encountering problems in the ease, speed, and legibility of his handwriting.

As the young preschooler begins to grasp a writing tool, he should be provided ample opportunity for free scribbling in the vertical position which brings into play large shoulder movements. Also, being near eye level, his visual attention soon is directed to the lines of scribbles which his own movement has produced. This important step should be available to children in nursery school and kindergarten and can be used at home to supplement the therapy program.

A large scribble board such as this would measure 6 feet to 8 feet in length and be attached to a smooth wall. To properly protect the wall, it is first covered with thin polyvinyl sheeting, secured with masking tape along the entire edge. Two widths of brown rolled wrapping paper the length of this space are taped to the board one below the other, and sealed in the same manner. The height and the expanse of such a scribble board invite sweeping exploratory arm movements. Heavy crayons or china marking pencils are strongly recommended for use in preference over lead pencils for the smooth flowing sensation of movement they generate. This is in contrast to the potentially irritating tactile sensation over a chalkboard.

The following adaptation of this method is particularly suitable for clinics. A hollow door is covered first with white paper; over this, sturdy vinyl sheeting is taped about the edges. The door is positioned horizontally, supported at a proper height on cabinet drawers and braced for use in a nearly vertical position. To motivate a child's involvement, age-appropriate pictures or drawings are placed beneath the vinyl for him to scribble over with the china marker, hiding them from view. In this repetitive scribbling task, the quality of performance can be seen to change from grossly erratic, random lines to a pattern which includes a greater preponderance of parallel lines.

Evaluation of Sample Performance of Number and Letter Forms (8.1)

If the child is in first grade or beyond when he enters therapy, or is in a

41. On two-inch lined paper, the child is asked to make his numbers *1-21*, or *21-31* for the older child, and print first the capital, then lower-case alphabet, or whatever portion of this is suitable, as a record of Hour 1 performance. Subsequent samples are taken for comparison at four- to six-week intervals.

kindergarten where pencil control has been trained, a sample of his numbers and letters is taken to record his baseline performance. Lines two inches apart are used, rather than lined pads, as a means of ferreting out subtle residuals of problems. In older children these residuals are less apparent unless they must adapt to using a spatial orientation to which they have not become accustomed.

Newsprint paper 12 *x* 18 inches is lined horizontally every 2 inches; this is secured with masking tape to a slightly larger piece of Plexiglas 1/8 inch thick for use at the desk. The Plexiglas provides a firm, smooth surface. It will not slip off if the child fails to secure it, and it is easily moved left and right to maintain optimal visibility and comfort for the child as he works.

A china marking pencil is preferred over a pencil because 1) its circumference is larger, which makes it easier for a young child to grasp, 2) it glides smoothly over the surface, giving a more pleasing sensation than would a lead pencil, and 3) it yields a width of line which is proportional to the size of a form to fit the 2 inch space.

The therapist sits on a low stool, opposite the child, to assure optimum eye contact as she speaks; this is especially important for any child who is obviously distractible and unable to listen well to verbal instructions. She first ascertains whether the young child can count and say any part of the alphabet. First he is asked to "make his numbers." He may need some help to keep the order in mind when he is concentrating on how to make them. It is helpful if he says the numbers aloud so the therapist is clear as to what number it is the child believes he is forming; sometimes the forms are quite unrecognizable.

First and second graders are asked to make the numbers 1-21. Children of age eight and above are asked to make the numbers 21-31. Upon completion of the numbers, the young child may be ased if he can make any letters of the alphabet or make his ABCs. The first grader would be asked to print the capital letters of the alphabet. As soon as the child starts to confuse capitals and small letters, he is again reminded to print the capitals. When he has finished, if it seems feasible, depending on the child's ability and the amount of confusion manifested, he would be asked to print the small letters of the alphabet on a second sheet. The child is asked to put his name on it; the therapist records the therapy hour and date on it.

Throughout the task the therapist immediately notes the sequence of those movements which are out of the ordinary by making the number or letter in her record in the same way as the child's with arrows numbered to indicate the sequence. Later these arrows are recorded on the child's drawing; reversals of patterns which are indicative of confusion are underscored.

The therapist would observe, for example, any time the child starts the number "1" from the bottom. Other observations would include whether the child's zeros are started at the bottom. Are they made in the clockwise direction? Are there any reversals in top-to-bottom orientation? For example, is the "4" made upside down? Are there any left-right reversals of numbers 2-9 being made in a mirror image, or any confusion of the number "3" with the letter "E"? Are the numbers made in a recognizable representation without any confusion? Are the double numbers reversed in sequence, so that "14" becomes for the child "4 — teen" and made as "41"? Are the double numbers appropriately spaced or are they run together and confused and without obvious individual identity? Do they touch the line, or are there "floaters"?

The therapist watches and records how the pencil is picked up and positioned. Is it clenched in the fist? Is the grasp tense? Is it held in a bizarre finger position or is it comfortably controlled in a more mature, tripod position? Does the child transfer the pencil from one hand to the other? How much tension and movement occur in the lips and tongue as the child directs the china marker?

Is the alphabet complete and the letters in the proper sequence? Is there confusion evident by combining capital and small letters of the printed alphabet or mixtures of printed form with script? Is the size constancy of letters and numbers fairly good or do they become progressively smaller or larger? Is the relative size inconsistent and erratic? Is the size totally inconsistent with the 2 inch space, ie, being less than ½ inch high or stretching beyond it? Are there "floaters" among the numbers or letters? Is greater skill evidenced in either the numbers or the letters?

The initial sample of numbers and letters is usually recorded during the first hour unless the child is obviously too young. After dominance has been confirmed, and prior to the left-right sensory identification being introduced, another sample is sometimes taken to see to what extent the left-right awareness has already become more integrated in relation to the work on the inflatables and hand dominance exploration. Even before any training per se is undertaken, there will often be a noticeable effect in reducing the disorganization and directional confusion which may have been exhibited in the initial sample of numbers and letters.

The procedure for training numbers and letters uses a left-right color coding which is consistent with previous work in P.P. 7. It cannot be emphasized too strongly that this color coding should never be used in isolation nor even as the primary means of directional orientation for numbers and letters; rather it provides information to confirm the direction for forming them and does so in a manner which is structured for the child's easy retrieval from memory.

As a means of alerting the tactile sensation for optimal control of the small, purposeful movements, the child is encouraged to hold a ⅜" dowel like a pencil and rub it back and forth over the textured scribble board for several minutes whenever he is going to practice his number and letter forms and also before each sample performance is to be taken. The textured scribble board, as it is called here, is formed of small prism-like areas throughout one surface of plexiglas, the primary intended use being to deflect the rays from fluorescent lights. This type of textured board is available at lumber companies in sheets 2 feet x 4 feet.

Also during the initial evaluation, motor control is observed with a pencil using the Visual Motor Integration Test by Beery and Buktenica.[1] This test has normative data from three to sixteen years. Its value is twofold; not only is the child's performance measured against that expected of children his age, but use of it for retesting provides the most obvious picture of change which can be recorded. The test is meaningful to parents and confirms to the therapist and teachers specific changes in motor control by relatively objective means. Retesting is done at three- to six-month intervals.

Concomitant with the above test, the Winter Haven Perceptual Copy Forms[2] is often administered. Retesting on this may be conducted more frequently, often monthly, during the period of time when attention is being concentrated on pencil control. This is economically advantageous, for the test is done on a blank sheet of paper; it is administered to children individually or in very small groups.

Bimanual Circles
(Early Bimanual Motor Integration) (8.2)

As soon as the child has performed satisfactorily in P.P. 7.2 — the introduction of the Positional Model — the use of these bimanual circles can be instituted at Level II. Two circles, one on the left in red and the other on the right in blue measuring about 19 inches in diameter, are drawn on a 30 x 40 inch piece of white paper and mounted on a ½ inch panelboard of the same size. This is covered with heavy transparent polyvinyl and secured around the edge with masking tape. The panelboard is placed horizontally in a near vertical position with red and blue circles left and right respectively, at a height where the midpoint would be near eye level for the child.

Holding a red china marking pencil in the left hand and a blue one in the right, the child is asked to place the hands together at the center point where the circles touch. The therapist tells the child to "Listen to the words and move your hands in the way the words tell you. Move DOWN and AROUND, move DOWN and AROUND, move DOWN and AROUND and STOP." These simple instructions are said to slowly establish a slow and even rhythm over a period of eight to ten seconds.

In the beginning the child will often move in a very irregular pattern, rushing on the inward-downward movement. In children who have poor postural and bilateral integration, one hand, usually the nondominant one, will lag behind the other noticeably. It can be helpful to the young child if in the beginning the therapist holds the red and blue markers while the child grasps the top of the adult's hands. In this "piggy-back" method, the pattern of movement and an even rhythm are conveyed to the child. One then watches as the child holds the markers to see whether there is sufficient carryover effect for the child to proceed independently.

When the movement is well controlled in speed and rhythm bilaterally, and the circles are of relatively equal size and contour, the child is ready for the next step. Proceeding as before, the child now moves in the opposite direction in accord with the words *up* and *around* for three repeats as before. It is not suggested that performance be perfected by extra practice in either of these two patterns. In any one session, they would be repeated no more than once or twice.

The next procedure, at Level III, is considerably more difficult and has been named the "locomotive." One should not proceed directly to this after the other two patterns have been achieved in therapy; preferably a "holding pattern" may be instituted for one or two months before introducing it. However, if on introduction of the two earlier methods the child can do them with ease, one would proceed to observe his performance using the locomotive technique.

In this locomotive technique, the child positions each hand at the point equivalent to nine o'clock. The child is asked to move his hands down and around simultaneously for three repeats, in a counterclockwise direction, in keeping with the more predominant movement in writing. To establish the rhythm, the words "CHUG-CHUG...CHUG-CHUG...CHUG-CHUG-CHUG" are voiced by the therapist in an obvious cadence.

Templates
(Gross Motor Organization of the Upper Extremities)[1] (8.3)

Large cardboard templates developed and marketed by the Winter Haven Lions Club Research Foundation are recommended for use in preference to those of plastic because they are less apt to slip when the child traces each of them in a vertical position. The forms and the order of difficulty as they are used in the holistic program are 1) circle, 2) square, 3) triangle, 4) vertical diamond, and 5) horizontal diamond. A scoring system has been adapted for use[2] primarily as a means of charting progress which can be meaningful and motivating to the child. The criteria for this numerical scoring are listed later in this text; the clinical observations which coincide with the three levels of performance in this program are cited in the OEPS.

The following general procedure is used in template training. When the child is still too active and disorganized to stand still for template training at the vertical position, use of them at desk level is recommended. Except for the fact that the paper is secured to a large piece of Plexiglas for desk use, the procedures are the same. The procedure used in the vertical position is described here in detail. A 12 x 24 inch piece of white newsprint is secured at the corners with masking tape. A "+" is placed approximately at midpoint in the left half of this sheet, which should be at the child's eye level; this is used as an important point of reference so the child can position himself properly each time before he starts to trace around the

42. Vertical positioning of the templates promotes good visual feedback of the movement; pressing hard with the nondominant hand helps to stimulate natural use of the hands together.

template. The template is first traced on the left hand side of the paper according to the "age formula." On the right hand side of the paper, after making a similar "+," the child makes a freehand drawing of the same form, but only once. This freehand form is then compared to the template, which is placed over it and traced only once with a crayon of a contrasting color.

Standing directly in front of the "+" with both feet flat on the floor, the child is asked to press his nondominant hand against the cardboard template to secure it as firmly as he can. The therapist also will need to help, but gradually she challenges the child to be increasingly responsible for securing the template, reminding herself not to do for the child what he can and should be doing for himself. He is urged to press the marker or large crayon firmly against the entire inside perimeter of the template, compelling the child to respond with equal force in each hand and stimulating integration of the two sides of his body. The significance of this integrated action of the hands, together with their overlapping movement in prone twirling, will have a definite influence on the child in helping him to spontaneously hold his paper for writing tasks.

A template for each of the five geometric forms is marked along its edge as described so as to structure the child's experience most effectively. For a right-handed child, the larger margin is positioned to the left for the nondominant hand to hold securely and then be marked appropriately. The template is positioned in the reverse, with the large margin to the right for left-handed

228

children, but the markings along the perimeter remain constant for both hands. The diamond template is the exception, being marked on one side to trace the vertical diamond and on the other to trace the horizontal one.

Movement around each form should progress in a counterclockwise pattern. While it is often difficult for the right-handed disorganized child to overcome the more primitive level of clockwise progression, it is even more arduous for the left-handed child to overcome this primitive pattern. The structure and markings of the templates greatly facilitate this change.

Upon completing the number of revolutions set by the age formula, the template in each case is removed; another "+" is placed at the midpoint of the right half of the same paper. The therapist places a dot at a point equivalent to that where the form had previously been started within the template. First the child is asked to think how it felt to trace the form around the template and then to make one as near as possible in size and shape as the one he has just traced. If the child proceeds in a clockwise direction, this is accepted without a word of correction and recorded by an arrow. Change will come about automatically and must not be the result of verbal reminders but rather as an indication of improved internal awareness and sensory organization.

Circle

The circular template is marked with arrows pointing inward at the twelve o'clock and six o'clock positions to help the child in counting as well as to regulate for him the tempo and rhythm. A line is drawn outward from the edge, at the one o'clock position, to serve as a starting point. An arrow from there, moving in a counterclockwise direction, clearly defines for the child which way to start. Now as the child's hand, holding the crayon, passes the arrow at the top, the therapist helps the child to structure the experience by counting aloud as follows: *one* — as it passes the point at the bottom she then says — *and* — structuring the experiences as this continues aloud, noting the number of repetitions which match the age formula. In the beginning, young children will be unable to count at the same time they are tracing. Gradually they will join in and, in time, should become independent in this while still maintaining a steady, slow tempo and rhythm.

Square

Beginning at the upper right-hand corner, an arrow points to the left and the word *count* is marked above. As the child moves in this direction around the square and establishes a slow rhythm by repeating the words of movement, which are likewise marked on the outer margins with arrows, he is helped to say: "ONE...DOWN...OVER...UP," as he moves along each side. The child is encouraged to push hard into each corner; this helps to retard the speed of the disorganized, hyperactive child as well as heighten the kinesthetic feedback from the impact. With the external structure provided by the firm template contour and the slow, rhythmic tempo, the hyperactive child is gradually able to exert greater internal control and organize his motor behavior more effectively. Used in this way, the square template, more than any other, clearly establishes in the child an awareness of the sensation of the horizontal and vertical directions through simultaneous multisensory avenues: visual, auditory, and tactile-kinesthetic.

Triangle

The outer margins of the triangle are marked in a similar manner, starting at the top. The count is made on the down stroke as follows: "ONE... OVER... BACK."

Vertical Diamond

Starting at the top and moving as always in a counterclockwise progression, the margin of the template is marked with arrows and the following words: "ONE...DOWN...UP...BACK."

Horizontal Diamond

Turning the template over and starting at the top to move counterclockwise, the template is marked with arrows and the following words: "ONE...DOWN... OVER...BACK."

Diamonds are the most difficult to reproduce because the oblique lines cannot be oriented with the ground, which is the most stable point of reference. The horizontal diamond seems more difficult because the top-bottom angles are more obscure than are the top and bottom acute angles of the vertical diamond. In reproducing the freehand drawing of the horizontal diamond, the tendency to err comes from extending the line along the lower left-hand side too far, usually protruding beyond the center or starting point of the angle opposite angle. Acute angles are apt to be reproduced more accurately than obtuse angles. This may be due in part to the fact that acute angles are visually more obvious; also, in tracing the templates, the tactile-kinesthetic feedback is stronger from tracing the acute angle than when tracing the obtuse angle.

The criteria for scoring performance has been adapted from the Winter Haven material,[2] as cited below. Its value is more for motivation of the child who needs positive feedback at this point in his program than it is for the therapist's assessment of his progress. Of greater importance than the score alone is the change in clinical observations cited in the OEPS for Levels I through III.

Circle	Starts at the top	1
(5)	Round	2
	Accuracy*	2
Square	Sides equal	2
(10)	Lines straight	2
	Corners closed	2
	Base horizontal	2
	Accuracy*	2
Triangle	Sides equal	2
(10)	Apex centered	2
	Lines straight, corners closed	2
	Base horizontal	2
	Accuracy*	
Vertical	Sides equal	2
and	Lines straight, no elbows	2

Horizontal	Points closed, sharp	2
Diamonds	Apex of top and bottom angles vertical	1
(10)	Apex of left and right angles horizontal	1
	Accuracy*	2

*Accuracy may be measured in either of the following ways:

1) Select the curve, the line or angle or a combination of these in the freehand drawing which corresponds most closely to the contour of the templates. Placing the template along the best corresponding features, trace around the template with another color. For a count of "2," no part of the form may be more than ½″ outside or inside the line of the template.

2) All lines are parallel to the template and may be ½″ or so smaller than or larger than the template.

The therapist must be alert to recognize various forms of disorganized motor behavior which often arise during template training. Residuals of poor postural and bilateral integration would be the most significant. This can be recognized by asking the child first to stand with his feet flat on the floor so that his head and eyes are in line with the "+" sign. It is important to observe any tendency for the child to resist crossing the midline of the body with his hand. For example, when the dominant right hand starts to move around the circular or square template and comes to the midline, the tendency of the child will be to shift the head and trunk to the left, or even step to the side, to thus alleviate the need for his hand to cross the midline of the body. Or the child may stand with all his weight on the contralateral foot, the other crossing over it. This is all done in such a natural and nonchalant manner that unless one is trained to recognize the significance of this behavior, its remedy will be ignored.

It is of interest to observe how long this pattern persists. It may be a solitary remnant of poor integration of the two sides, occurring only briefly, in a first or second grade child who has otherwise overcome any manifestation of this problem when rolling inside the carpeted barrel, twirling on the suspended tires or scooter board, and balancing on the inflatables. In this case, few if any verbal reminders to stand on both feet would be given, as the child would within the next few sessions make the necessary adaptive response to spontaneously stabilize his trunk as the hand crossed the midline.

Templates would also be used as an appropriate means for children 10 years old and older to reinforce hand dominance and develop better motor control. Reluctance when tracing around the templates may persist for four to six weeks. If children of ten and older are willing to do prone twirling on the scooter board, they will also be apt to demonstrate temporary reluctance to cross the midline, even at this age.

In adolescence, failure to cross the midline on large figure-eight drawings in P.P. 8.5 would be concomitant with these findings. To the extent that children through age ten will be agreeable, use of the scooter board is felt to still offer some therapeutic value for them. More acceptable as a primary means of developing better two-sided integration for older children, however, is the use of one of the inflatables for quadrupedal balancing. Within two months or at the maximum three months, the ability to stabilize the body during hand movements across the midline in the use of templates usually occurs spontaneously.

In the remaining cases, when it is clear during intermittent review of templates during this three-month period that the child will not be able to cross the midline automatically, then an occasional reminder or, as a last resort, a direct instructional approach is in order. The exact purpose of instruction here would be for the child to consciously force the hand across the midline while at the same time making every effort to stabilize the trunk. It will sometimes be appropriate to instruct the child to try to keep his feet flat on the floor. For some younger children too, an occasional nonverbal reminder such as this can be used:

> The therapist, standing behind the child, holds her left hand as a barrier so that his head does not shift away from the midline as he moves his pencil toward the left. Templates are being used in this instance as a means to an end to virtually force two-sided integration; their more obvious direct purpose would be to improve awareness of form and direction, and especially to develop better motor control of the dominant extremity.

It is impossible to assess the gross motor control of the dominant extremity when using template training in the vertical position without taking into full account the child's ability to maintain trunk stability by balancing and standing on both feet. Poor shoulder and hand-eye coordination in addition will be recognized by the irregularity of template tracing if he courses across the inside opening, or by the haphazard, forceful movements of the crayon as it jumps over the edge. An extremely light pencil grip will often signify that the child is tactually dormant and hypotonic, and needs further tactile input to be aware of how to hold and direct movements of the dominant arm and hand. All these points should be observed and recorded initially, as well as the changes as they occur.

The templates are presented in the order of their difficulty, the primary criteria for advancing to the next being relatively successful performance. The young child of first grade may perform too poorly on the circle to introduce the square for another three or four weeks. Other children, by contrast, may perform well enough that the circle and square are introduced the same session. After review of these, the triangle is introduced. The rate of advancement for each child is determined by his individual achievement.

As a means for improving gross motor organization in the dominant extremity, the primary focus of template training would be through the strong tactile-kinesthetic feedback. As a means of further enhancing this sensory input so as to make the individual more aware of joint positioning throughout the dominant arm, the following method is advocated. Starting out to trace around the template as before, the child is told that whenever he feels he is ready to do so, he should close his eyes and continue. It is of importance to therapists to note that blindfolds are not used for the following reasons: 1) closing his own eyes stimulates voluntary motor control, 2) blindfolds are irritating for many children because of tactile defensiveness, and 3) poor vestibular function makes it too threatening for many learning-disordered children.

By closing his eyes, the child's visual distractions are eliminated, and he can concentrate more fully on the position of the shoulder and elbow joints, especially at the points of impact at each successive corner of the square. Throughout the square, the child can sense clearly the direction, the speed, and the duration of the movement as the crayon courses along each side. The therapist can effectively augment his kinesthetic awareness by first telling him she will be tapping his shoulder or his elbow periodically while his eyes are closed, saying simply: "Think in your shoulder." "Think in your elbow." From this he will know that he is directing his full attention to the position and the direction of movement in that joint at the moment.

The follow-up freehand drawing of the square is started at the point the therapist designates on the right side of the piece of white newsprint paper. As the child places the crayon on that location, he is asked to again close his eyes and, before moving, to try to envision how it had felt when he had traced the form. After recalling the feeling as accurately as possible, he then tries to reproduce the same form with his eyes closed. Using this method, the point of closure often does not approximate the starting point, and the overall shape may not be as accurate as the one made with his eyes open. However, it is surprising how well a child can rely on this tactile-kinesthetic information. In fact, the length of a side or the angle the child reproduces can be remarkably close to the original. The degree of skill in reproducing the length of one side or the angulation of a corner is more relevant here than is the summation of parts which represent the whole form.

At this point the child's attention is directed to listening to the duration of the sound, together with the tempo of his movement, in addition to the sensation he perceives from the movement itself. Such a method can be very appropriate in establishing an awareness of the more refined movements of the dominant arm in the preadolescent and adolescent age groups, preliminary to the fine, sequential movements of script writing.

Kinesthetic Tag and Kinesthetic Baseball (8.4)

These two activities have been patterned after the technique used by Ayres in her standardized test for Kinesthesia,[3] because it is considered a valuable means of refining the child's skill. It should be remembered that this program is based on a holistic approach and that a formal evaluation is not conducted prior to, nor subsequent to, therapy. In those programs, however, wherein retesting in Kinesthesia is planned, one should not include these two activities because their use could invalidate retest findings.

A large piece of white paper is taped to one of the panelboards used in P.P. 7 and together these are then positioned in a near-vertical position at a convenient height for the child. The adult marks two dots which are 10″ to 12″ apart horizontally.

The child is asked to put his hand, which holds a crayon or marker, on the dot to the left. It is explained to him that after he closes his eyes, his hand will be moved from that dot to the other one and that while there, he must try to remember what it feels like in his arm to be there so that he will later be able to go back by himself.

In order for the child to concentrate on the kinesthetic feedback, he is asked to close his eyes; if the child is unable to do so, a manila folder is held in front of him to occlude his vision. The therapist lifts the child's hand, gliding it evenly and smoothly over the path, placing the crayon on the other dot. The therapist releases her grasp and the child waits there in silence to sense fully the sensory information until his hand is returned to the original spot. He is asked to try to tag the other dot as closely as he can. When he arrives at the point he perceives to be correct, he may be given a moment to adjust his arm position; this should not be an extended period, for the memory of the sensation is soon dissipated and the longer one "searches," the less accurate the response is apt to be.

A sheet of tracing paper is marked with progressively graded rings of 1, 2, or 3 inches in diameter to determine how close the child's terminating point was to the target. If in several attempts the response lies outside the 3″ ring, the activity should be discontinued for a month. When the child can tag the target occasionally within the 2″ or 1″ ring, then the procedure is continued with the dots placed vertically.

Kinesthetic baseball was designed along these same lines to appeal to boys, in particular, between seven and ten years. It is another means of gaining increased precision in their motor response, this time with oblique lines, which are more difficult. Since kinesthetic baseball requires that the child remain in the same standing position in front of home plate, it will necessitate that the child use the hand beyond the midline between second base and third and back to home plate.

A baseball diamond measuring 18 inches between bases is drawn on white paper, mounted on a panelboard, and covered with vinyl sheeting for use with a china marker. Each base consists of a dot ½″ in diameter, surrounded by rings measuring 1, 2, and 3 inches in diameter. The same procedure as that for tag is followed, moving from home plate around the bases. To motivate the child, he has three turns at each base to score a maximum of four points for the ½″ dot and decreasing one point for each successive ring. Scores may be used to measure progress in a way which is meaningful to the child and challenges his previous scores.

This technique is introduced during therapy but is preferably practiced at home with other members of the family. This is because of the time required, which is disproportionate for a balanced therapy program. It is also preferably done at home because it can be used as a means of fostering sibling relationships and a more positive interaction between them and the involved child. It is advantageous to the child in therapy to complete three repetitions of the same movement at each turn in order to help him concentrate on the kinesthetic input and refine his response. In this way, it also stresses the need to maintain as constant a standing position as he is able throughout each of these three repetitions. This can be used in school or clinic with two children competing. Beyond that, there may be too much undesirable background noise and movement of the other children, and this could easily reduce the child's concentration and detract from the value of the activity.

The first principle of promoting change in a holistic approach suggests moving along a continuum from maximal to minimal external structure. This principle is clearly illustrated here, moving from a task such as template training, which provides strong external structure and stimulates kinesthetic feedback regarding arm and shoulder movement, to kinesthetic tag and baseball. These two techniques represent the far end of this same continuum, since they provide a minimum of structure. Thus the child is required to exert increased internal control as he becomes able to do so. In kinesthetic baseball he must organize and monitor his own motor response, relying almost exclusively on the internal feedback about his position in space from those involved muscle and joint receptors.

Large Figure-Eight Patterns (8.5)

A large-scale vertical and horizontal figure-eight pattern is drawn in black on white paper measuring 30 x 40 inches and mounted horizontally on a panelboard of the same size. A black china marker is used to avoid generating any conflict or confusion relative to earlier color coding. By using black throughout, the child can clearly demonstrate whether he can move to the left or right on verbal instructions without having to rely on any color-coded visual clues. Foundations for a smooth, rhythmic, continuous sequence of movement used here in the figure-eight drawing evolved initially through the structured movement of template training and then the self-monitored control of shoulder motion in kinesthetic baseball.

In the procedure the child, facing the near-vertical position of the panelboard, places the marker on the center point and listens to the simple words of instruction which indicate for him to "loop to the top" and "loop to the bottom" in

43. As the therapist says, "Loop to the top, loop to the bottom," she watches to see whether there is any reluctance to cross over at the midpoint, resulting in an hourglass pattern, or whether a natural, continuous crossover pattern has developed first vertically, then horizontally.

a distinct, rhythmic cadence which is fairly slow. After the child has completed the third round trip, he is told to stop.

Useful observations can be made from this procedure. In particular, failure to cross the midline vertically is often the last remaining remnant of clinical evidence in older children and adolescents to indicate that in childhood there may have been some interruption or delay in development of bilateral and postural motor integration. Since this task is, by its size, an unfamiliar one, the individual would probably not have learned it as a splinter skill. Therefore, his actions will demonstrate to what degree his response toward crossing the midline has or has not been integrated for automatic use.

The therapist must be alert to observe every movement from the moment the instructions to move are given, for in older children and adolescents these faint remnants may be subtle and of short duration. However brief their existence, when also confirmed by historical data, these findings would strongly suggest some disruption in development had occurred in childhood. Relevant historical data would include 1) brief duration of creeping and crawling or avoidance of same, 2) delayed dominance, 3) reading and writing reversals, and 4) prolonged reluctance to secure the paper for writing, continuing even into adolescence.

The therapist notes whether the child balances equally on both feet and whether or not he shifts his body distinctly past the vertical midline when he follows the course of the figure-eight to the top and the bottom. It is insignificant whether the child moves toward the top along one side of the loop or the other. As the child reaches the end of the loop, the therapist must be ready to tell him promptly to loop to the bottom. In order to make the most valid observations, the therapist must present the changing instructions at the proper moment, and do so smoothly so that any hesitation or disorganization which shows up in the child's actions will not be the result of her own ineptitude.

The most critical observations come at the center point, so the therapist would be extremely alert to watch the child's movements each time he approaches it. Does the child automatically cross over to continue down the opposite side of the lower loop, or does he break this continuity and smooth sequence of movements to move along the same side in what is called the "hourglass" pattern?

For the therapist to make continuous observations and at the same time keep count of the number of times the child does and does not cross the vertical midline, an easy method has been devised. Each time the child crosses the midline, the therapist extends a finger on her right hand; when he fails to cross, she does the same on her left hand.

The rapidity with which these disorganizing, fragmented patterns may be resolved by some children into rhythmic, sequential movements suggests that their residual problem is minimal. Further exposure to this type of activity would be helpful in establishing a more consistent, stable pattern of bilateral postural and motor integration.

Vertical figure-eight patterns are not used in early assessment for children younger than eight when they enter therapy. After the child has progressed through P.P. 7.3 and 7.4, and when vertical figure-eight patterns are crossed more by purposeful intent than by chance, this task can then become an active part of the weekly therapy program.

By contrast to these remnants of the problem which are still evident into

236

adolescence, other children who are also in therapy at the age of five and six for problems other than postural and bilateral integration will make a very mature adaptive motor response, with smooth crossovers on the vertical figure-eight patterns, and also hold their paper for writing.

As soon as the child makes crossover patterns better than 50% of the time in the vertical figure-eights, the horizontal pattern is introduced. Starting again at the center point, the child is asked to "loop to the left" and "loop to the right" for three complete horizontal figure-eight patterns.

Some hesitation and disorganization in the sequence of movement may again arise and be resolved in a manner similar to that already described. The vertical and horizontal figure-eight patterns are designated as Level II difficulty. The "cloverleaf" patterns to follow are at Level III; they are not introduced until the child is at least 8 years old, and then only after movements of left and right in the horizontal figure-eights shows no residual confusion. Clover-leaf patterns can be an appropriate form of therapy to meet the needs of the adolescent, since it is sufficiently challenging that it does not insult them.

Starting at the center point, a review of several vertical patterns, followed immediately by several horizontal patterns, confirms in the child's mind the directional orientation and the tempo. Children may need to be slowed down for two reasons: First, they need sufficient time to listen and to interpret what they hear and act upon the instructions to move to any of the four loops. Secondly, the adult needs enough time to correctly anticipate in advance each of the two directions which can be executed without creating an awkward movement at the midline. The therapist must present these instructions so smoothly that no disorganization is precipitated by her own hesitancy. The child is told to be ready to loop to any one of the loops. He must not rush, and he must listen carefully.

Presuming the child moves up to the top along the right side of the upper loop, the basic cloverleaf pattern would be specified as follows: "Loop to the top...loop to the right...loop to the bottom...loop to the left." If the child moves first along the left side going toward the top, he must next be instructed to "loop to the left."

If the child does not move smoothly from the left side of the upper loop to the lower side of the right loop, but makes an abrupt change and a sharp angle to follow the upper side of the right loop, this is considered to be a residual manifestation of disorganized, fragmented motor behavior. The therapist stops him, to start again, without correcting the error. If this error is repeated, then it is too early for the child to engage in the task.

As soon as the child can smoothly execute two or three basic cloverleaf patterns, he would be ready for random cloverleaf patterns. Now it is mandatory that the therapist be able to carry out her responsibility without error. To do so, she observes a suitable formula. If the child is asked to "loop to the top" and he moves along the right side of this loop, then the only two possibilities open by which a smooth sequential pattern can be executed would be to "loop to the right" or "loop to the bottom." In other words, the therapist must recognize that if the child moves up the left side of the vertical top loop, she can depend on the fact that her next instruction will be correct if she asks him then to "loop to the left" next. In a similar manner, whenever the child is moving along the bottom of a horizontal loop, she can direct him to the bottom loop next. A smooth transition can always be made by instructing the child to move to the loop which is directly opposite the one he is then following, repeating this until one's thoughts are clear to proceed.

This activity will challenge the individual's ability to maintain smooth, well-controlled directional and crossover requirements for either the basic cloverleaf patterns or a series of random patterns. The child must be able to concentrate on auditory information and process it rapidly, while at the same time carrying out the movement patterns. As part of the program for adolescents and adults, they can try changing places with the therapist to verbalize these same instructions in the rapid order required. Indeed this does represent one of the most highly integrated activities within the entire program.

Fine Bimanual Motor Integration (8.6)

Under the OEPS heading Fine Motor Integration there is listed a series of graded activities, some of which are bimanual. If at this point in therapy there continues to be an obvious problem in bimanual action in dressing and in other activities of daily living which stem directly from bilateral incoordination of the upper extremities, then use of some of these activities can be helpful to supplement the more traditional means used in physical and occupational therapy.

Good integration of the two sides of the body was stressed early, in P.P. 2 and P.P. 6.1, to facilitate, among other things, the action of the nondominant hand to secure the paper for writing. Well controlled bilateral movements cited in P.P. 2 would be prerequisites for the child's development of some expertise in sports activities, eg, baseball, where he would face competition among his peers.

The bimanual movements of the upper extremities in P.P. 6.1 would relate more specifically to the action of the nondominant hand to secure the paper for writing. In treating the learning-disordered adolescent and adults, it is relevant to use some of the activities advocated here, eg, Labyrinth for a more mature level of fine bimanual action. The purpose is to further augment any of the gross motor activities such as the inflatables, usually used for early vestibular bilateral integration, which can also be used by adults. The rationale here would be that at least a greater consciousness and deliberate control of action between the hands may be developed through these fine bimanual tasks; whether more fundamental changes in vestibular bilateral integration can be accomplished beyond childhood is unknown; experience suggests that much of the improved functional performance can be sustained.

Activities recommended in this unit span Levels I through III. Many of these activities are recreational in nature and suitable for family use to supplement a therapy program. These are listed in the OEPS and graded according to the motor control required at the proximal shoulder joints to stabilize the arms for fine finger movements. These tasks are bilateral and require finely integrated control of both upper extremities. Noteworthy exceptions are Blockhead and the Magnetic Fish Pond which are included here because of the minute control and adjustments required in the shoulder of the dominant arm. When children play these games on the floor in the kneeling position, good body balance together with sustained head and neck extension against gravity are also required.

Development of Prehension, Initial Motor Control, Directional Awareness, and Sequence of Movements in Prewriting Pencil Exercises (8.7)

Throughout the initial evaluation of the child's sample performance with number and letter forms in P.P. 8.1, the therapist observes the child's prehension. In this section, continuing analysis is made of any remaining problems of pencil grasp and arm positioning which would interfere with writing ease. The palmar grasp, or fist clench on the pencil, should have disappeared before the child's sixth year; normally it is replaced with a tripod position much earlier. Poor positioning is often traceable to poor tactile system function.

The wide range of bizarre positions in which a child holds a pencil should be analyzed not only with regard to the fingers, but also in relation to the forearm and wrist. An example of this in one child was to position the palm slightly upward, with the wrist flexed; the forearm then is in a semisupinated position. For writing ease and efficiency, the forearm should be pronated slightly beyond the neutral position, with the wrist in a neutral or somewhat dorsi-flexed position. Steps should be taken in such instances to strengthen the pronators, eg, by pressing soft clay against a table top or by pushing aluminum foil against the textured surface of the plastic scribble boards used in the early steps of this program plan; this also gives localized tactile stimulation to the fingers.

Some children, especially those who are hypotonic, are unable to stabilize the thumb, index, and middle fingers in the normal tripod position. Exercise to strengthen the thenar eminence, the lumbricales, and the first and second dorsal interossei muscles is offered by means of wooden snap closepins. Whenever the more fanciful plastic toys in the form of clothespins called Clippy Clowns are available, they can entice and hold the child's interest and involvement longer. In the beginning, the adult usually holds the ⅜" dowel or lead pencil so the child can pinch the Clowns and align them along the dowel; preferably the nondominant hand holds the dowel as soon as possible so the child can direct his full attention to pinching the Clowns and aligning them on the dowel. The sooner he can also manage to hold the dowel in the nondominant hand, the better; not only is bimanual integration encouraged, the active role of the dominant hand becomes clear. Pictures in the Clippy Clowns box suggest pyramid building and other circus acts to delight young children. At the point of fatigue, the adult should terminate the task before the child switches to the nondominant hand. Pincer movements of the thumb and index finger may be strengthened by other means suitable for home programming such as shucking peanuts or shooting watermelon seeds. Whenever the normal childlike fun can be included, the interest and motivation is more apt to be sustained.

Children and adults who have been unable to develop sufficient grasp and control of the pencil with the normal tripod position will be seen using a variety of awkward grips. One of these is the resting of the pencil on the ring finger while the index and middle finger are placed along the pencil. Another is the immature thumb-index pincer pattern or a variety of positions in which the thumb is encased within the grasp of the fingers. If the tip of the thumb is not available then to stabilize the pencil, it will be ineffective in directing its movement.

44. This amusing picture invites the young child to "scratch his spots" to facilitate the early scribbling stage prior to establishing hand dominance; its vertical position involves visual awareness of this movement.

Teachers often see the child who is hyperactive and impulsive press so hard on the pencil in an effort to control it that the lead frequently breaks. As the tactile system function improves and better motor organization develops, the child will realize how he can function in a more controlled manner wherein he can apply less pressure and achieve better results.

To promote a more suitable tripod pencil grasp, a wooden dowel the diameter of the pencil is used to rub vigorously across the textured scribble board each session prior to practicing the prewriting and writing exercises. The child's hand is carefully positioned in the tripod position for this. It is more acceptable to him when rubbing the scribble board, since he is only stabilizing the dowel for wrist motion or gross arm action. The vibratory input helps alert the child to greater tactile awareness of how to stabilize the writing tool at the three pressure points of the tripod position. The child's attention is directed to recognizing how well he can feel it and how he can hold it comfortably. In pencil tasks which follow immediately, the child is asked to "get comfortable on the pencil" in hopes that the feeling of the tripod position will in these weeks come about automatically.

In the child of 8 years old and older who is often entrenched in using a poor pencil grasp, it is obvious that a shift to the tripod position will not come about automatically. Then it is discussed with the child, and he is asked to try the new position as he proceeds with the pencil exercises during these sessions. Since the older child will have already developed the sequential patterns of movement in conjunction with the faulty grasp, it may be too frustrating for him to change and would be a focus of resentment in some cases if expected to do so. Whether or not the child can use a tripod position, the same exercises for prewriting, printing, and script writing would be pursued.

At this point, the young child's attention is directed to recognizing how to start and stop the movement of his pencil and to control its motion along a prescribed course. Practice Sheet 1 has been designed for this purpose and is comprised of sets of vertical lines ¼″ apart and 2″ long, closed at each end. Another series of lines the same dimensions, below, run horizontally and at the bottom of the page. The vertical and horizontal lines of these same dimensions intersect to form three repeats of the "+." Sitting opposite the child, the therapist demonstrates how to start at the top of the vertical pairs of lines, likening it to riding his bicycle down the street while being cautious not to hit the curb on either side, and to stop when he reaches the bottom line. The child is offered a soft lead pencil which is easier to control than a ball point pen. A colorful felt pen is suitable as long as it does not squeak, since this can be particularly disturbing to any child who is auditorily defensive.

As the child starts from the top each time, the therapist says, "top-to-bottom," asking the child to join in saying this phrase as soon as he can manage that in addition to the concentration required to perform this motor task. It may be necessary to help him stop on time by saying, "top-to-bottom...and lift (the pencil)."

The same procedure is followed on the set of horizontal lines as on the previous vertical lines. This time the adult says, "left-to-right...and lift." At the bottom of the page, where these sets of lines cross, the sequence of these two basic movements is combined: "top-to-bottom and left-to-right." Upon completion, the child and adult may select the best two or three of each set of lines which merit

45. A small textured scribble board with pictures attached to the back is used at the desk to encourage proper tripod positioning on the pencil; awareness of this positioning is derived through vibration of the dowel against the plastic.

46. The child copies the number over the plastic page cover. Using a grease pencil, the child traces the number on the page cover before then drawing it in a similar two-inch square on the paper below, saying the rhyme, "Down and over.....and down once more, that's the way to make a four."

stars if they were within the lines and if they were started and terminated accurately. Using these criteria, opportunity is provided the child to assess his own performance with objectivity.

Directional Orientation Training to Numbers and Printed Letter Forms (8.8)

Once the child can maintain pencil control to draw between the ¼″ spaces vertically and horizontally in Exercise Sheet 1, he is ready to copy number forms from the Master Copy Sheets. Numbers in heavy black lines are superimposed on 2″ squares with a grid spaced at ½″ intervals and color coded for left and right to be consistent with the Positional Model. Practice Sheet 2 is designed also of 2″ squares with corresponding grids. The Master Copy Sheet of numbers 1-9 is slipped into a transparent page protector so that the child can trace over the numbers one at a time and, after each, attempt to reproduce it in one of the blocks of Practice Sheet 2 directly below. This Exercise Sheet, which can be mimeographed for school and clinic use, is folded into thirds to bring these blocks close together for good visual performance.

Throughout the Master Copy Sheets, arrows in red indicate when a number is started at the left of the center line, as do the numbers 2-7, while blue arrows indicate that numbers eight and nine start on the right side of center. The small numbers beside each of these arrows would indicate to the child the sequence of movements with which, for example, one would form a four. The numbers are traced and copied one at a time; they are sent home for further practice.

In addition to this procedure, a poem or saying is helpful to some very disorganized young learning-disordered children to provide the auditory structure together with the visual pattern. Various ones among these have been devised by teachers, parents, and myself and are often written on a Model sheet for the parents to also use at home, eg, "Down and over, and down once more; that's the way you make a four." This has been one of the most meaningful adjuncts to the visual-motor process, and in some cases, a technique which made the whole difference in the child's being able to perform. These sayings for numbers 1-9 are compiled in Appendix K.

Periodic rechecks are made throughout the program to see how much the child has integrated the number and letter forms for independent and increasingly automatic use. This is done by following the procedure described in P.P. 8.1 to document a sample performance of the way the child makes them, watching for any residual confusion in the sequence and the direction of movements.

The motor requirements for printing and script writing have been a longstanding interest for me. This aspect first drew my attention as an occupational therapist when working with severely handicapped adult polio patients, starting in 1949 at the Georgia Warm Springs Polio Foundation and continued during rehabilitation with both polio patients and arm amputees at Walter Reed Army Hospital. More recent observations and an analysis of the writing problems unique to the learning-disordered child started in 1964 while working with young children who were dependents of the armed forces at Walson Army Hospital, Fort Dix, New Jersey.

As the result of these analyses and observations, I have compiled a capital and lower case alphabet of printed letters and script which has been simplified so as to 1) reduce to the barest minimum the motor requirements of each, and 2) promote organization in otherwise disorganized responses of the learning-disordered child in learning to write. While the features of script writing will be defined in P.P. 8.9 to follow, the printed alphabets were designed with these specific features in mind:

1) the letters have been simplified so as to eliminate any unnecessary details;

2) these alphabets have been designed to be consistent in form with the printed letter forms used in P.P. 5.5 which emphasizes letter form recognition, and P.P. 4.8 to develop early visual tracking skill in the alphabet;

3) the letters of the lower case and the capital alphabet have been analyzed for the dominant features which they share in common, such as the vertical line, the oblique line, the circular form, or combinations of these;

4) a more nearly automatic function can be accelerated if the vertical line within the letter form is consistently first executed in the sequence of movements.

5) the vertical line provides a distinct and stable point of reference for the addition of curved lines or parts by contrast with the more primitive method in wide popular use which teaches the child to combine "sticks and circles."

In the alphabet as I have designed it, 16 lower case letters and 14 capital letters share the common feature of an initial vertical line. These letters are: a, b, d, f, h, i, j, k, l, m, n, p, q, r, t, and u, plus B, D, E, F, H, I, J, K, L, M, N, P, R, and T. The strong, stable, repetitive movement pattern of the vertical line which these letters share provide a frame of reference, or a figure-ground relationship, against which the child is able to concentrate on the differences, ie, the dots, the curves, and crosslines which are unique to that letter.

The basic motor patterns involved in printing have already been presented individually so that the child can concentrate fully on them one at a time. These include the vertical and horizontal lines in Exercise 1, the circular template, and the oblique lines of the triangular template. As he encounters each letter of the alphabet, he will then be able to focus on the sequence of movements required in combining these basic motor patterns. To organize the learning task in this way is less demanding and confusing than if the child were to ponder the seemingly unrelated characteristics of each letter when first learning to form them.

Among the learning-disordered children who have previously mastered the visual form recognition in P.P. 5.5 and the sequential order of the letters of the alphabet in P.P. 4.8, but who are having prolonged problems mastering pencil control to form the letters, grouping according to the dominant features which they share can augment the experience so that they can acquire pencil control more easily.

Emphasis on the initial vertical line which is advocated here helps to reduce those problems which can develop from the primitive technique using "sticks and circles." This latter method is contraindicated for the learning-disordered child who has problems with visual perception, motor control, and spatial relationships. The foremost reason is that there is a great similarity in the visual form of lower case letters, as shown in the groupings of these letters here and in P.P. 5.5. Identifying their likenesses and differences can be difficult for the child who has poor visual perception. If, in addition, the pencil control is so poor that the letter form is improperly executed, it can create erroneous feedback and cause further confusion in visual recognition of the form of the letter. By contrast with our usual thinking that the visual form perception is furthered by visual-motor experience, there can be a distinctly adverse effect. The learning-disordered child's motor control may be so poor that despite his erstwhile efforts to control the pencil, the results may nevertheless resemble disjointed, fragmented "sticks of spaghetti."

Fragmentation such as this further disorganizes and confuses the child by interfering with his ability to recognize and stabilize the whole-part relationships of the letter form. If the child's concept of single letter forms is hazy, then there is less chance for uniform and distinct spacing between letters within a word; as long as this persists, it will continue to jeopardize his word recognition. In light of this, it is possible that these factors can even create, or at least perpetuate, early reading problems. Whenever handwriting skills are promoted prematurely and the visual feedback is confusing, the chance is that problems in writing and reading will go hand in hand.

It would seem then that this simplified method of printing which requires the barest minimum of motor skills has become necessary because the training of pencil control has been started earlier and earlier, when the child is barely able to direct his movement. Here is one example of a direct effect which contributes to the child's confusion and continued disorganization, when the "stick and circle" method is followed with the letters "a" and "d." If the curved line or a circle of the "a" or "d" is formed first, as is commonly taught, then the child who has poor motor control and inept spatial relations will have difficulty subsequently in connecting the vertical line to the two ends of the curved portion. Equal difficulty will arise when trying to make contact with the curvature of the circle to form either of these letters clearly. The simple result is that the letter forms "a" and "d" are unstable this way and quickly deteriorate. If the circular and vertical lines are spaced too far apart, the intended letter will resemble a "cl" or a "ci," whereas when they overlap, they look more like a "¢" sign.

In clarification of one point, it was suggested in P.P. 5.5, which focuses on visual tracking to identify letter forms, that letters of the capital alphabet should be introduced before the small letters. Capitals may be recognized earlier by the child from seeing them on his toys, hence success is more assured. Of greater importance for stressing capital form recognition first is that it does not depend upon left-right identification and directional orientation, whereas this is a prerequisite skill for distinguishing those letters of the lower case alphabet which may be easily reversed. However, in relation to learning to print, greater emphasis is placed here on the small letters than on the capitals so as to expedite this skill and foster both writing and reading skills and to assure competence secondarily in other subjects whose mastery also depends on them. The method advocated in the holistic approach is the most relevant to the child because it is consistent with his prior learning experiences related to the Positional Model. If these methods are effective among children who have difficulties, one would expect they would be all the more appropriate for children in the normal classroom.

One question begs an answer here: Will difficulties arise for the child if the method used here greatly contrasts the procedures taught in school? If the underlying foundation skills have been adequately provided in therapy and the child has a good foundation in forming letters in the manner recommended here, he will usually be able to stabilize his own skills sufficiently so that he can continue without being confused even when another method is in use. It is the experience this method provides which develops in the child a stable point of reference by which to visually grasp the likenesses and differences among letters in addition to the automatic sequencing of movements which is relevant. In any event, good communication between therapist and teacher is important; the best interests of the child are the paramount consideration, should any conflict arise.

If the method presented in therapy will be in conflict with that emphasized in school, then the best decision may be to not introduce printing in therapy at all. The therapist would, however, continue to help the child to strengthen his fine motor skills, spatial relations, and directionality in the many ways indicated throughout these eight program plans. This influence will be helpful to him in acquiring a suitable printing pattern in school, although it may take longer to achieve the same results. Meanwhile, the therapist would continue to take samples of his performance in making the numbers and both printed alphabets in order to compare his progress against the baseline performance.

Training of Sequential Patterns of
Movement in Script Writing (8.9)

By contrast with simplified printed letters, script contains a wide variation of linear forms which, when analyzed, are found to consist of a series of circular and looped segments. The ease of continuity in moving from one to the other permits a smooth progression from left to right across the page. This continuity eliminates the directionality problems and avoids the fragmentation of the whole-part relationship of the printed letters and words. In fact, this very feature is the reason why early use of script instead of printing had long ago been advocated by some educators as a means of circumventing the problems of reversals prevalent among learning-disordered children. This alternative is not recommended presently for these reasons: 1) there are effective methods of teaching the child to print, 2) the motor patterns in script are too complex, and 3) letter reversals are only one symptom of a more basic problem of postural and bilateral integration.

Motor patterns used to form script letters have been analyzed here according to those movements used in the initial thrust or characteristic features of each letter. The majority of small and capital script letters include one of the loops of either the vertical or the horizontal figure-eight patterns (P.P. 8.5) or the movement used to transfer, for instance, from a vertical to a horizontal loop. As one example, the script letter *p* involves the sequential patterns of movement of first "the (clockwise) loop to the bottom," followed automatically by "the loop to the right," in the basic cloverleaf pattern stressed in P.P. 8.5. Five basic motor patterns have emerged from this analysis; combinations of them comprise each of the letters. Commonly used connectors are discussed later.

If the initial, and dominant, thrust can be instilled through the child's motor experience and memory for rapid retrieval, this will serve to activate the sequence of movement which follows in forming individual letters first and, in time, the sequential movement pattern of whole words. Until these simple repetitive movements can be executed in a more nearly automatic fashion, the child cannot direct his cognitive attention to the spelling of words nor the content of ideas he wishes to express. When the motor patterns for words do reach the level at which cognitive attention is no longer required, this memory of the sequential pattern of movement reinforces the spelling skill so that it can be maintained for the most part at a noncognitive level.

The script motor patterns are identified as follows:

    1) Horizontal figure-eight patterns, moving (from midpoint) UP and LEFT;

    2) Horizontal figure-eight patterns, moving (from midpoint) DOWN and RIGHT;

    3) Vertical figure-eight patterns, moving (from midpoint) UP and RIGHT;

1 and 3 combined in LOOP TO THE TOP and LOOP TO THE RIGHT;

    4) THE CLOSED LOOP;

    5) THE DOME.

Motor Pattern 1A: (Horizontal Figure Eights)
UP and LEFT

The child is instructed to practice tracing over the pattern in an unbroken, continuous pattern three times, applying greater pressure as he begins and moves from the midpoint, counterclockwise and to the left, around the loop, lessening the pressure as he approaches the midpoint and proceeds around the right-hand loop. He first traces over the letter several times. Then he traces the figure-eight three times, at the left side of the line, while keeping in mind the specific letter as he follows the principal thrust of the motor pattern which is characteristic of the letter. He practices making that letter along the line before going to the next line to start a new letter.

The following small letters and capitals have been included in this pattern. Practice sheets for these motor patterns are available commercially.

Up and Left

a o c d g q

A C E O Q G

Motor Pattern 1B: (Horizontal Figure Eights)
UP and RIGHT

In the same manner as for 1A, the child now moves from the midpoint to the right around the loop, putting pressure on the clockwise movement and lessening the pressure on returning to the midpoint before proceeding around the lefthand loop. It is not the initial thrust but rather the characteristic feature of these letters which involves the loop to the right.

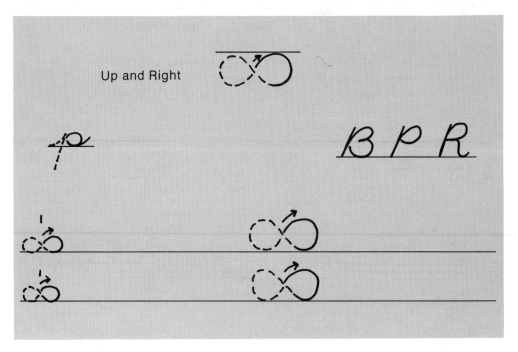

Motor Pattern 2: (Horizontal Figure Eights)
DOWN and RIGHT

The pattern is followed in the same manner as before, starting with the principal thrust down and right in a counterclockwise movement for the only letter using this pattern, the *D*.

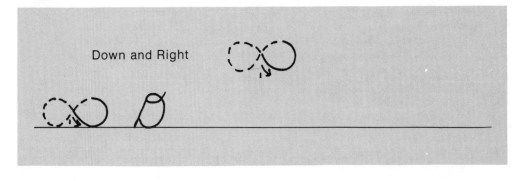

Motor Pattern 3: (Vertical Figure Eights)
UP and RIGHT

Following the arrow, start up and right, applying pressure to the solid line, continuing with lighter pressure over the dotted lines for three times, keeping in mind each letter in turn.

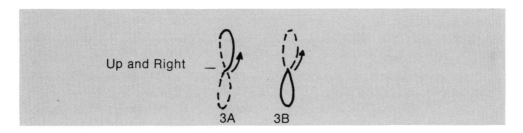

Motor Pattern 3B: (Vertical Figure Eights)
UP and RIGHT

Patterns 3A and 3B use the same vertical figure-eight pattern, but the principal thrust is on the up stroke in 3A and the down stroke in 3B, as shown by the heavy, versus light, dotted lines. Either of these basic motor patterns is combined with other motor patterns, eg, letter *g* combines patterns 1A and 3B, while the letter *h* combines patterns 3A and 5.

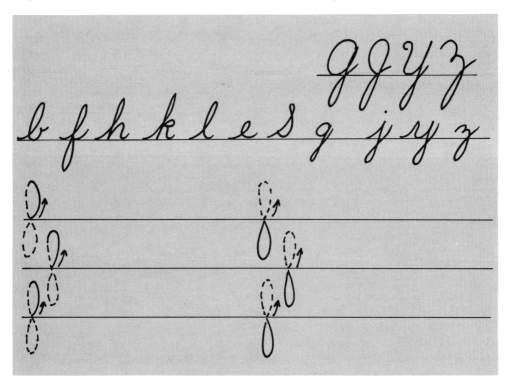

Exceptions to crossing the midline of the figure-eight.

f _____ *q* _____

Motor Pattern 4: The Closed Loop (long and short)

Practice is begun by forming the single, tall, closed loops with their connectors, as in the letter *t,* using a slightly slanted line to promote an easy flow of movement. Then attention is directed toward connecting the loops at the bottom, concentrating on the uniformity of the arc and the height of the loop. The child is also made aware of keeping a fairly small opening at the base of the *t* as compared to a child's early efforts where a "tentlike" form is often seen. Practice with each individual letter continues after tracing the model several times.

Long and Short

Motor Pattern 5: The Dome

Instructions for use are the same as above, starting practice with the arc by connecting the lines in as uniform a fashion as possible. The basic pattern is applied to these letters by first tracing the model letter and then making a series of each letter before practicing the next. As often as necessary, the child is urged to return to practice making the domelike shapes until these are smooth and uniform in size.

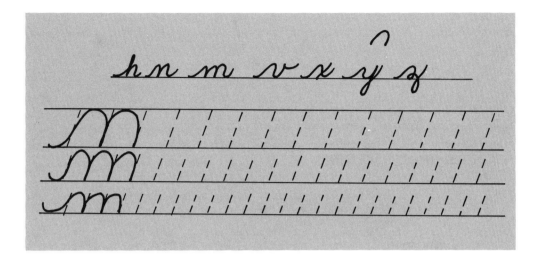

A slow writing pattern which may have been present throughout a child's early schooling can become a serious deterrent to academic advancement when a greater demand is made in the upper grades and beyond, especially in college. The goal would be to enable the child to start script writing as soon as he can begin to sequence the fine movement patterns, using a systematic method such as has been presented, so as to help him function at a more automatic level. Then his attention will not be diverted from the content of lecture material to the mechanics of writing while taking notes, nor will he be hindered by it when organizing ideas and concepts in writing.

One of the stumbling blocks to a smooth, continuous script writing is the hesitation which occurs in first joining letters together. This hesitation may persist even after the motor pattern for forming individual letters may be fairly well developed. To overcome the child's need to direct his conscious attention to the way letters are connected, an analysis has been made of the connectors between letters which occur most universally. Some are so commonplace that they are easily assimilated into the child's experience; it is the exception which presents problems and which prevents the child from acquiring confidence and speed in handwriting.

The most common connectors are an extension of the closed loop pattern, applying to the majority of script letters. An extension of the vertical loop in Pattern 3B is a common connector for letters which are included in that grouping. The "half dome" is often used to begin the script letters *a, c, d, g, o,* and *q.* The most troublesome connectors for beginners is called a "bridge" and is used following script letters *b, o, v,* and *w.* These letters, when followed by a vowel, will need appropriate adaptation and additional practice for most children. Between capitals and the first small letter, the use of connectors is optional; most often they would consist of the common connectors mentioned above.

To help the student practice these connectors and bring them into his conscious awareness as a preliminary step to more automatic function and improved speed in writing, words which include the various connectors are copied in a specified manner. The word *zebra* would be one selected for its various connectors; in

251

addition to the common connectors, there is an adaptation of the "bridge" between *b* and *r,* while the transition between the *r* and the *a* would be a "half dome."

The word to be practiced is written clearly at the top of a sheet of lined tablet paper by the adult. To practice in the proposed manner, the first letter is written three times; then the first and second are written along the same line for three times, followed by a similar repetition with the addition of each letter. Through this conscious, repetitive effort, concentrating on the formation of the individual letters as well as their connectors, the sequential patterns of movement will become more firmly established.

The following list of words has been prepared to provide ample practice:

boats	figure	acquire
zebra	joyous	waxing
quail	viewed	oasis
cadence	mixture	draft

The student may substitute words of his own choosing, but it should be kept in mind that words which are too long become tedious, while those which are too short do not provide sufficient practice. Six-or seven-letter words are suitable for older children; five-letter words are used for beginners. When writing these words, it will be helpful to the beginning student if the adult draws a light pencil line at midpoint between the lines to guide him in forming the lower half of the script letters at a more constant size and height.

To establish a baseline of function for students who have already been writing script but doing so with difficulty, a timed sample is made of his performance initially and then at appropriate intervals of six or eight weeks. Changes in the quality and the quantity of writing may become apparent; the observer can also determine the presence of consistent problems in individual letter forms or connectors which should be given additional attention.

A student who is 10 years old or older when starting therapy is asked to prepare the following writing samples at home between the first and second therapy sessions.

1) Using his most skilled handwriting, he is asked to copy material from a familiar printed text for a period of five minutes. This is timed by the adult so the child's full attention can be directed to the task.

2) At another time that week, or after sufficient rest of an hour or more so as to avoid tension and muscle fatigue, he is to copy the same material, this time writing as fast as possible during this five-minute period.

3) Students who are able are asked to take dictation for five minutes as the adult reads the material clearly and with an appropriate speed for the student to be able to copy as much as possible.

Sample #3 is taken to determine whether there may be any problem in taking lecture notes which would arise not so much from the motor problem as the auditory area. Through this dictation, the therapist can determine whether there is any difficulty in recognizing how to correlate the spoken word with the written word. Problems such as this should be dealt with directly within the more basic level of visual and auditory recognition and decoding of the visual and auditory symbols separately before they are integrated and coupled with the sequential motor patterns as well.

The principle of half-step progression whereby the student is enabled to master separately the various skills involved and integrate them by upgrading first and then the other would apply here. The problems which are represented in each student must be analyzed and dealt with on a purely individual basis so that the handwriting process can evolve successfully and the student can meet the increasing demands to effectively integrate numerous skills throughout the learning continuum.

References

1. Beery K, Buktenica N: Developmental Test of Visual-Motor Integration. Chicago, Follett Pub Co, 1967.
2. Perceptual Copy Forms, 1963. Winter Haven Lions Publications Committee, P O Box 1045, Winter Haven, Florida.
3. Ayres AJ: Southern California Sensory Integration Tests. Los Angeles, Western Psychological Services, 1972.

Summary Inventory of Foundation Skills for Academic Performance

The following inventories list summarily those foundation skills which, from a holistic point of view, are the necessary prerequisites to good academic performance. These skills are listed in sequence according to the relationship which experience with learning-disordered children suggests.

Pencil control for printing and script writing:

1) Establish early vestibular bilateral integration (P.P. 2).

2) Promote gross motor organization and sequential patterns in large movements (P.P. 3).

3) Establish early bimanual motor integration preliminary to hand dominance (P.P. 6.1).

4) Promote motor patterns in the hands in which they cross the vertical midline preparatory to securing the paper for writing, ie, the scooter board (P.P. 2.4). In a child of six and older, observe performance of the dominant hand in crossing the midline on large figure-eight patterns (P.P. 8.5).

5) Promote hand dominance exploration, selection, and confirmation (P.P. 6).

6) Promote tactile system organization through manual form discrimination (P.P. 1.4, 1.7).

7) Provide vertical scribble board experience to develop gross arm movement and early hand-eye awareness (P.P. 8).

8) Stimulate tactile awareness through use of the textured scribble board to promote a mature pencil grasp (P.P. 8.7).

9) Establish left-right sensory identification and body image (P.P. 7.1, 7.4).

10) Introduce the Positional Model as a basis for directionality (P.P. 7.2).

11) Apply Positional Model to identify reversible letters (P.P. 7.3).

12) Apply Positional Model to printing letters and numbers (P.P. 8.8).

13) Introduce small figure-eights and sequential motor patterns common to script writing (P.P. 8.9).

14) Strive for somewhat automatic control of script writing for speed to enable the individual to focus his attention to concentrate on expression of ideas and content (P.P. 8.9).

Proposed underlying foundation skills necessary for reading:

1) Promote early prone positioning to stimulate proprioceptive impulses through the neck extensors and enhance neural integration and maturation (P.P. 2).

2) Stimulate vestibular bilateral integration; enhance visuo-vestibular

integration and reduce motor disorganization as the eyes cross the midline (P.P. 2).

3) Develop adequate visual attention, fixation, and pursuit (P.P. 2.7).

4) Correlate manual form and visual form (P.P. 1.4, 1.7).

5) Establish a left-right tracking pattern (P.P. 5.5).

6) Promote visual recognition of letter form tracked along a line (P.P. 5.5).

7) Promote visual tracking by means of alphabetical sequencing (P.P. 4.8).

Proposed underlying foundation skills necessary for spelling:

1) Correlate the perception of manual form with visual form (P.P. 1.4, 1.7).

2) Establish letter form recognition of the printed letter (P.P. 5.5).

3) Establish concrete, tangible sequencing skill in size sequence (P.P. 4.1).

4) Same, in tactile sequence (P.P. 4.2).

5) Promote visual form recognition of the whole word as a unit (P.P. 5.6).

6) Establish visual sequencing skill (P.P. 4.5).

7) Establish auditory sequencing skill (P.P. 4.6).

8) Establish visual sequencing of letter order in words (P.P. 4.9).

9) Master the mechanics of pencil control to permit the child to focus his attention and concentrate on spelling skill (P.P. 8.8, 8.9).

(Spelling optimally is a combination of skills in visual memory of whole word forms, visual sequencing, auditory sequencing, and the memory and application of spelling rules.)

Proposed underlying foundation skills necessary for mathmetics. (Refer also to problem solving, which follows.)

1) Establish adequate pencil control to make the numbers legibly and in appropriate size to match the task (P.P. 8.8). (Continued use of oversized numbers and irregular spacing can deter the child's progress because it interferes with his being able to perform the task in the space provided on printed workbook pages.)

2) Establish sufficient visual figure-ground organization so as not to be confused and disorganized by math problems (P.P. 5.4, 5.8). (Meanwhile, reduce this aspect of the problem by cutting a window from cardboard which will isolate and direct his focus to one problem at a time.)

3) Establish body image as a forerunner to spatial relations (P.P. 7.4).

4) Establish awareness of spatial relations (P.P. 5.2, 5.7) to:
— maintain adequate size constancy of numbers,
— maintain proper spacing between double numbers,
— avoid numerical reversals (14 written as 41),
— prevent confusion by proper vertical alignment of numerical columns,
— establish early foundations in spatial relations for geometry, engineering, and architecture through early physical movement and experience with elementary three-dimensional spatial concepts.

5) Establish a basis for mathematical reasoning through experience with concrete objects to learn before and after, larger and smaller, more than and less than (P.P. 4.1 and others).

6) Establish auditory sequence, retention, and recall for an adequate grasp of problems and numerical statements in class (P.P. 4.6).

Proposed underlying foundation skills for problem solving:

1) Establish the early concept of sequence and order as a means of problem solving with tangible, three-dimensional objects:
— sequence by size (P.P. 4.1),
— tactile sequence and assembly (P.P. 4.2),
— problem-solving sequence and assembly (P.P. 4.3).

2) Establish early awareness of organization of objects through recognition of likenesses and differences, ie, features shared in common:
— sort and match color and forms visually (P.P. 5.1),
— sort and match three-dimensional manual forms (P.P. 1.4),
— sort and match linear form and design (P.P. 1.7).

3) Establish awareness of whole-part relationships:
— match halves of visual form units (top-bottom, left-right)(P.P. 5.1, 5.6).

4) Promote sensory system organization as a forerunner to recognition of relevant foreground from irrelevant background, sensory stimuli (P.P. 1, 5.4).

5) Promote abstract problem solving:
— sort (concrete or abstract) ideas according to the features they share in common,
— select ideas according to their relevancy (on a foreground-background basis) as opposed to viewing all ideas as having equal value,
— attempt to construct a conceptual framework of the problem,
— establish a logical sequence of steps through which to attempt a solution.

Task organization, attack, and closure:

1) Organize a task by identifying the scope and specifying clearly its end goal.

2) Identify the units or parts of the overall task.

3) Whenever practical, organize the task by grouping units together which require similar functions, skills, or equipment.

4) Identify the sequence of steps necessary in relation to the interdependence of individual units.

5) Sequence the "order of attack" of these steps further according to the urgency and relevance to the desired outcome.

6) Identify (to the child) when he has completed units within the overall goal.

7) When the child has brought closure to the task, either as it was originally defined or as it has been altered by time and circumstances, bring it to his conscious awareness.

The learning-disordered child is often fraught with failure and frustration in task completion with regard to school assignments and requests made of him at home. Such a child is so poorly equipped to organize his own actions that unless he is helped to develop skills that will enable him to "organize, attack, and bring closure" to a task, he will find even meager demands to be overwhelming.

257

Whereas the natural response of some adults is to challenge a child to perform better by holding out rewards for success, this will only intensify his anxiety over not being able to respond.

On the other hand, it will be more effective if parents, teachers, and therapists can follow the guidelines presented here to enable the child to turn his failures into experiences which provide him success in task completion.

Unless a child can first reap positive feelings about his capacity to achieve a goal or complete a task, there will be little motivation for him to try again. Failure to complete homework assignments is legend among learning-disordered children. For him to perform more adequately, the child will require those underlying skills described here. The therapist and parent should make a clear comment to the child to the effect that the task was completed as each opportunity presents itself among the Phase II activities. In so doing, the child's confidence about himself and his feelings of adequacy will shift in a more positive direction.

In the academic setting the child should at this time be presented assignments of short duration so that within his skill level he can also sense that completion of the task is within his grasp. The teacher will need to plan his homework at the level where he functions best, waiting to push on with new material until later. Again, the principle of "half-step progression" to success is aptly applied. Whenever such a child has completed an academic assignment, it would be most supportive to him if the teacher would clearly acknowledge it to him and possibly give him a grade or mark based on task completion as well as one for his competence with the subject material.

Organizing written assignments and examinations:

1) Assess any residual avoidance patterns which could be associated with inadequate pencil control and proceed to master the mechanics of handwriting so as to concentrate on expression and content.

2) Establish, through timed procedures such as visual tracking, a more acute awareness by which to measure the passage of time.

3) Determine the points cited under "task organization, attack, and closure" which are relevant to this task.

4) Organize ideas and concepts to be expressed on the basis of relevant versus irrelevant factors.

5) In a timed written examination, try to develop the following patterned responses:
— quickly assess the whole-part relationships within the examination,
— allot time proportionately to various parts according to their value in scoring,
— avoid bogging down in fruitless efforts on an early difficult question — be willing to leave it and return later if there is time,
— establish the habit of bringing closure by a quick review to check for essentials and to assure that important parts have not been overlooked.

Conclusions

Efficacy of This Approach

The holistic approach does in fact promote a composite, cohesive program of treatment for learning-disordered children. The goal of therapy for the learning-disordered child is to "bring organization out of disorganization in sensory input, motor output, social responses, and academic performance so that, insofar as possible, he can function as an equal among his peers." When the techniques are carried out as recommended, these goals can be closely approximated.

It has been demonstrated in the holistic approach that evaluation and therapy are inseparable. Most importantly, the holistic approach enables the therapist to make a continuous dynamic assessment of the problems — an assessment which is totally integrated with the corrective measures used to overcome them.

Five processes are identifiable along the learning continuum. These five — avoid, explore, organize, integrate, and conceptualize — become self-evident in treating the learning-disordered child. These processes are significantly more apparent in the learning-disordered child because he processes information much more slowly than does the average child.

Out of the author's longstanding process analysis, a fully integrated program has been devised. Throughout therapy the clinician makes continual process analyses as she observes the child's response to given tasks and experiences. Tasks are presented which will actively tap the needed processes and do so at a level and pace which are compatible with the child's capacity for success. By appropriately tapping the learning process specified in the hypothesis, the child is able to acquire the foundation skills. He cycles back to explore, organize, integrate, and conceptualize at higher and higher levels until he has mastered the basic requirements at least for handwriting, spelling, math, and reading.

The holistic approach has evolved from clinical research for the purpose of developing a practical and realistic as well as a comprehensive treatment program. It is my conviction that a parent-oriented focus is a necessary advantage in promoting the child's therapeutic program. Parent understanding and cooperation can be greatly facilitated through frequent reference to, and an understanding of, the Ongoing Evaluation and Performance Scale (OEPS), in addition to portions of this text. The OEPS serves as a useful avenue of communication for the therapist in helping the parents visualize the nature of the program and recognize how this therapy relates to their child's specific needs.

Modalities

It is my conclusion that in order for the therapist to fulfill her most critical early function, ie, to enable the child to move from an avoidance to an exploratory response, two factors are essential. First, motivating the child to spontaneously involve himself with activities which will reduce the sensorimotor disorganization requires that the modalities of therapy must have a natural attraction for children. Therefore, childhood toys and selected equipment must be used as the primary therapeutic modalities. Secondly, to enable the child to bridge the gap between avoidance and exploration, successful involvement on the part of the child must not depend upon verbal instruction; toys which permit a nondirective therapeutic technique are essential in the introductory portion of the child's program.

Value to Therapists

The holistic approach presented here stands as one model for therapy of the learning-disordered child. The primary value of this model to therapists is that its presentation is sufficient to permit even the beginning therapy student to envision a course of therapy through to completion. Through the concrete methodology described in the program plans, the clinician can make a valid, dynamic, week-by-week assessment of both residual problems and the changes toward their resolution. The therapist has at her fingertips planned protocols by which to recognize where and how to begin therapy. She can then select and upgrade the difficulty of the procedures so as to tailor a program which directly focuses on the child's changing needs. Through the coordinated use of the OEPS by the therapist and the parents, the therapist is able not only to communicate with them to foster their understanding, but through its use she can actively involve them as co-therapists. Without having to discuss details in the presence of the child, the parent is enabled to make more astute observations about the child's responses both in and out of therapy and to conduct a supplementary home program.

Inherent in the protocols of the eight program plans is the sequential gradation within and among the various tasks which enable the child to develop the needed skills. These plans, together with the Integrated Program Matrix, provide the therapist a clear, graphic illustration by which to effect a careful meshing of interdependent skills. These instruments also furnish specific indicators to show when the deficit skills have reached an adequate level of function so the child's program can be suitably terminated.

The greatest value of these instruments to the therapist is their usefulness as a viable training guide. The experienced clinician will quite easily assimilate these techniques and the sequence of programming so that, for her, charting minute changes will become less and less necessary. It is here that the value of the Summary Record Sheets will be realized as a means of recording quickly the updated performance levels for the various skills. Reference to the Integrated Program Matrix will help the therapist to maintain an operational structure for identifying and reaching the necessary goals.

"Hold" Patterns

Of special significance for the beginning therapist is the requirements of performance which are designated in the OEPS. These criteria for each step provide the therapist evidence to indicate whenever the child has reached a current plateau within a specific step or program plan. In such instances, while work could be continued on the other program plans, it should temporarily bypass this one until maturation and the integration of those underlying skills which are critical to further progress have been acquired. Inevitably there will be times when foundation skills which are crucial to a specific type of performance may as yet have eluded our awareness.

In many instances a purposely planned temporary "hold" pattern over four to six weeks is built into the child's therapy program. A defined period outside of therapy allows time for the child to consolidate his previous gains. This philosophy runs counter to the fears of many who feel that gains already made will be lost in the interim. Experience has led me to the conclusion that if the techniques of therapy have tapped the process which facilitate the development of the basic skills the child needs, these will not be lost. Instead, they will be further integrated through those natural encounters at home and at school which also tap these skills, and do so in the same way as other children. It is therefore appropriate to plan breaks after a certain period of weekly therapy in many cases, to await further maturation. Reasons for this would be that it prevents the pace of the program from lagging; to push hard to make further gains prematurely is not only nontherapeutic, it can be counterproductive, needlessly arousing antagonism.

These planned "hold" patterns are often suitable for the child who is functioning in the normal classroom despite his problems and makes progress in therapy at a fairly rapid rate; then a "hold" pattern is used to consolidate these rapidly acquired gains before again moving ahead to break new ground. On the other hand, a child in a slow-moving program may also need "hold" patterns built in, but for different reasons to be discussed later.

Duration and Termination of Therapy

Some general conclusions can be advanced about the duration of therapy which has been required for children to reach the desired goal of therapy, and that is for him to function insofar as possible "as an equal among his peers." Children who are typical of one group frequently seen here in therapy are those who are functioning marginally in kindergarten or the primary grades despite the fact that they have average or higher intellectual levels. Their distinctly disorganized and often hyperactive behavior is causing them distress and is disruptive to their relationships with teachers and peers. The hypoactive, slow-moving child, on the other hand, may be facing possible grade failure too; placement in a special class may be under consideration. The pattern of therapy sessions for a child who starts therapy early in the school year would, generally speaking, follow along these lines. Weekly sessions over two or three months would be followed by a "hold" pattern of increasing lengths of time throughout the first year. At the beginning of the next school year he would need three or four weekly sessions to give him a firm start. Review or reassessment to see how well his skills are holding under increasingly difficult academic demands would be scheduled as needed, possibly every six or eight weeks the second year. Resumption for a brief series of weekly sessions may occasionally be indicated to help him cope with some specific problems, such as spelling or geometry, for example, which require higher and higher levels of integration of many underlying skills.

With reasonable accuracy the therapist can pinpoint when progress begins to level off in the child's weekly program as a generalized widespread plateau becomes apparent. The duration of the "hold" pattern at that point depends upon the severity of the child's deficits and the length of therapy which had already been necessary to effect the progress which has been documented. A four, six, or even eight-week "hold" period may be appropriate, at which point his skills are reassessed. Resumption of weekly therapy is again up for consideration; repeating the "hold" pattern may be advised.

When reassessment after successive temporary "holds" such as these confirms that a more fixed plateau has occurred, the active therapy program is terminated. Resumption of weekly therapy at some point a year or even two years later may again be fruitful for children whose progress is very slow. Since the procedures advocated here also apply to children with mental retardation as well as the classical learning-disordered child who has normal intellect, annual reassessment and resumption of a limited period of weekly therapy to follow would sometimes be indicated.

The basis for termination of therapy among those children who continue to function in the regular classroom would be the completion of programming tasks which bring them up to those skills expected for their peer group. This would include the motor skills and the organization of information sufficient to meet and maintain grade expectations and a satisfactory social maturation commensurate with his age. Those skills which at the completion of therapy are still beyond their age and grade level (for instance, left and right crossover patterns or geographical orientation or script writing) can usually be acquired along with the other children in the class.

For the child who has had problems in sequencing gross and fine motor patterns, however, it would be advisable to have him return for a series of four or five sessions at the time script is to be introduced at school. A solid structure and foundation on which to acquire these sequential motor patterns will help to prevent subsequent problems as the demands of handwriting speed and the integration of auditory skills in order to take lecture notes increases.

Therapeutic Change

Results of the holistic approach have proven of value in expediting significant change both in the specific performance of the child and also in the parents' ability to cope more readily with their problems. Except in the more extreme cases, the expectation is that if a child is functioning for the most part at Level I, he will advance to Level II by means of the therapeutic effect. Among children of average intellect functioning in a regular kindergarten and first or second grade classroom, if he has moved from Level I to Level II in therapy, chances are he will have acquired the necessary foundations by which to acquire the additional skills in the academic setting just as the other children do. He will be able to advance to Level III performance without continued weekly therapy. Likewise, children who may be somewhat older and who are functioning at Level II when entering the program will generally advance to at least the early steps, if not perform at the top, of Level III in most areas.

For a further look at the changes which have been observed, it is necessary to identify various groups of children by the problems which are represented. Among those children, for instance, are those whom I classify by the term "psuedo learning-disordered." Most often after a course of therapy, their problems are reduced to those proportions commonly found among most children in the class; in other words, they are able to function as an equal among their peers in the academic setting. Depending upon the age of the child and the length of time he has been having academic problems, the duration of a therapy program will vary, but good results can be achieved by many children through an initial series of eight therapy hours or within a maximum of sixteen sessions overall, while at the same time remaining in the normal classroom.

Children who have moderately severe problems and who are already placed in a special class or in schools for their special problems can be helped measurably to make a better adjustment to many aspects of their academic and social setting; some of these children will return to the normal classroom. Short of that, use of selected portions of the therapy program can be appropriately resumed in adolescence to try once more for any gains from a sensory integrative approach. Then, with a final effort through instruction, he can be helped to learn to apply at a cognitive level some of those same skills whose procedures he was unable to perform earlier. The justification for therapy would be to help the child make the best possible prevocational adjustment with the goal of self-sufficiency through a sheltered workshop.

In general, adolescents and even adults who did not have therapy of this kind available to them as children will profit by having a program adapted for their needs. Adolescents and a few adults have been treated here over a period of eight to twenty-five hourly sessions with significant gains in accomplishing the desired levels of performance in those skills which are relevant to them.

There are also severely involved learning-disordered children who have attended this program who have also been medically diagnosed as having neurological problems of an organic nature; others are considered as being autistic. Some progress has been made to move these difficult-to-treat children farther along in Level I or to advance from Level I to beginning Level II skills in a few of the areas of the OEPS. Limited as this may seem, it is presumed to be at least the equivalent of progress made in other programs. Since many of the Phase I gross motor activities and many of the early Phase II desk tasks can be introduced in the absence of a child's expressive or receptive language skill, the holistic approach would seem to be a feasible avenue to follow. Not only may the child begin to function more spontaneously, but through these activities the meaning of words involving their actions could be directly instrumental in helping them develop better comprehension of the language involved. Programs such as this are conducted in close conjunction and cooperation with the speech and educational programs which are specially designed to meet the child's individual needs. After applying the hypothesis of the holistic approach to these children, I feel that more progress should be possible and that the learning processes can be tapped.

So far progress in the holistic approach is less striking among children with severe expressive and receptive language deficits as well as those who suffer severe and/or multiple handicaps to include partial blindness or deafness. However, considering the extent and the severity of the problems, perhaps the limited progress which can be observed among these children is even more noteworthy than that of the child who is helped to overcome his failures in the classroom.

Young children of three to five years of age upon entering therapy who are felt to be either retarded and/or have a severe expressive or receptive language deficit have been effectively helped by being seen in therapy twice a week as long as they continue to make steady progress; in some cases, intensive therapy such as this could continue for several years. In addition, they would continue to attend a specialized school or kindergarten education. Wherever therapy continues over a long period, planned vacation breaks are important in order to maintain the vitality of a program from the viewpoint of both the therapist and the child.

Clinical Research

The holistic approach has been presented as one model for therapy of learning disorders. In this book, I have provided the therapist a structure for observing and evaluating behavior in terms of clinical performance. I have presented a structure to envision steps along the learning continuum — steps which are attained by a carefully graded protocol. Through this structure the therapist can mitigate the disorganization in the child's sensorimotor, social, and academic behavior. By systematizing her observations, the clinical therapist is better equipped to investigate these aberrant forms of behavior.

Study of the methods which are effective with learning-disordered children suggests a rich field of investigation about learning generally. The impact of premature training of academic skills needs serious attention. Efforts directed here could measurably reduce the chance of needlessly creating "pseudo-learning-disordered children." It could greatly modify the extent of trauma on children who truly do have a learning disorder.

By their background and clinical experience, occupational therapists have a unique contribution to make in helping the learning-disordered child and his family. It is hoped that through this book they will be further inspired to do research not only to expedite therapy, but that they will be able to make a significant contribution to society by way of prevention.

Clinical Findings

A review of a sample caseload using current techniques points out the kinds of cases which have been treated here; these cases under age twelve are divided into five groups, A through E. The characteristics which identify each group are defined. A sample case study depicts the nature of a typical problem treated in each group, the duration of therapy, and the child's progress.

Group A represents individuals who required fewer than ten therapy sessions. Included here are children who were considered to have minor learning problems, whose needs could be effectively met within this brief period, and who were classified in some cases as having a "pseudo learning disorder," defined in this book. Fifteen children were seen for an average of eight sessions; problems of the pseudo-learning-disordered child would generally have been resolved by the conclusion of therapy.

Group B are those children most frequently referred to in this program. They include children who demonstrated problems within the spectrum of learning disorders, who are of average or above average intellect and who, although functioning only marginally, are in the regular classroom. This group was comprised of kindergarten, first, and second grade children who had not reached their eighth birthday when starting therapy. Fifteen children of kindergarten through second grade were seen an average of 22 sessions. These children generally arrived at a very adequate, often excellent level of performance in the normal classroom, and they also exhibited a greatly improved self-image.

Group C are children in the older counterpart of Group B, in third to sixth grade, not to have passed their twelfth birthday upon starting therapy. The emotional impact on these children may be such that they also suffered significant secondary emotional problems (true for both Group B and C). This is true because they are intellectually often above average and well aware of the fact that they are functioning inadequately in both academics and peer relationships. The failure, frustration, and damaged self-esteem are critical features to alleviate in therapy. Sixteen children in third through sixth grades were seen an average of 16 sessions, at which time they had reached a level of performance and ego development comparable to those children in Group B. At this age they were able to assimilate the steps of the program more rapidly than those in Group B.

Group D includes school-age children who are considered to be more severely involved. They may require partial or full-time assignment to special education classrooms; they may need individual tutoring; or they may have been detained for one grade in the normal classroom. This group also includes children who, because of the impact of their learning disabilities, may be functioning at a borderline retarded level of performance despite their adequate intellect. Eight children were seen an average of 32 sessions before their program was terminated. At that point some of these children were functioning at the level where they could succeed when assigned part time or full time to a regular class; some remained in a special classroom in their local school.

In *Group E,* 13 children were seen for a minimum of 10 and an average of 36 sessions each. Of these, three children are still in therapy after 30 to 80 sessions. Others have been terminated when a prolonged plateau in the child's performance in therapy is evident. The program was discontinued by an involved person other than the therapist for a variety of reasons, such as residential placement, family move, etc. None of the children in this group were able to be reassigned to a special education class in a regular school at the time when the child was being treated in this program. Group E spans the age range from three to nine years and includes the multiply handicapped, the more severely involved learning-disordered child with concomitant language problems, and those with severe developmental delays. Some children in this group clearly demonstrate organicity but do not have the motor impairments of the cerebral palsied child. A few are said to have autistic-like behavior; several have vision or hearing impairment together with other handicaps. All the children in this group attended special schools.

The purpose of presenting these five case studies, which are representative of their respective groups, is to illustrate the range of problems encountered. They provide an evolving picture of how these problems were identified and what changes took place. One case illustrates how the sensorimotor integrative techniques have been used from a holistic viewpoint to also reduce the effects of mental retardation.

In each of these cases the therapy would have spanned the relevant portions of each of the eight program plans. However, for obvious reasons, only the most pertinent aspects are described. Changes in performance have been charted along the Integrated Program Matrix for each case. When the child achieves the requirements cited in the OEPS, the therapy hour is noted in the appropriate block.

Case Studies

Sample Case from Group A

Tom, age six years and one month, was referred by the family because of the frustration and defeat the child was experiencing in trying to keep up with class expectations in the middle of his kindergarten year, particularly with regard to reading and writing. He was seen a total of nine sessions over a nine-month period. This was a normally healthy boy of above-average intellect who had no contributory family or medical history.

Evaluation

The initial evaluation of the child on Phase I activities revealed good gross motor coordination, as follows.

He involved himself immediately on the *indoor climber,* demonstrating exploratory activity which indicated he was functioning in high Level II and beginning Level III skills. On the *inflatables,* he showed organized patterns prone and in the quadruped position forward and back, left and right. In the *carpeted barrel,* he rolled over immediately with minimal fragmentation between revolutions, but had difficulty in maintaining hip and knee flexion, Level I. On the outside, he sat to balance with adequate trunk rotation and lifted himself up on his hands to shift body left or right, at Level II. On the *scooter board,* he clearly functioned at the top of Level II — prone, his trunk and hips were well stabilized; he had a good overlapping of the hands and a pivot prone posture at the end of the twirling arc, which he spontaneously demonstrated upon introduction of the activity. In the sitting position on the scooter board, he again demonstrated good two-sided integration with a well-stabilized "hand-over-hand" pattern to pull himself along on the overhead rope. He functioned consistently at Level II throughout the sitting posture; while trunk balance was adequate to turn around and maneuver without falling, there were no swing-through patterns attempted as yet.

In Phase II, timed hammering and crayoning samples demonstrated that productions of left and right were nearly equal, despite the fact that there was no overt confusion as to which is which by name, and the right has been the preferred one for pencil skills. However, residuals of confused dominance were clearly seen in the reversals of his numbers — 4, 7, 5, and 15. He wrote only capitals A, B, K, D, E, G when asked for the whole alphabet.

He demonstrated no top-bottom reversal problems in open-end nesting of the indented shallow squares, nor the closed-end nested eggs, but closed-end sequencing skills should nevertheless be reinforced.

It was concluded that vestibular bilateral integration was fair to good and that by a minimal amount of reinforcement, the foundations for hand dominance selection would be developed. Six weeks were recommended for his "exploration" of hand dominance at home by using the hammer to pound empty egg cartons and a three-foot-long piece of thick balsa wood. By doing this he would supplement the activity of the two intervening therapy sessions. Through cooperation of the teacher, the parents, and the therapist, efforts to teach reading and writing were curtailed until he had clearly established laterality with good hand dominance and directionality. The problem was felt to be one of minimal proportion, but if left untreated, the child would experience mounting frustration academically.

Therapy Program

By Hour Three inside the carpeted barrel, he functioned at the top of Level II and beginning Level III, no longer extending hips and knees, rolling without fragmentation, with head self-supported, off the floor throughout. On the outside of the barrel he also functioned at the top of Level II, beginning Level III. In the double suspended tires, he spent considerable amounts of time twirling at 60 RPM, returning again and again to repeat the action. His hands overlapped strongly; when only one hand was in use, it was his right.

He enjoyed twirling immensely; no subjective feeling of dizziness was expressed; nystagmus of minimal amplitude was briefly observed.

Seated on the scooter board in Hour Three, he had adequate motor control and trunk balance to hang onto the overhead rope, to swing through and back; by Hour Eight, he could make a 180° turn and gracefully execute elaborate patterns of movement at Level III.

By Hour Six, he performed well on the climbing ladder and used the jumping board with an excellent adaptive response, while giving intense stimulation to the joint receptors throughout all weight-bearing joints. He also did quite a bit of jumping rope at home.

On top of the carpeted barrel, in Hour Nine, he had complete control of his balance, at Level III, turning 360° as he rolled it across the floor on his hands and knees.

In Phase II, in Hour Three, six weeks after the initial evaluation, he was retested on the timed hammering test for hand dominance. Whereas the number of strokes was still equal (53 for the right and 52 for the left) during a 15-second period, the performance demonstrated significant contrasts. In the right hand, he held the wooden hammer so the flat face of it hit the paper, as opposed to striking the edge and skidding in an awkward manner with the left. A better clustering pattern of carbon marks were an obvious contrast to the lighter, more dispersed marks on the left.

Again, with timed crayoning as with hammering, the right was chosen for use first; in the right there was a good tripod grip, good control, and no attempts to transfer, whereas he tried to transfer from left to right twice and held the crayon awkwardly 4 inches from the tip. Strong contrasts in density were apparent between the two hands now, which were not evident in Hour One. The right is now felt to have been established by him as his dominant hand.

At this point the right-left sensory identification was introduced, followed by the Positional Model and its various applications, as well as the textured scribble board, Exercise #1 to establish top-bottom, left-right pencil patterns, and template training. Number training was introduced in the spring of his kindergarten year and was followed up with capitals after summer vacation at the time he entered first grade.

Body image, directionality, and spatial relations all developed without residual confusion. Occasional inverted placement was seen in the teens; sometimes the "7" would be reversed in "17," but the letters were quickly mastered. By the time he completed his program in Hour Nine, sample sheets of numbers, plus the capital and lower case printed letters on two-inch lined paper, were performed with only minor variations in size constancy and reversals in "j" and "z" alone; these forms no longer floated off the line.

Summary

Visual form recognition of the printed letters, visual pursuits, and visual tracking along the line developed well, and problems were reduced sufficiently so that frustrations in reading at the expected first grade level were largely mitigated. The ease with which this occurred, together with the absence of additional indicators of sensorimotor disorganization, suggest that this child would fall into the category described here as a "pseudo learning-disordered" child. Tom has continued to function very capably at his grade level over the last five years in a school which has exceptionally high academic standards.

Sample Case From Group B

Matthew, age six years and two months upon entering therapy, was referred by a learning disability consultant. He was in the first semester of kindergarten at the time, having spent an additional year in nursery school. Although he scored 129 IQ on the Peabody Picture Vocabulary Test, it was felt that he would have problems adapting successfully to the expectations of first grade the coming year because of the visual-motor incoordination, auditory distractibility, and poor organizational skills, particularly those that are required for third and fourth grades. There is no known contributory medical history.

Evaluation

When evaluated here, Matthew presented a picture of poor vestibular bilateral integration, confused dominance, and both tactile and auditory defensiveness. He was treated weekly through Hour Twelve and then on intermittent four and six-week hold patterns, with four months off during the summer. There were four consecutive weekly therapy periods at the beginning and at the end of his first grade year. The latter series of sessions emphasized the sequential motor patterns of script writing at the time when this was being introduced in his class. He has been seen a total of 24 therapy hours.

A summary of his initial performance in gross motor skills in Phase I is as follows.

On the *climber,* he functioned at Level III with minor exceptions such as use of one foot at a time to back down the ladder; he sought inverted positioning repeatedly, which is interpreted here as being a way of further stimulating the semicircular canals. When twirling in the *double suspended tires,* his hands were 180° apart, he used a heavy slapping pattern on the floor with both hands simultaneously, but later in the same time frame, he briefly positioned his hands near to, if not across, the midline; he sought the inverted head posture immediately in the supine position. On the *scooter board,* he performed kickoffs with adequate thrust in the legs, but trunk balance was unsteady, characteristic of Level I; hand action in twirling was similar to that in the tires, slapping the floor, first at 180°, then coming close to the midline. In the *carpeted barrel,* he functioned at Level II, inside and outside. On the inflated *"Moby Dick"* his prone thrust and alternating protective arm extension patterns were at Level II; prone and supine balance were under partial control, at Level I, on the large pillow or Space Ship.

Phase II findings showed that hand dominance was unconfirmed, although he preferred right in trained tasks such as pencil skills; disorganization present in writing numbers "one" and "nine" from bottom to top; capital letters were generally better organized, but F, J, and O were started at the bottom. Early organization of size sequence, and tactile sequence and assembly function, were adequate for him to recognize his errors and correct them.

Behaviorally, there was a false bravado about much of his gross motor work; his response became more appropriate within the first six months of therapy. His ability to interpret the meaning of verbal instructions improved; his auditory distractibility and his hyperverbal response were reduced but are still evident under stress. His balance, two-sided integration, and his ability to do motor planning in both gross and fine movements are comparable to his peers.

He has kept up with his class without undue strain. Now at the conclusion of therapy 18 months later, he is excelling in age-appropriate sports such as baseball, and he is developing good peer relationships. Although there is minimal, if any, obvious residual in his left-right confusion, it is recommended that Hebrew training be delayed for another year, when he will be nearly 9 years old.

Sample Case From Group C

Arthur, age ten years and three months upon entering therapy, was referred by a pediatrician whose neurological examination revealed a positive Prachtl sign and overflow movements; repetitive movements often got out of hand and explosive. He had a high activity level, seen by some observers as hyperactive. Etiology of these symptoms was unspecified. Pregnancy and delivery were uncomplicated; family history is noncontributory as regards the child's condition.

Arthur is a child of superior intelligence who is able to do school work well above his age level but has a great deal of difficulty with fine and gross motor skills. He is in a regular fifth grade but reads at the sixth-grade level with excellent comprehension. He has difficulty with his peers because he is far ahead of them mentally but cannot keep up with them physically.

Evaluation

In evaluation here, it was observed that Arthur exhibited poor vestibular bilateral integration with a dormant nystagmus, poor body image, tactile and auditory system dormancy, with poor motor planning secondary to the former, and with regard to the latter, a problem in processing and acting upon many verbal instructions, especially those related to directionality and spatial relations since these were concomitant problems.

His initial performance in Phase I tasks revealed a child who had great difficulty balancing on the *inflated pillow*, at Level I, and who needed constant counterbalancing efforts on the part of the therapist when he was lying prone lengthwise on "Moby Dick" — the most suitable because he is a large 10-year-old boy. In the *double suspended tires*, he sagged at the hips and neck, was unable to avoid hitting his knees on the floor, exhibited no prone twirling patterns, and functioned generally at the beginning of Level I. On the *scooter board*, he functioned also in Level I, with poor kickoff patterns and no spontaneous twirling. In the *carpeted barrel*, neck muscles were too weak to support the head off the floor while rolling inside the barrel, with head extended past the opening; he rolled back and forth and turned over within the barrel, without rolling it over (Level I). On the *climber*, he functioned at Level III, but this would not mean he would not have motor planning problems still; its use was continued primarily to provide heavy touch-pressure to limited weight-bearing areas of the body he could not see, as well as to promote sequential patterns of gross motor skills preliminary to script writing.

In Phase II the timed hammering and coloring tasks showed lack of confirmed dominance, with the left being the preferred hand and more skillful in trained pencil tasks than the right. The Visual-Motor Integration Test scored at eight months above his chronological age. Visual copying of a form was not a real problem academically; the problems in printing arose from confusion in directionality, where "b" and "d" were reversed, and the errors in auditory perception when letters such as "d" and "g" cause further confusion. (It was recommended after several months that the child also have language therapy.)

Serious problems in directionality and spatial relations persisted and were evident in the initial sample of numbers and letters on two-inch lined paper, made with a grease pencil. Numbers 3, 5, and 8 were made from the bottom up. Numbers and letters consistently float off the line. Letters, closely but evenly spaced, were minute but constant in size.

Body image testing of the back view reveals that left and right orientation were correct, but there was confusion (auditory component, plus body image) in locating the proper joint. The front view was totally reversed in left and right crossover patterns.

In nesting graded sizes of the open-end indented squares, there was profound top-bottom confusion; he nested them all upside down, with the smallest on the bottom.

Therapy

In therapy, Arthur made fairly steady and rapid progress throughout the program, which extended over 11 months; initially he attended therapy for 16 weekly sessions which were followed by a one-month hold pattern and then a summer break of five months, making 18 sessions in all.

By Hour Six, Phase I skills had improved significantly. Prone balance on the six-foot long inflatable, Moby Dick, was excellent; sitting balance on it was almost as good, supine balance was under fair control. During prone positioning across the midpoint of this 18-inch-high inflatable, the strength in the neck muscles had developed sufficiently to tolerate a two-pound weight, which was used to further stimulate the proprioceptors. This action of pushing forward hard with the legs and catching himself with extended arms against the floor activated the scapulo-thoracic musculature necessary for good stability in writing.

In the *double suspended tires,* he began to extend his head to the neutral position and above, from the previously flexed posture; the hips were partially extended, moving up from an angle of 90° flexion. In the tires, wide arc swinging, pivoting from the feet and knees, was his primary movement pattern. In Hours Seven and Eight, he began to twirl but again used his legs almost exclusively in an extremely awkward manner. It was not until Hour Nine that he sensed how to position himself in a more balanced way in the tires so that his arms could be activated for twirling. A random, occasional overlapping pattern emerged but was still very unstable. Meanwhile, from the beginning of therapy, he had repeatedly sought supine twirling, being positioned with his hips down, between the tires, and his head dropped down and backward. By Hour Seven, nystagmus was evident for the first time; subjectively, he expressed a feeling of dizziness and staggered after a prolonged period of 10 to 15 minutes of twirling both prone and supine, which he obviously enjoyed.

It is important to note by contrast that he was observed overlapping his hands at the midline during prone twirling on the scooter board three or four sessions earlier than he demonstrated this pattern on the double suspended tires. It is felt a heavy (or older) child such as this has a different center of gravity than that of a young child, and the legs are much heavier proportionally. In addition, his insensitivity to balance caused him to be unaware of how to shift his position forward so that some of the weight was supported. (He was never instructed to do so.) On the scooter board, however, the hips were much more apt to be supported, and the twirling could be activated by hand action alone.

The increasing strength of the neck muscles was also revealed in his response in Hour Six, when rolling inside the *carpeted barrel;* he now supported the head off the floor for one and a half trips across the room before resting it intermittently for the next two or three trips (20 feet in length). By Hour Eleven, he spontaneously positioned himself on hands and knees on the outside of the barrel, shifting weight to keep his balance and eventually to advance the barrel across the floor; until this time the barrel had to be partially stabilized for the sitting balance (Level I) and, at first, in the kneeling position (Level II). With his head in the closed end of the barrel, he demonstrated holding the knees and hips in flexion while rolling, but returned to an intermittent extension pattern as he fatigued.

He set his own goals for repeating the prone pushoff and return, with a forceful arm extension, while the weights were suspended around his neck. He advanced from 50 repeats in Hour Twelve to 75 and 100 in the next two sessions. By Hour Fourteen he reported he was doing headstands and that situps were easier in gym. In Hour Fifteen, he proudly reported a "B" in gym — his first! Self-confidence increased; peer relationships in group activities were at an all-time high.

In Phase II, random hammering on a 3 foot length of balsa wood revealed right-handed preference in Hour Two, but by Hour Three, all strokes were left-handed. Consistent home programming helped him establish a spontaneous hand selection by tapping the endurance level of the hand which is truly dominant; for him it was the left. In Hour Six he was retested on timed hammering and crayoning samples and demonstrated a significant shift to the left, by virtue of more skillful productions. Only at this point was it indicated to introduce the sensory identification of left and right, the Positional Model, and its various applications. Now pencil training proceeded using prewriting exercise #1, templates, copying numbers and printed letters from model sheets.

In Hour Eleven, another sample was taken of numbers and letters on a 2 inch line; numbers he made from 21-31 showed correct directional orientation and motor sequence from 21-29, but reverted to the bottom to top movements in making the "3s" which followed. He started to make O and Q from the bottom, then corrected himself. By Hour Thirteen, he demonstrated good directional organization throughout, working at a suitable pace instead of his previous haphazard, erratic manner. Printing on lined tablet paper was satisfactory, so the emphasis could now shift to script patterns. Body image testing showed no confusion even on crossover patterns, and no obvious residuals of confusion in various spatial relations tasks to include geographic orientation. Visual tracking was introduced in Hour Thirteen, following prior preparation on dot-to-dot alphabetical drawings; timing of his performance in visual tracking was not indicated until Hour Fifteen. By Hour Sixteen, he had completed the script motor patterns adequately, so the focus was placed on the connectors between script letters, and he was put on a hold period. Upon his return a month later, he was given a five-minute timed script sample to copy. Because it was acceptable in form and size constancy, the therapist could expect he would be able to function in current age appropriate demands for written work at school and to take notes rapidly during his future education.

The Beery-Buktenica Visual-Motor Integration Test was re-administered, and he now scored thirteen years and nine months, or two years and seven months above his age level, which reflects more accurately the intellectual and performance level of which he is capable. His fifth grade final report card listed all A's. He summarized his feelings clearly with the comment, "It wasn't as hard to get all A's this year as it was to try for B's last year." His entrance into sixth grade was very smooth and indicated no need for continued therapy.

Summary

A course of 18 therapy hours over an eleven-month period had proven successful in helping this boy, eleven years and two months old at its completion, to function as an equal among his peers, with particular regard to his motor skills and peer relationships. (Follow-up two years later confirms that there has continued to be an excellent adjustment throughout.)

Sample Case from Group D

William entered this program at age eleven years and eight months at the recommendation of friends of his family. He functioned within the average range of intelligence and may have had the potential to score higher had it not been for his prolonged, severe perceptual problems. William repeated fourth grade; he had received continued tutoring in reading and language skills over the past four years. Siblings are reported to have difficulties in spelling and math. The grandmother is said to be ambidextrous. William had used his left hand for writing until it was felt by a psychologist who evaluated him in the summer following first grade that he was not left-handed. It was recommended that he then use his right hand; subsequently he reverted to his left hand, which he has continued to use.

Evaluation

William presented a series of interrelated, complex problems which have continued to interfere with his learning ability. Foremost were his problems crossing the midline, poor vestibular bilateral integration with its natural sequelae of mixed hand dominance and left-right confusion, which was observed with the obvious "b" and "d" reversals. He had poor visual tracking left to right along a line, eg, on an eight-line page where he was to identify every "d," he omitted three out of twelve. He had poor tactile system performance, with faulty body image, and poor spatial relations secondary to inadequate function in both the tactile and vestibular systems. This was demonstrated in his inability to space letters within a word, between words, or on a line with any degree of constancy; he printed his name without leaving a space between the first and the last. It was surprising to observe that his age equivalency score on the Beery-Buktenica Visual-Motor Integration Test was eleven months above his chronological age. However, a lack of confidence in what he was doing was evident by his faint pencil lines. Despite the fact the results often met passing requirements for the item, the extent of his disorganization became apparent in the following observations. He made horizontal lines from right to left (not unusual for left-handed individuals); he made the first circle (Item #3) counterclockwise, starting at the top, which is desired. As he encountered more complex items which also included circles, his performance regressed, and some circles were then made clockwise; of these, one was begun from the bottom, a very primitive pattern. He was requested to make a five-pointed star and succeeded only on his second attempt. This I consider to be one of the prerequisite skills for success in cursive writing, since it requires mastery of a sequential motor pattern.

On the back view of the Body Image Test, the answers were correct, but they required considerable cognitive effort. When more than one process was involved, he repeated the instructions, eg, "put number 5 on his left ankle," before proceeding with the task. In the face view, he reversed all items. Top-bottom confusion was evident in reassembling the set of nested eggs. In nesting the set of hexagon cups, he failed to use his nondominant hand for assistance, a pattern which was consistent with his reluctance to hold the paper for writing.

Auditory perception problems contributed to his difficulty in processing the simple instructions in the Body Image Test and later were seen in his confusion in executing the movements "over" versus "down." It was obvious that his lack of constancy in identifying the visual form of letters had interfered with the reading process, yielding further erroneous feedback auditorily, eg, he misread "fur" for "fun" and "once" for "ounce." He was unable to maintain the necessary organization to say "after *a* comes *b*" in the dot-to-dot alphabetical drawing, which requires simultaneous visual, auditory-verbal, and sequential organization.

When he entered third grade, he was still unable to read. In repeating fourth grade, his grade scores by midyear were 6.0 in passage comprehension, 3.8 in word identification, 4.9 in word comprehension, and 3.0 in word attack.

In summary, from observations and background information, although he enjoyed playing various sports, it would appear that William has functioned in a mildly hypotonic manner; he demonstrated a dormant quality in the olfactory, tactile, and auditory triad, as well as a dormant mode in the visual-vestibular dyad. All of this led to poor sensory awareness, organization, and sensory integration with resultant disorganization in his academic skills.

Whereas William could process single skills or simple combinations of them, simultaneous processing of multiple skills, which are usually mastered by second grade, had seriously jeopardized his academic achievement. For instance, he lacked many of the skills necessary to compose a sentence, such as adequate visual form constancy, mastery of left and right directionality, and the application of this to letter and word forms. He also had difficulty in the spatial relations needed for positioning letters on the line and the proper spacing of letters within and between words. Furthermore he had not developed the sequential movement patterns to make his letters without giving undue cognitive attention to it. To master basic spelling requirements, one must have established a reasonable skill in the auditory-visual symbolic match and the auditory or visual sequencings of the letters. All of these skills had to be fairly well mastered before he could begin to concentrate on the cognitive aspects such as organizing the content or expressing the ideas he conceptualized. His severe auditory perception impairment was witnessed by his efforts to copy from dictation a four-line excerpt from the poem, "The Blu Skeys": "Pople come and peple go why they come non won nose. The woto is cole and clean and cler and anitmuls come with out ther fear." (sic)

Throughout the evaluation there was evidence of his lack of awareness of even the most fundamental forms of sequential organization. He was easily confused in the graded size relationships, of nesting items, was unable to maintain the sequential order of letters within the alphabet, except when said in a rushed version of the kindergarten song, and was unable to name the months of the year in their proper order.

Therapy

This boy was seen in therapy 37 times over a period of six months. The early course of therapy followed extensive work on gross motor skills, especially the quadrupedal balance on the inflated pillow and prone positioning over the carpeted barrel. This emphasized his use of the protective arm extension patterns. Weights over the back of the neck stimulated the proprioceptors of the neck extensors. Balance became more organized and rhythmic on the inflatables by Hour Seven. Sufficient skill for Level III was observed by Hour Sixteen. Eye pursuits, following the bead rolling along the three-foot-long tube, was adequate by Hour Seven. Using the Ann Arbor Tracking Program to track letters of the alphabet along a line, he demonstrated continued confusion and disorganization. His problems were due to poor visual form recognition as well as his auditory confusion over similar sounding letters , such as "u" for "q" plus the added demand of maintaining the sequential order of letters in the alphabet.

After a month of home programming to confirm his left dominance by hammering, directional orientation was introduced in Hour Five. Progress in directional orientation by applying the Positional Model to letter "b" and "d," the body image drawings and finally geographical orientation was slow and often regressed briefly between therapy sessions. A method which integrated the tactile, visual, and auditory-verbal responses was innovated to help establish memory patterns of spelling words and the multiplication tables for short-term and long-range recollection and recall. He made relatively good progress, but this may not be sustained unless used frequently.

He was able to use his imagination for clever ideas in essays, but he had no awareness of how to organize them so that the result was other than a series of simple, fragmented sentences expressing the content in a poorly organized manner. This problem was met by using the kind of frametray puzzles which he had previously assembled for visual figure-ground and spatial relations training. He was helped to visually identify from these the principal ideas and events. The therapist then took word-for-word dictation, assisting him as needed, to sense from this concrete structure how to expand and elaborate the theme, how to bridge disparate ideas with transitional words or sentences, and how to bring it to some conclusion.

Meanwhile, every possible effort was being directed toward improving the mechanics of his handwriting skills. Following extensive hammering and use of the textured plastic scribble board to yield tactile information as well as to confirm his left hand dominance, top-to-bottom and left-to-right movements were emphasized in the prewriting Exercise #1. Template training and tracing the 2 inch numbers, capitals, and lower case printed letter forms were stressed. Then, using 2 inch lined paper again, with the grease pencil, he was asked to copy sentences in print. Here his attention was directed to placement of the letter form on the line, the size constancy of letters, and the systematic spacing of letters within and between words. The next step was to try to apply the same skills on lined tablet paper. For brief periods, he would try to maintain the necessary control to copy a word or two, but as soon as there were more, or whenever it was necessary to use any additional process such as formulating an answer, the form deteriorated quickly. It was finally determined that at his age the most effective way to convey the sensory input would be for him to actually trace over the printed letters provided by the therapist. Hence the stories describing the puzzles were prepared for him page after page, skipping alternate lines throughout so he could clearly recognize and follow the movement pattern and spacing set up for him. As each theme was completed, he would be asked to go back and reproduce these same sentences without tracing them. There were some carryover effects, but whenever he had to use multiple processes such as formulating a test answer under the pressure of time, the results again deteriorated.

Script patterns were introduced in Hour Thirty, starting with individual letters which corresponded to each of the script motor patterns #1 through #5. When these were achieved,then the emphasis was put on the connectors. Following the same general progression, as in printed letters, eg, copying first words and then sentences, he finally was able to copy the material from his themes in script. However, he was not able at this point to take any dictation without again regressing in either his spelling skill or movement patterns or both. William's therapy was continued on a series of six-week hold patterns from Hour Thirty-four through Thirty-six.

Summary

It was felt that William had been brought as far as possible for the time being; it is possible that after a year or two, he could profit from some review. By then he may have matured to the point where he would have a more realistic sense of need and recognize the increasing academic demands for skill in both the mechanics of handwriting and the organization of content.

It is anticipated that William will always need an unpressured academic setting, with small classes such as those in a private school and with one-to-one supplemental instruction as needed. Presumably he will continue to have difficulty in acquiring new concepts and will have serious problems at higher levels of education both comprehending and taking lecture notes at the speed which most instructors deliver their material. Despite use of intensive sensory integrative techniques to make spelling easier, he still has a serious problem and will need help in learning even through slow, painstaking, and repetitive efforts.

Sample Case from Group E

Corine, who started therapy at 8½ years old, was referred from a special school for learning problems where she has been a student for the past few years. She has been diagnosed microcephalic. When last tested she was functioning at an IQ around 50, although she definitely has areas of performance which show better ability. Her comprehension is now at a second grade level; she has adapted very well in terms of social skills. Her limited visual-motor integration affects her academic performance most severely. The Beery-Buktenica Visual-Motor Integration Test scores at about the fifth year age equivalency, remaining relatively unchanged over the past eighteen months, in which she has had forty therapy sessions.

Some other changes which could not have been predicted have become evident by the way in which she can perform various therapy activities used to upgrade her sensorimotor organization, plus her improved social relationships and certain academic skills such as reading. Although sensory dysfunction is not the primary etiology, the same treatment techniques have been used to improve her learning ability and performance skills wherever possible.

Evaluation

During her initial evaluation, when 8½ years old, on the Phase I equipment, there was minimal involvement with each of the five basic pieces of equipment. On the *indoor climber,* she climbed up the first two steps of the ladder very slowly and then remained in a fixed position without further exploration, appearing fearful and anxious, especially when backing down. She was unable to comprehend the words "under," "over," or "through" with regard to the various parts of the climber.

Using the *double suspended tires,* she was fretful and resistant when in the prone position; she complained of a "headache" and sought relief from further involvement.

On the *scooter board,* she needed help to position herself on it, had no awareness of how to kick off and, even when helped, still could not initiate any action.

In the *carpeted barrel,* her entire attitude was negative; she was very upset with the unpredictable motion of the barrel and even when it was stabilized she would not involve herself. Similarly, even to sit and straddle the inflated *Moby Dick,* with her feet on the floor, caused too much anxiety, so its use was discontinued for the time being.

The vestibular system was functioning so inadequately that she was very unstable and apprehensive; this anxiety would have been intensified if at that point she had been urged to do more. She maintained a precarious balance within a very narrow range off dead center and was limited in her exploration. This restricted her opportunities to stimulate the maturation of the vestibular apparatus.

The problem was further complicated by the serious dysfunction in the tactile system known as "tactile defensiveness" which further prevents motor activity and integration between her tactile and vestibular systems. Her visual system has had little confirmatory information from either of these systems; as a result, the visual-motor integration and other underlying skills which she needed especially to form numbers and printed letters have been seriously impaired.

In Phase II, a request for her to make her numbers resulted in a barely recognizable series of numbers 1-5, floating far above the line, two inches wide; she was unable to print any capital letters. She tried instead to print her name. This effort produced a series of fragmented, disorganized lines, with indistinct form and directional confusion, eg, the opening of the "c" was turned upward, the "n" was reversed from top to bottom, becoming a "u," and the "r" became an "n."

She was unable to nest a series of six open-end shallow round cups and showed top-bottom confusion in closed-end nesting of six eggs. Left-right orientation on the body image drawings did not need to be tested to know that the directional confusion was profound. In an early problem-solving sequence and assembly task she was able to reassemble a simple six-piece plastic toy flower pot and flower. With only minor, self-corrected errors she could reassemble an early tactile sequence and assembly toy. Her recognition and matching of visual form far exceeded her ability to reproduce visual number and letter forms with a pencil.

Visual fixation on a still target in each of the four quadrants was up to age formula in all but one. Her visual pursuit of a marble in a tube was adequate for six out of eight trips.

277

Throughout the evaluation and many therapy sessions, her anxiety was expressed in a persevering manner, asking if this would be the last task, or if she would be going home now, despite the fact she seemed very pleased to continue and enjoyed herself.

Therapy

Throughout the first six to eight weeks of therapy, she continued to be resistant to involving herself on most of the five basic pieces of Phase I equipment, complaining of the sudden onset of headaches. During this time her father constructed a wooden climber for her home use. By quiet disregard of her negative attitude to these tasks, she gradually became more responsive to the invitational approach. She was allowed to maintain control of how fast to proceed. Once she began to achieve new steps, she became excited and continued spontaneously, having "bridged the gap from avoidance to exploration."

Initially as she began to explore the climber in her slow, laborious manner, she needed emotional support to help her continue in these new ventures. In Hour Six, she tried sitting on the top rungs, balancing with only one foot and without holding on; she was eager to go home to show her father. By Hour Eight, the continuity of her movement patterns had greatly improved; she jumped backwards off the ladder, with great glee, repeating it many times. She was very proud in Hour Fourteen of her ability to advance across the top. She found she could hang from the overhead rungs of a large outdoor jungle gym and do it better than her neighbor. The previous summer she had been fearful and unable to let go to drop to the ground, which she could do now. By Hour Seventeen, she had advanced from early stages of Level I to now be able to meet many of the requirements for Level III.

Initially, she was virtually immobile on the tires, keeping her knees in rigid extension. This was true even while the therapist helped her support her legs in an effort to have her feel a forward-backward movement in the prone position. By Hour Fifteen, she began to twirl and discovered the tires to be fun. She could now hold one leg in extension at a time, or both with her knees partially flexed. Most significantly, she no longer complained of early fatigue and pain in her neck from prone positioning. She did still complain occasionally about getting a headache from twirling. Her hands now crossed over the midline; nystagmus was evident for the first time, but with minimal amplitude. (She had resisted any prior efforts to assess the presence or absence of nystagmus.) In Hour Sixteen, she expressed her pleasure, saying she wanted to "twirl all day." Her legs could be kept in sustained extension for two to three revolutions as she twirled. The most apparent change was the lessening of earlier signs of anxiety and even a mildly depressive, or unresponsive face, which gave way to a much more relaxed, joyful expression. Most notable, her eyes had become widely alert as compared to their previously dulled look. She seemed to be a much happier child with more self-confidence and satisfaction from her increased capabilities.

On the *scooter board* she achieved a kick-off, feebly at first, on Hour Three, and being so pleased with her success, she returned to do it four or five times that session. By Hour Six the trunk was more stable so that she did not lose her balance and fall off as she had done, and she then began to twirl. As on the tires, she complained of her neck "hurting" in the prone position. By Hour Sixteen she demonstrated a more sustained hand-over-hand crossing pattern over the midline than on the tires; legs were maintained in strong extension as she proceeded to twirl very fast, with a heavy, rhythmic slapping cadence which caused her to be dizzy for five seconds or more after stopping. She then requested the twirling chair which heretofore she had rejected. She was twirled clockwise for a 15-second interval @ 36 RPM, with a resulting five or more seconds of nystagmus with minimal amplitude; she then rejected counterclockwise twirling. At about this time, Hour Eleven, it was reported by her parents that she had gotten "dizzy" as they sailed on a boat from Boston to Nova Scotia; it was her first such experience. At about this time, she was proud to report that she could go upstairs "two at a time...like the big kids."

On the *inflatables,* she sat astride the large Moby Dick to balance, with her feet on the floor. She then sought the supine rocking position in Hour Five during the same session when she accepted the supine positioning for brief twirling in the tires.

By Hour Eight she insisted on prolonged periods, eight to ten minutes duration, of heavy supine rocking where her head touched the floor at the end of each arc of motion; she giggled ecstatically, felt she could not get enough! On the inflatable at her school, she reported that no one could push her off from the kneeling position, as they had all the others in her group. By Hour Twenty-one skill on the inflatables, in nearly all positions, was at Level II and partially into Level III, balancing confidently and gracefully over a wide arc. In Hour Thirty-three she demonstrated an excellent response in Level III. Reports from school indicated she was now sitting more quietly in the classroom.

In the carpeted barrel, she showed minimal interest in rolling inside until after returning from her summer break at Hour Twenty-two. Since then she gradually came to function at Level II. In each of these five pieces of equipment, Corine moved from an almost total avoidance mode of response to a prolonged exploration of each, to organize her motor responses, integrate one sensory system with another, (tactile, vestibular, visual), and to draw needed elemental concepts of top-bottom, left-right, as well as a developing body image to apply in Phase II tasks.

In Phase II, the tactile system organization was painfully slow; early tactile discrimination of textured blocks and early form recognition of 3-D plastic animals, jumbo plastic baby snapbeads, and finally recognition of 2 inch size plastic freight cars were not fully mastered until Hour Twenty-three, eleven months from the beginning of therapy. Since then she proceeded to improve to the point where she could discriminate closely related 2 inch square aluminum linear forms which were as complex as differentiating five and six pointed stars, or recognizing a dollar sign from a treble clef and other similar forms.

Despite prolonged efforts to use sensory identification methods to help her to recognize left from right, and by introduction and application of the positional model, she continued to vacillate, particularly when more than one step was involved. For instance, in Hour Thirty-four she could correctly identify on the Body Image Test, back view, all joints as being left or right, as long as the instructions were broken down into "Find the right elbow...put #4 on it," but when asked to locate the "upper left hand corner" on a block, she was apt to be confused still, in Hour Thirty-eight.

Her pencil control with numbers and printed letters demonstrated only marginal change, still showing little awareness of direction, form, or firmness in executing them, and showing no ability to keep on the line or to maintain proper spacing between letters or words.

In Hour Thirty-three, to acknowledge her good efforts with numbers, several five-pointed stars were placed on the page, as is the custom, but they were made very rapidly so as not to train the child in a splinter skill. Suddenly she spontaneously started to make them herself and could do it fairly well. Because of this and her good sequential movement patterns on the climber, and also since only marginal progress would be possible for some time in printing, it was decided to introduce script writing in Hour Thirty-six. It was acknowledged that to maintain her interest and involvement it would be necessary to forego the more rudimentary techniques of Motor Patterns #1 to #5 and definitely try to teach a splinter skill. For example, words such as mom, dad, cat, horse, etc, which she could relate to, were used to motivate her. She could copy letters and words in a recognizable form on lined tablet paper. Her visual form perception and all the concomitant requirements for reading developed sufficiently enough for her to read independently for pleasure. To what extent she will ever be able to initiate and organize her own thinking in written form is not yet clear. However, as one stepping stone to prepare for this, the prerequisites were broken down into parts, eg, she was helped to organize the sequential order of her experiences of her birthday party by dictating these to the therapist. Months later this will be used when she is ready to copy it in script.

Summary

Throughout these 18 months of Corine's therapy, progress has been painfully slow in some areas, but nevertheless, she has never plateaued in progress across the board. Also, she had not reached a plateau in school at the end of the spring term as she usually had. It is felt that she will possibly continue steady progress such as has been described here and in many other areas outlined in the Integrated Program Matrix. Weekly therapy, except for vacations and long summer recesses, may continue to be appropriate for several more years. While it is expected she will always be functioning in the retarded range, it will be important for her intelligence to be retested after another year or more of therapy, when she will presumably be better equipped to function in test situations.

Corine has a very outgoing personality, expressing interest (albeit, occasional undue curiosity) about others. Social relationships with her peer group are encouraged through dancing classes and horseback riding, which she greatly enjoys. Her involvement with playmates has expanded this past year. She attends camp in a neighboring state several months each summer; she now talks about writing home from camp.

Predicting a prognosis for this child at the age of ten is difficult at best. It would, however, seem reasonable to expect that she will be able to be trained for at least a partially self-sustained form of employment in a sheltered environment when she reaches young adulthood.

Appendices

Appendix A

The Ongoing Evaluation and Performance Scale

Gross Sensorimotor Organization

Indoor Climber (P.P. 3.1)

Level I

1. ___ Terrified of the idea of climbing; avoids it by withdrawing from the apparatus ___ ; expresses fear of heights ___ ; prefers to remain uninvolved although gives no overt expression of fear ___ ; exploration minimal ___ ; stands on lowest rung of ladder ___ ; stands on lower, long crossbar ___ .

2. ___ Movement is laborious, clumsily executed ___ ; long periods of inaction when standing or sitting on climber ___ ; advances to second or third ladder rung ___ ; does not demonstrate alternating pattern of movement in legs when ascending the ladder ___ ; when descending ___ ; sequence of movement patterns poorly organized, hesitates before proceeding from one to another ___ ; unable to follow simple directions which indicate position and movement (under, through) ___ .

3. ___ Simultaneous movement of extremities and/or together with trunk motion is more by chance than plan (eg, use of arms and legs in climbing ladder) ___ ; moves from ladder to horizontal crossbar or reverse ___ ; shifts weight on feet to move along crossbar, from one ladder to other ___ ; can sit and balance on any rung or crossbar ___ ; stands on crossbars to extend head and shoulders through the spaces between overhead rungs ___ ; exploration is emerging and movement patterns are more complex ___ .

4. ___ Remnants of disorganization still evident. (eg, switches goals enroute when he verbalized a plan, or the adult asked if he could move from one ladder to the other) ___ ; moves from one end to other without touching the floor ___ ;

circles the climber without touching the floor _____ ; explores by climbing to the top of the ladder, then retreats before moving on to overhead rungs _____ ; discovers this activity to be fun _____ .

Level II

1. ___ Executes one pattern; stops to cognitively consider next move _____ ; soon runs out of new "tricks" _____ ; timidly proceeds across the top by sitting on overhead rungs _____ ; crawls up through and down through spaces between overhead rungs _____ .

2. ___ Volunteers for "follow the ladder" in a group _____ ; proceeds to explore without fear or hesitation, but not without exercising proper caution _____ ; develops a wide repertoire of "tricks" he is eager to demonstrate _____ ; exhibits exploration and daring in crossing overhead rungs, kneeling on hands and knees _____ ; hangs by hands on overhead rungs while feet climb ladder _____ ; hangs upside-down _____ .

3. ___ Goal direction is no longer disorganized _____ ; movement is organized, smoothly integrated from one pattern to next _____ ; comprehends verbal directions about movement _____ ; offers verbal description as to the plan of action he expects to pursue _____ .

Level III

1. ___ Initiates exploratory approach immediately; is self-motivated to continue _____ ; further complexities of movement, such as swinging, dangling, and balancing in any form, are readily explored _____ .

2. ___ Follows a series of one to three simple, verbal commands without becoming disorganized or losing goal direction ___ .

3. ___ Demonstrates a virtual "symphony of movement" with smoothly connected, well organized patterns _____ ; assertive, self-confident, displays an air or "pride" justified by his accomplishments _____ .

Suspended Equipment (P.P. 2.1)

Double Suspended Tires — Prone (P.P. 2.1)

Level I

1. ____ Avoids contact other than to push tires by hand ____; needs someone to hold tires in order for him to get into or climb on top ____; lies prone for brief periods only ____; in prone position head and legs sag into a downward, flexed position ____; brief periods of extension occur at head and neck during motion ____; child enjoys passive swinging ____; child pushes himself backward (bilateral arm extension) ____; pushes himself forward ____; head and hips are lifted in extension for brief periods ____.

2. ____ Child enjoys movement in tires; seeks more; begins to explore movement possibilities ____; signs of a twirling pattern begin to emerge ____; arms cross midline ____ (either direction).

3. ____ Head, neck and upper trunk demonstrate consistent extension ____; hips extend more frequently during twirling ____; hip extension is strongly activated by kick-offs from the wall ____.

Level II

1. ____ A consistent pattern of arms overlapping is observed ____; may reach speeds of up to 60 RPM ____; need to twirl seems insatiable ____.

2. ____ Consistent extension of head, neck, and upper trunk evident during any prone activity ____; hip extension more frequent and prolonged when twirling than heretofore ____.

3. ____ Need for excessive twirling in the prone position has apparently peaked and (over past few weeks) seems to be on the wane ____.

Double Suspended Tires — Supine (P.P. 2.1)

Level I

1. ____ Child does not show evidence of any desire to assume the supine posture in the tires ____; avoids any suggestion of same if it is offered ____.

2. ____ Child maneuvers into the supine posture or moves in such a way as to suggest he may be trying to do so ____; willingly accepts offer to help him get into supine posi-

tion _____; relaxes in the supine position _____; enjoys being twirled that way _____.

Level II

1. _____ Need for supine twirling seems virtually insatiable_____; asks to be twirled fast _____; returns to this position again and again _____; facial expression is one of distinct pleasure _____; twirling elicits "giggle signals" _____.

2. _____ Need observed above seems to be on the wane.

Level III

None

Twirling Chair (P.P. 2.6)*

Level I

1. _____ Prefers to avoid contact, declining the invitation to "ride" in the suspended chair _____; is accepting in a guarded way, but soon withdraws _____; slow twirling is initially acceptable (10-20 RPM); soon asks to stop _____; verbalizes some feeling of nausea _____. (This rarely occurs; the few children who would be so affected know from previous experience and appropriately decline the invitation.)

2. _____ Happy, eager to be twirled _____; slow twirling elicits no indication of distaste or discomfort _____; asks to be twirled faster and faster† _____; need for the stimulation of fast twirling seems insatiable _____; enjoys wide-arc swinging _____.

3. _____ Total absence of nystagmus (side-to-side eye movements) after twirling _____; trace nystagmus _____; no head-swinging during or after twirling _____; no staggering gait following it _____.

CAUTION: Since the child is a passive participant, use of this equipment should be limited to knowledgeable persons. By contrast, all other equipment is self-regulatory on the part of the child; it is thus unlikely that he would overstimulate his system.

†*The child's demands to "go faster" must be cautiously met during the first or second therapy sessions. The effect of twirling may be cumulative rather than immediate creating a feeling of nausea from too much stimulation. While one would normally not wish to put a child to such discomfort, the occurrence of such a response from the autonomic nervous system can be interpreted as a normal response, often absent among learning-disordered children.*

Level II

1. ___ "Giggle signals" erupt on slow twirling ____; on fast twirling, (60 RPM) ____; eyes tend to close during twirling, even when the child is asked to try to keep them open ____; head sways ____; staggering gait follows twirling sessions ____.

2. ___ Nystagmus elicited by 30-second duration of fast twirling in the clockwise direction ____; counter-clockwise-direction ____; nystagmus limited to minimal amplitude ____.

3. ___ Record of ratio scale between duration of stimulation and response:

	counter-clockwise	clockwise
Ratio of 6:1 nystagmus elicited (5 second nystagmus for 30 second @ 60 RPM).	____	____
Ratio of 3:1 nystagmus elicited (10 second nystagmus for 30 second @ 60 RPM).	____	____
Ratio of 2:1 nystagmus elicited (15 second nystagmus for 30 second @ 60 RPM).	____	____

Level III

1. ___ Ratio of 1:1 (10 second nystagmus for 10 second twirling @ 60 RPM) in clockwise direction ____; counter-clockwise ____.

2. ___ Moderate to maximal amplitude easily elicited ____.

3. ___ Head sways during, and/or after, twirling ____; staggering gait after twirling ____; now experiences the sensation of dizziness which most children normally report after such activities as being spun in swings or on playground or amusement park rides ____; wide amplitude and duration of nystagmus may have crested and begun to decrease with the same amount of twirling as before ____.

Inflatables (P.P. 2.3)

Level I

1. ___ Fearful, withdraws, rejects, avoids any invitation to involve himself with inflatables ___; timidly touches, pushes or engages in minimal contact with them ___; is willing to involve himself, but needs physical assistance to do so ___.

   The above statements do not apply ___; child launches into the experience with a haphazard, disorganized approach ___; hyperactivity and excitability are heightened ___.

   Protective arm extension is not evident ___; unaware of changing center of gravity ___; adult must control the movement of the inflatable to prevent the child from losing his balance ___.

2. ___ Efforts to balance are confined to sitting or lying, with arms or legs in contact with the floor ___; protective arm extension can be elicited with prone rocking ___; "giggle signals" erupt during prone rocking ___; during supine rocking ___; seeks inverted (eg, supine rocking) position repeatedly ___; slow rhythmic rocking is effective in subduing hyperactivity ___; seeks touch-pressure from inflatables ___.

3. ___ Protective arm extension is active ___; controls his sitting balance with feet on the floor ___; straddles inflatables to rock from side to side with feet intermittently off the floor ___; a trunk rotation pattern is emerging ___; arms cross the midline for balance ___; briefly sits Indian style on inflated pillows ___; rolls resistively across the series of inflated rolls (School of Porpoise) ___; enjoys balancing on his knees and falling safely ___; all above adaptive postural patterns are now functional ___.

Level II

1. ___ Needs no invitation, explores varied and random patterns ___; becomes aware of minute shifts in his center of gravity and strives to control same ___; "synchrony of movement" between trunk and extremities becomes evident ___.

2. ___ Recovers balance with speed and skill throughout a wider range ___; maintains balance in the kneeling position ___; kneels on pillows with hands free to maneuver the three foot tube while watching the movement of the rolling bead ___. (This requires a greater degree of

balance control directly from the vestibular system, inasmuch as the eyes would otherwise yield direct information about his verticality.)

3. ____ Maintains a well organized response in the Indian-style sitting position _____; controls balance very well kneeling on all fours _____; balances on knees _____ or prone____to execute well-controlled repetitions of movement forward and backward _____ and side to side _____; balances supine, with feet on the floor _____.

Level III

1. ____ At the outset the child organizes and controls movement so that any balancing requirement can be met safely_____; further exposure has reduced the cognitive element and enhanced a more automatic, integrative performance _____.

2. ____ Spontaneously initiates a 360° turn on his knees, balancing on large pillow _____; can repeat performance in either direction several times without losing balance _____.

3. ____ On the Space Ship in particular — since it permits the most extreme mobility with safety — the child demonstrates a "symphony of movement" which resembles a modern dance routine _____.

Carpeted Barrel‡ (P.P. 2.2)

Inside

Level I

1. ___ Displays total avoidance response _____; touches, looks in, reaches in, but avoids entering barrel _____; brief entry _____; lies down, virtually inactive _____.

2. ___ Movement is random rather than purposeful _____; can rock in a small arc from lying position _____; sitting position _____, kneeling position _____; can initiate purposeful, rocking movement _____; rolls over by accident _____; when head is at the open end during rolling, weak musculature in the neck causes his to rest his head on the floor ___; movement slow, laborious _____; between revolutions, movement is fragmented, halting, disorganized _____; rolls over in a cognitive, rather than well-integrated manner _____; when feet are at the open end, knees and hips remain extended during rolling _____; comes to the sitting position in a primitive manner, with bilateral hip flexion and little trunk rotation _____.

3. ___ "Walks the barrel" on hands and knees without rolling it over _____; makes more than one revolution in succession _____; halts to reposition himself for each repetition _____; exploration not fully self-motivated, needs some interaction with adult to sustain interest and involvement _____.

Level II

1. ___ Shows initiative and self-motivation to explore _____; shrieks of laughter arise or "giggle signals" are evident _____; prefers to roll with head in closed end _____; prefers to roll with head in open end _____; rolling pattern in either direction is readily sustained for three or four revolutions _____.

2. ___ Posture and movement patterns become more organized _____; knees and hips can be maintained in flexion during rolling _____; head is lifted off floor spontaneously during rolling _____; can come to sitting position with better trunk rotation _____.

3. ___ Fragmented, halting pattern between revolutions is decreasing _____; movement is faster and more forceful _____; a driving intensity is observed in rolling to the point that the need seems nearly insatiable _____.

‡*To promote hip flexion and a more advanced motor pattern than that used to roll on the floor without equipment, the bottom end of the barrel must be left intact.*

Level III

1. ____ Upon introduction to this equipment, spontaneously demonstrates an ability to perform the foregoing skills and proceed with a well-organized rolling pattern inside the barrel ____; needs brief exposure to assure suitable reinforcement ____.

2. ____ Smooth, continuous, automatic, well-organized rolling pattern is prevalent ____; fragmentation rarely, if ever, observed ____.

3. ____ The intensity of rolling, if observed at Level II, is now subsiding ____.

Outside*

Level I

1. ____ Moves barrel with his hands ____; avoids making any attempt to get on top of barrel ____; willing to get on with help ____; gets on alone (while barrel is stabilized) ____.

2. ____ Sits upright in rigid "stick-figure" posture ____; when his center of gravity shifts, there is a slight side-to-side movement of head ____; a hint of side-to-side trunk movement ____; no rotation of trunk observed ____; touches feet to floor more of the time than he stays on top ____; lies prone, making little postural adjustment with head ____; with trunk ____.

3. ____ Pattern of side-to-side motion of head and trunk rotation are beginning to emerge ____; arm reaches across midline for balance ____; pattern becomes more definite; can be repeated toward either side ____; can now be maintained for more than a chance interval of balance when center of gravity is shifted ____; can pull his feet up for longer internals (in contrast to the earlier pattern when he continually needed to protect himself from falling)____;

Level II

1. ____ A consistent pattern of head balance, trunk rotation, and the arm's moving past the midline is observed ____; sitting balance can be maintained for several side-to-side repetitions ____.

2. ____ Purposeful exploration of "cowboy" tricks on his "horse" emerges ____; while sitting, spontaneously lifts body weight on hands and arms to shift his balance as the barrel moves left or right ____.

*Caution: to avoid needless falls, and to mitigate the child's fear, the adult stabilizes the barrel during this early stage.

3. ___ From the sitting, straddled position, he spontaneously shifts to a kneeling posture ___ ; in this position, as the barrel begins to roll sideways, he can maintain his balance for brief periods ___ ; can purposely propel the barrel to his left or his right while on his knees ___ ; kneeling crossways of the barrel, he can "walk the barrel," using a well-organized pattern throughout the entire body ___ .

Level III

1. ___ Lying, sitting, or kneeling balance can be recovered over an increasingly wide arc of movement ___ .

2. ___ Increased sensitivity and awareness of minute shifts of balance enable the child to "hone his balancing skill" ___ .

3. ___ Turns a 360° circle repeatedly as he propels the barrel across the room on his knees ___ .

Scooter Board (P.P. 2.4)
Prone

Level I

1. ____ Child avoids any involvement with the scooter board by rejecting it or withdrawing from it ____; he is too poorly organized to get on independently ____; trunk control is so poor, he rolls off easily ____; moves scooter board by means of random, haphazard motor patterns ____; hands are inactive in moving scooter board, grasps it instead ____; prefers to avoid prone position after brief periods (10-15 seconds) ____.

2. ____ Arms function in bilateral arm extension to push self backwards ____; pushes self forward ____; twirling pattern is attempted ____; excessive, unrelated movement of legs and trunk observed during twirling efforts ____; arms are stretched out nearly 180° during twirling ____; in this extended arm position he uses wrist and finger action primarily ____; twirling is attempted through simultaneous contact of hands to the floor as they are positioned in nearly 180° ____; shoulder action during twirling increases ____; hands are now coming closer to the midline of the body ____; hands cross over occasionally when twirling in either direction ____; legs still drag during twirling ____; pivot-prone posture absent in twirling ___; fatigue noted earlier in prone positioning is no longer apparent ___.

3. ____ Shows poor motor organization in positioning his legs in "frog-leg" position for kick-offs ____; head sags, lacks pivot-prone posture after kick-offs ____.

4. ____ A spontaneous twirling pattern is initiated on introduction of scooter board, with traces of above disorganization patterns evident ____.

Level II

1. ____ Skillfully maneuvers obstacle course using arm action ___; in twirling, arms cross midline half the time ____; consistent crossover pattern observed in each direction ____; hands are more forceful in twirling than before ____; hands pound floor heavily ____; trunk and hip stability sufficient to keep their action to a minimum ____; feet no longer drag during twirling ____; pivot-prone posture active ____.

2. ___ "Frog-leg" positioning is automatic for kick-offs ___;
kick-off pattern well organized, both legs function with
equal, simultaneous, forceful thrust ___; pivot-prone
pattern observed ___.

3. ___ Heavy pounding seen earlier is diminishing ___; pivot-
prone pattern consistent with sustained endurance ___.

Sitting, Kneeling

Level I

1. ___ Prefers to avoid scooter board in sitting position ___; unable to get on independently ___; unable to position
feet in cross-leg position alone ___; feet fall off frequently ___; trunk balance can be maintained briefly
while in motion ___; unaware of how to pull on the suspended rope for the "Ferry Boat" ride to propel himself___.

2. ___ Uses one-handed grasp on the rope ___; uses a disorganized two-handed procedure ___; a random, irregular
hand-over-hand pattern is emerging ___.

3. ___ Trunk balance is adequate to make a 10'-12' Ferry Boat trip
without falling ___; attempts simple swing-to- and
swing-through patterns holding on to overhead rope ___;
if he swings through too far, is unable to recover from semi-
suspine position ___.

Level II

1. ___ "Hand-over-hand" pattern on rope is well organized, consistent ___; sufficient goal-directed performance to make
a round trip on "Ferry Boat" without becoming disorganized and losing the goal ___; balance adequate to turn
around, back up and maneuver, rarely falling ___.

2. ___ Motor control in arms and trunk organized enough to swing
through under the rope, turn around and return ___;
usually can recover from near-supine position to a sitting
posture ___.

All Positions

Level III

1. ___ All patterns of head, trunk, and extremities are well organized in moving the scooter board, so that elaborate and complex patterns can be executed ___.

2. ___ Patterns of movement are done in smooth succession, with
rhythm and grace, taking on the aspect of a modern dance
routine ___.

3. ____ Capability for all requirements on scooter board is adequate upon introduction; needs minimal, if any, reinforcement ____ .

Gross Motor Organization (P.P. 3.2-3.5)
Total Body

Level I

1. ___ Avoids the most elemental crawling activities ___ ; body image is so poor that child tends to hit the back of his body or head against surfaces he tries to crawl under ___ ; trips easily ___ ; willing to explore by climbing through, over, into spaces and objects early patterns of movement in structured, "near the floor" activities (eg, horizontally placed ladder; self-assembly Playhouse) ___ ; can originate and explore new variations of "near-the-floor" movement patterns (eg, hula hoops) to structure for himself the repetitions of movement.

Level II

1. ___ Movement and standing balance skill is well enough organized to walk along a marked course on the floor without depending on wild arm movements ___ ; can do this on elevated equipment (balance beam, stepping stones) ___ ; performs activities requiring standing balance on one leg ___ ; can jump rope when it is turned for him ___ ; can organize total body movement well enough to turn rope himself for jumping ___ .

Level III

1. ___ Instability of this suspended, highly unstable equipment requires more motor control and balance than he has, so he avoids it ___ ; engages in it minimally ___ ; explores cautiously ___ ; engages in extended exploration, elaborating on new-found skills ___ .

Refining Sensory System Organization and Integration
Olfactory Awareness and Discrimination
(P.P. 1.3, 1.5, 1.8)

Level I

1. ____ Responds to one or more items from the "Olfactory Zoo" with an overtly defensive response ____ ; collateral data from this sensorimotor history confirms this type of response ____ ; this defensive response is not otherwise confirmed; seems to be a random finding, which is not repeated ____ .

2. ____ Makes no overt response to scent on "Olfactory Zoo," which is fairly intense ____ ; gives a subtle response to suggest he may be aware of some incoming stimuli, but cannot identify them in relation to the object at hand ____ ; gives a fleeting response, briefly directing object toward his nose ____ ; gives a definite, distinct motion to "smell it" ____ ; wets his lips in response to a food scent ____ ; offers it to the parent for them to experience ____ .

3. ____ Verbalizes or demonstrates some association (eg, "May I have some gum?" to peppermint) ____ ; makes a direct statement about the aroma ____ ; makes gross distinction between pleasurable aromas of food and distasteful scents as camphor or medicinal odors ____ ; attempts to identify an appropriate association for each item in "Olfactory Zoo" ____ .

Level II

1. ____ Correctly identifies scented "scratch and sniff" paper matching one picture among three which would have obviously contrasting scents ____ ; correctly identifies food scents which are closely related (eg, lemon and orange) or other objects of more subtle or closely related scents (pine and cedar for older children) ____ .

Level III

1. ____ Correctly matches pairs of unmarked strips of "scratch and sniff" paper to each other in a manner upgraded for age and experience ____ ; identifies scents of eight to ten items ____ .

Tactile Discrimination and Manual Form Perception (P.P. 1.4, 1.7)

Level I

Matching: Gross Contrasts

Two sets of each of the following are prepared. The child feels an object from one set beneath the surface of the desk, or behind a screen, and matches it from among the set of objects which are visible.

1. ___ Matches familiar three-dimensional objects which differ widely in texture and form, eg, pine cone, wad of cotton, ball, jacks, piece of fur, walnut.

2. ___ Matches varying textures of cloth, sandpaper, carpeting, etc, mounted over pieces of wood six inches in length.

3. ___ Matches elementary geometric forms found among early childhood toys, eg, large threading beads, jumbo snap beads, magnetic forms.

Level II

Matching: Minute Contrasts

1. ___ Matches more minute contrasts of 3-D forms in the method described above in Level I: Sets of small plastic animals ___; freight cars ___; circus cars ___; matches any of these with a trial-and-error approach nearly half the time ___; matches all pieces of each set ___; accurately matches forms when freight cars and circus cars are mixed ___.

2. ___ Matches embossed aluminum 2-D form of simple, closed, linear designs, in Set #1A ___; same for Set #1B ___ perceiving the relationship of the lines to the perimeter.

3. ___ Same as above — designs upgraded to include open-end forms, plus tangential and intersecting lines as in Set #2A ___, same for Set #2B ___, perceiving the relationship of intersecting lines.

Level III

Matching: Minute Contrasts

1. ___ Same as above; designs upgraded to include more elements, closer in their similarity, in Set #3A ___; same for Set #3B ___ perceiving relationship of lines having great similarity.

2. ___ Same as above; designs have a closer relationship of one element of the form to another, in Set #4A ___ ; same for Set #4B ___ perceiving lines, elements of which appear in each pattern.

Auditory Localization and
Discrimination (P.P. 1.6, 1.9)

Level I

Localization

1. ____ With head positioned at the closed end inside carpeted barrel, child listens to determine whether a soft clap emanates from one side of the room or the other. Rolls to that side correctly part of the time _____; each time _____.

Direction

1. ____ Sitting in a chair, with eyes closed, the child can localize whether the sound of a bead in a plastic tube is rolling toward him _____; away from him _____; coming from back to front _____; from front to back _____; left to right _____; right to left _____.

Early Auditory Matching

1. ____ Is not able to match one animal sound cylinder with another _____; matches obviously contrasting sounds (cow, cat, bird) _____.

Level II

Discrimination

1. ____ In Set #1, some errors are made _____; matches set #1 without error _____.

2. ____ In Set #2, some errors made _____; matches Set #2 without error _____.

Visual Attention, Fixation,* and Pursuits (P.P. 2.7)

Level I

Visual Attention

1. ___ Child cannot direct his visual attention, is very distractible _____; a moving object which produces some sound will attract his attention briefly _____; he will watch and play with a rolling object or marble on a track _____; visual attention follows changes in direction of moving target___.

Visual Fixation

1. ___ Child will direct visual attention to an object of interest such as liquid, or pebble, infant hourglass which attracts his visual and auditory attention _____; lying supine, can fixate on hourglass or color-shaded pen light held midline 3 feet to 4 feet above him for two to four seconds _____.

2. ___ While supine child can voluntarily maintain visual fixation for two to four seconds in each quadrant, ie, upper left, lower right _____.

3. ___ Child can visually fixate on a still target such as the hourglass in each quadrant up to age formula.†

Pursuits

1. ___ Child, in supine position, tries to follow a moving stimulus (rolling bead in 3 foot tube) from side to side, but loses it at midpoint _____; eyes rush to the end ahead of the tube _____.

2. ___ Can pursue target side to side with only minor disorganization and disruption at midline.

3. ___ Can pursue target between various positions around the clock face.

Level II

Fixation

1. ___ In a sitting position, against a nondistracting background (eg, blank wall) can fixate on color-shaded penlight held 4 feet away, for half the child's age formula _____; up to age formula _____.

Pursuits

1. ___ In sitting position, facing nondistracting background, can

*Fixation is used here to mean to concentrate focus of eyes or attention.
† Age formula means one successful repetition for each year of the child's age.

follow bead in tube part of the time, but often becomes disorganized in this pattern at the midline or beyond it _____; follows bead more often without losing it (repetitions equal half the child's age formula) _____; functions up to age formula _____.

Level III

Pursuits

1. ____ Performance in following the bead in the tube is upgraded so that the child functions before an actively moving, highly distractible background (eg, people moving in the room, seated before the television screen, etc) up to age formula _____.

Visual Form Perception (P.P. 5.1, 5.2, 5.6)

P.P. 5.1, 5.2

Level I

1. _____ Requires maximum structure (box with transparent lid) to sort two or three colors of poker chips or colored discs_____; needs moderate structure (cupcake tin) to sort four or more colors _____ ; matches single color disc or block to proper spot on master card picturing six or more colored spaces. _____ . (#N-100 Color Disc Counters, #N5-2 Everyday Object Counters, #286-1 Real Things Counters by Philip and Tacey, from Constructive Playthings.)

2. _____ (a) Inserts single 2-D cardboard puzzle pieces of whole objects (Playskool Fit and Find Series, Animals #3101, Things That Go #3102, Playthings #3103, Things in My House #3104) _____ .

   (b) Inserts simple, solid 3-D forms into firm contours (Playskool Playchips #120; Simplex Posting Box #201; Wooden Form Boards #N33, Galt; #790 Playskool; #327 Simplex) _____ .

   (c) Inserts multiple object forms into a firm contour (Simplex #310 Cars & Trucks; #309 Dogs; Europlastic Primary Puzzle #407 and Educational Zoo #213; Simplex Playboards #180, #190 and others with knobs attached)___.

   (d) Inserts geometric forms of subtle contrasts into soft pliable contours (Fit-A-Space forms by Lauri) _____ .

3. _____ (a) Visually matches pictures of simple, whole objects to single master card of six to nine objects (Picture Lotto #255, Platt & Munk; Object Lotto #127, Ed-u-Cards; Bilderlotto #15.002, O. Maier; Zoo Lotto #101, Ed-u-Cards) _____ .
   Matches pictures correctly when two-four-six master cards are in view _____ .

   (b) Matches picture to picture when one is rotated 90°, as in dominoes (Simple Picture Dominoes #111, Ed-u-Cards, #102 Ed-u-Cards; #3510, Shackman) _____ .

   (c) Matches visual form having more subtle likenesses and differences (Learning Lotto, Colors & Shapes #T880, O. Maier; Garden Lotto #15.018, O. Maier; Matching Pictures #2 Ben-G; Learning Lotto-Shapes #E667, Creative Playthings; Noel Picture & Shape Sorting Cards Box A & B, Philip & Tacey or Sorting and Sets 81-160, NYT Teaching Resources, same but small) _____ .

4. _____ (a) Matching halves of pictured objects top to bottom (Kiddie Cards or Ed-u-Cards; Children of the World, Mini-Puzzles J-1600, Creative Playthings) _____ .

(b) Matches halves left and right (Playskool Matchups: Colors and Things #7107, Animal Homes #7105, People and Their Jobs #7106; Object Dominoes, Abbatt); Animals J-1600 and Houses J-1600. _____ .

(c) Matches halves in a more complex arrangement (Animal Puzzle Dominoes #Q7, Abbatt) _____ .

(d) Combines multiple sections in a whole-part relationship (Ed-u-Cards, What's Missing Lotto #120, Easy 3's Card Game) _____ .

5. ___ Matches visual form by association or by elementary abstract concepts (Missing Faces #1, Ben-G; Word-meaning Puzzle #3, Ben-G; Go Together Lotto #121, Ed-u-Cards; Animal-Bird-Fish Card Game; Frame Tray-Opposites #4416, Western; Flannel Board Opposites #7824, Milton Bradley) _____ .

(P.P. 5.6)

Level II

1. ___ Has developed adequate organization of visual information to select whole form from a visual figure-ground pattern. Can match single cards to one master card _____ ; two, four _____ . (Find-It #L-551, Galt; Lotto #15.008, Maier; following Playskool Series — very suitable, not currently on the market: How We Travel #96905, How We Live #96903, What's In A Store #96904, Life On The Farm #96902).

2. ___ (a) Maintains adequate whole-part relationships of objects with (Plastic Transportation Puzzle E19, Europlastic; Car Capers #1189, Spears) _____ .

(b) Recognizes whole-part relationships of geometric forms and spaces, eg, two triangles form a square or diamond. (Small Parquetry Designs I P-116, DLM. This series of designs is continued in Level II, Spatial Relations) _____ .

3. ___ Maintains whole-part relationships of visual form upgraded to stress subtle differences of both form and position and to include a left-right component (Reading Fun #2, Ben-G; Picture Readiness, Dolch; Simplex Inset Boards, Houses #306 or Chickens #326; Two Dimensional Plastic Form Puzzle #E-376, Europlastic; Noel Picture and Shape Sorting Boxes C, D, E, Philip & Tacey; Same and Different Design Cards P212, I, II, DLM; Perception Plaques — Faces, Creative Playthings; Matching Cards 81-170, NYT Teaching Resources; Look Alikes 811-150, NYT Teaching Resources) _____ .

Level III

1. ___ Maintains adequate organization to select whole form from

a visual figure-ground with variable depth perceptions and subtle color tones. (Traffic Lotto #6891, Carlit; Animal Lotto #6556, Carlit) _____ .

2. _____ Functions adequately to recognize visual form upgraded to stress subtle differences and multiple left-right factors. (Simplex Inset Boards: Flowers #325, Ships #311, Windmill #307; Galt, Find-A-Pair Matching Cards #104; Same or Different Design Cards P212, Series III, IV, DLM; Learning Lotto Same and Different #670, Creative Playthings; Learning Lotto Small Differences E671, Creative Playthings.) _____ .

3. _____ Form and word recognition adequate to be successful in identifying differences in Continental Press, Seeing Likenesses and Differences, Level 2.

Visual Figure-Ground (P.P. 5.5, 5.8)

Level I

1. ___ Traces with finger, or pencil, the course of lines from one point to the other on Frostig Figure-ground Sheets #1-#4 ___ .

2. ___ Traces with pencil the course of the lines from one point to the other on Frostig Figure-ground Sheets #5-#15 ___ .

3. ___ The child can locate either end of a strand of beads of the 3-D visual figure-ground task found in a clustered four-strand set ___ .

Level II

1. ___ The Visual Figure-ground exercises one through six by K-Dee are designed to strengthen this skill; the child can maintain sufficient organization to visually pursue the course of lines from end to end as they overlap and intersect without being diverted or distracted to another line ___ .

Level III

1. ___ Dvorine Plates, used to identify color blindness, provide figure-groud experience in tracing subtle colored trails embedded in a similar background. Presents no problem ___ .

Spatial Relations (P.P. 5.3, 5.7)

Level I

1. ___ Using a maximum structure of a transparent ½″ plastic grid, insert pegs (blocks) into grid with overlay method, using graded designs: 1 ___ horizontal and vertical sequence; 2 ___ chair; 3 ___ school bus. (If grid 10 x 13 blocks is not available, adapt larger Mosaic Frame and Pegs, #82-165, NYT Teaching Resources Co.)

2. ___ Same as above, with pattern ahead of grid, to upgrade spatial relations and develop early visual memory, preparatory to copying from chalk board, a transition method.

3. ___ Parquetry Blocks #306 Playskool. Successful using overlay method ___ ; transition method ___ .
    (Supplemental or alternative: Peg Board M128 and Peg Board Designs P150, DLM and Magnetic Form Board #402, Playskool, Colored 1″ Cube Designs #111, DLM).

Level II

1. ___ Using ½ inch plastic grid & blocks above, following designs in half-scale, are upgraded for difficulty; 1 ___ house; 2 ___ locomotive; 3 ___ windmill; 4 ___ funny face; 5 ___ dinosaur; 6 ___ kitten; 7 ___ gingerbreadman; 8 ___ .

2. ___ Small Parquetry Designs I, P-116, DLM and wooden chips W-115.

3. ___ Small Parquetry Designs II, #179, DLM.

(P.P. 5.7)

Level III

1. ___ Using ½ inch plastic grid and blocks, full scale designs here are coded for form and color to require a higher level of integration involving decoding, visual memory, and spatial relations: 1 ___ locomotive; 2 ___ house; 3 ___ flowers.

2. ___ Colored 1 inch cube Designs in Perspective #112, DLM or Plain 1 inch cube Designs in Perspective #118, DLM (used with colored cubes #111 and plain cubes #117, DLM).

3. ___ Small Parquetry Designs III, P180, DLM, outline of design only, requires abstract conceptualization of whole-part relationships of geometric forms.

Graded Integration of Spatial Relations and Visual Figure-Ground (P.P. 5.4, 5.9)

Level I

1. ___ Level of function requires use of single unit puzzles ___ . Level of function in spatial relations is pre-elementary; can be successful using puzzles (5-7 pieces) ___ ; elementary (8-13 pieces) ___ .

2. ___ Level of function in visual figure-ground is pre-elementary ___ ; elementary ___ .

     ___ *   ___ *
     ___   ___
     ___   ___
     ___   ___
     ___   ___

Level II

1. ___ Level of function in spatial relations is intermediate (14-35 pieces) ___ .

2. ___ Level of function in figure-ground is intermediate ___ .

     ___ *   ___ *
     ___   ___
     ___   ___
     ___   ___
     ___   ___
     ___   ___

Level III

1. ___ Level of function in spatial relations is senior (36-48 pieces) ___ .

2. ___ Level of function in figure-ground is senior ___ ; advanced

     ___ *
     ___   ___ *
     ___   ___
     ___   ___
     ___   ___
     ___   ___

*Open spacing allows the therapist to list, in their order of difficulty, titles of puzzles available for use in the program.

Sequential Organization
Sequencing by Size (P.P. 4.1)

Level I

Open-end Sequencing

1. ____ Uses random placement; by chance nests three or four units of a simple form (round or square) ____; force is used as a solution ____; tries to put a larger one into a smaller one ____; sequences five or six units with less trial and error and more purpose ____; self-correcting responses emerge ____; good organization in sequencing ten to twelve units ____.

____ 1	____ 5
____ 2	____ 6
____ 3	____ 7
____ 4	____ 8

Supplemental size sequencing   ____ 1
with maximum visual-tactile   ____ 2
feedback: (flat wooden pieces of   ____ 3
graded size, eg, apples, by Simplex)

Closed-end Sequencing

1. ____ Among six unit closed-end sequencing tasks, early trial and error efforts are unsuccessful ____; primitive methods used for open-end tasks are applied here (eg, bottoms are nested first, then tops added) ____; problem-solving methods emerge from trial and error to enclose each whole unit in the proper sequence ____; nests more advanced units (eg, inverted bowls or drums) with only marginal success using the primitive pattern above ____; more mature pattern emerges to pronate and supinate forearms in nesting this set ____; mature pattern of action such as this consistently maintained ____.

____ 1	____ 4
____ 2	____ 5
____ 3	____ 6

Stacking

1. ____ Stacks any of the sets below which have a tapered core, thus offering maximum feedback ____; same, with center post and feedback from graded sized discs ____; stacks with minimal trial and error any item of six units or more without a core ____; can stack any number of units above

shoulder and eye level and maintain adequate motor control and sequential organization _____ .

_____1   (tapered core)
_____2   (tapered core)
_____3   (center post)
_____4   (no core or post)
_____5   ”   ”   ”   ”
_____6   ”   ”   ”   ”
_____7   ”   ”   ”   ”
_____8   ”   ”   ”   ”

Level II

None

Level III

None

Tactile Sequence and Assembly (P.P. 4.2)

Level I

1. ____ Child's tactile system (together with visual system) is too disorganized to grasp the concept that smooth junctures convey the correct sequence and that "bumps" mean they are incorrect ____; tactile system yields sufficient feedback to recognize errors and be self-correcting ____; units below are ¾ inch thick, so present obvious contrasts; child can organize these with minimal trial and error ____.

   ____1   ____4
   ____3   ____5
   ____3   ____6

Level II

1. ____ These items, which contain from nine to sixteen units each, are only ⅜ inch thick, thus offering less obvious tactile feedback. Tactile system organization is adequate to sequence three or more of this group with only minimal trial and error ____.

   ____1   ____6
   ____2   ____7
   ____3   ____8
   ____4   ____9
   ____5   ____10

Level III

None

Problem-Solving Sequence and
Assembly (P.P. 4.3)

Level I

None

Level II

1. ___ Disassembles object _____; efforts to reassemble object result in a random, purposeless, disorganized response to single (6-piece) unit _____; disorganization apparent in trial and error approach, but interest is evident _____; increased organization, less trial and error in 6-piece units _____ .

2. ___ Disassembles and reassembles any 6-piece unit with interest, intent, and success _____; same, in units of more pieces _____; successfully explores more than one way of reassembling pieces which are interchangeable (Fun Flowers, Engine, Magic Box).

    _____ 1   _____ 4
    _____ 2   _____ 5
    _____ 3   _____ 6

Level III

1. ___ Items below are reassembled with much trial and error _____; errors are recognized and self-corrected where total problem is visible in a small area, ie, on table _____; same, in assembly of a large item where only parts of problem are visible at one time _____; shows a well-organized problem-solving approach throughout _____ .

    _____ 1   _____ 3
    _____ 2   _____ 4

Time and Temporal Sequencing (P.P. 4.4, 7.5)

Level I

Application of Positional Model to Telling Time

1. ___ Recognizes on Panel #4 (the color-coded clock face) the side which indicates the minutes before and after the hour ___; the child has learned to tell time ___.

Level II

Temporal Sequencing

1. ___ Recognizes the natural sequence of events in his day ___; can apply this in organizing sequential Picture Cards depicting daily events ___; same for longer time segments, such as night and day cycles, seasons, plant growth, etc ___.
2. ___ Names the days in the week ___; names which day follows another ___; which day comes before another ___.
3. ___ Names the months of the year ___; which month comes after ___.

Level III

Temporal Sequencing

1. ___ Arranges important historical events, which are in keeping with the the child's grade level, in their proper temporal sequence (eg, discovery of America, birth of Lincoln, invention of the airplane) ___.

Auditory - Verbal Sequence (P.P. 4.6)

Level I

None

Level II

None

Level III

Auditory Sequence

1. ____ Words: Repeats the sequential order of three simple, familiar objects ____; repeats in proper sequence four or five objects of two and three syllables ____ when age appropriate, sequences five to seven multi-syllable words, some of which sound similar ____.

2. ____ Numbers: Repeats the sequence of three numbers ____; four or five numbers ____; six or seven numbers ____; can repeat numbers in reverse order ____.

3. ____ Letters: Repeats the sequence of three letters to spell a familiar word ____; can do the same for four or five-letter words ____; spells at the class level in school ____.

Visual Sequence (P.P. 4.5, 4.9)

Level I

1. ____ Within a structure (plastic grid or the equivalent) the child can overlay color blocks to match the pattern below ____; demonstrates a left-right progression in doing this ____; when a set of four one-inch color cubes is placed in a left-right sequence and exposed for five seconds before being shuffled, the child can reassemble them in the correct sequence ____; he can do this for five blocks ____; for six blocks ____.

2. ____ In the same manner, can sequence correctly a series of three small uniform pictures of familiar objects ____; can do the same for four or five blocks ____; for six blocks ____.

Level II

1. ____ Child can sequence correctly wooden letter blocks to spell a three-letter word ____; four or five-letter work ____; six-letter word ____.

2. ____ Can correctly identify graded set of minute differences in Same or Different Design Cards, #P212, by DLM.

Level III

1. ____ With minimal error can identify from Same or Different Word Cards, P211 by DLM: five cards ____; fifteen cards ____; twenty cards ____.

2. ____ Can idenfity the letters of the same sequential order in Continental Press Series, Seeing Likenesses and Differences, Level 3 ____.

3. ____ Can analyze their pages for their differences and formulate a statement which conveys this concept. (See text, P.P. 4.9).

Dot-To-Dot Alphabetical Sequencing (P.P. 4.7)

Level I

1. ____ In early alphabetical dot-to-dot drawings listed in #3 below, the child is unable to maintain the proper sequence of letters ____ ; has partial success, when the circular pattern of the drawing suggests the sequence ____ ; points out sequence adequately while the adult draws the connecting lines ____ ; when the adult provides the verbal structure by saying "after ____ comes ____ " the child can furnish the letters in their proper sequence ____ .

2. ____ The child can follow the dot-to-dot pattern but does so in such a rapid, disorganized manner that there is little integration of the visual, the verbal, and motor processes involved ____ .

3. ____ The child can function in a sufficiently organized manner to successfully connect the dots in alphabetical sequence, saying "after ____ comes ____ " with some assistance.

   ____ 1 Ice cream cone (A-J)   ____ 4 Bicycle (A-Z)
   ____ 2 Stop sign (A-J)   ____ 5 Telephone "
   ____ 3 Clock (A-Z)   ____ 6 Face   "

Level II

1. ____ Rushed, erratic responses are coming under better control, along with the verbal structuring of performance (by saying "after ____ comes ____ ") ____ ; child can initiate this voluntarily at least half the time ____ .

2. ____ The child is well organized in his performance ____ ; integration of the visual, verbal, and motor response is evident ____ ; spontaneously verbalizes "after ____ comes ____ " ____ .

3. ____ The child can successfully complete the drawings in which there is irregular placement of the letters of the alphabet to challenge the skill level.

   ____ 7 Typewriter (A-Z)   ____ 8 Ship (a-z)

Level III

1. ____ Some hesitation exhibited over sequence or constancy of letter forms between small and capital alphabets ____ ; errors are self-corrected ____ ; absence of any confusion over small and capital letters even though they are purposely placed in proximity to distractors ____ .

   ____ 9 Football player   ____ 10 Lunar module
        (A-Z and a-z)   (A-Z and a-z)

Visual Tracking (P.P. 5.5, 4.8)

Level I

Three gradations of difficulty are to be found in each of these seven exercise pages:

Exercise 1 ____ O C G Q S U
         2 ____ B D E F H I J K L P R T
         3 ____ A K M N V W X Y Z

Exercise 4 ____ a c e o s
         5 ____ i j l t
         6 ____ b d f g h k p q y
         7 ____ m n r u v w x z

1. ____ Within the first gradation at the top of each exercise sheet, the child can identify each repetition of a letter arranged in a random order except for these problem letters among the capitals ____; lower case letters ____; he identifies correctly letters in the first gradation on exercise sheets circled: 1 2 3 4 5 6 7.

2. ____ Within the second gradation in the center of each exercise sheet, the child experiences occasional omissions or error among these capitals ____; lower case letters ____; child performs within this gradation with few if any errors, often self-corrected or initially successful with exercise sheets circled: 1 2 3 4 5 6 7.

3. ____ Within the third gradation at the bottom of each exercise sheet, the child experiences occasional omissions or error among these capitals ____; lower case letters ____; child performs within this gradation with few if any errors, often self-corrected or initially successful with exercise sheets circled: 1 2 3 4 5 6 7.

Level II

1. ____ In elementary visual tracking the child can maintain the sequential organization of letters of the alphabet when these stimulus letters are placed at short, fairly rhythmic intervals, as in Exercises 8 and 9 ____.

2. ____ In Ann Arbor Tracking Programs, Letter Tracking, Section I, performance is within acceptable limits, but reveals some hesitation, omissions, or errors ____; individual is confident enough to be timed ____.

     timing for most paragraphs in Section I is between 1½ to 2 minutes ____;
     timing for most paragraphs in Section I is between 1 to 1½ minutes ____;

timing for most paragraphs in Section I is under 1
minute _____ ;
timing for most paragraphs in Section II is between 1½ to 2
minutes _____ .

Level III

1. _____ Timing for most paragraphs in Section I around 30 seconds.

2. _____ Timing for most paragraphs in Section II around 45
seconds.

3. _____ Timing for most paragraphs in Section III around 60
seconds.

Individuals in high school or beyond may strive to improve
their scores and to progress to Sections IV and V.

Development of Fine Motor Control

Early Bimanual Motor Integration (P.P. 6.1, 8.2)

Level I

1. ____ Actively engages in forceful pushing together and pulling apart of toys or activities which are the most age-appropriate.

Level II

1. ____ *Large Bimanual circles:* "Piggy-back" method required initially _____; sufficient carry-over effect to proceed independently _____; proceeds down and out with relatively well-controlled speed, rhythm, size, and contour _____; same for up and out progression _____.

Level III

1. ____ *Locomotive technique:* With each hand positioned at a point equivalent to nine o'clock, the child moves his hands (counterclockwise) down and out together. For three or more revolutions the child can maintain a smooth pattern with the hands in corresponding positions around the circle _____.

Dominance Exploration, Selection, and Confirmation (P.P. 6.3, 6.5)

Timed Hammering Sample

Hand selected first:

_____ / H- _____	_____ / H- _____	_____ / H- _____
Initially	*Initially*	*Re-Check*

Level I

1. _____ Hand dominance is not yet established when the following indications are present:

	H- _____	H- _____
Number of strikes with one hand is nearly equal the other (2/3 or more)	_____	_____
Density of carbon impression nearly equal for both hands	_____	_____
Density of impression, or control, or other features such as clustering is better on the hand not used for pencil tasks	_____	_____
Dispersal of strikes is more prevalent than "clustering" of impressions in each hand	_____	_____
Tension in the face, and protrusion or movement of the tongue is evident during this procedure	_____	_____

Level II

1. _____ Hand dominance is emerging as evidenced by a contrast in the motor control between the two sides:

	Date _____ H-		Date _____ H-	
	Left	Right	Left	Right
Number of strikes is greater in:	_____	_____	_____	_____
Fewer skid marks appear in:	_____	_____	_____	_____
Greater density of carbon appears in:	_____	_____	_____	_____
Greater "clustering" is evident in:	_____	_____	_____	_____

	H-		H-	
Tension in the face, and protrusion or movement of the tongue is less, or absent, when using:	___	___	___	___
Attempts to transfer hammer to:	___	___	___	___
Indicates or verbalizes preference for:	___	___	___	___

Level III

1. ___ Hand dominance has been established if:

	Date ___ H-		Date ___ H-	
	Left	Right	Left	Right
A greater number of strikes exceeds the lesser number by 50%, the greater number being in:	___	___	___	___
Hand and arm control is definitely better in:	___	___	___	___
Clarity, density and extent of clustering are distinctly better in:	___	___	___	___
Facial tension less or absent when using:	___	___	___	___
Attempts to transfer hammer to:	___	___	___	___
Indicates or verbalizes preference to:	___	___	___	___

Timed Crayoning Sample

Hand selected first:

___ / H- ___	___ / H- ___	___ / H- ___
Initially	Re-check	Re-check

Level I

1. ___ Hand dominance is not yet established if the following indications are present:

	H- ___	H- ___
Grasp of crayon about equal in each hand:	___	___
Motor control to direct crayon about equal:	___	___

321

Density of productions is relatively equal: _____ _____

Tension in the face, protrusion or movement of the tongue is evident during this procedure: _____ _____

Level II

1. _____ Hand dominance is emerging as evidenced by contrast between the two sides:

	Date _____ H-		Date _____ H-	
	Left	Right	Left	Right
Visual attention better with:	_____	_____	_____	_____
Grasp of crayon is better in:	_____	_____	_____	_____
Motor control to direct crayon is better in:	_____	_____	_____	_____
Less effort to perform with:	_____	_____	_____	_____
Density is definitely greater in:	_____	_____	_____	_____
Evidence of smooth, parallel lines is greater in:	_____	_____	_____	_____
Transfer attempts toward:	_____	_____	_____	_____
Verbalizes preference for:	_____	_____	_____	_____
Facial tension, etc, less when using:	_____	_____	_____	_____

Level III

1. _____ Hand dominance has become established when:

	Left	Right	Left	Right
Better motor control is obvious in:	_____	_____	_____	_____
Transfer attempts toward:	_____	_____	_____	_____
Verbalizes strong preference for:	_____	_____	_____	_____
Facial tension, etc, less when using:	_____	_____	_____	_____

Gross Motor Organization — Upper Extremities (P.P. 7.2, 7.3, 7.5, 7.6)

Positional Model and Its Application

Level I

1. ____ Left-Right Sensory Identification:
   Confusion over left and right hands is evident during this procedure _____; right hand can be associated with heavy, blue weight with some consistency _____; left hand can be associated with red crayon _____; left-right confusion not apparent here _____ .

2. ____ Positional Model: (red crayon — left hand; blue — right hand)
   Holding the proper color crayon in each hand, at bottom of Panel #1, can follow these instructions without confusion _____; "one, two, go up to the top...three, four, come down to the bottom."
   (Child asked to place both hands at the centerpoint before executing the following) "One — two, move your hands apart...three, four, bring your hands together"; timing and movements are erratic, haphazard _____; timing and movements are rhythmic, smooth, well controlled _____ .

Level II

Application to Direction and Reversible Letters

1. ____ Identifies these positions on the Positional Model

top _____	upper _____	b from d _____
bottom _____	lower _____	p from q _____
left _____	upper left-hand	
right _____	corner _____	
no residual confusion apparent on these _____ .	lower right-hand corner _____	

Level III

Application to Geographical Orientation

1. ____ Identifies these positions in relation to the Positional Model

North _____	East _____	Northeast _____
South _____	West _____	Southwest _____

2. ____ Using black and white grid, Appendix J-9, Items #1-4, can be performed with minimal error _____ .

3. ____ Using black and white grid, Appendix J-9, Items #5

(Weathervane) and #6 (Windmill) can be performed satisfactorily with only minor, self-corrected errors _____ .

Application to Body Image (P.P. 7.4)

1. ____ Recognizes and locates obvious joints on himself _____ ; correctly identifies those joints which are on his left _____ ; on his right _____ ; using back view of Body Image Drawing (enlarged version or page size) the child correctly identifies the joints by left and right _____ ; on the ten-item Body Image Test (back view) confusion over left and right is apparent _____ ; confusion not apparent on Body Image Test (front view) _____ .

Level II

1. ____ Body Image and directionality concepts adequate to imitate varied positions of legs and arms (demonstrated with Looney Links, G. I. Joe, etc.) when both face the same direction _____ .

Level III

1. ____ On the ten-item Body Image Test front view demonstrates residual left-right confusion _____ ; responds with less confusion throughout the procedure, which uses the blue weight (right hand) together with the body image drawing, (front view) _____ ; no evidence of confusion in Body Image Test (front view) _____ .

Templates* — Vertically Positioned (P.P. 8.3)†

Level I

1. ____ Responds to request to position himself directly in front of the "+" sign before starting to move the marking tool** _____ ; standing balance often shifts to the leg opposite the dominant hand _____ ; as the right hand comes nearer to the vertical midline of the body, the head tends to move to

*See text for scoring guide.
†See Program Plan 8 in text for a description of the way young children may use templates at desk level. This is done simply to create an initial awareness of changes in direction long before the children are ready to work for these and other goals in the vertical position.
**Jumbo crayons are recommended for use by young children because they do not break under the pressure which is desired to train control in the shoulder muscles; china markers, also known as "grease pencils" are preferred when breakage is no longer a problem because the point yields a more precise line along the edge.

the left or the whole body shifts laterally _____ ; same in reverse for left-handed child _____ .

2. ____ Grasp of marking tool is primitive, awkward _____ ; grasp is adequate, mature _____ ; pressure is faint _____ ; pressure is excessive, and erratic _____ ; poor shoulder control causes marking tool to jump over the edge of the template frequently _____ ; poor motor control in arm and shoulder makes irregular lines within the template _____ .

3. ____ Scores less than full count (5) on circle _____ ;
Scores full count more than once on circle _____ ;
Scores at least half score on square (out of 10) _____ .
Scores at least half score on triangle (out of 10) _____ .

Level II

1. ____ Voluntarily positions himself directly in front of the "+" sign; needs no reminders _____ ; stands more frequently with weight balanced on both feet, but some shifting with hand movement is still apparent _____ ; head control at the midline is more stable during arm movement _____ .

2. ____ Exerts and controls pressure of marking tool adequately _____ ; movement is evenly controlled against edge of template _____ ; rarely bumps the edge or makes irregular marks within the space of the template _____ .

3. ____ Scores full count (5) on circle _____ ;
Scores between 7 and 9 on square _____ ;
Scores between 7 and 9 on triangle _____ ;
Scores half count or better (out of 10) on vertical diamond _____ ;
Scores half count or better (out of 10) on horizontal diamond _____ .

Level III

1. ____ Automatically stands with body weight distributed on both feet _____ ; automatically maintains head at the midline without being tense or exerting effort to do so _____ .

2. ____ Motor control of shoulder, arm, and hand is very good ____ ; traces templates up to "age formula" without irregular marks within _____ .

3. ____ Scores full count (5) on circle _____ ;
Scores full count (10) on square _____ ;
Scores full count (10) on triangle _____ ;
Scores between 7 and 9 on vertical diamond _____ ;
Scores between 7 and 9 on horizontal diamond _____ .

Kinesthetic Tag & Baseball (P.P. 8.4)

Level I

None

Level II — Tag (horizontal and vertical):

1. ____ In first few attempts, response lies outside the three inch target _____;
scores within a three inch circle repeatedly _____;
scores within a two inch circle repeatedly _____;
scores within a one inch circle repeatedly _____.

Level III — Baseball (oblique):

1. ____ Scores within a three inch circle repeatedly _____;
scores within a two inch circle repeatedly _____;
scores within a one inch circle repeatedly _____.

Large Figure-Eights (P.P. 8.5)

Level I

None

Level II

1. ____ In the large vertical figure-eight, child does not cross the midline at centerpoint; an "hourglass" pattern prevails _____; shows hesitation, disorganization, and confusion as he approaches the centerpoint _____; crossing the midline is by chance, not purposely repeated _____; hesitation and disorganization at centerpoint are less apparent than indicated above _____.

2. ____ Crosses vertical midline less than half the time _____;
crosses vertical midline more than half the time _____;
crosses vertical midline almost every time _____.

3. ____ Fails to cross midline during the horizontal figure-eight pattern _____; hesitation and disorganization at centerpoint are apparent _____; crosses by chance; does not repeat it _____; crosses about half the time _____; crosses almost every time _____; hesitation and disorganization are seldom apparent vertically _____; or horizontally _____.

Level III

1. ____ Control of speed and direction adequate to introduce the basic cloverleaf _____ .

2. ____ Makes two complete cloverleaf patterns without missing one crossover _____ .

3. ____ Maintains smooth, well-controlled directional and crossover requirements for random patterns _____ .

Fine Bimanual Motor Integration‡ (P.P. 8.6)

Level I

1. ____ Bilateral shoulder control sufficient to control rolling bead in three foot plastic tube, to stop at specified point _____.

2. ____ Bimanual motor integration is sufficient to: string beads _____; use sewing cards _____; use Lego blocks, Build-O-Fun or equivalent _____.

3. ____ Shoulder control in dominant arm refined by: Magnetic Fish Pond _____; Blockhead _____.

Level II

1. ____ Fine bimanual motor integration adequate to use hand operated and/or power toy sewing machine _____; spirograph _____; erector sets _____.

Level III

1. ____ Fine bimanual motor integration and control adequate to use games involving control of rolling marble or ball such as any of the following: Labyrinth, Roll-A-Score, Tippecanoe, or Skill-Roll-Ball.

Directional Orientation to Number and Letter Forms (P.P. 8.8)

Level I — Numbers:

1. ____ On 12″ x 24″ paper, with lines two inches apart, child's efforts to control writing tool fail to render more than a chance number or letter from memory _____; without any visual clues to copy, can make a recognizable representation of numbers 1-10 _____; some numbers drawn from bottom to top _____; top-bottom reversals are evident _____; left-right reversals are evident _____.

2. ____ None of the above features of the child's numbers are currently present when asked to make numbers 1-10 from memory _____; confusion over double numbers, (ie, 14 is made "41") _____; confusion about spacing between double numbers _____; size constancy is poor _____.

3. ____ Order reversal of teens and other double numbers is no longer apparent ____; spacing problems have been resolved _____; size constancy fair to good _____.

‡Many of these activities are most suitable for supplemental home programming.

P.P. 8.8, 8.9

Level II — Printed Letters:

1. ____ Prints a recognizable representation of letters in his name from memory ____; prints letters A-E from memory ____; prints alphabet from memory with obvious problems, but with sequential order reasonably correct and complete ____.

2. ____ Top-bottom reversals are evident ____; size constancy is poor ____; spacing between letters is erratic ____; letters do not touch the line consistently ____; problems cited above are not currently apparent ____.

3. ____ There is inconsistency between capitals and lower case letters ____; there is inconsistency between use of the printed form and script ____. Problems cited here are no longer apparent ____; maintains adequate sequential organization of motor patterns to draw a five-pointed star, a prerequisite indicative of ability to sequence script motor patterns ____.

Level III — Script:

1. ____ Copes reasonably well with motor patterns of the letters of the script alphabet.

2. ____ Has a fairly fluid, automatic use of "connectors," as practiced in suggested list or substitutes for these practice words ____.

3. ____ After several weeks of practice, in comparison with the child's original specimen, a five-minute timed performance of script writing copied from a text shows:

   (no) (some) (marked) improvement in readability
   (no) (some) (marked) improvement in speed
   (no) (some) (marked) improvement in ease of
                           performance
                      other ____

Summary Record Sheets

Summary Record Sheet
Phase I
Gross Sensorimotor Organization

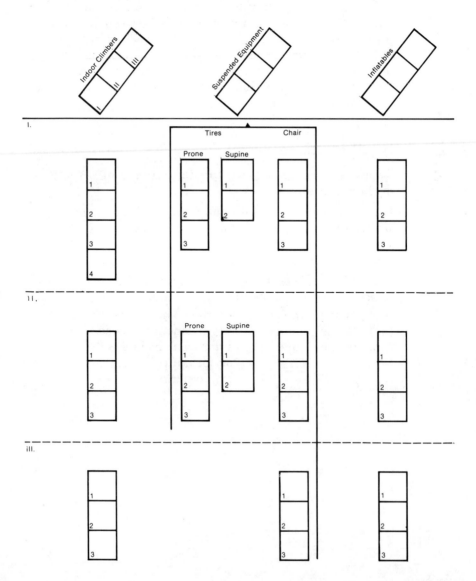

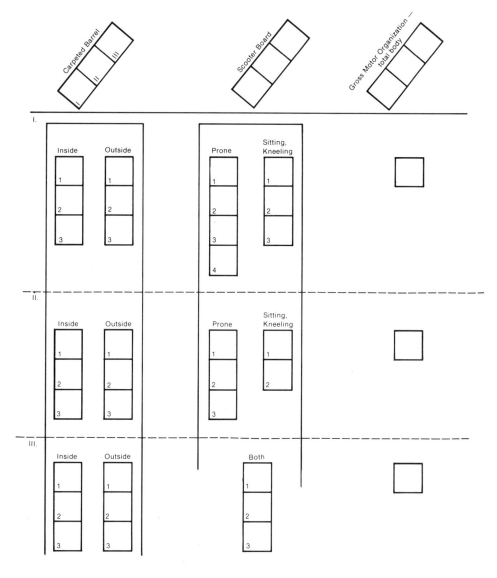

Summary Record Sheet
Phase II, Section A
Sensory System Organization
and Integration

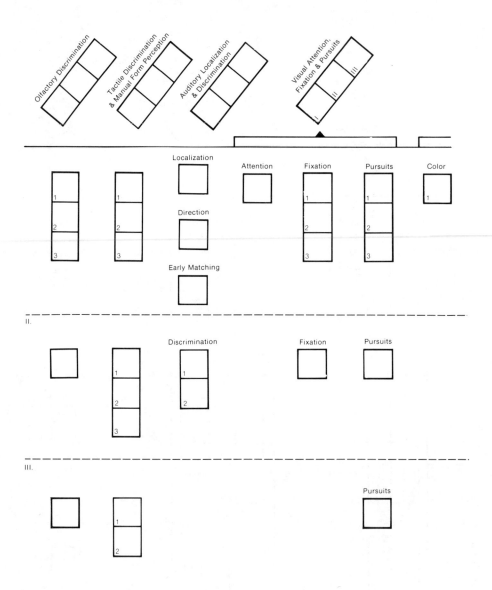

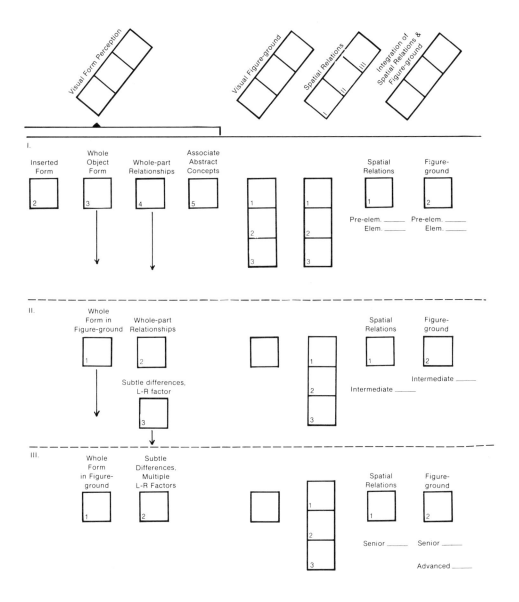

Summary Record Sheet
Phase II, Section B
Sequential Organization

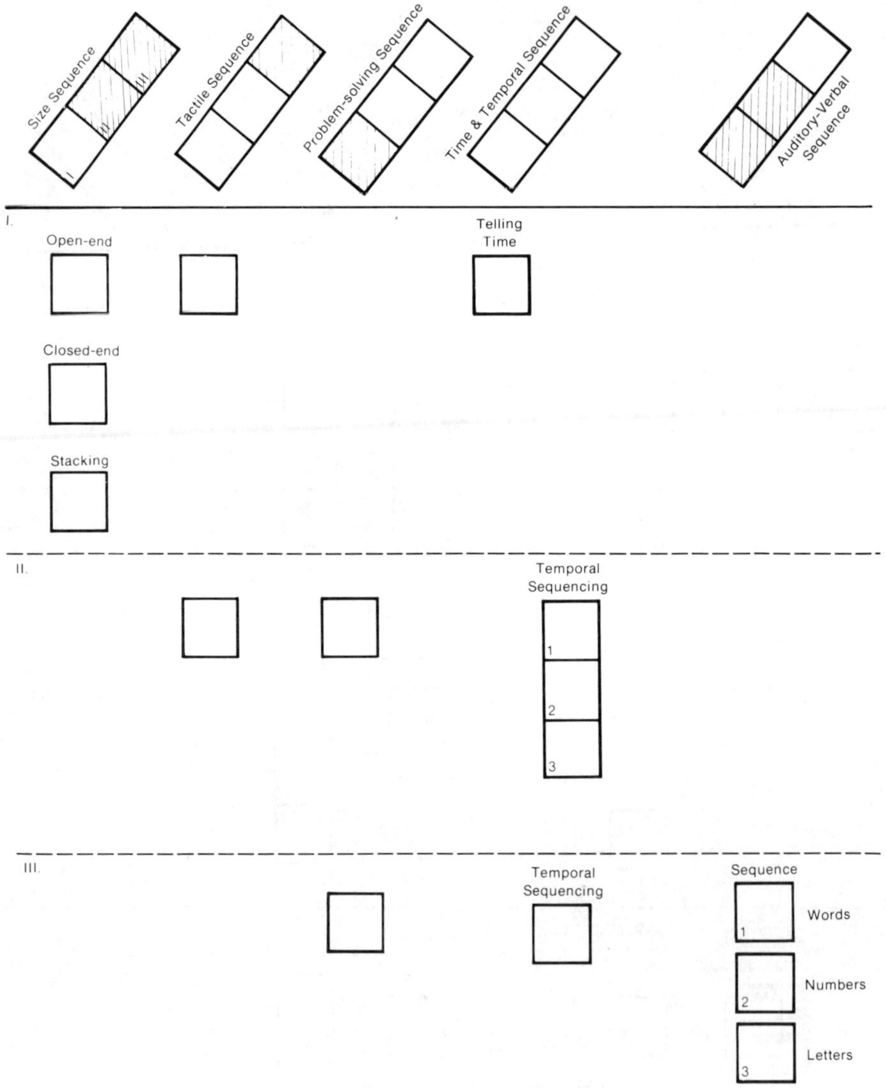

Size Sequence   Tactile Sequence   Problem-solving Sequence   Time & Temporal Sequence   Auditory-Verbal Sequence

I.

Open-end   Telling
Time

☐   ☐   ☐

Closed-end

☐

Stacking

☐

II.

☐   ☐   Temporal
Sequencing

1
2
3

III.

☐   Temporal
Sequencing ☐

Sequence

1	Words
2	Numbers
3	Letters

334

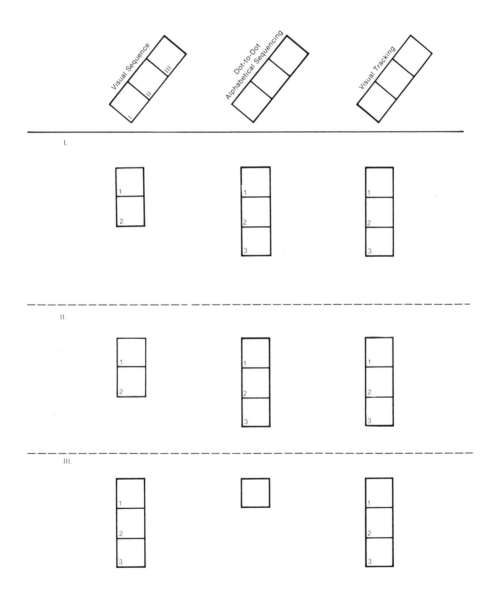

I.

II.

III.

Summary Record Sheet
Phase II, Section C
Development of Fine Motor Control

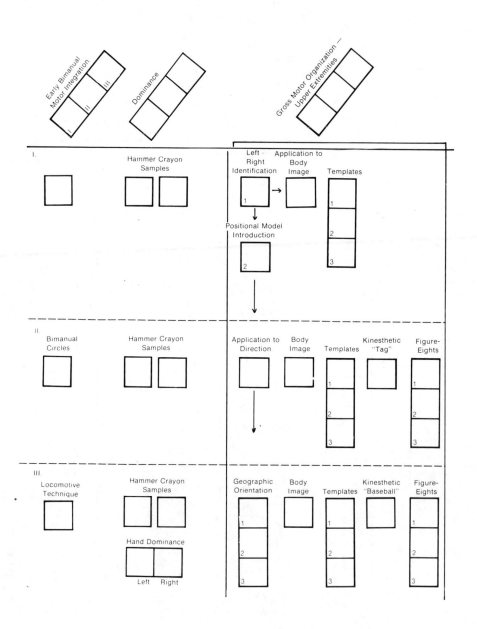

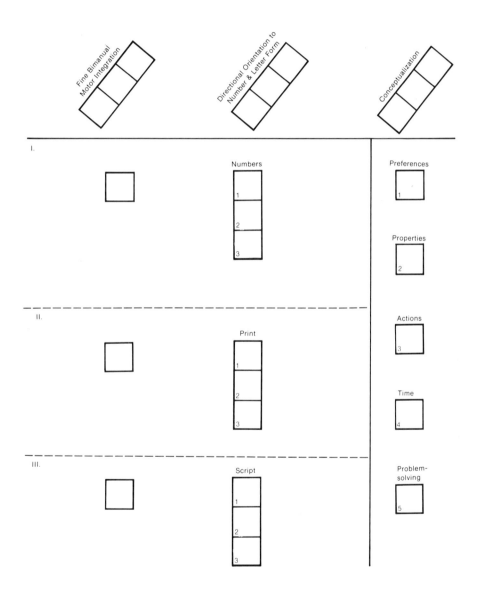

Appendix C

The Program Plans

Program Plan 1
Reduction of Avoidance Behavior in the OTA Triad

Initial Phase

1.1 Promote early tactile system organization and activate it in a pivotal role

Promote tactile system organization to reduce the defensive mode:

    Indoor climber
    Carpeted barrel
    Inflatables
    Towel rubbing and brushing

Promote tactile system organization to reduce the dormant mode

1.2 Recognize the olfactory system as a barometer of change

1.3 Decrease the defensive response of the auditory system

Early Sensory Discrimination

LEVEL: I   II   III

1.4 Tactile discrimination and manual form perception

1.5 Olfactory awareness through the Olfactory "Zoo" (Olfactory Awareness and Discrimination)

1.6 Early auditory matching of sounds (Auditory Localization, Discrimination and Sequence)

Refining Sensory Discrimination Skills

1.7 Manual form perception (continuation of 1.4)

1.8 Olfactory discrimination (continuation of 1.5)

1.9 Auditory discrimination (continuation of 1.6)

Program Plan 2
Reduce Avoidance Behavior in the Gravity-Activated
Visuo-Vestibular Dyad

Reduce residual influences of gravity-activated postural reflexes and promote gravity-related responses to integrate the two sides of the body and establish motor function across the midline.

LEVELS: I II III

2.1 Double suspended tires (Suspended Equipment)

2.2 Carpeted barrel

2.3 Inflatables

2.4 Scooter board

2.5 Jumping board (Gross Motor Organization)

Activate the extraocular muscles through the pivotal role of the vestibular system

2.6 Twirling chair (Suspended Equipment)

Promote voluntary oculomotor control independent of head movement

2.7 Visual attention, fixation, and pursuit

Program Plan 3
Bridge the Gap Between Avoidance and Exploration
to Organize Gross Motor Skills

Prerequisite to this, or ongoing with it, would be activities of Program Plans 1 and 2

Early noninstructive exploratory motor activities:

LEVELS: I II III

3.1 The indoor climber

3.2 Structured "near the floor" gross motor organization

3.3 Unstructured "near the floor" gross motor organization

3.4 Vertical balance and movement from a stable base

3.5 Balance and movement from an unstable base

Program Plan 4
Development of Elementary Concepts Through Sensory Sequence, Order, and Organization

Prerequisite to this, or ongoing with it, would be activities in Program Plan 2.

Level   I   II   III

4.1 Sequencing by size

4.2 Tactile sequence and assembly

4.3 Problem-solving sequence and assembly

4.4 Temporal Sequence (Time and Temporal Sequence)

4.5 Early visual sequence (and its application to visual memory)

4.6 Auditory sequence (and its application)

4.7 Dot-to-dot sequence of drawings of numbers and alphabet (Dot-to-dot alphabetical sequence)

4.8 Visual tracking of the alphabet

4.9 Visual sequence (of letter order in words)

Program Plan 5
Visual Form, Spatial Relations, and Visual Figure-Ground

Prerequisite to this, or ongoing with it, would be activities in Program Plans 1.4, 1.7, 2, and 7.

LEVELS: I   II   III

5.1 Color recognition, matching, and sorting

5.2 Visual form

5.3 Elementary spatial relations

5.4 Graded integration of spatial relations and visual figure-ground (puzzles)

5.5 Visual figure-ground

5.6 Visual form

5.7 Spatial relations

5.8 Visual figure-ground

5.9 Graded integration of spatial relations and visual figure-ground, continued (puzzles)

Program Plan 6
Dominance Exploration, Selection, and Confirmation

Prerequisite to this, or ongoing with it, would be activities in Program Plan 2.

LEVELS: I   II   III

6.1 Early bimanual motor integration

6.2 Nondominant "finger drawing" and scribbling

6.3 Presence or absence of established hand dominance observed in the:
   Hammer sample
   Crayoning sample

   (Dominance Exploration, Selection, and Confirmation)

6.4 Nondirected dominance exploration*

6.5 Document dominance shift or selection*

   Hammer sample
   Crayoning sample

6.6 Confirm the roles of the dominant and subdominant hand*

   Hammer and peg sets
   Cutting with scissors

*Continuation of unit cited above.

Program Plan 7
Directional Orientation

Prerequisite to this, or ongoing with it, would be activities in Program Plans 2, 3, and 6.

7.1 Establish a sensory identification of left and right

Gross Motor Organization — upper extremities — to develop awareness of position and direction

7.2 Introduction of the Positional Model

7.3 Early application of the Positional Model to directionality (top-bottom, left-right, b - d, p - q, N S E W)

7.4 Application of Positional Model to body image

7.5 Application of Positional Model to telling time (Time and Temporal Sequence)

7.6 Application of Positional Model to geographic orientation

Program Plan 8
Scribbles to Script

Prerequisite to this, or ongoing with it, would be activities in Program Plans 1.4, 1.7, 2, 6, and 7.†

8.1 Evaluate sample performance of number and letter forms

As a guide for initial and ongoing evaluations, use Directional Orientation to Numbers (Level I) and Letter Forms (Level II) below.   LEVELS: I   II   III

Gross motor organization to develop control of arm movement:

8.2 Bimanual circles (Early Motor Integration)

8.3 Templates (Gross Motor Organization of the Upper Extremities)

8.4 Kinesthetic "tag" and "baseball" (same)

8.5 Large figure-eight patterns (same)

Fine motor organization and movement sequence:

8.6 Fine bimanual motor integration

8.7 Develop prehension, initial motor control, directional awareness and sequence of movements in prewriting pencil exercises (Practice Sheet #1)

8.8 Train directional orientation to numbers and printed letter forms (Directional Orientation to Number and Letter Forms)

8.9 Train sequential patterns of movement in script writing (Directional Orientation to Number and Letter Forms)

†These prerequisites stress tactile system organization for prehension (P.P. 1), vestibular bilateral integration (P.P. 2), dominance exploration (P.P. 6), and directional orientation (P.P. 7). In addition, use of large scale vertical scribble boards, both textured and nontextured, are important in developing prehensile awareness and alert initial hand-eye awareness to guide early motor control.

Appendix D

The Integrated Program Matrix

Program Plan*													
#1	1	2	3	4	5	6	7	8	9	▓	▓	▓	▓
#2	1	2	3	4	5	6	7	▓	9	▓	▓	▓	▓
#3	1	2	3	▓	▓	▓	▓	(2.5)	5	▓	▓	▓	▓
#4	1	2	3	4	(7.1)	5	6	7	(5.5)	(5.6)	▓	▓	▓
#5	1	2	3	4	5	6	7	8	9	▓	▓	▓	▓
#6	1	▓	▓	2	3	4	5	(6.5)	▓	▓	▓	▓	▓
#7	▓	1	2	(6.5)	3	4	5	(6.1)	6	4	5	6	▓
#8	▓	1	2	3	4	5	6	7	8	(7.3)	▓	▓	9

*Numbers in parentheses indicate the precise prerequisite required.

Appendix E

The Sensory Avoidance Profile

Supportive Evidence

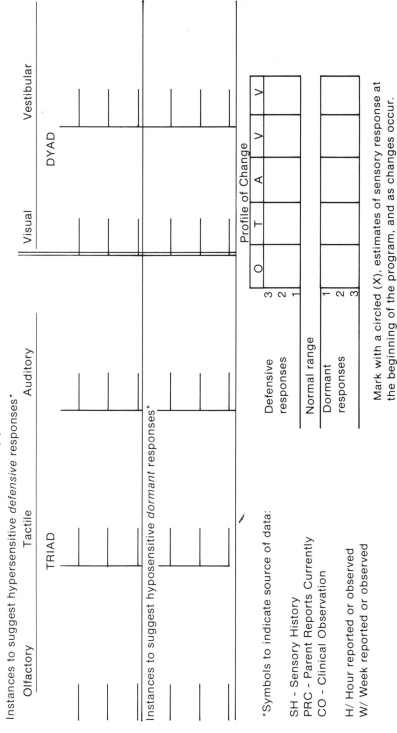

Instances to suggest hypersensitive *defensive* responses*

Olfactory	Tactile	Auditory	Visual	Vestibular
	TRIAD			DYAD

Instances to suggest hyposensitive *dormant* responses*

*Symbols to indicate source of data:

SH - Sensory History
PRC - Parent Reports Currently
CO - Clinical Observation

H/ Hour reported or observed
W/ Week reported or observed

Profile of Change

	O	T	A	V
Defensive responses	3			
	2			
	1			
Normal range				
Dormant responses	1			
	2			
	3			

Mark with a circled (X), estimates of sensory response at the beginning of the program, and as changes occur.

347

Appendix F

The Sensorimotor History

F-1 The Cover Letter to Parents
F-2 Sensorimotor Questionnaire
F-3 Key to Sensorimotor History

Appendix F-1: Cover Letter to Parents

Dear Parents,

Your child has been referred for therapy to help him become better organized in his ability to cope with problems of learning and behavior. Learning disorders can occur in children who have normal levels of intelligence; perceptual-motor dysfunctions may further complicate the problems of children who are considered retarded. Many children have what is called a developmental "lag"; while this can occur from a variety of reasons, often the cause is not readily identifiable in relation to a specific child. As a therapist, I am concerned with helping your child to improve his performance level and rate of maturation; the specific cause of this condition does not alter the methods used for therapy.

The goal of this program is to enable a child who may exhibit disorganized behavior in the classroom and/or at home to become better able to cope with the demands of his situation. This is done by helping him in four ways:

1) to recognize and assess more accurately the nature and quality of sensory information coming into his body from all the senses: smell, touch, hearing, vision, and balance. From this sensory information he comes to relate better to his immediate environment; thus, can feel more secure in it and learn from it.

2) The child is helped to develop more control and organization of his movement patterns through his senses (touch, balance, and vision) to replace "senseless," random, haphazard motions.

3) the child is helped to recognize concrete concepts of sequential organization through early tangible experiences, such as graded sizes of objects, so as to form a foundation for developing abstract concepts (eg, sequential steps in problem solving) later.

349

4) The foundation skills above are applied to help him develop those specific skills required for pencil control and handwriting, math, spelling, reading, the organization of academic tasks.

In order that I may grasp a more complete picture of the nature of the problem, I am asking you as parents to compile data about your child's early sensorimotor and developmental responses and current features of the problem as you see them. The enclosed questionnaire can be answered by checking the answers, but feel free to expand on any point.

Through such data I can more quickly develop a comprehensive impression of your child's strengths as well as problem areas. In so doing, the most efficient methods of therapy can be utilized.

All material will be handled confidentially and released only with your written permission.

Sincerely,

(Miss) Barbara M. Knickerbocker

Appendix F-2: Sensorimotor History Questionnaire

Date _____

CHILD'S NAME _____ BIRTH DATE _____

Please think of the various stages of your child's development, considering behavior which comes to your mind as you answer these questions. What do you recall as being different from other children you know? Were there times when his behavior was difficult to cope with in the family unit? Are there solutions you have found for any of these problems of behavior which have helped?

The following questions are posed to help in compiling a more complete picture of your child in his infancy and early childhood and at present. Some of these questions may refer to children who are older than your own. Kindly cross out the verb tense which does not apply. Check the choice which applies: Yes, No, or N/A (not old enough yet, or for other reasons, nonapplicable). Add narrative information which would also be important.

1. GROSS MOTOR ORGANIZATION. (proprioception to include tactile, kinesthetic, and vestibular information, plus the visual system.)

	YES	NO	N/A
1.1 Are his movements slow, plodding, deliberate?	___	___	___
1.2 Does he seem to be hyperactive, eg, in "perpetual motion" from sun-up to sun-down?	___	___	___
1.25 Did you ever use an infant plastic carrier for this child?	___	___	___
1.26 Did you use the infant plastic carrier infrequently (eg, once a week or less)?	___	___	___
1.27 Did you use the infant plastic carrier regularly for feeding?	___	___	___
1.28 Did you use the carrier and/or the car seat on a daily basis to transport the child, and the carrier regularly for feeding, play time, and napping?	___	___	___
1.29 Did he, as an infant, play and nap on a flat surface, eg, crib, playpen, floor, carriage, stroller, in contrast to being secured in a semi-reclined, seated position?	___	___	___
1.3 Was the creeping and crawling phase brief or almost entirely omitted?	___	___	___
1.31 Was the creeping and crawling phase unusually prolonged?	___	___	___
1.4 Did he sit, stand, or walk early?	___	___	___

	YES	NO	N/A
1.41 Did he sit, stand, or walk late?	_____	_____	_____
1.42 Is (was) he slow in learning to hop on one foot?	_____	_____	_____
1.43 Is (was) he late to learn how to skip?	_____	_____	_____
1.5 Is (was) he late to ride a tricycle?	_____	_____	_____
1.51 Is (was) he late to ride a two-wheeler with and without training wheels?	_____	_____	_____
1.6 Does he seem to misunderstand the meaning of words used in relation to movement?	_____	_____	_____
1.7 Has he ever gotten car sick?	_____	_____	_____
1.71 Does (did) he get nauseous and vomit from other movement experiences?	_____	_____	_____
1.72 Is he able to give adequate warning of these feelings?	_____	_____	_____
1.73 Does he seek quantities of twirling on piano stools or equivalent?	_____	_____	_____
1.74 Does he seek quantities of stimulation on rides at amusement parks?	_____	_____	_____

2.0 FUNCTION OF THE OLFACTORY SYSTEM

	YES	NO	N/A
2.1 Does (did) he seem to be highly sensitive to scents and odors?	_____	_____	_____
2.2 Does (did) he seem to lack a normal awareness of odors readily perceived by others?	_____	_____	_____
2.3 Does (did) he express any strong likes or dislikes toward food smells? Explain.	_____	_____	_____
2.4 Does (did) he express strong dislikes toward other scents? Explain.	_____	_____	_____

3.0 TACTILE SYSTEM: (to include perception of pain and temperature)

	YES	NO	N/A
3.1 Does (did) he seem to lack the normal awareness of being touched?	_____	_____	_____
3.11 Does (did) he seem overly sensitive to being touched?	_____	_____	_____
3.12 Does (did) he dislike being held, cuddled?	_____	_____	_____
3.13 If he likes to be cuddled or touched now, has this undergone change, from disliking it earlier?	_____	_____	_____

	YES	NO	N/A
3.14 Does (did) he seem excessively ticklish?	___	___	___
3.15 Does (did) he seem easily irritated or enraged when touched by siblings or playmates?	___	___	___
3.16 Does (did) he seem to pick fights at school, for example, standing in line on the playground?	___	___	___
3.17 Does (did) he have a strong need to touch objects and people?	___	___	___
3.18 Does (did) he like to touch animals?	___	___	___
3.19 Does (did) he dislike the feeling of certain kinds of clothing? Name.	___	___	___
3.20 Are (were) his sleep patterns in infancy and/or childhood irregular?	___	___	___
3.21 Is it difficult to get him to sleep now?	___	___	___
3.22 Is he an early riser, immediately on the go?	___	___	___
3.23 Did he cry excessively in infancy?	___	___	___
3.30 Does (did) he seem to lack the normal awareness of cold outdoor temperatures?	___	___	___
3.31 Does (did) he overdress, seeming to be unaware of excessive summer outdoor heat?	___	___	___
3.32 Does (did) he often seem to feel room temperatures in marked, or some, contrast to what others find comfortable?	___	___	___
3.33 Does (did) he seem overly sensitive to water temperature for a bath, wanting it to be noticeably cool?	___	___	___
3.34 Was (is) he overly sensitive to food temperatures, wanting them to be noticeably cool?	___	___	___
3.35 Does (did) he seem overly sensitive to rough textures in food?	___	___	___
3.36 Does (did) he strongly dislike the feeling of showers, outdoor sprinklers?	___	___	___
3.37 Does (did) he prefer tub baths over showers, if both were available (and he was old enough to take showers)?	___	___	___
3.40 Does (did) he seem almost unaware of, or "stoic" over, painful experiences such as having shots, stitches, dental work?	___	___	___

	YES	NO	N/A

3.41 Is (was) he often unaware of brusies, cuts, and bleeding gashes from playing, until someone brought it to his attention? ___ ___ ___

3.42 Does (did) he play with toys appropriate for his age? ___ ___ ___

3.43 Does (did) he play with the graded sizes of nesting toys in childhood? ___ ___ ___

3.44 Does (did) he like puzzles, manipulative toys? ___ ___ ___

3.45 Is (was) he clumsy in playing with toys? ___ ___ ___

3.46 Does (did) he engage in any prolonged play activity at home of his own volition? ___ ___ ___

3.47 Is (was) this in direct contrast to reported distractibility in the classroom, where he has trouble paying attention to the task at hand? ___ ___ ___

3.48 Is (was) he overly destructive with toys? ___ ___ ___

3.50 Are (were) manipulative hand skills difficult for him? (eg, use of spoon, cut, etc) ___ ___ ___

3.51 Does (did) he have greater than average difficulty learning to put on clothes over his head, out of his visual range? ___ ___ ___

3.52 Does (did) he have prolonged confusion over putting the right shoe on the right foot? ___ ___ ___

3.53 Does (did) he have particular difficulty with executing sequential movements in dressing tasks, such as buttoning, connecting jacket zippers, tying shoes? ___ ___ ___

3.60 Does (did) he have extreme difficulty learning to hold a pencil or crayon in a 3-point, or tripod, position? ___ ___ ___

4.00 AUDITORY SYSTEM:

4.05 Has he ever had any ear trouble? Specify. ___ ___ ___

4.10 Is (was) he particularly distracted by sounds, seeming to hear sounds which go unnoticed by others? ___ ___ ___

4.20 Does (did) he often fail to listen, or pay attention, to what is said to him? ___ ___ ___

	YES	NO	N/A
4.30 Does (did) he often fail to follow through, to act upon requests to do something, to understand instructions?	___	___	___
4.40 Is (was) he unable to function if two or three steps of instruction are given to him at once?	___	___	___
4.50 Does (did) he talk excessively?	___	___	___
4.55 Does (did) talking by others stimulate him to be overly verbal?	___	___	___
4.60 Does (did) this talking interfere with his ability to listen?	___	___	___
4.65 Do sounds in the classroom easily distract him?	___	___	___
4.70 Are (were) any sounds frightening to him which would not normally convey alarm for other children of the same age?	___	___	___
4.75 Are (were) sounds around him, such as a refrigerator, fluorescent light bulbs, heaters, distracting?	___	___	___
4.80 Is (was) speech development delayed?	___	___	___

5.00 VISUAL SYSTEM:

	YES	NO	N/A
5.10 Is (was) he highly distracted by visual stimuli?	___	___	___
5.20 Does (did) he have poor attention span at school?	___	___	___
5.30 If the above is true, can he nevertheless sit at home alone for extended periods to play with toys or objects of interest?	___	___	___

(Academically related points regarding visual perception are contained in the following unit.)

6.00 ACADEMICALLY RELATED QUESTIONS: (omit those which are not age-appropriate) Teachers' reports and conferences from previous years would be helpful, as well as discussion with his teacher about some of the following:

	YES	NO	N/A
6.10 Is (was) he noticeably distractible in class?	___	___	___
6.11 Does (did) he function significantly better in a one-to-one relationship to do school assignments than in class?	___	___	___

	YES	NO	N/A

6.20 Is (was) his posture generally poor and slouched? _____ _____ _____

6.21 Does (did) he frequently prop his head and his hand while reading or writing at the desk? _____ _____ _____

6.23 In writing tasks does (did) he often have to be reminded to hold the paper for writing? _____ _____ _____

6.30 Is (was) there prolonged confusion over which hand is dominant? _____ _____ _____

6.31 Is (was) he persistently confused over which hand or foot is left and right? _____ _____ _____

6.33 Is (was) he easily confused in cross-over patterns to find the right side of a person facing him? _____ _____ _____

6.40 Do top-bottom reversals in numbers appear? (Explain) Does he make his numbers upside down?) _____ _____ _____

6.50 Are numbers or printed letters made backwards? _____ _____ _____

6.51 Does he reverse the sequential order when he "teens," eg, "14," by forming the "4" and then placing the "1" in front of it? _____ _____ _____

6.52 Does he confuse letter reversals such as "b" and "d"? _____ _____ _____

6.53 Does he confuse reversible words, eg, "dog" and "god," "saw" for "was"? _____ _____ _____

6.54 (If the child is studying Hebrew) does the problem of reversals in letters and words in English re-appear after having been reasonably well mastered earlier? _____ _____ _____

6.60 Is there an undue amount of confusion in recognizing letters in Hebrew which have great similarity in form? _____ _____ _____

6.70 In laboratory sessions, in cooking class, or shop work, is there a significant problem in coping with written instructions? _____ _____ _____

6.80 Does he find gym, and participation sports in general, distasteful? _____ _____ _____

6.90 Please cite any additional information teachers say are problems at school, either academically or behaviorally:

	YES	NO	N/A

7.00 SOCIAL ADJUSTMENT

7.10 Does this child find it hard to make friends among his peers?

7.20 Does he prefer the company of adults, or children who are older, who allow him more room for his mistakes?

7.30 Does he tend to play with children who are one or two years younger than he?

7.40 Is he a loner?

7.50 Does he express feeling of low self-esteem?

7.60 Does he frequently express feelings of failure and frustration?

7.70 Would you say he is discouraged and depressed?

8.00 PROFESSIONAL WORKUPS: Evaluations from the following are available and will be forwarded.

> Physician
> Psychologist
> Teachers

9.00 ADDITIONAL COMMENTS, DATA:

Appendix F-3: Key to Sensorimotor History

Groups of answers tend to suggest that the least one of the reasons cited below the answers could contribute to the problems in question.

1) GROSS MOTOR ORGANIZATION

Yes: 1.1, 1.31, 1.41, 1.42, 1.43, 1.5, 1.51
Hypoactive, possibly a hyposensitive, dormant response within/or poor integration between the tactile, vestibular, and visual systems.

Yes: 1.2, 1.3, 1.4
The opposite of the above, hyperactive, may be secondary to hypersensitive or defensive responses in the tactile system; poor balance.

Yes: 1.6
Poor auditory perception

No: 1.29, 1.7, 1.71, 1.72   Yes: 1.27, 1.28, 1.73, 1.74
Dormant quality to the responses of the vestibular system and poor integration between the balance and the visual systems.

No: 1.25, 1.29   Yes: 1.26
Opportunity available for early proprioceptive facilitation to extraocular muscles.

No: 1.28
Suggests it was not used to excess, and probably did not contribute to poor visuo-vestibular development.

2) OLFACTORY SYSTEM

Yes: 2.1, 2.3, 2.4
Hypersensitive, defensive olfactory system.

Yes: 2.2
Hyposensitive, dormant olfactory system.

3) TACTILE SYSTEM

Yes: 3.10, 3.30, 3.31, 3.32, 3.40, 3.41
A hyposensitive, dormant tactile response.

Yes: 3.11, 3.12, 3.14, 3.15, 3.16, 3.19, 3.20, 3.21, 3.22, 3.23, 3.33, 3.34, 3.35, 3.36, 3.37.
A hypersensitive, defensive tactile response.

Yes: 3.3, 3.17
An emerging pattern from an earlier hypersensitive response, or after a prolonged dormant response, changing toward a more normal level.

No: 3.18
May (among other factors) tend to suggest hypersensitivity to contact with him which is unpredictable or out of his control.

No: 3.43, 3.44, 3.46   Yes: 3.45, 3.47, 3.48, 3.50, 3.51, 3.6, 3.61
Poor manipulative skills from either a hypo or hypersensitive response, yielded inadequate or inaccurate information for him to motor plan, eg, manipulate hands easily.

Yes: 3.51, 3.52
Poor body image, left-right confusion.

4) AUDITORY SYSTEM

Yes: 4.10, 4.20, 4.30, 4.50, 4.55, 4.60, 4.65, 4.70, 4.75
Auditory defensiveness.

Yes: 4.20, 4.30, 4.80
Auditory dormancy.

Yes: 4.40
Either of the above two reasons, plus a basic lack of awareness of sequential ordering about what goes on in the environment; basic to auditory memory.

5) VISUAL SYSTEM

Yes: 5.10, 5.20
Visual figure-ground problem, or visual distractibility, a form of defensiveness.

Yes: 5.30
Although the immediate problem suggests poor visual attention, it may be that tactile defensiveness prevents the child from focusing on tasks when others, especially children whose movements are unpredictable, are in his immediate vicinity.

6) ACADEMICALLY RELATED QUESTIONS

Yes: 6.10, 6.11
Visual distractibility and tactile hypersensitivity, together or alone.

Yes: 6.20, 6.21
Poor motor development and strength in trunk; may be a long-term carry-over from inadequate proprioceptive stimulation and early balancing and lack of prone positioning in infancy.

Yes: 6.40
Directional confusion, poor body image and spatial relations.

Yes: 6.23, 6.30, 6.31, 6.33, 6.50, 6.51, 6.52, 6.53, 6.54
Inadequate early integration of the two sides of the body, secondarily resulting in left-right confusion, poor body image, and spatial relations.

Yes: 6.8
(Same as above), plus poor motor planning skills and poor sequencing of motor patterns.

Yes: 6.6

Possible minor or latent difficulty in visual form, so that when the visual form differences are minute, as in this case, the problem becomes apparent.

Yes: 6.7

Auditory perception and/or poor sequential organization or procedural steps in carrying out instructions.

7) SOCIAL ADJUSTMENT

Yes: 7.2, 7.3

Avoidance of competition when skills are inadequate; ego development suffers and he moves in circles which are not competitive.

Yes: 7.1, 7.4, 7.5, 7.6, 7.7

Poor sensory integration yields poor motor skills and the feeling of inadequacy. With poor ego development, there is a tendency to withdraw; this is intensified with repeated failure and frustration. Initial withdrawal may be related to tactile defensiveness.

Appendix G

Hourly Record Sheet

NAME _____ DATE _____ Advanced Plan and Record of Hour _____

PHASE I: Gross Sensorimotor Organization.
Climber _____; Barrel _____; Inflatables _____; Scooter Board _____; Tires _____; Chair _____; Other _____

PHASE II: (A) Refining Sensory System Organization and Integration
Olfactory: Scented "Zoo" _____; Olfactory system discrimination _____;
Tactile: Rubbing with Towel _____; brushing _____; textured blocks _____; early 3-D manual form _____; small 3-D manual form, freight cars _____; circus cars _____; 2-D linear aluminum form _____;
Auditory: Localization _____; direction _____; early discrimination, animal sound cylinders _____; sound cylinders, Set #1 _____; Set #2 _____;
Visual: attention _____; fixation _____; pursuits _____;
color matching _____; form matching _____; visual fig.-ground _____; sp. rel. (grid & blocks) _____; integrate spatial relations and visual figure-ground using frametray puzzles _____; Spatial relations, assemble: 3-D cube Designs in Perspective (DLM-112 or 118) _____; Parquetry Designs I (DLM-116) _____; Par. Des. II (DLM-179) _____; Par. Des. III (DLM-180) _____; (These require conceptualizing whole-part relationships of geometric forms within a space.)

PHASE II: (B) Sequential Organization
Size: nesting, open-end _____; nesting, closed-end _____; stacking _____;
Tactile Sequence and Assembly: _____
Problem-Solving Sequence and Assembly: _____
Temporal Sequence: of incidents _____; days of the week; _____; months _____;
Auditory Sequence: numbers _____; words _____; letters _____;
Visual Sequence: color cube patterns _____; pictures _____; letters _____;
Alphabetical Sequence: dot-to-dot drawings _____; tracking _____;
PHASE II: (C) Continued next page.

KEY
✓ plan to do, coming hour
✗ activity used
↟ upgrade
℞ review

361

PHASE II: (C) Development of Fine Motor Control

Elicit purposeful response (in infants) _____ ;

Random hammering _____ ; textured scribble board _____ ; early bimanual integration _____

Large bimanual circles _____ ;

Left-right sensory identification _____ ; Positional Model _____ ; application to b-d _____ ; application to body image (back) _____ ; (front) _____ ;

application to direction _____ ; application to geographical orientation _____ ;

Templates (desk level) _____ ; vertical _____ ; large figure-eights _____ ;

Pre-writing Exercise #1 _____ ; model sheets to copy numbers _____ ; to copy printed CAPS _____ ; to copy lower-case letters _____ ; practice

sheet stressing line-size-spacing _____ ;

Script Motor Patterns: 1 2 3 4 5; connectors in script _____ ;

Evaluate:

Timed hammering _____ Body image (back view) _____ VMI _____ Sample: Numbers _____ CAPS _____ LC _____

Timed crayoning _____ Body image (front view) _____ b - d reversals _____

362

Appendix H

Source List

Sources

The equipment, toys, and early academic materials are listed here in the same sequence as they are presented in the program plans, Part III of the text. Within individual units they are listed in their order of increasing difficulty. The items cited here have proven to be constructive, and some even critical, to the smooth progress along the developmental hierarchy. For this reason the original identity and source is included even though some of these have become unavailable on the market. Insofar as possible, those items which are felt to be most critical to this progress and which are no longer available from their original source may be carried by another source (K-DEE); current substitutes will be suggested as necessary.

* *Abbott Ltd*, London. (Has gone out of business; many of their products are recognized by therapists by this name, hence it is included. Some of these prducts are carried by other British vendors; imported to US).

Achievement Products, P.O. Box 547, Mineola, New York 11501.

* *Ambi* (Europlastic Subsidiary) Amsterdam, Holland.

Ann Arbor Publishers, P.O. Box 388, Worthington, Ohio 43085.

Ben-O Products, East Williston, New York.

Blockhouse, 1107 Broadway, Toy Center North, New York 10010.

* *Brio*, Osby, Sweden (some toys imported to US).

Childcraft Educational Corp, 964 Third Avenue, New York, New York 10032.

Child Guidance, P.O. Box 113, Bronx, New York 10472.

Continental Press, Elizabethtown, Pennsylvania 17022.

Creative Playthings, Box 330, Princeton, New Jersey 08540.

Developmental Learning Materials, 7440 Natchez Avenue, Niles, Ill 60648.

Edu-U-Cards, 60 Austin Boulevard, Commack, New York.

* *Europlastics*, Amsterdam, Holland (distributors, Childcraft).

Follett Publishing House, Chicago, Illinois.

* *Galt*, Brookfield Road, Cheshire, England.

Ideal School Supply Company, 1000 South Lawrence Avenue, Oak Lawn, Ill 60453.

Irwin Toys Inc, 200 Fifth Avenue, New York, New York 10010.

* *Kiddicraft*, Kenley, Surrey, England.

† *K-DEE*, Box #6149, Lawrenceville, New Jersey 08648.

* Included to help domestic and foreign therapists identify the items. Many of these are imported and sold through Blockhouse, Childcraft, DLM, and local stores which carry imported toys.

† A series of K-DEE (Knickerbocker Developmental and Education Enterprises) toys has been designed for the purpose of arousing in the young preschool child initial cause and effect relationships which would precede the performance outlined in these program plans.

* *Kouvalais Toys,* manufactured in Greece, imported to US.
  Lauri Enterprises, Philips-Avon, Maine 04966.
  Maggiore, Old Beth Page, New York, (Action Climb-A-Roo — #5400.)
* *Merit,* Potter's Bar, England.
* *Otto Maier,* Ravensburg, West Germany.
  Milton Bradley, Springfield, Massachusetts.
  New York Times Teaching Resources, 334 Boylston Street, Boston, Massachusetts 02116.
  Norstar Toys, Inc, The Toy Center, 200 Fifth Avenue, NY, NY 10010.
  Playskool Inc, 3720 North Kedzie Avenue, Chicago, Illinois 60618.
* *Philip & Tacey,* 69-79 Fulham High Street, Fulham, London SW6.
  Platt & Munk, The Toy Center, 200 Fifth Avenue, NY, NY 10010.
  J A Preston Corp, 71 Fifth Avenue, New York, New York 10003.
  Questor Eductional Products Company, Bronx, New York 10472.
  Shackman, 85 Fifth Avenue, NY, NY.
* *Simplex Toys,* manufactured in Holland; imported by Childcraft, DLM, and others.
* *J W Spear & Sons,* Green Street, Brim'sdown, Enfield, Middlesex, England.
  Tupperward, Orlando, Florida.
  Western Publishing Company, Racine, Wisconsin.

Sources and Identity of Therapeutic Modalities

Program Plan 1

Texture blocks	K-DEE**
3-D plastic floating toys, 5415, Irwin	
Olfactory Zoo	
Bird-animal sound cylinders	K-DEE
3-D plastic freight cars	K-DEE
3-D plastic circus cars	K-DEE
2-D Embossed Linear designs	K-DEE
Olfactory Discrimination cards	K-DEE
Sound cylinders, AP 530, 530-1	Achievement Products

Program Plan 2

Inflatables	K-DEE
Scooter board	K-DEE
Jumping Board	K-DEE
Tires (red)	go-go tires by Marx
black, tire swing	#3773, Irwin
Twirling chair	(local furniture import store)
Liquid Hourglass	K-DEE
Marble Railway	K-DEE

** Send self-addressed envelope to K-DEE, Box 6149, Lawrenceville, NJ for the most current source of item(s) needed for your program.

Program Plan 3

Indoor climber for home and clinic use	Maggiore (# 5400)
Cloth tunnel, AP 271	Achievement Products
Self-assembly Playhouse	K-DEE
Plans for self-assembly playhouse	K-DEE
Stepping stones R752	Creative Playthings
Balance Beam AP300	Achievement Products
Rope Ladder	Irwin (#3522, Tarzan Climbing Ladder)
Knotted Climbing rope	Irwin (#3522, Tarzan Climbing Ladder)

Program Plan 4

Open-end sequencing by size:

Shallow round cups (11)	Child Guidance, Ring-A-Round #10
Deep round cups (12)	Playskool
Nesting cups with handles (10)	15831CG16, Blockhouse
Shallow square cups (9)	Square Pyramid, 1326/E509 Blockhouse
Deep square cups (10)	Child Guidance Learning Tower #90
Hexagon (10)	Child Guidance
Indented square, shallow cups (8)	Kiddicraft, Vari-form pyramid

Closed-end sequencing:

Nested wooden dollars, numbering 3 to 10,	Korea, Japan, Russia
Nested eggs (6)	#1033, Playskool
Nested Houses (5)	Japan
Barrels (7), Kitty in the Kegs,	#80 Child Guidance
Handy Boxes (6)	#1M-101, Childcraft, or Cannisters #335, DLM
Nested drums (10)	#1M-316, Childcraft, or Inverted Bowls, Playskool
Family (7)	Shackman

Tactile sequence and assembly:

Level I:

Ring-A-Bell (6)	#4050, Merit
Pyramid Tree (5)	Kiddicraft
Build-up Cat (7)	#303, Kouvalais
Build-up Dog (7)	#304, Kouvalais
Twirling Tower (6)	K-DEE
Giraffe (9)	#31743, Brio
Duck (9)	#31728 Brio

Level II:

Teddy Baby (9)	#31721/1, Brio
Parrot (9)	#31725/1, Brio; 971-31725, Blockhouse
Soldier (10)	#31730/1, Brio; 968/31730, Blockhouse

Windmill (10)	#31738, Brio
Percy Penguin (13)	#31723, Brio

Problem-solving assembly:

Fun Flowers (6 ea.)	Child Guidance
Iron	#7660, Merit
Activity Engine	#7500, Merit
Habitat	E-400, Ambi, Childcraft
House Building Set	Brio
Swiss Chalet	K-DEE
Self-assembly Playhouse	K-DEE

Dot-to-dot alphabetical sequence	K-DEE
Visual letter forms, LC & Caps	K-DEE
Initial visual tracking exercises	K-DEE
Letter Tracking	Ann Arbor Publishers
Same or Different Design Cards	#P-212, DLM
Same or Different Word Cards	EP-211, DLM
Seeing Likenesses & Differences, Level 3	Continental Press

Program Plan 5

Visual form perception:

Compartmental box with transparent slotted lid for sorting	K-DEE
Bunte Baloone	#14.206 Maier and local toy importers
Hide-A-Peg Set	K-DEE
6" x 6" transparent plastic box	K-DEE
Color Pattern Board	#6001, Ideal
Grid & Block Set	New York Times Teaching Resources
Graded patterns for Grid and Block Set	K-DEE
Parquetry Blocks, #306	Playskool
Frostig Program for the Development of Visual Perception by Marianne Frostig & David Horne	Follett
Dvorine Psuedo-Isochromatic Plates	Preston
Linjo by Otto Maier	local toy importers
Hex — by Spears	local toy importers
Visual Figure-Ground Exercises #1-6	K-DEE

For convenience in conducting a program, many items used for visual form perception are identified in the OEPS. Obviously, many more items are included than would be needed to conduct most programs. The purpose of this is to help the therapist in the proper grading of these toys to insure successful mastery of even minute increments of difficulty and smooth progression along the hierarchy of the child's development; this is critical in the treatment of the more severely impaired child.

Program Plan 6

Build-O-Fun	Tupperware
Skaneateles train track	local toy stores

Program Plan 7

Body Image Drawings, 8" x 10"	K-DEE
Patterns for direction and geographical orientation	K-DEE

Program Plan 8

Lego	local toy stores
Tinkertoy sets (wood and metal)	
Large scale plastic tinkertoy sets	Questor
Labyrinth	Brio, and local toy stores
Roll-A-Score	toy and game shops
Visual-motor Integration Test by Beery-Buktenica	Follett
Winter Haven Perceptual Copy Forms	Winter Haven Lions Club Research Foundation, Winter Haven, Florida
Templates	Winter Haven Lions Club (same as above)
Blockhead	local toy stores
Magnetic Fish Pond	Merit, local toy import stores
Clippy Clowns	#344, Norstar Toys
Prewriting Practice Sheet #1	K-DEE
Practice Sheet #2 for numbers, printed letters	K-DEE
Master copy sheets for numbers and	
Master copy sheets for numbers and printed letters	K-DEE
Script motor pattern practice sheets	K-DEE

Appendix I

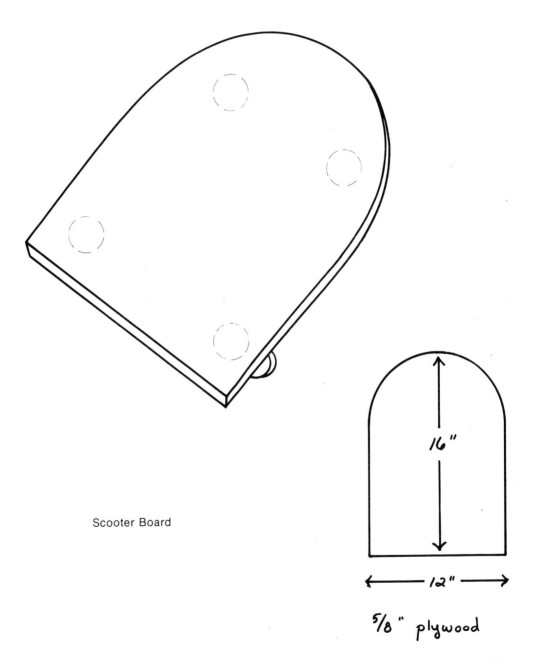

Scooter Board

16"

12"

5/8" plywood

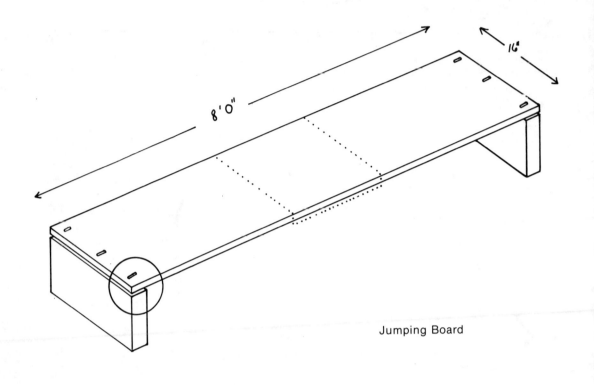

8'0"

16"

Jumping Board

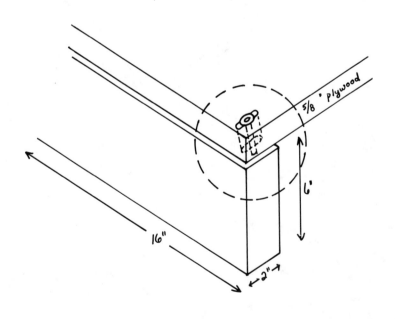

5/8" plywood

6"

16"

2"

Appendix J

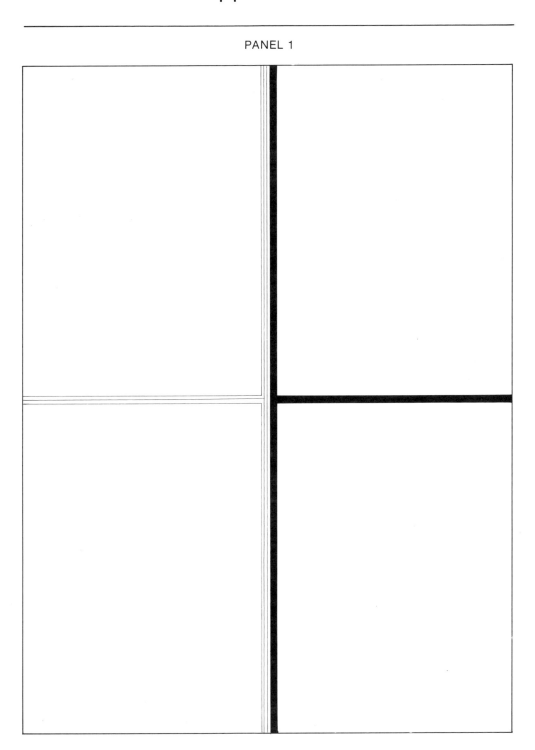

PANEL 1

371

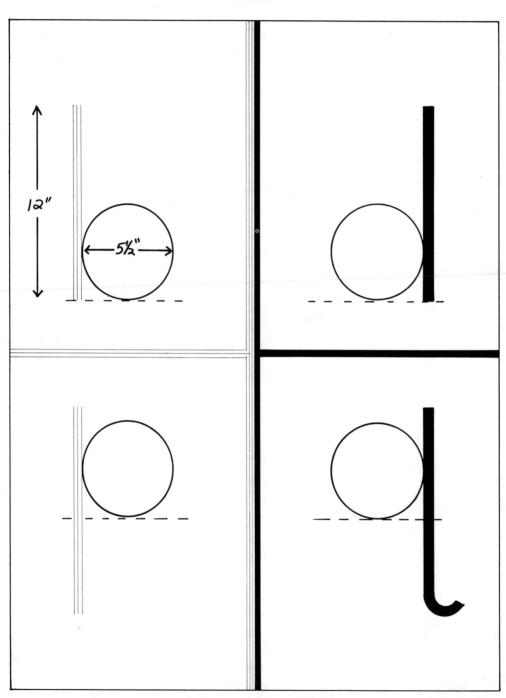

PANEL 3

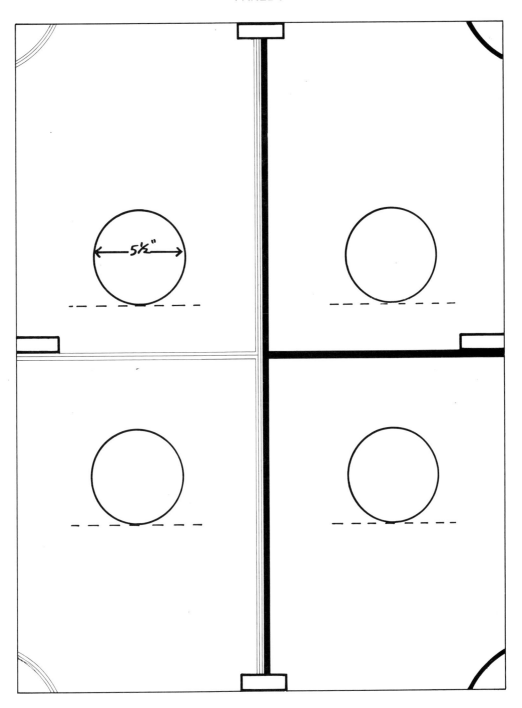

PANEL 4

374

PANEL 5

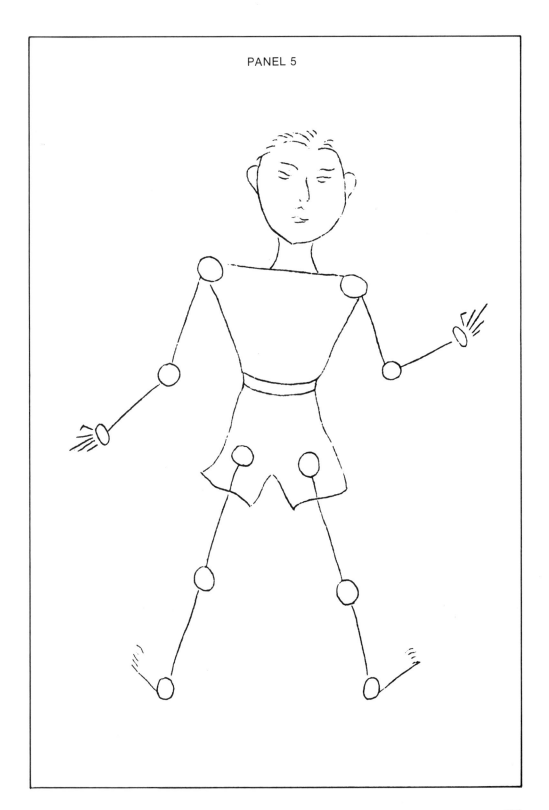

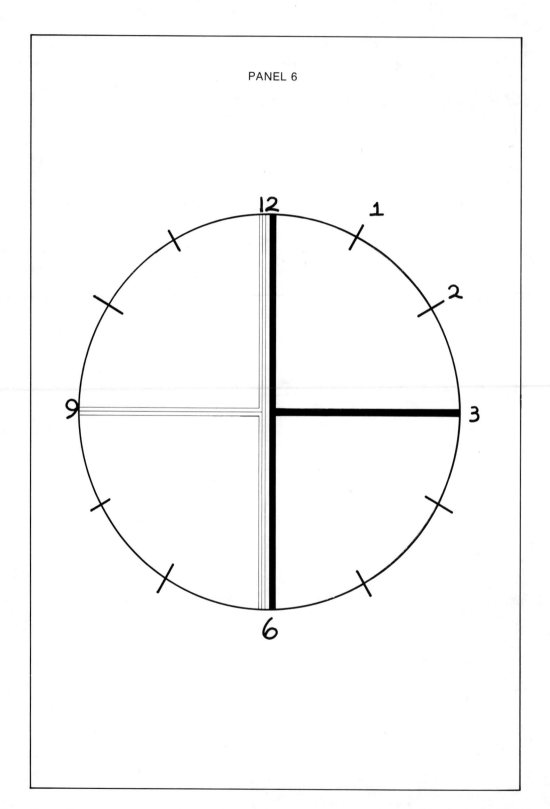

PANEL 6

PANEL 7

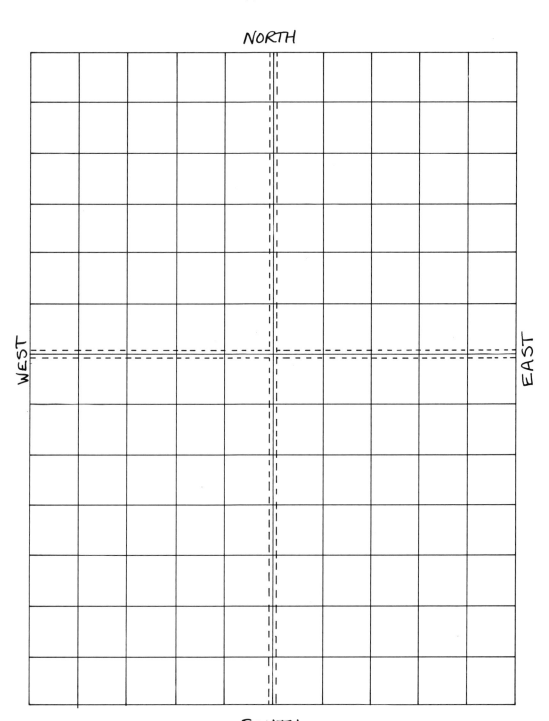

PANEL 8

378

Appendix K

Top to bottom,
makes a ONE.

Go 'round the top,
Thru the center
To the bottom and over.

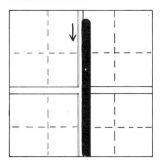

Loop to the center.
and loop once more.

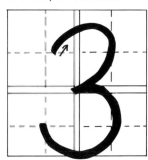

Down and over,
and down once more
That's the way to
make a FOUR.

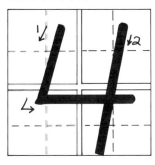

Short neck, body fat.
Number FIVE wears a hat.

circle down and
around the town.

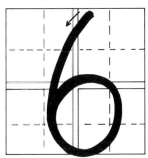

Across the top and
Down from heaven.
That's the way to
make a SEVEN.

Make an "S" and
then up straight.
That's the way to a
make an EIGHT.

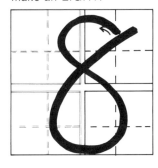

Make an oval,
and down the line.
That's the way
To make a NINE.

Master Copy Sheet #1: Directional Orientation to numbers 1-9. © Copyright 1971, Barbara M. Knickerbocker, OTR.

379

Index

H

I

J

K

L

W